A PATTERN OF CATECHISTICAL DOCTRINE,

AND OTHER MINOR WORKS

OF

LANCELOT ANDREWES,

SOMETIME LORD BISHOP OF WINCHESTER,

WIPF & STOCK · Eugene, Oregon

Wipf and Stock Publishers
199 W 8th Ave, Suite 3
Eugene, OR 97401

A Pattern of Catechistical Doctrine, and Other Minor Works of Lancelot Andrewes, Sometime Lord Bishop of Winchester
By Andrewes, Lancelot
ISBN 13: 978-1-60608-123-5
Publication date 3/17/2009
Previously published by John Henry Parker, 1846

NOTICE.

The present volume contains five different works, by Bishop Andrewes:—

I. Pattern of Catechistical Doctrine.

II. Judgment of the Lambeth Articles; annexed to which is the

Judgment of the Censure upon Barret.

III. Form of Consecration of a Church and Churchyard.

IV. Summary View of the Government both of the Old and New Testament: whereby the Episcopal government of Christ's church is vindicated.

V. Discourse of Ceremonies retained and used in christian churches.

Of these works,

1. The first was probably Andrewes' manual of college lectures, and the folio volume which appeared in 1642, calling itself "The Morall Law expounded, 1. largely, 2. learnedly, 3. orthodoxly, That is, The long expected and much desired work of bishop Andrewes upon the Ten Commandments: being his Lectures many years since in Pembroke Hall chappell, in Cambridge, which have ever since passed from hand to hand in manuscripts, and beene accounted one of the greatest treasures of private libraries, but never before this published in print," seems to be nothing

more than notes taken down by Andrewes' pupils from his lectures orally delivered out of the above manual. Another work also appeared in 1650, and was reprinted in 1675, called "The Pattern of Catechistical Doctrine at large; or a learned and pious Exposition of the Ten Commandments, with an Introduction containing the use and benefit of catechising, the general grounds of religion, and the truth of christian religion in particular; proved against Atheists, Pagans, Jews and Turks. By the right reverend father in God, Lancelot Andrewes, late bishop of Winchester. Perfected according to the author's own copy, and thereby purged from many thousands of errors, defects, and corruptions, which were in a rude imperfect draught formerly published." This volume is simply the work on the Moral Law put into shape; and it is done by very competent hands, but being less than even the former was, the production of Andrewes himself, it could by no means be admitted into an edition of his works.—Of the original work of Andrewes, the Pattern of Catechistical doctrine, an edition appeared in 1630, and another in 1641, with here and there a new sentence introduced; but all apparently from the same hand, and the new matter consisting probably of notes which had afterwards come to light. The later edition has been followed in the present publication.

2. The documents which make up the second work, the bishop's Judgment, namely, of the Lambeth articles, and of the censure upon Barret, are sufficiently explained by the contemporary histories, e. g. Strype's life of Whitgift.

3. The Form of consecration of a church and churchyard, gives its own history.

4. Of the fourth document, the Summary view of the government both of the Old and New testament, no more perhaps can now be known than is expressed in the title-page at the beginning of it.

5. The same account may be given of the concluding treatise, the Discourse of ceremonies retained and used in christian churches. The prefatory notice, from which an extract is given p. 365, gives an account of the document which is probably the true one. The treatise itself, as printed in 1653, is obviously the work of a man of great reading; and it is equally manifest that his manuscript was left in a state which made it very hard for the unlearned persons whose hands it fell into, to decypher it. The mistakes which appear in the printed edition are manifold and absurd, but the present editor found reason to be convinced as he proceeded, that the work would reward a very laborious examination, and such it has accordingly received.

There are now but a very few references in the whole book which have not been verified; a statement which they who know the works of that period will understand the importance of. The toil which this has required, the strange disguise under which some of the names were lurking,—Agesilaus, the holder of a remarkable view, turning out after every biographical notice of every Agesilaus had been ransacked, to be no king of Sparta, but the philosopher Arcesilas, (p. 26), —the Rabbi Abbidelus, after being hunted through all the regions of Hebrew literature, disclosing himself as the ancient historian Abydenus, (p. 49),—the people called Caes, after having been nearly abandoned as a lost nation, turning out to be the people called Seres, (p. 375),—"Outerus's ancient descriptions," found by a happy conjecture to be Gruter's valuable work in disguise,—these and the like are recollections for an editor, but of little interest to others.

Only one other particular need be mentioned in which the present volume exhibits a departure from the former edition of the same material. In verifying the texts of The Pattern of Catechistical Doctrine, the Editor found the reference to be almost as often wrong as right; and then to identify it was frequently a matter of the greatest difficulty, the allusion in the writer's mind having often been in the highest degree remote and indirect; yet were the trains of thought which suggested the references so rich and fertile frequently when developed, that it seemed a duty to bestow upon the work any amount of pains rather than let the allusions be lost. It was from being struck with the beauty and significance of these allusions in many cases, that the Editor was led to adopt the practice of putting texts at full length when they could be advantageously introduced into the paragraph, instead of leaving the reader to search them out, or not to search them out, in his Bible. This is the only particular in which the text of the present edition differs from the former, a change which the reader of the work will not be displeased with. The table of Contents at the beginning of the volume, (the several lines of which are introduced as a running sketch of subjects in the body of the work also,) and the Indexes at the end, are new.

CONTENTS.

I. PATTERN OF CATECHISTICAL DOCTRINE.

II. JUDGMENT OF THE LAMBETH ARTICLES.

A PATTERN

OF

CATECHISTICAL DOCTRINE.

WHEREIN MANY PROFITABLE QUESTIONS TOUCHING CHRISTIAN RELIGION ARE HANDLED,

AND

THE WHOLE DECALOGUE SUCCINCTLY AND JUDICIOUSLY EXPOUNDED.

WITH ADDITIONS.

B

PART I.

THE PREFACE OF THE CATECHISM.

CHAP. I.

OF CATECHISING.

Warrant of a Preface.

FIRST, let us see the warrant of a Preface, before we come to the work itself of catechising.

Clemens Alexandrinus intending his Pedagogy, or his Book of Instruction for young christians, and Cyril writing several catechisms for the same purpose, build themselves on David's example[a]; and we have it Psalm xxxiv. 11, where David being about in few words to set down the whole sum of religion, beginneth with this as his preface, "Come, children, hearken unto me, I will teach you the fear of the Lord." "Come children;" therefore we may make a Preface, or Introduction.

Preliminary observations.

And in this Introduction these three things are to be considered,

- that children ought to be instructed;
- the manner of this instruction;
- what is required of the catechised, that the exercise may be fruitful.

The knowledge of these points is necessary; because in scripture[b] Pharaoh maketh a scoff of it that their children should go with the Jews into the wilderness to worship God,

[a] [i. e. do as David did, in writing a preface or introduction. There is not either in Clement's or Cyril's work any particular allusion to David's practice.]

[b] [Exod. x. 8—11.]

as if children had nothing to do in such a work; and because Aristotle[c] and some other philosophers held that young ones were not fit auditors of moral instructions; and the orator[d] said that youth should take his course, *donec deferbuerit*, 'till the heat of folly was spent.'

Whatever these heathens said, the practice of most of them hath been contrary to these speeches; Phocylides[e] would have *παιδ' ἐτ' ἐόντα*, the little ones, taught in their tender years; and to that end Solon[f] left his sacred admonitions, and Pythagoras[g] his Golden Verses; and Plutarch[h] delineated a course for children's education; Athens also had a great care of instructing their youth, and then only permitted them to carry torches in their solemnities when they had made some progress in their literature; and Aristotle himself, *De repub.* vii.[i], holds it necessary that children be taught the instructions of virtue as soon as may be; and Tully[k] also elsewhere injoins that in tender years youth are to be kept in and restrained from lust and pleasure. The third witness is good both for the truth, and against themselves: where the one speaks concerning youth what their temper often is, not what it ought of right to be; the other in a plea oratoriously rather than truly, to excuse a young man's wild courses.

§ 1. *That children ought to be instructed.*

To proceed then;

First, the instruction of children is proved,

1. From the end of the Law; Psalm cxix. 9, "Wherewithal shall a young man cleanse his way? by taking heed thereto according to Thy word;" the Law is not only given for those of riper years, but even for the younger men to cleanse their ways.

2. From the Law itself; Deut. vi. 7, "thou shalt teach them diligently unto thy children;" and Exod. xii. 26, sqq., "it shall come to pass, when your children shall say unto you, What mean ye by this service? that ye shall say, It is

c [Eth. Nicom., lib. i. cap. 1. vol. ii. p. 1095.]

d [Pro M. Cœlio, § 18. vol. vi. p. 92.]

e [In Plutarch, De lib. educand., vol. vi. p. 10.]

f [Vid. Æschin. cont. Timarch. init. p. 296.]

g [See "List of Edd." &c. end of this vol.]

h [Vol. vi. init.]

i [Cap. 14, sqq. vol. ii. p. 1333, sqq.]

k [De Off., lib. i. cap. 34. vol. iii. p. 213.]

the sacrifice of the Lord's passover," &c.; children must be taught the meaning of the passover. And by their doings, whether they be godly and religious, or wanton and wicked, they shall be judged; *judicabuntur semitis suis,* Prov. xx. 11, "even a child is known by his doings, whether his work be pure, and whether it be right."

3. They are partakers of temporal blessings if they do well, Psalm cxxvii. and cxxviii., and of temporal curses, doing ill, 2 Kings ii. 24; "he turned back and looked on them, and cursed them in the name of the Lord; and there came forth two she bears out of the wood, and tare forty and two children of them."

4. In Golgotha are to be seen sculls of all sizes. Death, the reward of sin, cometh upon the young as well as the old; little and great, all must come to account and be judged; Rev. xx. 12, "I saw the dead, small and great, stand before God."

5. From the gospel; Christ at twelve years old submitted himself to be catechised; Luke ii. 46, "they found Him in the temple, sitting in the midst of the doctors, both hearing them and asking them questions;" and *omnis Christi actio nostra instructio,* 'every action of Christ is our instruction,' John xiii. 15; "I have given you an example that ye should do as I have done."

6. Christ reproved those that forbad little children to come unto Him; Matt. xix. 14, "suffer little children, and forbid them not, to come unto Me."

7. He allowed of Hosanna sung by them, Math. xxi. 16, Mark xi. 9; "have ye never read, Out of the mouth of babes and sucklings Thou hast perfected praise?"

8. He chargeth Peter to feed not only His sheep, but His lambs; and His lambs first, for the increase of the whole flock.

9. That our nature being then quick and prone to evil, may be turned to good. If children can say, 'Baldpate' to Elisha, why should they not say, 'Hosanna' to Christ? And that time is to be taken which is fittest for every thing; but this age is fittest to be taught, both in respect of the general duty, and docility, so that like a new mortar it savoureth that which is first beaten in it; as also for that

they are not yet acquainted with the cares of this world, with ambition, with adulterous acts, malice, &c. Therefore as saith Austin, *adhibetur magister extrinsecus ut sit intus*, 'children ought to have a governor and instructor without them till they have the grounds of religion in their hearts to be a governor and teacher within them;' so that when they come to years they cast not off subjection to government, but change their governor, lest having a governor neither within nor without, they should be sons of Belial, without any yoke or government.

§ 2. *The manner of this instruction.*

Secondly, for the manner of this instruction; it is Teaching or Catechising; "I will teach you," or, "I will catechise you."

The duty of the catechist, or him that doth catechise, is to make his doctrine easy to enter, by giving it an edge and perspicuity of method[1].

This teaching by way of catechising differeth from the other teaching which we call preaching, on this manner;

preaching is
- *a.* the dilating of one member of religion into a just treatise,
- *β.* for all ages,
- *γ.* without repetition by the hearer;

catechising is
- *a.* a contracting of the whole sum,
- *β.* chiefly for children,
- *γ.* to be repeated by the catechised.

There may be a summary of doctrine.

And here arise certain questions;—

Quest. 1. Whether there may be such a sum or not?

Ans. And that there may we see;

a. Matt. xxii. 37, sqq.; Christ drew the whole law into two heads, love to God and love to our neighbour; "thou shalt love the Lord thy God with all thy heart, and with all thy soul, and with all thy mind; this is the first and great commandment: and the second is like unto it, thou shalt

[1] *κατηχεῖν, resonare.* שנן *acuere, i. e. efficere ut penetret commodius.* שנה *repetere, sicut in acuendo.*

love thy neighbour as thyself; on these two commandments hang all the law and the prophets."

β. John iii. 16; Christ catechising Nicodemus drew the gospel to this head, "so God loved the world," &c.

γ. Eccles. xii. 13; Solomon draweth all the duty of man to these two, "fear God, and keep His commandments."

δ. Heb. vi. 1. Paul draweth the foundation of religion to these two, repentance and faith; "repentance from dead works, and faith toward God." So Acts xx. 21, "repentance toward God, and faith toward our Lord Jesus Christ."

ε. The learned think that the sum of teaching is meant by Paul, 2 Tim. i. 13, "the true pattern of the wholesome words;" Rom. vi. 17, "the form of the doctrine;" Rom. xii. 6, "the proportion of faith."

ζ. The physicians have aphorisms; the lawyers, instituta; the philosophers, isagoges; and why not divines, epitomes?

η. One calleth the two heads to which Christ drew the Law and the prophets, *sepem legis*, 'the hedge of the Law,' lest we might waver and wander *in infinito campo*, 'in an infinite field.'

The fruit of this.

1. We may refer all our reading to these two heads.

2. We see God's goodness in making things which are necessary to be known, easy, as the sermons of the Apostles when they baptised so many hundreds in one day; and those which are not easy, not so necessary.

Here take these two provisos;

1. They are inexcusable which seek not to know things so easy, 2 Pet. iii. 18; 1 Cor. xiv. 20; Ephes. i. 13;

2. We must continually proceed, and still seek for more and more knowledge; for as in some places of the scripture the lamb may wade, so in others the elephant may swim, and we must search both; for we shall never be free from this, "search the scriptures," John v. 39.

Religion may be so taught.

Quest. 2. Whether it may thus be taught?

Ans. Yes; and this is demonstrated,

1. Before the flood, Gen. iv. 3, 4, the word was taught by tradition, and not by writing; and therefore they reason probably that say, without this the worship of God could not have continued. Surely Cain and Abel's sacrificing must needs be taught by their father Adam; and of him Abel must necessarily learn what was typed and signified by his sacrifice, and thereupon be remarkable for his faith, Heb. xi. 4. Adam doubtless would teach his children what God taught him and Eve, that "the seed of the woman should break the serpent's head."

2. After the flood till Abraham's time there was no other way of teaching but by traditions, which, as some think, were put in writing by the gentiles and were called the books of the Sibyls.

3. In Abraham's time we consider,

a. that he taught his, Gen. xviii. 17. 19, "I know him," saith God, "that he will command his children and his household after him," &c;

β. what he taught them, Gen. xvii. 1, "I am the Almighty God;" xviii. 18, "Abraham shall surely become a great and mighty nation, and all the nations of the earth shall be blessed in him;" xxii. 18, "in thy seed shall all the nations of the earth be blessed;"

γ. the fruit of his teaching, in his son, Gen. xxiv. 63, he went to pray; and in his servant, v. 12, he prayed before his business. This servant also at the end of his business concludes with prayer and thanksgiving for his good success, Gen. xxiv. 27; "he said, Blessed be the Lord God of my master Abraham, who hath not left destitute my master of his mercy and his truth; I being in the way, the Lord led me to the house of my master's brethren." His care also of performing his master's business shewed well how he was religiously instructed, Gen. xxiv. 33; where he would not eat till he had declared his message.

4. In the time of the Law, Deut. vi. 7, "thou shalt teach them diligently unto thy children," &c.

5. The practice hereof we see in David, Psalm xxxiv. 11; and Solomon testifieth of David, Prov. iv. 4, "he taught me also," &c.; 1 Chron. xxviii. 9, "and thou Solomon my son," &c.; in Solomon to his son Roboam in the first six chapters of the Proverbs; in Jehoiada, 2 Kings xii. 2, to Joas the young king, who "did that which was right in the sight of the Lord all his days wherein Jehoiada the priest instructed him." After the captivity, it appears by Josephus and the Jews' Talmud that there were between Antiochus' and Christ's time four hundred houses of catechists, whither their children being once thirteen years old were sent to be catechised; the Pharisees also had a special care to train up their novices, though in many things corruptly, and taught them the letter of the Law. To these Paul may seem to have relation, Rom. ii. 18. *κατηχούμενος ἐκ τοῦ νόμου*, 'catechised in the Law.'

6. See the practice of it also in christians, Eph. vi. 4, *ἐκ- ρέφειν*, 'to train them up continually,' *ἐν παιδείᾳ*, &c. 'in instruction;' 1 Cor. xiv. 19, *ἵνα καὶ ἄλλους κατηχήσω*.

Examples of those that were catechised;—Theophilus, Luke i. 4;—Apollos, Acts xviii. 25;—Timothy, 1 Tim. iii. 15; both are included, Gal. vi. 6, "let him that is taught in the word communicate unto him that teacheth in all good things."

What effect the Apostles' and their followers' catechising had, Hegesippus[m] testifies, saying that hereby it came to pass that no known commonwealth in that part of the world was inhabited which within forty years after Christ's passion felt not a great shaking of its heathenish superstition. Julian the apostate[n], the grand and subtle enemy of christianity, perceiving this, inhibited and suppressed all christian schools and places of catechising and teaching the liberal arts; and if this tyranny had not been as a cloud soon passing away, it might have been feared that his policy would in short

[m] [Vid. Euseb. H. E., lib. ii. cap. 23. p. 77; lib. iii. cap. 20. p. 109. cap. 32. .127; lib. iv. cap. 22. p. 181.]

[n] [Aug. De Civ. Dei, lib. xviii. cap. 52. vol. vii. p. 535; Socr. H. E., lib. iii. cap. 12. p. 187; Theodoret. H. E., lib. iii. cap. 8. p. 129.]

time have overshadowed all religion. By our catechising the papists have lost ground of us, and can never recover it again unless by a more exact course of catechising than ours.

§ 3. *The duty of the catechised.*

Thirdly, the duty of the catechised is, often to go over the same matter, as the knife doth the whetstone; and to repeat it till they have made it their own. The parts of his duty are to Come, and Hear.

First, to come.

First, we must come;

1. This is that that the prophet speaks of, Psalm xl. 6, 7, "then said I, lo, I come;" that he rejoiceth at, Psalm cxxii. 1, "I was glad when they said unto me, let us go into the house of the Lord;" Esay ii. 3, "come ye, and let us go up to the mountain of the Lord;" for in the temple one day is better than a thousand elsewhere, Psalm lxxxiv. 10.

2. The cause of our coming must be in respect of God, because He hath said, Come, though no man were any way to be respected.

3. We must be absent from no part of catechising, for unless we have all we can make no profitable building.

4. We must not any way excuse our absence, for we see them blamed that made excuses, Matt. xxii.; though the things were indifferent which they alleged, yet when they hindered them from God they were sin. No pastime, that was Esau's trade, Gen. xxv. 27; nor sluggishness, as Esay xxix. 10, "the spirit of deep sleep;" nor idleness, as Matt. xx. 6, must keep us from the house of God.

5. Because every one that cometh is not welcome, but such as come prepared, as 2 Chron. xxix.; many things are unperfect for want of preparation; and 1 Chron. xxix. 18, David prayed to have their hearts prepared; so in giving of the Law, Exod. xix., and in giving of the gospel, Matt. iii. 3, preparation is enjoined;—therefore it is necessary we come prepared:

And with what preparation.

And this preparation standeth in two points;—

a. That which is Acts xi. 23, a settled purpose of heart to abide in the doctrine of God, to put it in practice, to rule our lives accordingly, Psalm cxix. 9; for without this all is of no effect. A young man, Psalm cxix. 9, must rule himself according to the word, that he may cleanse his ways thereby; it availeth not to hear God's word, unless we do it. The pharisees' corrupt doctrine was leaven, wholly infecting their disciples; but Christ's doctrine was leaven, whose property it is, 1 Cor. v. 6, to turn the whole lump into the property of itself, and this seasoned His scholars perfectly with christianity.

β. When our hearts are prepared, we must then pray for wisdom, Psalm cxi. 10; James i. 5; 1 Kings iii. 6, 7; Matt. xxi. 22, that we may feel the sweetness of it, that that may breed delight, and delight diligence to attain it. We must also pray that God's word, likened to nails and goads, Eccles. xii. 11, may be fastened in our hearts, and that we may be bettered by His sharp threatenings, and incited to all godly actions by the goads of reproof, as well as comforted and cheered up by the honeycomb of His mercies.

Secondly, to hear.

Secondly, it is required that we hear; Luke xiv. 35, "he that hath ears to hear, let him hear;" Mark vii. 6, a man may be *præsens absens*, 'near in body, far off in heart.' We think all the preparation to be in the speaker and none in the hearer, but Christ saith, Luke viii. 18, "take heed how ye hear;" and His reason is, he that heareth well shall have more good things revealed unto him than he heareth; but he that doth not, shall have that knowledge taken from him which he hath. And the gentiles were not far from the truth, who held that a solecism and absurdity might as well be committed in our hearing amiss, as in our speaking amiss; this Esay found true, when the people came near God with their mouths and lips, but had their hearts far from Him, Esay xxix. 13; their ears heard not well, nor conveyed the message well to their hearts.

What faults to be avoided herein.

And in our hearing four faults must be avoided;

1. we must not stare here and there, but having our eyes fastened on him that teacheth, still attend him; Luke iv. 20,

"the eyes of all them that were in the synagogue were fastened on Him;"

2. not hanging the face, 2 Cor. ix. 7; God loveth cheerfulness, as in the giver, so surely in the hearer; Col. iii. 23, "whatsoever ye do, do it heartily;"

3. not moving the body to and fro, as if we were weary;

4. not gaping, as if we were fit to sleep; but as the heathen before their sacrifices had one that stood up and cried, *hoc agite*, 'do or intend this;' so we must intend what we are about, that we may so hear as to remember; for if we hear and remember not, we are like an hour-glass, which as soon as it is full runneth out again. The word must have recourse to our hearts, for *quod cor non facit non fit*, 'that which the heart doth not, is not done.'

And lastly, we must so remember it as to practise it. And that is indeed the best examination of our hearing, *à posterioribus; antecedentia* are not so sure; a man may guess of the goodness of the mould, but he knoweth what it is when he seeth the corn; for as there is *febris spuria*, 'a bastard fever,' which only hath the same *symptomata*, 'signs,' which true fevers have; so there may be *spuria pietas*, 'bastard godliness.'

How we should examine what we hear.

Finally, our examination of that we hear standeth in three things,

1, searching and enquiry, Esay viii. 19, "should not a people seek unto their God?" John v. 39, "search the scriptures;" Rev. ii. 2, "thou hast tried them which say they are apostles, and are not, and hast found them liars;" Acts xvii. 11, they "searched the scriptures daily, whether those things were so;"

2, meditation, Gen. xxiv. 63, "Isaac went out to meditate;" Psalm i. 2, "in his law doth he meditate day and night;" 1 Tim. iv. 15, "meditate upon these things;"

3, conference, Luke xxiv. 17; Gal. ii. 2.

Thus then I conclude as Cyril[o] did his preface,
meum est docere, ''tis my work to teach;'
vestrum auscultare, 'yours to learn;'
Dei perficere, 'God's to give a blessing to both.'

[o] [Procatech., cap. 17. p. 13.]

The foundation of our catechising, in Four Questions.

The course of religion which we are to treat of is likened to a building; he which is to teach is likened to a builder; the principles of religion are called a foundation; that must be digged deep till we come to the rock, that our building may not be shallow upon the earth without foundation. The builders of our age dig not deep enough; they dig not to the rock; now to dig till we come to the rock that we may build surely thereupon, is after this manner;—

If any ground of religion be set, we must seek whether the ground be true; and if it be scripture, we must seek what the regard of God is toward man, that He would give him the scripture, or His word; then we must know whether He be a God. But our builders presuppose that God is, and that the scriptures are true, (as they are indeed,) and so presupposing it never seek for reasons to prove it, and by that means build upon such a slender foundation that they leave advantage to the adversary; for we know that many have gone about to undermine the very foundation, and say plainly there is no God; and we know also that when the devil hath brought his winds and his storms, he hath shaken the very saints of God because they have not built deep enough.

Therefore that we may begin at the very rock, we will ask these four questions;

1. Whether there be a God or not: against the Atheist.

2. Whether He hath that respect of man, that He would give him His word to reward the good and punish the evil: against the Epicure.

3. Whether the scriptures be His word and true, or not: against the Turk.

4. Whether our religion be truly grounded on His word: against the Jews and papists.

CHAPTER II.

OF THE FIRST QUESTION: WHETHER THERE BE A GOD.

Our warrant for the FIRST is, Heb. xi. 6, "He that cometh to God must believe" first, "that God is."

And here we note three things;

1. That the fruit of our religion and our felicity is, to come to God; that is the end of our journey.

2. The means to this is, to believe; that is the way to the end.

3. That God is, is that which we must believe.

§ 1. *Of the first point, that the end of our journey is, to come to God.*

I. First, the end of our journey is to come to God.

The phrase of 'coming' used in our vulgar tongue, as 'coming' to wealth, honour, learning, may shew us thus much in christian wisdom; that while man kept God's commandments and submitted his wisdom to God, he was partaker of God's goodness and happiness, but desiring to depart from God, he fell in extreme misery;—first, into sin; secondly, into shame; thirdly, into fear; fourthly, into travail; fifthly, into death.

But all who come again unto God shall find remedy and deliverance from all these, and enjoy felicity.

Arguments against the other supposed ways of happiness.

Men think they may be happy by other means than by coming to God; as the worldling by wealth, the politician by honour, the epicure by pleasure, the stoic by virtue, the platonist by contemplation.

Against these we will make short exceptions.

Against the first, wealth.

1. Wealth is not desired for itself, and therefore cannot be felicity; all the wealth we have is for but food and raiment; and what is the use of them but to keep our body and nature lest it fail, and not to amend it; but that which is felicity must do both.

2. The end of man is better than man; but no man will give

his life for the whole world, therefore riches being worse than man cannot be man's end, and so not felicity or happiness.

3. If wealth should be felicity, then a man should be esteemed by that which he hath, and not by that which he is, and so his purse should be better than himself; but as we do not esteem a sword by the scabbard, nor a horse by his trappings, so not a man by his wealth.

4. The good that cometh by wealth is to spend it, and so to part from it; but it should be absurd to part from felicity; and therefore wealth cannot be happiness.

Against the second, honour.

1. They bring themselves from this, when they say *honorem esse virtutis umbram,* 'honour is the shadow of virtue;' for who knoweth not that we must leave the shadow and follow the body; therefore even by their own account rather virtue than honour is true felicity.

2. If honour should be happiness, then many should be unhappy to honour one and to make one happy.

3. If they be honoured by some, they may be despised by others or at another time, and so not happy; and if it be answered that they must be *honore digni,* they fall into virtue again.

4. *Honor est bonum sine serâ aut clave,* 'honour is a kind of good which is neither under lock nor key;' it hangeth on other men's mouths, and therefore hath no stability; as we see in the Jews' honouring of Christ, one day they would have made Him a king, but within few days after they crucified Him.

Against the third, pleasure.

1. Pleasure is for sensible things, and therefore inferior to man who is a reasonable creature, and so not his end, and therefore not felicity.

2. The very beasts have pleasure at liberty, without seeking any private place, or without any remorse of conscience, which man that setteth so much by pleasure, cannot have; and yet they will not say that beasts have felicity; but *apage felicitatem quæ latebras quærit,* 'away with such an happiness as hides itself in corners,' as pleasure doth.

4. They say themselves pleasure is not good but in medio-

PART I.

crity, and so they leave pleasure and cleave to mediocrity; whereas if it were felicity the more of it the better it were.

3. We call him continent that abstaineth from pleasure, and continency is a virtue; shall we then say that he is continent or virtuous that abstaineth from felicity?

Against the fourth, virtue.

1. Moral virtues are to pacify our affections, or for the rule of our actions and works; and so not for themselves and therefore not felicity.

2. Justice is to keep peace; fortitude to make peace; therefore not for themselves, therefore not felicity.

3. Prudence, which they call the chief virtue, is nothing but to direct us to the end, and not the end itself, and so not felicity; and so seeming to teach us to shoot, they take away the mark.

Against the fifth, contemplation.

1. It is absurd in nature, that any thing should have *generationem longam,* 'a long time to be growing,' and *fruitionem brevem,* 'a short time to be enjoyed in;' but this is so long in getting that it never comes to enjoying, always in conceit and never in act, and so not felicity.

2. They testify of themselves that they never attained it. Socrates was wont to say, *hoc solum scio me nihil scire,* 'this only I know that I know nothing;' Aristotle, that he had *γλαυκοὺς ὀφθαλμοὺς in contemplandis entibus cœlestibus,* 'owls' eyes in contemplating heavenly essences;' Simonides[p], that by longer meditation he was the further from the knowledge of God; Heraclitus found it so deep he could not sound it. *Maxima pars eorum quæ scimus est minima pars eorum quæ nescimus,* 'the greatest part of things we know is the least of things we know not.'

Thus much of these five severally.

Now generally against them all.

They set down for their felicity two things,

the first, *terminus appetitûs, αὐτάρκεια,* 'satisfaction of the appetite;'

the second, perpetuity.

[p] [Cic. De nat. deor., lib. i. cap. 22. vol. ii. p. 415.]

There is wanting in them, first, satisfaction.

First, for satisfaction of the appetite;

1. To come to any thing but to God, satisfieth not our appetite; for all the world is too little for it, because it was ordained to receive God: and without God there is no universal good; then there is some want, then a desire of that which wanteth; and so the appetite not satisfied, but for want thereof unquietness, and so no felicity.

2. Ἐπιθυμία, 'a desire,' they derive of *θυμεῖν*, *ardere*, 'to burn,' and so we say *ardens appetitus*, 'a burning or earnest desire;' now if a man heap never so much wood on a fire, it will not quench the fire, but make it bigger and apt to receive more; and so this fervent and burning desire is never satisfied but in God, but still more and more inflamed; *quomodo igitur ejus sitim extingues cujus sitis ex potu crescit*, 'how will you quench his thirst whose thirst increases by drinking?'

3. These things are not made to fill the appetite, no more than learning to fill a bag, or the air to fill him that is hungry. And as Alexander wept when there was not another world for him, so all they that go about to satisfy their appetite with any thing beside God do but more and more increase their appetite; and whether they be given to pleasure, or to the desire of wealth, or honour, or whatsoever, the more they have the more they would have; and they deal as Theocritus saith of the covetous man, first he saith, *mille meis errent in montibus agni*, 'may I have a thousand lambs feeding on the mountains,' and having gotten *mille agnos*, then *pauperis est numerare pecus*, ''tis a sign of a poor man when one can count his cattle.' [Idyl. xvi. 90. p. 582.]

Therefore we conclude hence, that all these ways are like drink to a man that is troubled with a dropsy; they satisfy not our appetite; and so we cannot make them the end of our journey, nor be happy by them; and so not possible to have an end but in God.

There is wanting in them, secondly, perpetuity.

The second thing in their felicity is Perpetuity;

1. Where perpetuity wanteth, there is fear of losing the good we have, and so unquietness, and therefore no felicity; but this perpetuity is in none but in God; for all other

PART I. things either pass from us, or we from them, as one saith, *si non habent finem suum, habebunt finem tuum,* 'if they have not their own end, they shall see an end of thee.'

2. That they are uncertain we see, as money for thieves, merchandise for the winds, cattle for the rot, building for the fire; and all uncertain.

3. Man's life is also uncertain, as we see by daily experience; and then seeing one of these must needs depart from the other, neither of them can be the felicity of the other.

In coming to God, are both of these.

On the other side, by coming to God there is both satiety and stability; both satisfaction of the appetite, and perpetuity and continuance of that satisfaction. For as Christ saith to the woman of the water, John iv. 14, so we may say of God, He is the fountain, and he that drinketh of Him, he that hath Him, shall never thirst; he shall be satisfied, and that not for a time, but with stability for evermore.

The experience of this coming to God, we see in David, Psalm xvi. 11, "with Thee is fulness of joy for evermore." And Solomon found by experience the vanity and emptiness of all other things whatsoever, as appeareth in his book of Ecclesiastes.—Yea the heathen themselves confess this; as before Christ, Sibylla[p] confesseth that the union of man with God is true felicity; and Plato, *De repub.*, lib. x.[q]; Pythagoras[r] in his Golden Verses;—since Christ, as Plutarch, Simplicius[s], Jamblichus[t], Aphrodiseus[u].

So that it is proved	by answer to their several exceptions, by demonstrative arguments, by experience, and by confession of the heathen,	that God is our felicity.

And so we may conclude this point with that of S. Augustine in his Meditations[x], *Domine creasti nos ob te, nunquam quietum cor erit donec pervenerit ad te,* 'Lord, Thou hast

[p] [Lib. iv. lin. 24. sqq. p. 37.]
[q] [Vid. § 12. sqq. p. 214.]
[r] [Vid. p. 4. sup.]
[s] [Comment. in Epictet., p. 218.]
[t] [De Myst., sect. x. passim, præsert. capp. 1, 5—8.]
[u] [Alexander Aphrodiseus, or Aphrodisiensis, a commentator on Aristotle.]
[x] [Vol. vi. Append. vid. pp. 123 A, 125 B, 126 A.]

created us for Thy own sake, our hearts will never be at quiet till we come to rest in Thee.'

Thus much of the first point, that the end of our journey is to come to God.

§ 2. *Of the second point, that the way to come to God, is by belief.*

II. The second point is, the way or means to come to God, which is belief.

To come to God there are two ways, { by reason, or / by faith. }

The Manichees[y] held that error, that by cunning and reason we should come to God, and not by faith; which opinion is next unto atheism. This the Manichees held in a bravery against christians, because they well knew that the philosophers would rather submit to their sect, opening *fontem sciendi*, 'the fountain of knowledge,' than to the christians, laying on them *jugum credendi*, 'the yoke of belief;' and this was the cause that some philosophers, who became christians, were first drawn into Manicheeism, and afterwards were won thence to the orthodox doctrine of Christ. And such be they whom the learned in our days call *quæristæ*, which will have a reason for every thing: as, Why thus, and not rather thus? and therefore so far as they see reason, so far they will go, and no further.

Now then we must prove that faith is the best way, and reason the worst.

We cannot come to God by reason.

1. If by knowledge only and reason we could come to God, then none should come but they that are learned and have good wits, and so the way to God should be as if many should go one journey, and because some can climb over hedges and thorns, therefore the way should be made over hedges and thorns; but God hath made His way *viam regiam*, 'the king's highway.'

2. Many are weak natured, and cannot take the pains that is needful to come to knowledge; and many are detained by the affairs of the commonwealth.

[y] Aug. De util. cred., cap. i. § 2. vol. viii. p. 45.

3. Many are cut off before they come to age to understand reason and to attain knowledge.

And so we see that few by reason can come to God.

Faith not a sign of lightness.

Object. And whereas they object against faith, as Porphyry did against the christians in his time, that it is a sign of lightness and credulity, which might breed occasion of doubting whether they were in the truth or no; which objection hindered many in that time;

Ans. 1. We answer them by themselves; for they say themselves, that *nemo credulus nisi qui credit stulto aut improbo,* 'no man is counted credulous but he that believes a fool or a knave;' which two things are both excluded from God, and it were blasphemy to say otherwise; and so remaineth no place for credulity in believing of God. Besides, our believing is grounded on the word of God; which word, though it was delivered by the ministry of men, yet was of great power; as plainly appeareth, for those very men, first, healed leprosies, dropsies, men possessed with foul spirits, palsies, &c., all diseases; cures far beyond the strength of physic's skill; secondly, they raised divers from death; thirdly, they shook the powers of Heaven; fourthly, unlettered and plain men in one day became skilful in all tongues. Therefore what was done by them had the divine power working by their ministry, and was far above all human abilities.

2. Lightness is more in reason than in faith; for when there were two hundred and forty-eight sects of philosophers, and every one had a diverse felicity and divers reasons, there must needs be many crooked ways, and so, much doubting of the one side and credulity on the other.

3. In the knowledge of *prima entia,* 'first essences,' they are in the dark; for the principles of reason are from the sense, but God is above sense and reason, and beyond both.

4. Themselves dispute that God is above all reason of man. And therefore we cannot come to God by reason.

We cannot come to God save by belief.

Now to shew that there is no other way to come to God, but belief.

1. If they should in any matter be driven to prove every thing by reason, it would drive them into madness.

2. No man can make demonstration of every thing, no not in matters of the world; a man cannot make a demonstration that his father is his father, or that he is his son; so that there must needs be belief.

3. If a man should say he hath seen such and such a place, he can make no demonstrative reason of it; for the circumstances are not capable of demonstration, and no more is God, being the end of our journey.

Of belief.

Thus much for the necessity of belief;—now for belief itself.

1. *Oportet discentem credere,* 'a learner must believe;' we must lay hold of that we hear; but this belief at the first is not perfect, *nam quod recipitur in imperfectum est primo imperfectum,* 'for that which is received in an imperfect body is at the first imperfect;' wood in the fire is first warm before it burn; it hath *calorem alienum,* 'heat from another,' before it have *proprium,* 'its own' heat; so the learner must first take *ex aliena fide,* 'of another man's credit;' Esay vii. 9, *nisi credideritis non stabiliemini,* 'unless you believe ye shall not be established.'

2. We must try and prove those things which we thus receive, either *à priori,* or *à posteriori; quia ut virtutum reliquarum, ita et religionis principia nobis innata habemus,* 'by what is precedent or consequent,' 'for we have inbred in us the principles, as of other virtues, so of religion;' and reason uncorrupt always agreeth with God's word, and so God sends us often to nature; so the Apostle, Acts xvii. 24, &c.; Rom. i. 20, "the invisible things of Him from the creation of the world are clearly seen, being understood by the things that are made."

3. When we have thus strengthened our faith, we must yet look for a higher teacher; for though faith be a perfect

way, yet we walk unperfectly in it, and therefore *in iis quæ sunt supra naturam soli Deo credendum*, 'in things above nature we must believe God only;' so that we must look to God for His spirit and inspiration.

4. This inspiration cometh not at the first, and therefore we must, as they say, *festinare lentè*, 'make haste with leisure,' to avoid rashness; as Esay xxviii. 16, *qui crediderit non festinabit*, 'he that believes maketh not haste,' so we must wax perfect by little and little, and ever be building "to our faith, virtue; to our virtue, knowledge; to our knowledge, temperance; with temperance, patience; with patience, godliness; with godliness, brotherly kindness; with brotherly kindness, love," 2 Pet. i. 5; and though we build slowly, yet ever be sure to build on the rock.

Thus much for the second point, that the way to come to God is by belief.

§ 3. *Of the third point, that God is that which we must believe.*

III. The third point is, that God is that which we must believe; that there is a God.

For the preparation to this point we will first note

Four errors of Satan.

1. Autotheism; he persuadeth man that he shall be God. So he did Adam; but in the very same day it was proved false, for when Adam hid himself and was afraid, he shewed plainly that he was not God; (and here note that, as we fell from God by unbelief, so we must come to Him by belief.) So Alexander's flatterers said he was a God[z], and he persuaded himself no other, till he saw his own blood. So Claudius thought himself God, till the thunder made him afraid, and then he was glad to hide himself and to say, *Claudius non est deus*, 'Claudius is not a god.'

2. Because God, when man was fallen and had undone himself, made him garments, shewed him how to dress the earth which by the influence of heaven should yield him food, and gave him the use of the rest of the creatures, and thus was an help and stay to man, and man cannot stand

[z] [Vid. Plutarch, Vit. Alexandri, vol. iv. p. 68.]

without Him, therefore the devil persuadeth by a false conversion that of what man or thing soever we receive any good, that is our god; so saith the philosopher, τὸ τρέφον θεός ἐστι, *quod nutrit Deus est*, 'that which nourisheth us is God.' And this is polytheism, to have many gods, or more gods than one.

3. Because among so many gods there was no true God, it came in question whether there were a God or not, and so came atheism, to deny that God is.

4. The end why the devil doth all this is that they should worship him; so did Julian the apostate; and so by conjuration the devil worketh feats and maketh men believe that he is a god, and so they worship him.

But our drift is most especially against the third of these, atheism.

Account of atheism.

They that stand in defence of atheism set down these five heads;

that there was a time when men wandered like beasts;

after wandering they came into society;

they ordained laws unto themselves to preserve their estate;

these laws were not able to bridle them;

by that mean they invented that there was an ἔκδικον ὄμμα, 'a just eye,' to see them even in secret, so that by this invention they might be afraid to do evil.

This is that which the atheists say for themselves.

The theory false.

But all these are taken away by this, that laws were not before religion, but on the contrary religion long before laws; for in Homer's time they had religion, though they had no laws; and it is manifest that laws came into the world a thousand years after religion, to tame those brutish men which like horses and mules would not be tamed by religion.

But more particularly against these; and first, that religion is no vain invention.

1. The universality of the persuasion of God in all

nations and all places, proveth it, in as much as there is no history which sheweth the manners of any people, but it sheweth also their religion; yea all both new and ancient commonwealths had always something which they worshipped and called in their language God.

2. If it be here said that one nation received religion of another, that is also an argument against them; for they are so far from taking it one from another, that there is as great variety herein as may be, even of those that are borderers one to another; some worshipping invisible things, some visible, as the heavens and elements; yea, some a red clout hanging on a pole, and some that which they met first in a morning.

3. Falsehood claims no kindred of time, but truth only is time's daughter; therefore every thing that is besides truth, by invention or whatsoever, will be worn out; but religion was, is, and shall be perpetual; therefore no invention of man.

4. If it be here said that religion continueth so long because it is so necessary to keep men in awe, that is also another argument against them. For falsehood and truth cannot agree; and they dare not say that policy is a feigned thing; and therefore if religion do uphold policy, it must needs be true and not feigned, for truth needs not falsehood to maintain it. And that religion upholdeth all policies and all commonwealths, we may see plainly; for take away religion, and take away,—first faith, that one shall not trust another; secondly, temperance, that concupiscences shall not be bridled; and thirdly, submission to governors;—and where would then the commonwealth be?

How it arose.

Now secondly, we can shew against atheism the person, the time, and the place of forging of it. For Ham the youngest son of Noah, whom the heathen sometimes nominate, after he had the curse of God and of his father, he first took stomach against God, and began this atheism, to deny God, in Egypt, in *anno mundi* 1950, as Josephus reporteth; and secondly, seeing he was deprived of all joy of the life to come, he gave himself to all sensuality and to witchcraft, and so to the devil.

So that in him we see these two causes of atheism; first, a stomach, and desire to revenge; and secondly, sensuality; which come of the two parts of our mind, *θυμὸς* and *ἐπιθυμία*, understanding and will.

1. For the first of these; stomach we may see in Diagoras[a], who, as Diodorus Siculus reporteth, having written a book of verses and made it ready to be set forth to his commendation, was by stealth deprived of it; and when he had called him that had stolen it before the senate of Athens, he sware that he did it not, and so was quit, and afterwards set the book out in his own name; which when Diagoras saw, and that he was not presently stricken with a thunderbolt, he became an atheist. The reasons of Diagoras are very frivolous, and such as in that great confuting world none would vouchsafe to answer; for thus he reasoned; Saturn, Mars, Juno, &c. are no gods, therefore there is no God at all; as if he should argue, Many seem to be good scholars which are not so, therefore there are no good scholars at all.—Likewise it is testified[b] of Porphyry and Lucian, which at the first were christians, and receiving injury by the church, the one by words, the other by blows, in a spite and stomach against the church, became atheists.

2. For the second, which is sensuality; Epicurus himself and Lucretius[c] say that they have an excellent benefit hereby that become brutish, and think that the soul is not eternal or immortal.

But the very heathen confute them here.

a. For the first, in things which are corrupted, corruption taketh hold both of the thing itself and of that whereby it liveth, both at once; but in ages when the body is most weak, the mind is most strong, and therefore eternal.

β. Secondly, the soul, the more it separateth itself from the body, the more perfect it is, as in temperance, justice, learning, and other virtues; and therefore in the greatest separation, namely, after death, it shall be most perfect.

γ. Thirdly, the soul is the subject of truth, which is eternal.

[a] [Suidas, art. Diagoras, p. 933.]

[b] [Nicephorus, lib. x. cap. 36. vol. ii. p. 88. D.]

[c] [Lib. iii. 16. et passim.]

PART I.

And thus we see that atheism may be referred to these two causes, stomach, and sensuality. As Arcesilaus[d], seeing the way to knowledge to be hard, yet because he would needs be a philosopher, denied that there was any knowledge, so these atheists, seeing it is somewhat painful to live a religious life, say that there is no religion.

The doctrine false: shewn first, à priori.

Now to shew there is a God.

1. The reason of the philosophers is manifest to prove that there is a God, namely, that there is a first mover and a first cause of all; for if this were not so, there should be before every mover, another mover, and so *in infinitum*. And if the causes were infinite, they should either have infinite motion and so infinite time, or else infinite things should move in finite time, both which were absurd. As also seeing the inferior thing moved doth not move without a superior mover, if there were not a supreme and first mover of all, there would not be at all any effect or motion of these inferior things.

2. The second reason to prove that there is a God, is from the spiritual nature of man; for there is in man a spirit set upon mischief to do hurt both to body and goods, which would have destroyed all before this time if there had not been a superior power to resist this evil, and that is God.

3. A third reason is from the frame of the world, and from thence many reasons may be gathered.

a. Though we dig long before we come to the head of a spring or the root of a tree, yet we know the spring hath a head and the tree hath a root; so we may think that the world had a beginning, as we see in the figure of it; and Damascene[e] reasoned very demonstratively that it had a beginning, because it is always in alteration and change.

β. The agreement of so many divers things sheweth that of necessity there must be some modulator of such a harmony.

[d] [Cic. Acad. i. 12. vol. ii. p. 75; Brucker. Hist. Phil., vol. i. p. 746; Bayle, art. Arcesilaus.]

[e] [De fid. orthod., lib. i. cap. 3. vol. i. p. 126 A.]

γ. Experience teacheth us that all things in the world had a beginning; as commonwealths, laws, learning, &c. Diodorus saith, that laws came from the Jews and commonwealths from the Chaldeans, &c.

δ. Pliny's whole Natural History was written to this end, to shew that all things had a beginning.

Object. 1. And for that which they say against this, that *ex nihilo nihil fit*, 'of nothing can be made nothing;'

Ans. We answer, there is *alia conditio rei dum fit, alia factæ; nutritur quisque in conceptu per umbilicum, post conceptum per os,* 'the condition of a thing in the making, and of it made, is different; we are nourished in the womb by the navel, after our birth by the mouth;' in generation it is so, but before generation it was not so.

Object. 2. And for that they say we cannot tell whether the *motus* or *movens* were *prior*, 'the motion or mover were first;'

Ans. No more can we tell in this sensible thing of the *systole* and *diastole*, 'the rising and falling of our pulse,' which was first; yet we know that this pulse had a beginning from the heart, so both *motum et movens*, 'that which moves and the mover,' from God.

So then there was a beginning;

And if there were, it was either by chance, nature, or God.

First, not by chance; proved thus;

a. If a man should see but a cottage or stye in a desert, he would conceive there had been a builder; and if a man should spy a triangle, as Aristippus did, he would say somebody had made it. For so in common talk we attribute no generation or effect to chance, but corruption and mishap we call mischance; as when we say such a house was burnt by fire, we call it a mischance.

β. If it were by chance, then there should be no order; but in the world there is an excellent order and harmony, yea, no confusion, except it be in the corrupt actions of men.

Secondly, not by nature, as appeareth thus;

a. By nature we understand the continual course of all things; now if all things should have their beginning by nature, then they should bring a natural reason of all things;

but that can they not do, as of the ebbing and the flowing of the sea, of the colours in the rainbow, of the strength of the nether chap, and of the heat in the stomach, which consumeth all other things and yet not the parts about it.

β. The virtues they make not all natural, but are fain to make some heroical to come from God.

γ. If nature were the first and chief cause of all things, then nothing should be done against nature; but we see things fall out contrary to nature, as the sun to have an eclipse in the full of the moon, and such like.

Thirdly, seeing neither by chance nor nature, it followeth therefore that all things had their beginning from God.

Shewn, secondly, from things without us.

Which we prove also further thus;

1. All the prophecies shew the same. And these prophecies we see to be marvellous, if we mark them; Isa. xlv. 1, of Cyrus, a hundred years before Cyrus was born;—1 Kings xiii. 2, of the birth of Josias, three hundred years before it came to pass;—Josh. vi. 26, the building of Jericho, five hundred years before it was re-edified; and fulfilled, 1 Kings xvi. 34.

2. Also the power and art in the creation shew plainly that it was of God, Acts xvii. 27. And even them whom miracles would not move, have the least things of all made astonished and confounded, and forced them to confess God's power; as Pliny wonders at the gnat so small a creature yet making so great a buzzing, and so also at the butterfly; so Galen[f], when he had profanely written of the excellent parts of man, when he came to one of the least, stood astonished, and is compelled to name God.

And thus by those things which are without us we may see that there is a God.

Shewn, thirdly, from things within us.

Now also by those things which are within us.

1. *From our souls.*

We have an immortal soul, as we proved before; then

[f] [Lib. iii. cap. 10. vol. iii. p. 237.]

this soul must either be the cause of itself, or have some other cause.

Of itself it is not the cause; for,

a. we know not ourselves, neither our own parts, no not by anatomy, and therefore we cannot be the cause of ourselves;

β. our parents know not what they begot or conceived, and the cause being reasonable must know the effect;

γ. we are not able to command the parts, nor to stay in ourselves the natural motion in the pulses, and therefore we must of necessity have a cause; and there is none in the world that hath reason, but man, and none above reason, but God.

Therefore as Aratus his poem is, Acts xvii, "we are His generation," and Rom. i. 19, "that which may be known of God, is seen in His creatures."

2. *From principles of truth therein.*

In our souls are principles of infallible and demonstrative truth; as to honour our parents, to do as we would be done to, to defend ourselves, to keep promise, &c.; which principles hold with all men, unless they be horribly profane. Amongst which principles this is one, that there is a God, and that God ought to be worshipped; and howsoever other of these principles fail, yet this never faileth, for though men be never so much bent to other wickedness, yet before they be utter atheists, they will worship some one thing or other as God.

How it cometh that there are atheists.

Quest. If it be questioned here, how then cometh it that there are some atheists?

First, we may answer with Seneca, *mentiuntur qui dicunt se non sentire esse Deum, nam et si tibi affirmant interdiu, noctu tamen et sibi dubitant,* 'they lie that say they think there is no God; for though they affirm it to thee in the day time, yet they doubt of it in the night with themselves.'

Secondly, it is true that a man may harden his own heart much, and proceed in great perverseness; and indeed some make their hearts fat, and are sick with the pleasures of the world; yet whatsoever he be, if God put His bridle into his mouth, those sparks and notions that God hath put into every man's soul will break forth, and the darkness shall not always be able to obscure the light; as if God vex them with any of these three;

[v. 489 sqq.] *α.* first, with trouble, as in Æschylus his tragedy called Persæ, when they must needs fall into the hands of the enemy unless they be holpen, then though they were never so evil, they would down on their knees and pray to God;

β. secondly, with sickness, as a philosopher and an atheist called Diogenes being afflicted with sickness and pain of the strangullion, detested his opinion;

[vol. vi. p. 270.] *γ.* thirdly, with age; so Cephalus in Plato, *De Repub.* i., in his age said to Socrates, whilst he was a young man he never thought there were any Styx, but now in his old age he became to doubt, What if there be one?—So that these three things do make the most wicked to confess God.

3. *From the distinction of good and evil.*

By the distinction of good and evil. We see, Gen. ix. 22, Ham could perceive it was not good to lie as his father did naked;—Gen. xiv. 21, the Sodomites would recompense good for good;—so Gen. xxvii. 41, though Esau will kill, yet not whilst his father lived;—so 2 Sam. xvi. 17, Absalom though he were in war against his father yet he could rebuke unkindness towards a friend. So then when the most evil would seem good, and being very evil in themselves, yet rebuke evil in another, this is really to distinguish between good and evil. Now there must be a ground of this distinction; and it is not of man, as Pyrrho would have it, for then every thing at man's appointment should be good or evil; and therefore the ground of this distinction must be from a higher nature, and that is God.

4. *From our conscience.*

Also we may see there is a God by our conscience, God's deputy; else why should the wicked be troubled in conscience if there be not a God?

Object. If any say they are thus troubled lest they should be revealed, and so the law should take hold of them;

Ans. Let them do some heinous deed in the wilderness where none seeth them, yet they will never be quiet, but the conscience will beat and whip the soul; yea, they will tell it themselves either in sleep or in madness, or at least they will be afraid that the bird in the air will tell it; and their worm never dieth; Esay lxvi. 24, "their worm shall not die, neither shall their fire be quenched."

5. *From deaths of atheists.*

To conclude this point, this may be a manifest argument to prove that there is a God, that even they which have denied Him in their lives have approved Him in their death;

α. Pherecydes[g] an Assyrian being merrily disposed at a banquet amongst his friends, bragged how long he had lived and had never done sacrifice to any god; but his end was miserable, for he was devoured of lice;

β. Diagoras[h] for his damnable opinions was the cause of the destruction of the whole country of Melos, for revenge of his atheism;

γ. Julian[i] the apostate being shot in the bowels with an arrow as he was in battle against the Persians, pulled out the arrow, and receiving the blood as it gushed out into his hand, cast it into the air crying, *Vicisti Galilæe,* 'Thou hast overcome me, O thou Galilean,' and so died blaspheming;

δ. Lucian[k] going to supper abroad left his hounds fast when he went, and as he returned home having railed against God and His word, his dogs fell mad and met him and tore him in pieces;

ε. Apion[l] scoffing at religion and chiefly at circumcision, had an ulcer the same time and place, as Josephus reporteth;

ζ. Machiavel rotted in the prison of Florence, as the Italians write.

These and a number of atheists more, though they denied God in their lives, yet by their deaths they have approved that there is a God. And therefore as it was written on Zenacharib's tomb[m], *εἰς ἐμέ τις ὁράων εὐσεβὴς ἔστω,* 'he that

[g] [Diog. Laert., vol. i. p. 90. Jambl. De Vit. Pythag., p. 252.]

[h] [Thucyd., lib. v.]

[i] [Theodoret. H. E., lib. iii. cap. 25. p. 143.]

[k] [Suidas, col. 2338 A.]

[l] [Cont. Apion., lib. ii. § 13. vol. ii. p. 1374.]

[m] [Herod. Euterp., cap. 141.]

beholds me, let him be religious and acknowledge God's hand;' so say we, let him that looketh on the death of these men learn to be godly, learn to acknowledge that there is a God.

And thus much of that first point against the atheist.

CHAPTER III.

OF THE SECOND QUESTION: WHETHER GOD BE A REWARDER OF GOOD AND EVIL.

The SECOND point is, that He hath regard and is a rewarder of good and evil.—For we must not only know the essence and being of God, by which little glory cometh to Him, and less profit to us; but we must also know His providence; and they which deny His providence are semi-atheists, as the Epicures, who though by the reasons of the heathen they confess there is a God, yet they deny His providence utterly, and therefore are half-atheists.

§ 1. *Opinions concerning providence.*

Of His providence there are four opinions;

1. That there is none at all, but that He doth as it were draw the heavens a curtain betwixt Him and us;

2. That there is a providence, but it is of general things not of particular;

3. That there is a providence, both of general and particular things, but it is idle and not rewarding;

4. That there is a providence both of general and particular things, which rewardeth good to the good and evil to the evil; and this is the truth which we hold.

Objections against a providence considered.

For the first their reasons are three;

a. first, the adversity of the good and prosperity of the wicked; for, say they, if there were any Providence, he would see that it should be *bonis benè, malis malè*, 'well with the good, ill with the wicked;'

β. the abuse of gifts; for Providence would have given

the use with the gifts, or else would not have given so good gifts to them that should use them so ill;

γ. the evil effects in natural and moral things; and God would not suffer so much evil if He had any care or providence over the affairs of men.

For answer to the first.

We must know there is no man absolutely good, or absolutely evil; but as the best have some evil, so the worst have some good; and therefore God will punish that evil which is in the good with temporal punishments, and give temporal blessings to the evil for the good that is in them; that seeing all good must be rewarded with good and all evil with evil, the good of the good might have an everlasting reward of good, and so contrariwise the evil of the evil might have an everlasting reward of evil.

For answer to the second.

The same answer may serve against the second; for as, if it had been only *bonis bene*, 'well with the good,' the devil would have said, "Doth Job serve Thee for nought?" so here, if God had given to all the use with the gifts, the devil would have said, "Job can do no other but serve God, it is no praise to him:" but when some that are wicked have as good gifts as the godly, and do notwithstanding abuse them, it taketh away this exception of Satan, and maketh much for the praise of the godly and the glory of God in them.

For answer to the third.

Those things which come so to pass, God hath no part in the doing of them; for though the power that does them be from God, yet the power is in the soul, and the soul faulteth not, but the crooked body the instrument of the soul, God so permitting it.

And of this permission of evil we have three reasons;

a. God permitteth evil, that is, the defect of good, *per privationem gratiæ*, 'by depriving men of His grace,' or else there would not be,

PART I.

first, such perfect resemblance of chiefest good; nor
secondly, any variety of things by degrees, but only one good thing; not
thirdly, any order; and *ordo mater pacis*, 'order is the mother of peace.'

β. Sundry virtues should be superfluous, as justice and fortitude; and it were unseemly to make all the parts of a man's body of like dignity.

γ. That God should be loved in the highest degree; *nam bonum carendo magis quam fruendo cernitur*, 'for good things are discerned rather by wanting them than by enjoying them.'

And generally, God permitteth evil that a greater good may come of it; as by the greatest evil and most wicked action that ever was, namely the betraying of Christ, came the greatest good to man, that is, salvation.

§ 2. *That there is a general providence.*

Now to prove that there is a providence, and that not only in general but of particulars; and that not by nature or chance, but as it reacheth to every one, so it rewardeth good to the good and evil to the evil.

For the first, general providence;

1. It is natural for every thing to have *στοργὴν*, 'a natural love,' toward that which it bringeth forth; and all men call *ἀστοργίαν*, 'want of natural love,' a vice; but there is no vice in God, and therefore *στοργὴ*, 'a natural love,' and so a providence;

2. Things are yet daily in generation; and no wise man leaveth off his work before he have finished it; therefore God is not without providence.

And a particular providence.

For the second, particular providence;

1. Aristotle[n] saith, and so it is also proved by others, that the sea is higher than the earth; and they can render no reason why it should be kept from overflowing the land, and therefore it is God's providence;

[n] [Meteor., lib. i. cap. 14. vol. i. p. 352.]

CHAP. III.

2. Plotinus[o] reasoneth from the plants which grow between a fruitful and a barren ground, and shoot all their roots towards the moist or fruitful soil; and so from the lilies, which shut themselves with the sun, lest they should receive evil and corrupt moisture in the night;

3. That there is a providence, David of the birds saith, The young ravens are fed of God, being forsaken of their dams, and left bare; for out of their dung ariseth a worm which creepeth to their mouth and feedeth them.

4. Wild beasts
- *a.* rest in the day time when man goeth forth, Psal. civ;
- *β.* are not so fruitful as the tame;
- *γ.* keep in holes and desert places, though they be desirous of prey.

5. All creatures living
- *a.* know the place of their nourishment, as the lamb her own dam;
- *β.* distinguish their own nourishment;
- *γ.* avoid that which may hurt, as the lamb doth the wolf.

6. Men love their own children, though they be never so crooked and untoward.

7. The sudden cry of all things, *quasi vox naturæ clamantis ad dominum naturæ,* 'as if the voice of nature did cry to the God of nature;' which comes at some sudden fear, as though there were no help but in God.

And thus we see the providence of God in particulars; of which Theodoret[p] wrote ten orations against those which thought providence to be as a clock whose plummets were wound up in the beginning and go ever after of their own accord.

§ 3. *That providence is not by nature, or chance.*

For the third, that providence is not by nature, or by chance.

First, not by nature.

1. Because the means work nothing of themselves, neither can bread nourish without the staff of bread, which Christ calleth the word of God; and unless that be added to the

[o] [Ennead. vi. lib. 7. cap. 15. fin. p. 708.]

[p] [Vol. iv. p. 482, sqq.]

PART I.

bread we shall decay, and, as Agge i. 6, put our wages into a bottomless bag. And this is called by philosophers, infusion into nature; for we see the best meats will not nourish some, nor the best complexion prolong life, without this infusion; and therefore there is another cause beside nature, which is God's providence.

2. Because we see the things brought to pass without the means; as God created the light before the sun, that we might know that it dependeth not of the sun; so did He make the fruit with the seed in it.

3. Because there are some effects, and some things done contrary to nature, and against nature: as Christ with clay healed the eyes, whereas the nature of clay is to put them out; Elias mended the salt water with salt; so the christians with meanness and simpleness overcame the great and learned philosophers.

Secondly, not by chance.

1. We see the contrary in that which they attribute most to chance; as in war, *sors domina campi*, 'chance is the lady governess of the field,' so the heathen and profane men were wont to say; but we christians know that God is a man of war, and fighteth for His servants and gives them victory, or else for their sins and to humble them giveth them into their enemies' hands and maketh them lords over them. And the heathen themselves made their worthies, Diomedes, Ulysses, &c. prosperous by the assistance of some god; and even in the heathen stories often there goeth a vow before war, and after the victory the performance.

2. We see it in drawing of lots by the mariners, when it fell upon Jonas.

3. We see it in the chief chance, that is chance-medley; it is providence; for Cambyses[q] lighting off his horse, after he had been shewing great cruelty to them of Athens, his sword flew out of the scabbard and slew him.

4. The philosophers call chance but a remotion of the cause; and therefore providence cannot be ascribed to chance or nature.

[q] [Herod. Thal., cap. 66.]

§ 4. *That providence reacheth to every one.*

For the fourth, that providence reacheth to every one, and rewardeth.

First, to every one, every *individuum*.

1. Providence is a part of prudence, which is busied *circa res practicas*, 'about things tending to practice,' which are *individuæ*, 'particulars.'

2. All the qualities of God are equal, but His power is over all, therefore also His providence; and it is sure that His power reacheth to every thing, for *virtutis est maximæ pertingere quam remotissima*, 'it shews the greatest power to reach to things most remote.'

3. It is better to have provided for every particular than if only for the general: and therefore is Mithridates[r] commended for calling all his soldiers by their particular names.

And reward.

Now for reward. Though we be bound to serve Him, yet the rather to move us He will reward us; and if any say He rewardeth some but not all, His rule is, *dabo huic novissimo sicut et tibi*, 'I will give to this last as I give thee.'

Thus much against the Epicure; that God hath regard, and is a rewarder of good and evil.

CHAPTER IV.

OF THE THIRD QUESTION: WHETHER THE SCRIPTURES BE GOD'S WORD.

The THIRD point of the four general points is, that the scriptures are God's word, and true; and so are not either the oracles or the miracles of the heathen or Turk.

The ground for this is 1 Cor. viii. 5, 6, "though there be many gods that are so called, yet to us but one God."

r [Qu. Cyrus? vid. Val. Max., lib. viii. cap. 860, "De Cyro et Mithridate regibus," fol. 309.]

<table>
<tr>
<td>And here note four ways</td>
<td>that the heathens which continue in America and in the east isles and a great part of Tartary,
that the Turk,
that the Jews,
that the christians,</td>
<td>walk in.</td>
</tr>
</table>

Of all which there is but one true and the rest false; and therefore let us have a care to apprehend the truth, and not to hang our religion on our country where we were brought up.

§ 1. *Of the way of the heathen.*

First for the way of the heathens.—They exceeded all men indeed in all wisdom philosophical, but wanted the true wisdom of godliness and true religion.

I. Against their many gods S. Paul hath two arguments together in one place, proving that there must needs be but One,

1. *ἐξ οὗ τὰ πάντα·* He from whom all things are, can be but One; as we see,

a. in superior things, so many motions from one, so many lights from one; and

β. in inferior things, so many roots, so many members, so many streams, so many veins, all from one head;

2. *εἰς ὃν τὰ πάντα, in quem omnia concurrunt,* 'to Whom all things tend;' for there can be no mutual order *nisi sit in uno conjunctus,* 'unless it be united in one;' and therefore one, and but one God.

II. Pythagoras saith that there is an infinite power, or else our reason should exceed the Maker thereof. For what finite thing soever is, we can comprehend it; and if the power be infinite, the subject wherein that power is must needs also be infinite, or else *adjunctum excederet capacitatem subjecti sui,* 'the adjunct would exceed the bounds of his subject;' and there can be but one infinite subject, and therefore but one God.

III. If there be many, yea, or but two gods, and both omnipotent, then, as Lactantius[s] saith, they must be either

[s] [Div. Inst., lib. i. cap. 3. vol. i. p. 9, sqq.]

1. equal, and then either { agreeing, and so one superfluous; or disagreeing, and then all would be dissolved; or,
2. unequal, and then one would swallow up another.

Testimonies against it, from heathens themselves.

These reasons were not hidden from the heathen themselves, for,

α. Pythagoras[t] bade his scholars search till they came to *μονάδα*, that is 'unity,' in everything.

β. Aristotle hath his *primum, ante quem non sunt alia,* 'first, before whom nothing was;' and that there is *primum ex primis*, the 'first of all first,' that is, God.

γ. Zeno hath this saying, *dicite plures et dicite nullum,* 'say there be more gods, and say there be none at all;' so polytheism is next to atheism.

δ. Plato[u] in his epistle to Dionysius warneth him to mark that when he beginneth to write of a certain truth, he beginneth with *θεὸς*, 'God,' but when he writeth that which is doubtful, he begins with *θεοὶ*, 'gods;' and so partly for fear and partly for love, that they would not trouble the commonwealth, they dissembled the truth.

ε. Sophocles[x] saith, *εἷς ὁ θεὸς*, *unus est deus*, 'there is one God.'

Augustine[y] *De civ. Dei*, lib. iv. cap. 24, saith that some excuse the heathen, and say that they gave their gods those names which they had, only to shew their effects, and not as having any such conceit that they were gods indeed; which if it were so, then it seemeth in their own consciences they were convicted that there was but one true God.

§ 2. *In particular, of the heathen gods.*

To come more particularly to the heathen gods.

1. They commanded images to be erected to them, and told the fashion that they were of, as Porphyrius saith; but no infinite thing can be resembled by any shape, therefore they were not infinite, and so no gods.

[t] [Brucker. Hist. Phil., vol. i. p. 1049.]

[u] [Ep. xiii. ad fin. vol. ix. p. 156.]

[x] [Euseb. Præp. evang., lib. xiii. cap. 13. p. 680.]

[y] [Vol. vii. col. 106.]

PART. I.

2. They forbid nothing but outward things, therefore are men and no gods.

3. They challenge but some particular honour, as Origen saith, some for medicine, some for wisdom, some for war, &c.; but God is universal and to be universally honoured, therefore they were no gods.

4. As Cyril said against Julian[z], (which made Julian to stagger,) the sin of the body defileth the soul; now their religion was only in offering frankincense and such outward oblations, and therefore could not cleanse the soul.

5. Their manners, parents, and birth is set down

by
- poets, Hesiod;
- philosophers, Tullius *De naturâ deorum;*
- Cyril against Julian;
- Augustine *De civitate Dei;*
- Eusebius *De præparatione evangelicâ;*
- Cyprian *De vanitate idolorum.*

And Alexander[a] having private talk with Leo a priest of the Egyptians, was by him certified that the Grecians had their gods from the Egyptians, and Romans from the Grecians, or else from Asia by Egypt, and that the Egyptians could in their chronicle shew their progeny, as Hermes Trismegistus.

6. They were not only men, but wicked men, yea and some of them harlots, as we may see in Eusebius *De præparatione evangelicâ;* Cyril; Josephus *In Apionem;* Athanasius; Tertullian.

7. They not only worshipped men, and wicked men, but even beasts also.

Of the worship of men.

Quest. And if it be asked, how came men to be worshipped? and more, how came they to worship beasts?

Ans. First, of the worship of men there are two causes.

1. Because Cham had persuaded them that every thing that did them good was their god, and so they worshipped those that did deliver them either from peril, evil beasts, or evil men.

[z] [e. g. lib. ii. p. 45; lib. x. p. 338, et passim.]

[a] [Aug. De civ. Dei, lib. viii. cap. 5. vol. vii. col. 194; lib. xii. cap. 10. col. 309.]

2. Because as Porphyry, out of a writer not now extant, called Sanctonicanus, saith, Ninus[b] having gotten renown by his father, set up an image to remember him after he was dead; and that his memory should be the more famous, he made to it a sanctuary, that whoso fled to it were saved, what evil soever they had done. And therefore many that would flatter Ninus, and seem thankful, appointed a day in the year to meet at it and to be merry, and so it grew afterwards to be worshipped.

And of beasts.

Secondly for the worship of beasts.—Plutarch[c] speaking of Isis and Osiris, saith that Osiris, that he might the better govern the people, set up signs at the places of division, as he divided them, and gave to some a dog, to some an ox, to some a clod, to some a crocodile, for a sign; and afterward forgetting to what end those signs were set up, they worshipped the signs; he that lived by the ox, worshipped it, he that lived by the water, worshipped the crocodile, &c.

Of the miracles and oracles of the heathen gods.

Quest. Here also may be asked how they came to work miracles, and to give oracles as they did use to do?

Ans. First, for miracles; true miracles do always profit, as the healing of the blind or lame; but they did none such, neither could the magicians do any such, and therefore their miracles were not true miracles.

Secondly, for oracles; they spake not, but the devils in them; and if they gave any answers, they were as often false as true, and always ambiguous, as Eusebius saith, no more than a politic man may conjecture by the good or evil disposition of the cause.

But more plainly to prove that they were devils, in their cruelty they would desire men to be offered unto them; and when they were more mild they would have stage-plays, and

[b] [Vid. Hieron. in Ezech. xxiii., vol. iii. col. 856; in Osee ii. col. 1251; Ambros. in Rom. i. 23, vol. ii. append. col. 33; Cyril. cont. Julian., lib. iii. ad fin. vol. vi. p. 110.]

[c] [Vol. vii. p. 492, sqq.]

specially that wherein were gladiators, in which his chance was counted the best that could kill the other.

Thus much against the way of the heathen.

§ 3. *Of the way of the Turk.*

The second way is that of the Turk, who doth substitute Mahomet, and will not have Christ, because they think Him not to be the last prophet; and therefore they follow altogether a religion devised by Mahomet.

Against Mahomet's doctrine;

1. It must not be disputed of, whereas truth loveth trial; and to set down that for a rule is as much as if he should say, It is good money, but weigh it not.

2. It hath fables and false tales in it, as Andreas Maurus[d], a Saracen, and bishop there, noteth nine hundred untruths in the Alcoran; whereof two in the eighth section are very gross; one, that Abram was the son of Lazarus; the other, that Mary the mother of Christ was the sister of Aaron[e]; which are both, as all the rest, manifest untruths.

3. In that everything in it is sensible; as sect. xvi. Mahomet himself said he felt the hand of God seventy times colder than ice; and that one angel had seventy thousand heads[f]; and that the devil is circumcised, and such like.

4. The promises in it are carnal pleasure, fit for nobody but Heliogabalus, cap. xxxv., lii., and liv.

5. The precepts which are in the lxv. chapter of the Alcoran are indulgent to perjury; and cap. xliii., *impium non ulcisci*, 'it is impious not to revenge a wrong;' and that they may have many wives; also they favour adultery; a man may have four wives and five concubines, cap. xxiii.; none must be accused under four witnesses; also they allow men to couple themselves with beasts, and to spoil one another's goods.

6. The miracles which he pretendeth, had no witness, nor any possibility of truth; as, that an angel when he was a child opened his heart, and took out that lump of blood

[d] ["Confusio Sectæ Mahometanæ, à Joanne Andreâ, Mauro," &c.] Lond. 1734.]

[e] [Ut sup. p. 51. Sale, p. 251, 4to.

[f] [Ut sup. p. 106.]

which is the cause of sin; as though the cause thereof were not spiritual.

7. The means of propagation of his kingdom, cap. xv., was by the sword and by compulsion; whereas the truth doth draw men of their own accord.

8. Lastly, the effects, perjury, murder, &c.

Therefore Mahomet with his doctrine is false and to be shunned.

§ 4. *Of the way of the Jews.*

The third way is the way of the Jews.

The contentions between the Jews and us are concerning Christ, whom they deny, and we profess.

The Jews hold the Old testament for true, and also certain of their own writers; therefore from hence we draw some arguments against them.

And herein the Jews hold three errors concerning Christ;

that the Messias shall have a princely court at Jerusalem;

that Christ is not that Messias;

that that Messias is yet to come.

Against their first error.

1. Esay liii. 6, "upon Him was laid the iniquity of us all;"

Psalm xxii. 16—18, "they pierced My hands and My feet," &c.; "they part My garments among them, and cast lots upon My vesture;"

Dan. ix. 26, "the Messias shall be slain," &c.;

Zach. ix. 9, "rejoice, O daughter Jerusalem, behold thy King cometh unto thee," &c.

Out of these places the chaldee paraphrase, Rabbi Jonathan, R. Simeon, R. Moses of Nisa, R. Hatzadok, and all the ancient rabbins, might and did gather that Christ should be such a one as these places describe Him; and therefore in the gospel they sent unto John a poor man, saying, "art thou He, or shall we look for another?"

2. In Agge ii. 8, "the expectation of the gentiles." But if He be a king of the Jews only, the gentiles would not look for Him, for it is against nature to desire a stranger to be

their king; and forbidden, Deut. xvii. 15, "one from among thy brethren shalt thou set king over thee; thou mayest not set a stranger over thee, which is not thy brother."

3. The Messias must bring felicity to all men; but how should an earthly king profit Abraham, or the dead? and if the dead should rise again, all Jerusalem were not able to hold them.

Against their second error.

1. Gen. xlix. 10, Jacob's prophecy that the sceptre should not depart from Judah nor a law-giver from between his feet, until Shiloh come; but it was then departed when Christ came; therefore Christ is that Shiloh or Messias.—The sceptre was in Judah till the captivity; and in the captivity they had one of their brethren called the king of captivity; and after the captivity it continueth till Aristobulus and Hyrcanus, who striving for it were both dispossessed, and Herod an Idumean placed in their room; and then came Christ, as was prophesied.

Object. The Maccabees were of the tribe of Levi, not of Judah.

Answ. The prophecy is divided, that there shall be a king or law-giver till Christ, and Simeon Justus was the last of the levites.—And if they understand the prophecy of the tribe in general, that the tribe shall last in Judah till Christ, by reason of the word שבט, we see that after Christ came, and after the dispersing of the Jews, there neither was nor is any tribe, but they are all mingled one with another; the emperors labouring still to root out the Jews, and especially that tribe, and so made them to confound the genealogies.

2. Dan. ix. 24, seventy weeks, which are four hundred and ninety years, ended at our Saviour's death.

3. Agge ii. 9, "the glory of the second temple shall be greater than the glory of the first;" and how should that be without the Messias? for the first was far more glorious outwardly than the second.

And we see in their Talmud, chap. iii.,

1. The disciples of Hillel[g], seeing the first seven weeks,

[g] [Petr. Galat., lib. iv. cap. 19. init.]

Dan. ix. 24, fall out so justly, looked for the coming of the Saviour in those days, being long before the full due time, because they read in Esay that the Lord would shorten those days. CHAP. IV.

2. Esay ix. 7, למרבה with ם final, themselves took for a great mystery, and that ם in that place signifieth six hundred, for six hundred years between Christ and Esay.

To the which arguments we may add,

1. The continual sending to and fro of the Jews to John baptist, which is a manifest token of their looking for Christ at that time.

2. The great company of false Christs and deceivers, more at that time than ever before or since, either eight or ten, as Josephus witnesseth in his sixteenth, seventeenth, and eighteenth books, Judas, Theudas, Galonites, Athronges, &c.; insomuch that there were four hundred drowned at once following Bar Cosba the younger, whom all the rabbins, excepting one, confessed to be Christ.

3. Suidas mentioned out of Theodosius a noble Jew, that [Col. 1751.] before Christ did rebuke the scribes, they marvelling at His wise answers and questions, made Him one of the priests, and entered His name Ἰησοῦς ὁ υἱὸς Θεοῦ καὶ Μαρίας, 'Jesus the son of God and of Mary,' otherwise He being of the tribe of Judah could not have been suffered to preach at Nazareth, Luke iv.; at Capernaum, Math. xi. 23.

4. The destruction of the second temple, which could not be before Christ; Luke xix. 43, "the days shall come upon thee that thine enemies," &c.

5. The desolation of the Jews, prophesied Amos ii. 6, and Zach. xii. 2, 3; and we see how Vespasian offered them peace, and they would not; which made the first breach;—secondly, he brake into their city at Cedron, where they took Christ;—thirdly, on the same feast day that Christ was taken;—fourthly, he whipped them where they whipped Christ;—fifthly, he sold twenty Jews for a penny, as they sold Christ for thirty pence. So that he must needs be the Messias, for the selling and crucifying of whom they were so handled.

Against their third error.

The arguments that proved Christ to be the Messias prove also that He is not yet to come.

Yet we may see out of themselves;

1. They could not build the temple at the emperor Julian's commandment, for fire flying out of the earth[h].

2. They have been deceived in the prefixing of times; insomuch as now, whereas the mean Jews were wont to hire the scribes and rabbins to teach them, now the rabbins are glad to hire them to hear them.

3. There is now no Bethlehem where He should be born.

4. Themselves confess that He was born before the destruction of the second temple, but they say He lieth yet hid; but that is confuted by Augustine.

5. They say the world must last but six thousand years; two thousand before the Law, two thousand under the Law till Christ, and two thousand after Christ under grace; and there are past already five thousand and some odd hundreds, and therefore their expectation of Christ yet to come is now vain, and their religion false and erroneous.

Thus much against the way of the Heathen, Turk, Jew.

CHAPTER V.

OF THE FOURTH QUESTION: WHETHER OUR RELIGION BE TRULY FOUNDED ON GOD'S WORD.

The fourth way is the way of christians, or christian religion; which is all one with the FOURTH general point which is set down before, and therefore we will handle them both together, and therein prove that our religion is truly grounded upon the word of God.

The ground for this is 2 Pet. i. 19, "we have a most sure word of the prophets," &c. where the apostle teacheth us that we have the Law from God immediately, and all other scripture by the ministry of men, but yet so as they spake nothing but that which the Spirit of God commanded them and inspired into them, and therefore that which they delivered we must hold for a most sure and infallible truth.

[h] [Chrysost. de S. Bab. § 22. vol. ii. p. 574.]

§ 1. *Of our religion, as the same with the Jews'.*

Now to prove that christianity is true religion.

Shewn true, from its antiquity.

I. The ancienty of it; for,

a. seeing man must come to God, and religion is the way, it must needs be as ancient as man is, or else should man have been destitute at that time when he wanted religion; and,

β. this religion is *copula relationis,* 'the tie and bond of relation' between God and man, and therefore must be of the same continuance with the *relata.* Therefore Tertullian[i] *Adversus hæreticos* saith *prima sunt vera,* 'the first things are true;' and the philosophers call *prima entia verissima, quia ut verum est affectio entis, sic falsum non entis,* 'things first existent are most true, for truth is an affection of being existent, as falsity of non-existency;' *nam falsum non potest subsistere in suo, quia non est, ergo subsistit in alieno,* 'for falsity cannot subsist in its own, because it is not, and therefore subsists in that is another's,' so that *verum est prius,* 'truth is before it.' Now we say,

γ. that our religion is the same which the Jews had before Christ; for as the Law is nothing else but the old gospel, so the gospel nothing but the new Law; the Law *evangelium reconditum,* 'the gospel under veil,' the gospel *lex revelata,* 'the law unveiled;' and therefore our religion the same that the Jews had before Christ, and so the most ancient of all other religions.

It is the parent of heathen religion.

a. As for the heathen fables, it began with their gods Hercules and Æneas, &c. about the Trojan war, which was after our religion three thousand years; and Orpheus the first poet was after Moses eight hundred years, as Strabo[j], Plutarch[k], and Diodorus Siculus[l] testify. And the most ancient records of the heathen began in Solon's time, which was when Crœsus was, which was in the time of Cyrus and Esdras; and Herodo-

[i] [De præscript. hær. passim., p. 202, sqq.]

[j] [Lib. xvi. vol. ii. p. 1103.]

[k] [e. g. De mus., vol. x. p. 654.]

[l] [Lib. i. cap. 94. vol. i. p. 105.]

PART I. tus the most ancient of their writers beginneth his story with Crœsus.—Therefore what God soever they had, their worshipping of God came from the Jews, as the Frenchmen had their Druids from the Romans, and the Romans from the Grecians, and the Grecians from Cecrops an Egyptian; and so the Carthaginians from Cadmus a Phœnician; and those two countries Egypt and Phœnicia, with the Mediterranean sea, do compass about Judea; so that all their religion came from the Jews.

β. So the wise men of Greece asking their gods whence that knowledge of arts should come, received this answer, *μόνος ἤδ' ἄρα Χαλδαῖος σόφος·* that is, *solus utique Chaldæus sapiens est,* 'the Chaldean alone in this very regard is wise;' which *ἤδ' ἄρα* noteth some particular part of the Chaldeans, which is the Jews. So saith Orpheus [m], when God was angry He destroyed all, and left it *uni Chaldæo.*

γ. And Plato in his Epimenides referreth all *uni barbaro,* 'to the barbarian alone [n].' If we ask who this *barbarus* should be, the Egyptians call him 'Theut [o],' which signifieth 'a stranger,' meaning Abraham; for so Origen against Celsus [p], and Josephus against Apion, say plainly that when the heathen conjure they would say, *per deum Abraham,* 'by the god Abraham.'

δ. Likewise Phocylides [q] his verses are plainly translated out of Moses. And themselves say that Plato had his wisdom from the Egyptians. And Strabo saith that Pythagoras had conference in the mount Carmel, lib. xvi. Eusebius *De præp. evang.* [r] saith, that although Aristotle was never in Egypt, yet all his conference was with an Egyptian, as Clearchus a peripatetian testifieth of him.

ε. And it is found that some of the Old testament was translated before the Seventy, and the old poets would have translated the whole into greek, but that for strange visions and sickness they durst not.

ζ. So it appeareth that in every famous nation God had

[m] [Euseb. Præp. evang., lib. xiii. cap. 12. p. 665.]

[n] [See also the expressions of the platonist Amelius concerning St. John, in Euseb. Præp. evang., lib. xi. capp. 18 fin., and 19. pp. 540, sqq.]

[o] [Ubi sup. lib. i. cap. 9. p. 31.]

[p] [Lib. i. cap. 22. vol. i. p. 339 C.]

[q] [See "List of edd." &c., end of this vol.]

[r] [Lib. ix. cap. 5, sq.; p 409, sq.]

ever some register; as in Egypt, Manetho[s]; in Chaldea, Berosus[t]; in Asia Minor, Abydenus[u], &c. So Herodotus hath the story of Sennacherib[x]; the edict of Cyrus[y]; all Daniel, though somewhat corruptly.

η. Josephus lib. xi[z]. as Augustine, lib. viii. *De civ. Dei*, saith, that Alexander being in Babylon would have the Jews to help to build a temple to the image Belus, and because they would not he went up to destroy them, but Jaddus being priest met him in his priest-like apparel, whom when Alexander saw he fell off his horse and worshipped, and told his nobles the cause, namely, that God which commanded him to conquer the earth appeared unto him in that shape.

θ. Also by the library of Ptolomy in Alexandria was the Jews' religion spread abroad.

ι. So Laertius[a] writeth that Epimenides being asked the cause of a great plague in Athens, answered that it was from a higher power, and that for the staying thereof they must sacrifice τῷ ἀγνώστῳ θεῷ, 'to the unknown god,' for so they entitled their altar, Acts xvii. 23.

κ. And the Romans called their temple which they built to Bacchus for victory, *templum pacis æternum*, 'the everlasting temple of peace,' because Delphos told them it should stand *dum peperit virgo*, 'till a virgin brought forth a child,' but as soon as Christ was born it fell.

And thus do the heathen prove the antiquity of our religion and therefore the truth of it.

Shewn true from other reasons.

II. A second reason for the proof of christianity, is the preservation of God's word, whereon our religion is grounded. Notwithstanding the Jews were hated, imprisoned, and contemned, yet not one tittle of this book perished; whereas all other knowledge is corrupted and perished, though it have been much made of and greatly esteemed; therefore this is the truth which we hold.

s [Joseph. cont. Apion., lib. i. § 14. vol. ii. p. 1336.]

t [Ibid., § 19. p. 1342.]

u [See Fabricius, ed. Harles. art. *Abydenus*, vol. i. p. 197.]

x [Euterp. 141.]

y [Clio, ad fin.]

z [Ant. Jud., lib. xi. cap. 8. § 5. vol. i. p. 503; Orig. cont. Cels., lib. v. § 50. vol. i. p. 616.]

a [vol. i. p. 81.]

PART I.

III. The certainty of our religion; whereas all others are
1, unperfect, 2, contradicting one another,
3, counterfeit, 4, full of question,
ours is not so.

1. Unperfect; so are all other religions, going on by little and little, and so coming to what perfection they can; whereas God's law was once given, and then all, and therefore perfect at the first; and so perfect as that nothing hath been added thereunto or may be detracted from the same, but only it hath been made more plain and open.

2. Contradictory; so are man's laws, and religions that are human; in men's laws there is yea, nay; but in God's laws, yea and amen, 2 Cor. i. 20. And the fathers by seven rules of contradictions have reconciled all that the malicious could object.

3. Counterfeit; insomuch that they have hidden their wisdom as much as they could; but God hath shewed His to all that it might be seen; yea, the christians have had it in their frontlets and in their guards, and such open places; nay more, they have died for confession of the truth thereof.

4. Questionful; the latter writers correcting and descanting upon the former; but none of the prophets ever called in question that which other had said, but proved and strengthened it.

IV. A fourth reason for the proof of christianity is from the end of it. The end of other religions is, as an unregenerate man's end in all his actions, only themselves; but that religion which attributeth all to God,—"every good gift and every perfect gift is from above, and cometh down from the Father of lights," Jam. i. 17,—is the true religion; but no religion except christianity doth attribute all to God, but respect and seek man, either in whole or in part.

V. The precepts in man's laws do neither command all good nor restrain all evil; so the Athenians had their *græca fides*, 'grecian fidelity,' and the Spartans, *furtum spartanum*, 'the lacedæmonian theft;' the seventh commandment is wholly broken of them, and so the whole first table;

but on the contrary this religion of ours both commandeth all that is good and also restraineth all that is evil.

VI. The laws of men are restrained according to the time, place, and person; as the wise men answered the king that would have married his own sister, that indeed there was a law that a man might not marry his own sister, but they found another law that the king might do what he would; and so the king should have more liberty to sin than the subject. But the precepts of our religion are general to all alike; so that to the king as well as to the subject we say as John baptist said to Herod, *non licet tibi,* 'it is not lawful for thee.'

VII. There is no religion but this that reacheth to the heart; for except only this there is not one law that hath in it *non concupisces,* which pulleth out as it were the very core of sin.

VIII. The Trinity, Creation, and Incarnation, the true metaphysics, are only in this, and only to be conceived and understood by this religion.

IX. Not to hide the faults of our own father is unnatural, to cover the evil of our friends and country is natural; therefore that which plucketh out this course of nature must be a thing supernatural and above nature; but Moses was contented to speak in discommendation of his own stock, and spared not his brother Aaron, nor his sister Miriam, no not his own self sinning at the waters of strife; therefore this is only the truth.

X. All other laws teach us to enlarge kingdoms and to be in favour with princes; but this our religion supernaturally teacheth us that live, to hate life. And so the prophets did not seek the favour of princes, but reproved them to their faces; and therefore this is that truth which is not ashamed, and is that truth which cannot proceed of man.

XI. As God is a spirit, so His worship must be spiritual; and such is the religion that is described in the scriptures, without image or shadow; and as we reprehended other religions before for worshipping many gods and having many mediators; so here we say, they worship not one God, because their worship is not spiritual but corporeal; for God requireth the heart, and therefore the true religion which is of God must be spiritual; but all other religions, as they proceed from man, so man himself being corporeal, the worship that he prescribeth must needs be corporeal, and therefore not the true religion.

XII. As we before reproved their miracles, so now in defence of our own miracles we say,

α. they are not hidden, but are done before Pharoah and all his servants, Exod. vii. 20;

β. also ours are fruitful and beneficial;

γ. and lastly, they cannot be done by any of the magicians; for what magician did ever part the sea or make the sun to stand or go back, or brought manna from heaven raining down?

XIII. As for our oracles, they are not flattering, no not to please the king, *φιλιππίζειν*, 'to say what king Philip would;' nor are they doubtful, as those of the heathen were; but whereas their prophecies come not to pass, ours do certainly come to pass, some one hundred, some three hundred, some a thousand years after, as the enlarging of Japhet's tents, Gen. ix. 27.

And these reasons prove the truth of our religion jointly with the Jews'; so far as they held with us and did not depart from us.

§ 2. *Of our religion as different from the Jews'.*

Now follow proper reasons for the truth of christianity.

First, for the credit of the gospel.

The witnesses thereof were the evangelists and apostles. Now in every witness we note two things, skill, and honesty; both which were in them;

1. for skill;—they write not by hear-say or report, but as St. John saith, 1 John i. 1, "that which we have seen and handled," and none durst ever write against them in their own times nor since;

2. for honesty;—it had been folly in them to lie for nought; as Tacitus [b] saith, they testify best *quibus nullum est mendacii præmium,* 'who get no benefit by telling a lie;' and we know they had nothing for their labour, yea they lost their own lives for it.

Secondly, for the story, 1. *of the birth of Christ.*

a. Sibylla [c] almost setteth down every action and circumstance; and by this many have been turned to christianity, as Marcellinus and Secundanus.

β. And for this cause both Vespasian and Augustus would have destroyed all the Jews, but especially the tribe of Judah.

γ. And Rhodigin [d] and Volateran leave us this of credit, that there was an altar in Egypt that was dedicated *virgini pariturœ,* 'to the virgin bringing forth a child;' like as that same *templum pacis,* 'the temple of peace,' should stand, *donec virgo peperit,* 'until a virgin brought forth a child.'

δ. So doth also Postellus shew that there was another altar intitled *ara primogenito Dei,* 'an altar to the first born son of God.'

ε. Also Augustus [e] understanding by the wise men that both he and all the people should worship one that was born, would not be called *dominus orbis terrarum,* 'the lord of the whole world,' as he was before, but gave up that title.

ζ. Also for that in the day of His birth there appeared three suns; but especially that of the star, whereof Pliny [f], lib. ii. cap. 25. witnesseth, calling it *stella crinita sine crine,* i. e. a comet; but it was a plain star; of which many meditating have turned to the truth, as Chæremon among the stoics, and Challadius among the platonists, who thereupon went to Jewry and became Jews.

2. *Of the death of Christ.*

a. The ancient Egyptians, when they write *vitam æternam,* 'everlasting life,' they write the sign of the cross, wherein howsoever they were directed, the mark was like

[b] [Hist., lib. iv. cap. 81.]

[c] [Præsert., lib. viii. p. 61, sqq.]

[d] [Lect. antiq., lib. ix. cap. 19. col. 478.]

[e] [vid. Sueton. Vit. Octav., lib. ii. cap. 53. vol. i. p. 178.]

[f] [vol. i. p. 179.]

and agreeable to the action of Christ's death upon the cross to purchase for us everlasting life.

β. The universal eclipse and earthquake which was at that time that He died; for by no natural causes can all the earth move, but it must have something to stay upon, confessed by Pliny[g], lib. ii. cap. 25. Phlegon Trallianus' Chronicle[h]. Neither is it by nature that the sun should be eclipsed the fourteenth day of the moon, when the moon was just at full, quite against the rules of astronomy.

γ. In the reign of Tiberius the falling of the oracles; as Plutarch[i] writeth, "there came a sound to the mariners that great Pan was dead;" which great Pan who it was, all the wise men could not tell; and Nicephorus[k] reporteth that the oracle at Delphos said it was *παῖς ἑβραῖος*, *puer hebræus*, 'an hebrew child.'

δ. Ambrose, Justin Martyr[l], and Tertullian[m], as Eusebius[n] saith, testify that Pilate himself did witness in a letter to the emperor Tiberius all these things of Christ Himself, His life, death, &c.

Thus much for the credit of the gospel, and the story of His life and death.

Thirdly, for the progress of christianity.

The greatest arguments for the proof of christianity are drawn from the proceeding and going forward of christianity, contrary to man's reason; for,

1. Whereas reason will have apt instruments to every action, and the matter well disposed to work upon;

a. there was no instrument more unapt than the twelve apostles, neither noble men nor learned, but poor simple souls;

β. so the matter also to work upon, which was the world, was altogether unprepared; for we see both Jew and gentile hated the poor servants of Christ, the apostles; Ulpian the chief lawyer, Galen the chief physician, Porphyry the chief aristotelian, and Plotinus the chief platonist, were utterly against them; so was Libanius and Lucian, the chief scholars;

g [ibid.]
h [Euseb. Chron., p. 77.]
i [De orac. defect., vol. vii. p. 651.]
k [lib. i. cap. 17. vol. i. p. 83 B.]
l [Apol. i. § 48.]
m [Apol. cap. xxi. p. 20 D.]
n [H. E., lib. ii. cap. 2. p. 47.]

Julian forbad[o] schools of religion, and the liberal arts, and made false dialogues between Christ and Peter to induce youth to the hatred of christianity; also they prepared for them and put them to great torments, insomuch that four thousand christians have been executed at once.—And though the instrument were so mean and so weak, and the matter so froward and stubborn to work on, yet we see how christianity hath prevailed; which is a great proof of the truth of it.

2. The precepts of this religion are not as those of the Turk, whereof we heard before; but here instead of revenge, "love your enemies:" instead of lust, "look not on a woman to lust after her;" instead of covetousness, "be ready to part with and leave all;" yea, it doth not allow us the least thought to use at our pleasure, *non concupisces*, 'thou shalt not covet.'

3. The promises of our religion are not worldly pleasures, as other religions do promise, but contrary; "they shall whip and scourge you; they shall bind and lead you whither you would not;" *tollat quisque crucem, relinquat omnia*, 'let each man take up his cross and leave all." So that as one said, This is not (according to man's reason) to say, *sequere me*, 'follow me;' but rather, *mane post me*, 'tarry after me;' and rather terrifying than inducing. And thus therefore in this new regeneration there is a resemblance of the first creation; for as there was all things of nothing, so here all things contrary to reason; and nothing is set to confound something, that we may see it to be the finger of God.

4. At the Turk's beginning there was in all the world idleness, palpable ignorance, and very few learned men, and so the more easily drawn to follow him; but when Christ began, and in the times presently after, the world was full of wise and learned men, as Paulinus, Clemens, Ambrose, Origen, Austin, &c. that were to be converted by simple men, that God might shew the power of His might above all.

5. The conversions also to christianity prove the truth of it. Paul before he was converted was a wise and learned man, in great reputation and in way of preferment, and especially then when he had received the greatest authority

[o] [Socr. H. E., lib. iii. cap. 12. p. 187.]

and was made most strong against Christ; in so much as Porphyry saith, it was pity such a man should be bestowed upon our religion; and yet then he was turned clean another way against that he was before, and was glad to tread many a hard step. So was Origen [p], Ammonius' scholar, a magician, content to be a poor catechist in Alexandria, every day in fear of death, when he might have been with his fellow Plotinus in great authority and favour, if it had not been for christianity.

6. Their conversions were not only strange, but likewise also there were never such true conversions as of those which were converted to christianity; no such sound repentance, no such true justice and fortitude, no such constancy in affliction, yea even to death, nor any such willingness to endure it, insomuch that it was a proverb amongst those that lived in those days, *soli christiani mortis contemptores*, 'christians only are willing to die;' which appeared well in the woman that ran to the fire, her child in her arms, lest the christians should be burned before she could get to them to be burned with them.

7. The miserable end of the persecutors of the christians, (Herod eaten with lice, Judas hanged himself, and all the emperors came to miserable ends,) saving Libanius that went to Basil and became a christian: whereupon Tertullian writing to Scapula [q] saith, *si nobis non parcis, tibi parce; si non tibi, Carthagini*, 'if you will not forbear cruelty toward us, forbear it towards yourself; if not towards yourself, forbear it towards Carthage.'

8. The devil's testimony against himself; all the art magic that ever they had could never call up Christ; Plotinus and Apollonius [r], and divers heathen that raised up the image of Jupiter and other heathen gods, did assay to bring up likewise the image of Christ, but could not effect it; He is not subject to that power; nay, Julian [s] could not raise up the devil in that place where Babylas the martyr was burned at Antioch.

[p] [Euseb. H. E., lib. vi. cap. 2, sq. p. 257, sqq.]

[q] [Ad fin. p. 71 D.]

[r] [vid. Philostr. Vit. Apollon. Tyan., lib. i. cap. 5. p. 170.]

[s] [Socr. H. E., lib. iii. cap. 18. p. 194.]

9. This religion of ours is that which feareth not the face of man, but Christ must be confessed and professed before all men and at all times; nay, it is not afraid of Styx nor all the stygian lakes of hell, but hell itself quaketh and trembleth thereat.

And therefore this is the supernatural, true, and the only true religion.

§ 3. *Of our religion as different from the Papists'.*

Now in the way of christianity there is yet no difference between the papists and us; let us therefore see wherein they and we differ.

Because they build themselves on the word of God, and so do we, but of a diverse meaning; we must look therefore for a right way to the interpretation of the word.

The question between us is of the means of interpretation.

And this is the main question between them and us, Who have the true means to interpret?

They have the Fathers, Councils, the Church and the Pope. We have not so. But as it is 2 Pet. i. 20, the scripture is of no private interpretation; so to make it plain what we hold, we will first lay down these three grounds;—

1. That as to the eunuch, Acts viii. 31, so much more to us there is need of an interpreter.

2. That there is a certain and infallible interpretation; else if we were always uncertain, how should we build on the rock?

3. As we must take heed of private interpretation, not to distort the scriptures; as Hilary saith, *non afferre sensum ad scripturas, sed referre*, 'not to devise a sense for scripture but to give it its proper sense;' so must we, as 1 Cor. xii. 10, hold, that God hath given the gift of interpretation, which gift is not given to any but those which are in the church, 1 Cor. ii. 10—14, and of those not to the common sort of every private man, but to the learned. And seeing it is, 1 Cor. xii. 11, *singulis prout vult*, 'to each man as God pleaseth,' it is not to be restrained to some one bishop, as

the gross papists do. But Stapleton[t] when he had proved all that he could, yet at last he was fain to confess that God doth extraordinarily give this gift to others, as well to Amos a herdsman, as Jeremy a priest, lib. X. cap. 7. But Andradius[u] leaned to the other side, saying that the bishop must approve their gifts.

Now for the sense of the word. It is well said in law, that *apices juris non sunt jus*, 'each small quiddity of the law is not the law,' so say we, the letter is not the word of God, but the meaning, and that is it which we seek; and for the meaning Thomas Aquinas[v] saith,

1. in a matter of faith or manners we must take the literal sense;

2. for other things we may make a tropological sense;

3. there is but one true sense of one place;

4. that is it which the construction will give, if there follow no absurdity.

Now for the examination of the sense, because we must never look to stop their mouths, but they will still wrangle, we must therefore bring them to one of these;

1. to that, Tit. iii. 11, "being condemned of himself;" to drive them to condemn themselves in their own heart;

2. because the devil so blindeth some that they will not understand, therefore the second thing we must drive them to is that of the 2 Tim. iii. 9, that their ἄνοια be ἔκδηλος, their 'madness' be 'manifest.'

Of our means of interpretation.

The means for interpretation as we allege them, are six.

1. The first, wherein they and we agree, is prayer[x]; so saith Augustine, *oratio postulat, lectio inquirit, meditatio invenit, contemplatio dirigit*, 'prayer requesteth, reading searcheth, meditation findeth, contemplation directs.'

The second, third, and fourth[y], are for the phrase of speech, viz.

2. Conference of places, Augustine *De doctr. christ.* lib. ii.

t [Princip. fid. demonstr. method., lib. x. cap. 7. p. 374, sqq.]

u [Defens. Trident. fid., lib. ii. passim, e. g. p. 246.]

v [Summ. fid. Pars i. qu. 1. art. 10. Quodl. vii. artt. 14, 15. Gal. cap. iv. lect. 7.]

x [Stapleton, lib. x. cap. 10. p. 381. lib. xi. cap. 9. p. 418.]

y [ibid. pp. 418—437.]

cap. 8[z]; the less plain must be referred to the more plain; Acts xvii. 11, 12, "they searched the scriptures daily, whether those things were so; therefore many of them believed."

3. *Inspectio fontium,* 'to look to the original,' as, for the New testament, the greek text; for the Old, the hebrew; Augustine *De doctr. christ.* lib. ii. capp. 10—14[a].

4. The acquaintance with the manner of dialect, that we may know the Holy Ghost's tongue, Heb. v. ult., having our "senses exercised to discern."

The two last are for the word; the two following for the whole sentence and chapters.

5. That which they call *oculus ad scopum,* 'the eye intent to the scope,' 1 Tim. vi. 20, "avoiding profane and vain babblings, and oppositions of science falsely so called;" mark the end of the writer; for so saith Hilary, *ex causis dicendi doctorum habemus intelligentiam,* 'by finding the cause why a thing is spoken, we attain the understanding of that which learned men spake.'

6. To look to *antecedentia* and *consequentia,* with every circumstance.

And for these means we must note, that they are to be referred diversly to divers things, some to one and some to another, and not all to everything. And therefore Stapleton in reproving these means committed a double error; first, because he saw that some one of these was not necessary to some one thing, he thence concluded that it was not necessary at all; and secondly, because he saw that to something none of these severally could serve, he thereupon concluded that they were not at all sufficient.

Of the papists' means of interpretation.

Now the papists' means are these; beside prayer, wherein they agree with us, they set down these means also;—

The fathers; the councils; the pope; and the church.

They say all these are true means of interpretation.

We say, No; for

1. For the fathers and the councils we say, if there be doubt in the scriptures, there is much more in the exposition.

[z] [vol. iii. col. 23.]

[a] [ibid. col. 24, sqq.]

PART I.

2. For the pope and the church, we must first see whether the pope stand in the truth or no; and whether their church be the true church or no; and so looking well into their means we shall find that they are so far commendable as they use ours, and no farther.

1. *Of the fathers.*

For the fathers; they say their exposition is true; now that must needs be meant when they agree all in one, or else which of them shall we believe? But we shall not find one place of a hundred which they all expound alike, so that few of their expositions should be received. And as Basil saith of Dionysius[b], Epist. ix., that they wrote many things ἀγωνιστικῶς, *disputationis gratiâ*, 'by way of dispute,' not δογματικῶς, *definitivè*, 'according to their own judgment.' And Augustine being oppressed with authorities of the fathers saith, he regardeth not *quis, sed quid.* And Paul saith, Gal. i. 8, "if an angel from heaven teach any other doctrine let him be accursed." And the papists themselves refuse the most, yea almost all of the fathers, expounding this, *tu es Petrus*, 'thou art Peter,' *de fide, non de personâ*, 'of his faith, not of his person.' So in the division of the commandments, they take against all but Augustine[c].

2. *Of the councils.*

For the councils; they have two parts;

1. The action; and therein there is such error that they are fain to lay all upon the canon, saying it makes no matter how the premises be, so the conclusion be good.

2. The canon; and thereof we see some plain opposite one to another; as in the two general allowed councils, the one of Constance[d], the other of Basil[e]; whereof the one setteth down that the councils could err, and so also the pope, and

[b] [vol. iii. p. 90.]

[c] [Quæstt. in Exod., lib. ii. qu. 71. vol. iii. part i. col. 443. Serm. ccl. ad fin. vol. v. col. 1033. Serm. ix. de dec. chord., vol. v. col. 52. Cont. Faust., lib. xv. cap. 4. vol. viii. coll. 274, 278.]

[d] [vol. xxvii. col. 519, sqq.]

[e] [vol. xxix. col. 1, sqq. See also Patricius, "History of the Councils of Basle, Florence," &c., and Turrecremata's speech at the Council of Florence, Harduin's Councils, vol. ix. coll. 1081, sqq. and 1235, sqq.]

that the council was above the pope, the other affirmeth quite the contrary. CHAP. V.

3. *Of the pope.*

For the pope; Damasus a pope, as Hierome saith, subscribed to heresy; Liberius[f] an enemy to arians, subscribed after to that heresy; Honorius[g] was condemned in the sixth general council of Constance in seven canons and seven actions, *propter subversionem fidei*, 'for subverting the faith.'

4. *Of the church.*

For the church; all the East, which is half, do not hold their supremacy. And if we should follow their bishops, many of them have been arians, so that here is both ambiguity and peril. And so Basil[h], cap. xxvii. *De Spiritu Sancto*, saith, that *mersio in baptismo*, 'dipping in baptism,' was at first but *una*, 'one,' and then *trina*, 'triple,' and then *una*, 'one' again; so in one of these must needs be error.—So that all these grounds are every one severally proved to be false.

Now to prove them false jointly, lest we fall into Stapleton's fault[i]; they all failed in this, the ministering of the Lord's supper to infants, whereas Paul saith we must examine ourselves, &c., which infants cannot do.

And so both jointly and severally their grounds are false, and ours are the only true means of interpretation.—And if they will do as Stapleton doth, who maketh the interpretation personal, they fall into that extremity that he doth, saying, that the interpretation of an unlearned bishop is better than the interpretation of any other learned man; which, as the rest of their religion, is a most miserable, detestable error.

And thus much for the Preface.

f [Lib. de Vir. illustr. cap. 97. col. 918. in opp. S. Hieron. ed. Vallars. ad calc. vol. ii.]

g [Harduin, vol. iii. col. 1422.]

h [vol. iii. p. 55.]

i [vid. p. 57. sup.]

PART II.

OF THE LAW OF GOD.

Now religion hath two parts, the Law, and the Gospel.

The romanists pervert this order, teaching the gospel before the Law; Hosius[k], Canisius[l], and the last Tridentine council[m].—But that is an unnatural order, for the Law and the gospel are two covenants;—

a. the one made between God and Adam, on God's part to perform him paradise, on Adam's part to perform obedience; but Adam having strength to do this, and abusing the same, incurred the forfeiture of this covenant, which was the danger of hell and the penalty of death;

β. when this covenant was broken a new was made, that Christ to God should make perfection, to us should restore that we had lost; and on our side, that we should perform perfect obedience, but by Christ; and this is the covenant of faith.

And this course of teaching by humiliation, is usual, that by the Law we might see what we are.

a. This course God Himself useth, first to Adam, *ubi es?* there was the Law; after that, *semen mulieris,* there was the gospel;

β. after the flood, God taught Abraham the Law first, Gen. xvii. 1, *ambula mecum et esto integer,* 'walk with me and be perfect,' afterwards the gospel, Gen. xxii. 18, "in thy seed," &c.;

γ. Moses in Deuteronomy; first the Law, then the gospel;

δ. Esay, in his first thirty-nine chapters the Law, afterward the gospel;

ε. Paul to the Romans (which epistle is called the sum of religion) from i. 18. to vii. 15. the Law, afterwards the gospel;

ζ. the form of instruction Heb. vi. 1. is thus; repentance by the Law, faith by the gospel.

[k] [vol. i. cf. p. 313. cum præcedd. et sqq.]

[l] [Opus Catechist. Cf. cap. iii. q. 5. p. 74. cum præcedd. et sqq.]

[m] [Catechism. Concil. Trident. "Pars 3tia De Dei præceptis in Decalogo contentis."]

CHAPTER I.

OF GOD'S LAW IN GENERAL.

§ 1. *What is contained in God's law.*

In God's law as in every good law are,
the word, this;
the manner, thus;
the reward to the good and punishment to the evil.

I. The action consisteth of these two,
not doing evil, doing of good, } the breach hereof is { commission, omission.
For doing good there are these three, Tit. ii. 12,
1. *piè*, 'piously' toward God;
2. *sobriè*, 'soberly' toward ourselves;
3. *justè*, 'justly' to our neighbours;

Augustine hath three rules for these three;

For the first, *deterius subjiciatur meliori; quod commune habes cum angelis, hoc subde Deo*, 'let the worse part be subject to the better; that which thou hast in thee as have the angels, make it subject to God.'

For the second, *quod commune habes cum brutis, hoc subde rationi*, 'that which in thee is like to that in brute beasts, make it subject to reason.'

For the third, *fac quod vis pati*, 'do as thou wouldest be done unto.'

The corruption of these is the transgression of the law; when we come to this,

1. as Satan said to Eve, *dii eritis*, 'ye shall be gods, be not subjects;'

2. *quod libet, licet*, 'what it pleaseth any to do, that is lawful to be done;' as they did *videre et nubere*, 'see and marry,' no restraint of lust by reason;

3. that of Machiavel, *quod potes fac*, 'do all thou canst.'

II. Next the action followeth the manner, Thus. And to this is required that we do,

1. *toti,* apply all our strength and power, as Gen. xxxi. 6, Jacob to Laban;
2. *totum,* all that is commanded, Gen. vii. 5, Noah in the ark;
3. *semper,* always, as Job all his life.

III. For the reward and punishment, we cannot escape both; *aut faciendum, aut patiendum,* 'either we must do our duty, or suffer for neglect thereof.'

The reward is to the good,

In temporal things, Gen. xxxix. 3, Joseph's master for his sake.

In eternal things, Gen. v. 24, Enoch.

The punishment to the wicked,

In temporal things, as Adam and Joseph's brethren.

In eternal things, as 1 Pet. iii. 19, the spirits now in prison.

§ 2. *Of the law written in men's hearts.*

Obj. But why may we not live now without the law as well since Moses as before?

Ans. They lived not without law, but they had a law, Rom. ii. 14, even *effectivè,* in the hearts, a thing equivalent to the law; and thereby they could accuse and excuse themselves, even by the witness of their own consciences, the effect of the law being imprinted in the hearts of all men by nature.

The Jews had the law in their hearts.

First for the Jews, to prove that they had the effect of every commandment in them before the Law.

1. Gen. xxv. 2, "put away the strange gods."
2. Gen. xxxi. 34, idols. Gen. xxxv. 4, ear-rings.
3. Gen. xxiv. 3, "swear by the Lord of heaven."
4. Gen. ii. 3. and Exod. xvi. 23, rest of the sabbath.
5. Gen. xxvii. 41, "days of mourning for my father."
6. Gen. iv. 9, Cain hideth his killing of Abel.

7. Gen. xxxviii. 24, the whore Tamar to be burnt, and xxxiv. 31, "should he deal with our sister as with an harlot?"
8. Gen. xliv. 7, "God forbid we should steal."
9. Gen. xxxviii. 20, Judah kept promise, not lying or deceiving by untruths.
10. Gen. xii. 17, and Gen. xx. 3, Pharaoh, and Abimelech; it was sin to look on a woman with lust after her.

Also the gentiles had both the ten commandments;

Secondly, not only the Jews but the gentiles also had the same law by nature in their hearts; though some of the commandments more manifestly than other some.

Manifestly six, namely the third, fifth, sixth, seventh, eighth, and ninth.

Somewhat obscurely four, the first, second, fourth, and tenth.

For the most manifest commandments;

The third was a law of the Egyptians, as Diodorus Siculus[n] saith, *μὴ ὀμνύε*, 'swear not,' *nisi morieris*, 'unless you will die.'

The fifth; Homer[o] saith of one that had a misfortune, it was *quia parentes non honoravit*, 'because he honoured not his parents.'

The sixth is a rule even in nature, *homicida quod fecit expectet*, 'let the homicide expect that which he hath done to another.'

The seventh, Stephanus[p] out of Nicostratus, *fuge nomen mœchi si mortem fugies*, 'fly the name of an adulterer if thou wilt avoid death.'

The eighth, Demosthenes[q] against Timocrates repeateth it as Solon's law in the very words, 'thou shalt not steal.'

The ninth, in the twelve tables, *Tarpeio saxo dejiciatur*, 'cast him down from a high rock[r].'

For those they had somewhat obscurely;

n [vid. lib. i. cap. 77. vol. i. p. 87.]

o [The reference is to Il. P. 302, but the passage is misunderstood.]

p [In Stephanus's "Comic. Gr. (i. e. Nicostr. all.) sententiæ," this passage is not found.]

q [vol. i. p. 732 sqq.]

r [Leew. De jur. civ. Rom., p. 284. Aul. Gell., lib. xx. cap. 1. fin. p. 291.]

PART II.

For the first, Pythagoras said, "If a man come and say, I am God, let him create another world, and we will believe him."

For the second, they agreed that every god should be worshipped as he himself thought good; and this is the very foundation of the second commandment.

For the fourth, little can be found, but sufficient for their condemnation; they knew[s] that *numerus septenarius est Deo gratissimus,* 'the number of seven was most pleasing to God;' and it was *numerus quietis,* 'the number of rest;' and thence they might have gathered that God would have His rest that day. And so the seventh day after birth, they kept *natalitia,* 'the feast of their nativity;' and the seventh day after death, their funeral feasts or exequies.

The tenth, their laws never touched; yet the scope of them was *τὸ μὴ ἐπιθυμεῖν, non concupiscere,* 'not to covet;' and Menander saith that they should not covet so much as a button.

And the three rules above given.

Now to prove that the gentiles had also the grounds of the three former rules.

The action, This.

On Delphos' door[t] were written all the three rules.

1. *εἶ.* signifying that if any man would ask counsel of the oracle, they should do whatsoever the god commanded them; and this is *subde Deo.*

2. *γνῶθι σεαυτὸν,* 'know thyself' to be better than a beast; *subde brutum rationi.*

3. *μηδὲν αἱρεῖν,* no covetousness; and this is justice, *fac quod vis pati,* 'do as thou wouldst be done to;' which sentence Severus the emperor used to malefactors in every punishment, and caused it to be graven upon his plate.

The manner, Thus.

1. *toti, ἢ ὅλος ἢ μὴ ὅλως,* 'either fully with all thy strength, or not at all.'

2. *totum;* they set a mark upon Cæsar[u], and Euripides[x],

[s] [See Beyerlinck's Magnum Theatrum, art. Numerus septenarius.]

[t] [Plutarch, περὶ τοῦ ΕΙ ἐν Δελφοῖς, vol. vii. p. 512.]

[u] [Cic. De off., lib. iii. cap. 21. vol. iii. p. 280; Suet. Vit. Jul. Cæs., cap. 30. vol. i. p. 44.]

[x] [Phœniss., lin. 538.]

which broke justice *regni gratiâ*, 'to get a kingdom;' and Plutarch[y] compareth our duties to a fish which eaten sparingly hurteth, but being eaten up all it is medicinable.

3. *toto tempore*, 'continually,' for they compared their good man to a *tetragonismus*, all sides alike, as a dye; no cameleon or unconstant.

Reward and punishment.

They say God hath a sheet of parchment[z] made of the skin of the goat that nourished him, wherein he noteth all men's deeds, rewarding to the good, *tres gratias*, 'three graces' in this life, and *campos elysios*, 'the elysian fields' in the life to come; and to the evil, three *erynnyes* in this life, and Styges, Tartarus, Cocytus, answerable to Tophet, or Gehenna, in the life to come.

And so the Jews before the Law, and the gentiles both before and since, having both the effect of the law and the grounds of the rules, are, as Paul saith, Rom. i. 20, inexcusable.

§ 3. *Questions hereupon.*

Object. But if the law were in their hearts before, to what end should it be written?

Answ. Adam's fall broke it in pieces, and afterwards it grew dimmer and dimmer daily, and the shards smaller, so that they could hardly be put together; and therefore, lest that which was in the heart should be clean put out, it was necessary it should be written.

Quest. How grew the law darker and darker?

Answ. 1. Men did what they could to put it out; for when they communed with their own hearts, there was straight an accuser; so that they durst not look into themselves, but as Augustine saith, *facti sunt fugitivi à cordibus suis*, 'they became fugitives from their own hearts;' and therefore it was necessary they should have the law before their eyes, that so it might be brought to their hearts, *unde fugerunt*, 'whence they fled.'

2. There came a *superseminator*, who sowed after the good seed was sown; the devil put false principles into their

[y] [Athen., lib. viii. cap. 3. p. 337.]

[z] [Parœm. Gr. ed. Gaisford. Zenob. Cent. iv. pr. 11.]

heart, and choked up the true; as, *dii eritis; bonum est quod prodest,* 'ye shall be gods; that is good for you which makes for your benefit,' and such like.

Quest. But is any man able to fulfil the law?

Answ. Paul sheweth from Rom. i. 18. to chap. vii. 13, both Jew and gentile to come short herein, as that the very best, even the regenerate, faileth in the manner; he doth it not *totus,* with all his strength and power; for there is a law in his members that rebelleth against God's law.

Object. But how is God just, to command a thing impossible?

Answ. 1. Though the matter be never so crooked to work upon, yet the rule must needs be straight.

2. Seeing God is perfect, His law must needs be perfect also.

Quest. But why then were not we made able to do that which God commandeth?

Answ. Adam was made able; but he was like an evil servant, receiving money of his master to do his business, which he maketh away; or else he is made drunken therewithal, so that he cannot do his master's work.

CHAPTER II.

OF MOSES' LAW IN PARTICULAR.

§ 1. *Of the preparation.*

But to come in particular to Moses' law.

And first, of the Preparation, which hath his ground, Exod. xix., and standeth upon three heads.

The first beginneth, v. 4; where by a commendation of God's benefits Moses maketh us willing to hear. We are in God's hands as the pot in the hands of the potter to be used at his pleasure, and therefore if He allure us Who might command us, we ought in all humility to attend. Moses telleth them v. 4,—

"You have seen what I did to the Egyptians;" which argument ought to be of no less force with us, for we have also been delivered from the spiritual Egypt, from the devil and sin, as also from death, and judgments due for sin.

"And how I carried you upon eagles' wings."—There be wings of God;

a. His providence, whereby He being infinite and eternal hath respect unto the meanest things upon earth, Ps. cxiii. 5, 6, "Who dwelleth on high, who humbleth himself to behold the things that are in heaven and in the earth;" even our hairs are numbered, Mat. x. 30;

β. His special love, from whence flow the peculiar graces of election, redemption, justification, sanctification, the ministry of the word, but above all, the good things of the life to come, which are such which the eye hath not seen, 1 Cor. ii. 9.

The second part of the preparation is to make us apt, as the other was to make us willing; and this beginneth at v. 7. unto v. 12;—

"Sanctify the people;" for if a clean thing be received into an unclean it will be polluted.

The time of preparation is there set down, two days. This sanctification was to them in ceremony, and such things as were figures unto them are examples to us, 1 Cor. x. 11, and every ceremony hath his equity. And the equity of this ceremony is this, that some due preparation is necessary to the service of God.

a. Ver. 10; "let them wash their clothes," saith God by Moses. Garments in the Old testament were either *vestimenta,* or *stolæ,* inward or outward; and those garments became stained by two means, by touching him that had an issue, or if a man had an issue within himself. Answerable to the first is the pollution which we receive by evil example; to the second, that which we have by natural corruption. In respect of both these there is need of washing, for no unclean thing was permitted to enter into the temple, as in the New Jerusalem, Rev. xxi. 27. The means to cleanse us is the baptism of the Spirit, wherewith we must labour daily to be cleansed, expressing the virtue thereof in the practice of mortification and new obedience.

β. The last part of their sanctification Moses may seem to add of himself, v. 15, "come not at your wives." The equity

PART II. of this ceremony is, that even lawful things, when they hinder God's service, must not be used.

The third point of their preparation is mentioned v. 12, and repeated again v. 21, that the people should not pass their bounds; the morality whereof is this, that we pass not the marks that God hath set in knowing His will, but content ourselves with the knowledge of such things as are necessary to be known. We must know that hidden things belong to God, revealed to man, Deut. xxix. 29; we must not desire to be overwise, Rom. xii. 3; nor eat too much honey, Prov. xxv. 27; nor doat about questions whereof cometh nothing but strife of words, 1 Tim vi. 4; for as Augustine saith, *qui inventa veritate ulterius quærit, nihil quærit præter mendacium,* 'he who finding the truth, seeketh further, he seeketh for nothing but a lie.'

The fourth part of their preparation is taken from the circumstance of the manner of delivering the Law, beginning at the 16th verse, expressed also Heb. xii.; which was by dark clouds, thunder, fire, trembling of the mount, &c., to stir them up to reverence, both in attention and practice.

This argument should move us also, for if the delivery of the Law was so terrible, what shall the requiry be?

α. It was delivered by angels, but God Himself shall require it.

β. It was delivered in clouds, it shall be required in darkness and terror, Amos v. 18, 19; Joel ii. 10.

γ. For the thunder in the delivery, there shall be a fearful noise at the dissolution of all things in the requiry; 2 Pet. iii. 10, "the heavens shall pass away with a great noise."

δ. For the earthquake, it shall not be of one mountain alone, but of the whole world; Heb. xii. 26, "yet once more I shake not the earth only, but also heaven."

ε. For the sound of the trumpet, there shall be such a sound as shall raise up the dead, John v. 25, "the dead shall hear the voice of the Son of God; and they that hear shall live."

ζ. And as the giving of the Law made the people and Moses to quake, so the requiry shall make the elect to be afraid, 1 Pet. iii. 14, but the wicked to hide themselves in dens and rocks, Rev. vi. 15.

And thus much of the Preparation.

§ 2. *Of the end of the Law.*

Now of the end of the Law.

1. It giveth no perfection.
2. It is our schoolmaster to Christ.

I. It giveth no perfection, Heb. vii. 11. For though as Solon's law carried the mark of the author's mildness, and the laws of Draco of his cruelty, so likewise God's laws, of His holiness, righteousness, and goodness; yet it brings no perfection, as the gospel doth. To which end consider these circumstances;

1. The place where the Law was given was a vast and barren wilderness; even so all the souls that have been since Adam, none have been added unto God by the Law, Gal. v. 3, 4. Ismael must be cast out, and only Isaac, which is born supernaturally, can have the possession, for the inheritance is by grace. Again, mount Sinai was such a hill as no man might ascend unto it; but Sion the hill of grace, must be ascended, Esay ii. 3.

2. The circumstance of the person by whom the Law was delivered proveth it, for,

a. if any should have perfection by the Law, then doubtless Moses by whom it was given; but he transgressed it, Num. xx. 12, and so could not enter into Canaan;

β. again, Moses his miracles were altogether destructive, as the plaguing of Egypt, the drowning of Pharoah, &c.; but the miracles of grace were lively, as the raising of the dead, healing of the sick, &c.;

γ. lastly, Moses his face did shine so bright, that no man might behold him but through a veil, which veil did prefigure Christ, 2 Cor. iii. 7.

3. The tables were broken before they were delivered, which the fathers affirm to signify the frustration of the Law.

4. The time of the delivery of the Law was when the people were committing high treason against God, worshipping the golden calf, *ergo,* unfit to receive the Law, or any perfection thereby.

PART II.

5. The blast of the trumpet was terrible at the giving of the Law, but in the beginning of the gospel the angels sang praises unto God.

II. The Law is our schoolmaster to bring us unto Christ; for by the Law we call ourselves to account; this shews us our talent, and so brings *remedium ignorantiæ,* 'a remedy for our ignorance;' then, finding our debt so great and sin so strong, we are brought to repentance, and this is *remedium superbiæ,* 'a remedy for our pride;' then it remaineth, that being not able to discharge this account, we seek for a surety, and this is Christ; and thus the Law leadeth us to Christ.

§ 3. *Of the sum of the Law.*

Now of the sum of the Law.—The Law containeth two things, God's Authority, and Charge.

Of God's authority.

I. The authority is the prerogative royal whereby every prince doth all things within his dominion, and it is the common reason of all the commandments.

This authority of God is expressed by { His Name, His jurisdiction, His excellent acts.

1. His Name is יהוה, the name of His nature; that τετραγράμματον, 'name of four letters,' so much talked and writ of. Some think that of the three letters the first signifieth power, the adjunct of the Father; the second knowledge, the adjunct of the Son; and the third love, the adjunct of the Holy Ghost; and the doubling of the two letters, the two natures of the second Person.

This name is derived of היה or חיה, 'to be,' *quia Deus est a nullo, per nullum et propter nullum,* 'because God hath being from none, subsists by none, hath none for whom He is existent,' Rom. ii. 36. God is absolute of Himself, and therefore hath no commission from any; but all the princes of the earth have their commission from Him, and *ergo* they insert this clause into their title, *Dei gratiâ,* &c., for all other things depend upon Him, but He upon none, Ps. civ.

2. His jurisdiction is twofold,
   α. general over every creature,
   β. particular over His church.
   Deut. x. 14, 15; "Behold, the heaven and the heaven of heavens is the Lord's thy God, the earth also, with all that therein is; only the Lord had a delight in thy fathers to love them, and He chose their seed after them, even you above all people, as it is this day."

3. His excellent acts appear,
   first, in that the state of the Israelites was a most vile and miserable servitude;
   secondly, in that they were strongly delivered, with the destruction of their enemies.
   And these things belong also unto us, their temporal afflictions and deliverances being but a figure of those from which we are delivered.

And thus much of the authority.

Of God's charge.

II. Now of the charge; which is nothing else but the ten commandments. Which we call Moses' law in this respect; because howsoever the Law was at first ordained and given by God Himself in tables of stone, Exod. xxxi. 18, yet when the tables by means of their idolatry were broken, Exod. xxxii. 19, Moses wrote it again, Exod. xxxiv. 28, and from thence it is called Moses' law.

Division of the commandments.

For the division of the commandments, it is double;

1. from the subject, and so it is divided into two tables, Deut. iv. 13, "He wrote them upon two tables of stone;"

2. from the object, and so it is divided into the love of God and our neighbour, Matt. xxii. 37; and therefore Paul calleth love, the subject of the law, 1 Tim. i. 5, Rom. xiii. 8; for the true love of our neighbour doth always presuppose the love of God.

Now in resolving these ten commandments into two tables, there arise two doubts;

First, between the Jews and the christians; the Jews

would have the fifth commandment to be of the first table, because it belongeth unto superiors; but then it should be appropriate unto God, which cannot be, because there is in it also a duty to be performed to inferiors.

Secondly, between the papists, and the protestants and lutherans; for they make one commandment of the two first, and two of the last; against the most of the fathers, and so they break their own rule; again, the tenth commandment is all but one verse, and no wise man would thrust up two laws within one period.—Their reason why there should be but three commandments in the first table is very weak, viz. because there are but three Persons in the Trinity; but with as good reason we may answer that the fourth may be added because of the Unity.

What is required in a law-giver.

In a law-giver are required, { wisdom to make just laws, authority to enact them, and to command them to be kept.

1. The wisdom of God clearly appeareth in these His laws, because,

a. 'tis the people's wisdom to observe them, Deut. iv. 6, "keep therefore and do them, for this is your wisdom;" and foreign nations profess, "surely this people is a wise and understanding people;"

β. and for the laws themselves, "what nation," saith Moses, "hath statutes and judgments so righteous, as all this law?" Nor can it otherwise be, for God, whose laws they are, is "wonderful in counsel," Esay xxviii. 29.

2. God's authority and power is manifest,

a. because He with a mighty hand brought Israel out of Egypt; and in many wondrous works He shewed His almighty power; these go beyond all titles of princes which they prefix before their laws;

β. but farther, God in the second commandment proclaimed Himself a jealous God, able to punish offenders, ready and in mercy to deal with such as observe these laws;

In the third commandment He teacheth us not to hold guiltless them which take His name in vain;

In the fourth commandment His making of heaven and earth may assure us of His authority to command all things in heaven and earth, as their Lord and Master.

The commandments contain our duties to

- God
  - perpetual,
    - inwardly, ... *Com.* 1.
    - outwardly in
      - gesture, *Com.* 2.
      - speech, *Com.* 3.
  - temporal, ... *Com.* 4.
- our neighbour
  - in act or intent,
    - particularly .... *Com.* 5.
    - generally on
      - himself,
        - his life, *Com.* 6.
        - his wife, *Com.* 7.
      - his gifts,
        - his goods, *Com.* 8.
        - his name, *Com.* 9.
  - in very motion, ... *Com.*10.

§ 4. *Of the interpretation of the law.*

The commandment is a perfect law, and therefore forbiddeth and commandeth all things that must be left undone or done; but not the hundredth part of this in the bare words without exposition, therefore there must be an interpretation.

Quest. From whence shall we have this interpretation?

Ans. Of the levites, God's angels and ministers, Deut. xvii. 9; Mal. ii. 7. And this interpretation must be examined by the rules of interpretation, which are two;

extension, for the breadth of the commandment;

limitation or restraint, for the narrowness.

First, by extension.

For extension, the Jews set down thirteen rules, reduced by christians to these six;

1. Every precept is both affirmative and negative, *fac et non fac*, 'do this; and thou shalt not do this;' Ps. xxxiv. 14, "fly evil, do good;" according to the logic rule *à contrariis*, 'from contraries.' And by this rule the rabbins gathered two hundred and forty-eight affirmative precepts, according to the number of the joints of our body; and three hundred and sixty-five negatives, after the days of the year; both

added make six hundred and thirteen, according to the letters of the ten commandments in hebrew.

2. Every precept containeth all the species that are under it; they are reduced by *par*, and *æquipollens*, that which is 'equal' and 'of like force;' if it is *impar*, 'unequal,' *à minori*, 'from the less to the greater,' as, we must honour our parents, much more God.

3. Every precept is spiritual, Rom. vii. 14; *humana lex ligat manum et linguam, divina verò ligat animam*, 'human laws bind the tongue and the hand, God's laws bind the soul and the heart;' John iv. 23, God will be worshipped in spirit and truth.

4. All the means to any offence are forbidden, and to the things commanded the means are also commanded; and this is *ambulare per viam regiam*, 'to walk by the king's high way.'

5. All the signs are commanded and forbidden as well as the things themselves; as,

Esay iii. 16, "the daughters of Zion are haughty, and walk with stretched forth necks and wanton eyes, walking and mincing as they go, and making a tinkling with their feet:"

1 Tim. ii. 9, "that women adorn themselves in modest apparel, with shame-facedness and sobriety; not with broidered hair, or gold, or pearls, or costly array;"

Zeph. i. 8, "I will punish . . all such as are clothed with strange apparel," &c.

6. We must not be accessaries to any fault, for the principal doers and consenters are both alike.

How we may be accessary to sin.

And we may be accessaries to other men's sins, { in unlawful things, and / in lawful things.

In unlawful things.

In unlawful things there are six partakings;

1. *Jussio*, 'a command,' as,

Esay x. 1, 'they that decree wicked things;'

Dan. iii. 4, Nebuchadnezzar, for his image;

1 Sam. xxii. 18, Saul to Doeg, for the killing of the priests;

Acts xxiii. 2, Ananias commanded to smite Paul.

And this may be also by writing,

2 Sam. xi. 15, David concerning Uriah;

1 Kings xxi. 10, Jezebel concerning Naboth.

2. *Permissio*, 'a permission,'

Lev. xx. 4, "if the people of the land do any ways hide their eyes from the man when he giveth of his seed unto Molech, and kill him not,"—

Rom. xiii. 4, "he beareth not the sword in vain;"

1 Sam. iii. 13, "his sons made themselves vile and he restrained them not;"

1 Kings xx. 42, "thou hast let go out of thy hand a man whom I appointed to utter destruction, therefore thy life shall be for his life;"

John xix. 16, Pilate delivering Jesus to be crucified.

And therefore the magistrate hath the sword put into his hand, *ut mali si non dimittant voluntatem, amittant facultatem peccandi*, Augustine; 'that if wicked men will not lay aside the will to sin, they may have taken from them their ability to sin.'

3. *Provocatio*, 'provocation,' Job ii. 9, Job's wife; 1 Kings xxi. 25, Jezebel; Gal. v. 26, "provoking one another."

4. *Consilium*, 'counsel,'

Ps. i. 1, "walking in the counsel of the ungodly;"

Gen. xlix. 6, "O my soul, come not thou into their secret; unto their assembly, mine honour, be not thou united;"

Ezra iv. 5, the people of the land "hired counsellors against them to frustrate their purpose;"

2 Sam. xvi. 21, Ahitophel's counsel to Absalom;

Mark vi. 24, Herodias's counsel to her daughter;

John xi. 49, Caiaphas to the chief priests and pharisees;

Acts xix. 26, Demetrius to the craftsmen against Paul.

5. *Approbatio*, 'approbation,' Rom. i. 32, favouring the wicked;

a. whether it be directly approving them, as 1 Tim. v. 22, laying on of hands;

β. or being an instrument by action;
2 Sam. xi. 16, Joab for the slaying of Uriah;
Acts viii. 1, Saul consenting to Stephen's death;
Ps. l. 18, 'thou art partaker with the adulterer;' whereas we ought to find fault with offenders, Lev. xix. 17, "thou shalt in any wise rebuke thy neighbour, and not suffer sin upon him;" for as Augustine saith well, *quemadmodum malus sermo ducit in peccatum, sic silentium relinquit in peccato*, 'as evil speech draws men into sin, so silence lets them sleep secure in sin.'

6. *Defensio*, 'defence,'
Prov. xxiv. 24, "he that saith unto the wicked, Thou art righteous,"—
Prov. xvi. 29, "a violent man enticeth his neighbour, and leadeth him into the way that is not good;"
Ps. lv. 21, "the words of his mouth were smoother than butter, but war was in his heart;"
Esay v. 20, "that call good evil, and evil good," excusing it, as Ezek. xiii. 10—16, "daubers;" an example hereof we have in Ahab's false prophets, 1 Kings xxii. 6—11.

In lawful things.

In lawful things also another man's sin we may be partakers of; for

a. if that we are to do be not in the commandments, and we know that the use thereof will offend our brother and be a stumbling-block unto him, we must not use it for his offence;

β. but if it be in the commandment, we must do it whatsoever come of it; for as Augustine saith, *malo ut scandalum committatur quam ut veritas omittatur*, 'I had rather that offence should be taken than that the truth should be lost.'

And thus much of the extension of the commandments.

Secondly, by limitation.

For the limitation or restraint of the commandments, it is and hath been much abused; as we see,

a. in the pharisees restraining *non jurabis*, to *non pejerabis*, or *non jurabis per Deum*, 'thou shalt not swear,' to 'thou shalt not forswear,' or 'thou shalt not swear by God;' but our Saviour reproveth them by the first rule of extension;

β. for *non occides*, 'thou shalt not kill,' that is, say they, *non occides innocentes*, 'thou shalt not kill the innocent;' but Christ by the third rule of extension sheweth that it reacheth to anger, which is equipollent to murder;

γ. so for adultery; they would have as many wives as they list; but Christ by the fourth rule of extension taketh away the means of adultery, that we must not look on a woman to lust after her.—So that we may err in restraining too much.

Rules of limitation.

And therefore in restraining we must observe these three rules;—

1. Dispensation; and this is rather God's right than other princes', for God doth according to equity, but they oftentimes by affection. We see God Himself dispensed with the second commandment in setting up the brazen serpent; but this rule is not for our times, to follow examples that are dispensive, unless we have the like dispensation.

2. The second rule of restraining is from the nature of the precept, affirmative or negative; the affirmative bindeth us not *ad semper*, 'to be ever doing it,' as the negative doth; and this rule is sure and infallible.

3. The third rule is altered by divers occasions, and is called *antinomia*, 'a conflict of laws,' when one law is opposite to another, and so one of them must needs have a restraint.

How act in an antinomia, or conflict of laws.

And for our direction in this restraint we must understand that *nemo est inter duo peccata, quin pateat exitus sine tertio*, 'no man is so straightened between two sins but that a way of escape lies open without a third sin;' and we may obtain this *exitus*, or deliver ourselves, on this manner;—

1. if the precepts that seem repugnant may be agreed, there is no more to do but to reconcile them; wherein Herod erred, for he needed not to have performed his promise, for his oath was no oath;

PART II.

2. if they cannot be agreed, *agat id ad quod est obligatus,* 'let him do that to which he is obliged.' For,

a. God hath ordained things in their order;
His own glory, which passeth every man's salvation;
our salvation;
the salvation of others; and

β. every one of these must be respected in his order;
first, God's glory;
secondly, our own salvation; and
thirdly, the salvation of our brethren.

Examples of antinomia.

And this *antinomia* we may consider,

1. Between the first and fifth commandments; but this conflict is easy, for how can we obey man, when God which is stronger holdeth us back? and again, we are not bound to obey them further than they are bound to obey God, so that our rule must be, Honour them so, as God be not dishonoured.

2. Between the first three commandments which are perpetual, and the fourth which is temporal; every man's reason will prefer the perpetual before the temporal.

3. In the second table, "thou shalt not kill," and yet we must give *cuique debitum,* 'to every man his due that he deserveth,' and some deserve death, and therefore it were injustice not to give it them. Or else we may answer, that it is God's cause to execute the just office and duty of a magistrate, and we may do that in God's cause which we may not do in our own; and it is God's commandment that he that will not have the direction of the law must have the correction; *aut faciendum aut patiendum,* 'either he must do the duty of the law or suffer the penalty thereof,' as we have shewed before.

For the solution of a doubtful commandment.

Every doubt may be referred to one of these;

1. Obscurity, when both parts be doubtful whether we should do it or not do it, and here we must take the *minimum;*

2. Controversy, when there be great reasons on both sides, and here we must take the *maximum.*

General observations on the commandments.

There are yet three general things to be noted in every commandment.

1. That they are all in the second person singular; whence we learn,

 α. that they appertain to all alike;

 β. that they must be particularly applied.

2. That they are all with the verb of the future tense; whence we observe,

 α. that we have broke them in times past;

 β. that the keeping of them should continue with us for ever, even so long as it may be said, "thou shalt."

3. That they are for the most part of them negative; whence we note,

 α. the confirmation of the rule of extension to include the affirmative, for *qui prohibet impedimentum præcipit adjumentum,* 'he that forbiddeth what hindereth doth command what furthereth;'

 β. that we are more fit by nature to receive a countermand than a commandment, because we are by nature full of weeds which must be rooted out before any good thing can be planted in us.

And now to come to the exposition of the commandments themselves.

THE FIRST COMMANDMENT.

§ 1. *Necessity of this commandment.*

The first commandment is *primæ necessitatis,* first and necessary to be regarded; it was never dispensed withal, nor ever shall be.

It is propounded negatively, "thou shalt have no other god before Me," (the affirmative part was prefixed, "I am the Lord thy God,") and is quoted by Christ, Matt. iv. from Deut. vi. 13, "thou shalt worship the Lord thy God, and Him only shalt thou serve."

What is contained in this commandment.

The first commandment hath in it three things,

1. We must have a God;
2. Him for our God;
3. Him alone, and none else.

1. We must not be our own gods, for so came the first mischief, "*dii eritis;*" so that we must not do or judge after our own affections, but acknowledge a superior to teach us to know good and evil, and when it teacheth, obey; for so religion doth follow God.

2. All other gods are no gods, and therefore their service error and their religion false.

3. None but He can reward and punish as He can, and therefore He alone must have the glory.

Of the sins opposite thereto.

The sin opposite to the first of these, is Profaneness, whe[n] a man will be under no yoke or law, but do what seems good in his own eyes and stands with his own fancy and affection.

The sin opposite to the second, is False worship and false religion, done to other gods, or strange gods (so as an harlot is called strange flesh; strange worship is put for idolatry and false worship).

The sin against the third, is that called by Elias the Halting between two opinions, the blending and mingling of religions; such was their error who served God and Baal; and such was the Samaritans' humour, who feared Jehovah when he sent lions among them, and yet worshipped the gods of the nations whence they came.

How we are led to these sins.

To these three the devil brings us by three helps;

1, being himself Belial, a master without a yoke, he lets his servants have their own will, and this following our licentiousness is the next step to atheism;

2, he suggesteth unto us a desire of novelties, as he enticed Solomon to see what religions are in the world;

3, he putteth into us a desire to reconcile God and mammon, to join temporal commodity with the service of God, thinking to have a paradise on earth and in heaven also. CHAP. II.

Reasons against these sins.

Against these therefore our reasons to maintain the three former propositions are these;

1, all things else are satisfied but man, and the defect in man came by the fall of Adam following his own will, and therefore we must hearken to a superior, and that is God;

2, it is manifest that we must have a true God, for the greatest deceiver that ever was would not willingly be deceived himself;

3, if we join any thing with Him, it must needs be of a lower nature, and so detract from His honour.

Object. Seeing idols are nothing, 1 Cor. viii. 4, and therefore no gods, and all things in the world are no gods; it may seem strange to bid us have no other gods, when there are none.

Answ. To have, is to acknowledge or account; so the meaning is, we must not have any other gods in account or estimation, we must account nothing as god but God alone; God the Lord we must have for our God, and Him alone.

And Him we must have, in knowledge, and in regard. For the first commandment is divided as the soul is; now the soul hath two parts;—

1, the mind or understanding, whose duty is to know God, for *ignoti nulla cupido*, 'no man desireth the thing which he knoweth not;' and knowledge breeds faith; as St. Augustine saith, we may desire things which we have not seen, but never those things which we have not heard of. Therefore where of two things one dependeth and followeth on the other, if the first be taken away the second shall never be fulfilled; so then that on the second place we may love God, it is first required that we should know Him;

2, the will and affection, whose duty is to regard God and to love Him; so God must first be known; then loved; and love breeds obedience.

PART II.

§ 2. *Our worship of God founded on His attributes.*

God is known by His attributes, which are ten; majesty, truth, unchangeableness, will, justice, mercy, knowledge, power, ubiquity, and eternity.

The two essential attributes are, His

justice, mercy; } of these we must have { knowledge, love.

If to justice and mercy we add the other eight, we shall know Him the better and love Him the more.

From knowledge apprehending { justice mercy } come { fear and humility, hope and love.

The fruit of hope is invocation, prayer, and thanksgiving in acknowledging whence we have received the ground of our hope.

The fruit of love is obedience, whereby we conform ourselves and our wills to God's will, and willingly bear and undergo whatsoever it pleaseth Him to lay upon us.

In these the worship of God consists, yet scripture sometimes mentions but one of these, as

John xvii. 3, "this is life eternal, to know Thee the only true God;"

Eccles. xii. 13, "fear God and keep His commandments; this is the whole duty of man;"

Rom. viii. 24, "by hope ye are saved."

The mentioning of one includes the rest, because none of them is above and without the other.

Of knowledge.

First, for knowledge.—There is in all the above-named virtues an inchoation in this life, and a consummation in the life to come; the schoolmen term them a first and second perfection; therefore our knowledge here is but a taste of the blessed knowledge hereafter. So then, as the apostle makes a first and second resurrection, and he is said to be blessed who hath his part in the first, because he shall partake of the latter also: so there are two knowledges; the first is *fides,* 'faith;' the second is *visio Dei,* or *vita æterna,* 'the beatical vision;' and blessed is he who hath his part in the first knowledge, for he shall also enjoy the second; such is the order of God's goodness in these things, that none have their portion in the second knowledge or resurrection, who had not their share in the first.

The law is *doctrina agendorum;* every action must be with a motion, every motion with a will, will with a desire, desire with knowledge; therefore take away knowledge, and take away all.

Whether ignorance may be excused.

Some argue out of Acts xvii. 30, that God regarded not the time of that ignorance; and so labour to excuse ignorance as no sin, when it is, as they call it, invincible, namely,

in children, } which have not the use of reason;
in fools, }

in them which have lost their knowledge by disease or sickness;

when the means of knowledge cannot be had.—But this is not invincible; for the law of nature may teach them.

But indeed none of these can take away the sin; they only lessen the same, and excuse *à tanto,* but not *à toto.*

But there are two kinds of ignorance worse than these, namely,

1, *affectata ignorantia,* 'affected ignorance,' when they will not understand; Ps. xxxvi. 3, "he hath left off to be wise;" and this many skilful men have; being desirous to remain in an error or a sin, *nectunt argumenta,* 'they solder together arguments' in defence of it.

2, *supina ignorantia,* 'wretchless ignorance,' *quando habent à quo discant et tamen non discunt,* 'when they may learn and will not.'

To know God aright we must *removere impedimenta,* 'remove all lets,'

a. within us, our own reason, Deut. xii. 8.; Eph. iv. 17; 2 Cor. x. 5.

β. without us, { traditions, 1 Pet. i. 18;
customs of the time, or } 2 Chron. xvii. 4.
fashion of the place, }

Rules concerning knowledge.

1. The measure of our knowledge must not be slight; we must know the true Shepherd's voice, John x. 16; give a reason of our faith, 1 Pet. iii. And that we may do this the better, it is necessary the teachers themselves be not out of course; for as Chrysostom saith, no marvel if there be a mist in the meadows, when the tops of the mountains are covered with darkness.

2. To our knowledge we must add practice, for as in anatomy the veins come from the heart to the hands, so in divinity the life of that which is in the heart is practised in the hand.

Thus much of knowledge.

Concerning fulness of knowledge;—We are commanded to be men in understanding, to proceed from being babes, nourished with milk, to be able to digest strong meat; for God hath poured His spirit on all flesh, Acts ii. from Joel ii.; all His children are taught of God, Esay liv. 13; the people which before sat in darkness, after Christ's time saw a great light. The same is held out to us, so that all the earth might be full of the knowledge of God, Isa. xi. 9, if men were laborious to teach it, and the rest swift and desirous to hear it.

Of faith.

Now the fulness of knowledge bringeth a second duty, which is a full persuasion, a constant faith.

Of the kinds of faith.

In divinity there are three kinds of faith;
- general, Hebrews xi. 6, that God is;
- legal, to believe the law, the promise, the punishment, and the reward, John v. 46;
- evangelical, which is not for this place.

We are now to speak *de fide legali*, 'of the legal faith,' whose object is, Heb. iv. 2, "the word of God."

Of the means of faith.

Faith is *cœlestium et terrestrium*, 'of heavenly and earthly things;' the second a means to the first.

To *fides terrestrium,* 'the belief of earthly things,' there are sometimes means and sometimes none.

We must believe whether we have means or no means.

If we have means, we must,

a. Use them; not seek extraordinary, when we have ordinary; but yet

β. Not trust in the means; neither

our art, Hab. i. 16, "they sacrifice unto their net, and burn incense unto their drag;"

our goods, Job xxxi. 24, "if I have made gold my hope, or have said to the fine gold, thou art my confidence;"

mighty men, Psalm cxlvi. 3, "put not your trust in princes, nor in the son of man."

1. For a right judgment of them, Deut. viii. 3, we must know that it is not bread, but God's decree, which nourisheth.

2. For the right use of them, because without God's blessing they are nothing, therefore seek strength for them from a further power than is in them; 1 Tim. iv. 4, 5, "every creature of God is good, and nothing to be refused, if it be received with thanksgiving, for it is sanctified by the word of God and prayer."

§ 3. *Of fear.*

The duty of faith is to stir up Fear.

The object of fear is principally God's judgment and justice; in which judgment do concur all things that may cause fear, for it is,

1, *futurum,* 'a thing to come,' Matt. xxiv. 6; though all this be thus, and thus, yet the end is to come, and shall be worst;

2, *propinquum,* 'a thing which is near at hand;' because God is every where, and all things are naked before Him, as it is, Heb. iv. 13;

3, above our resistance, Ps. cxxx. 3, "if Thou, Lord, wilt be extreme to mark what is done amiss, O Lord, who may abide it?" 1 Cor. x. 22, "do we provoke the Lord to jealousy? are we stronger than He?"

And this hath it in four things;

a. punishment, 2 Cor. v. 10, "for we must all appear before the judgment seat of Christ, that every one may receive the things done in his body, according to that he hath done, whether it be good or bad;"

β. fearfulness, violent fire, Heb. x. 27, "a certain fearful looking for of judgment and fiery indignation, which shall devour the adversaries;"

γ. suddenness, 1 Thes. v. 3, "when they shall say, peace and safety, then sudden destruction cometh upon them, as travail upon a woman with child, and they shall not escape;" Prov. i. 27, "when your fear cometh as desolation, and your destruction cometh as a whirlwind," &c.;

δ. it is without remedy.

Now as judgment is the object of fear, so because *metuitur ille qui malum infligere potest,* 'we fear him who can inflict some evil upon us;' therefore in God we consider,

1. His authority, He is a king, Mal. i. 14, "I am a great king, saith the Lord of hosts;" God above all, Isa. xlix. 24, 25;

2. His power, mighty and furious;

3. That we all lean and depend upon Him, and He seeth and knoweth all our faults.

Fear is of two kinds.

1. *Timor servorum,* 'a fear of servants;' of a defect in ourselves: and this a good fear, Rom. viii. 15; it is best of all to be a son, but better a servant than an enemy; as Augustine saith, *si non potes propter amorem justitiæ, fac propter timorem pœnæ,* 'if thou canst not do it for the love of justice, do it for the fear of punishment.'

2. *Timor filiorum,* 'the fear of sons,' which proceedeth of love, Ps. xix. 9; love casteth not out this fear, 1 John iv. 18, but we must make it as Solomon saith, Prov. i. 7, the beginning, and Eccles. xii. 13, the end of all.

Here are forbidden,

a. hardness of heart, Eccles. viii. 11, when "because sentence against an evil work is not executed speedily, therefore the heart of the sons of men is fully set in them to do evil;" and, β. want of fear, Ps. l. 21, "thou thoughtest wickedly that I am even such a one as thyself; but I will reprove thee, and set before thee the things that thou hast done."

Means to beget fear in our hearts.

I. The consideration of such scriptures as set forth God's judgments,

Heb. x. 31, "it is a fearful thing to fall into the hands of the living God;"
— xii. 29, "for our God is a consuming fire;"
Isa. lxvi. 15, "behold the Lord will come with fire, and with His chariots like a whirlwind, to render His anger with fury, and His rebuke with flames of fire."

II. The consideration of those *tria novissima*, 'the three last things' befalling us;

1, our end by death; Ps. xc. 12, "so teach us to number our days, that we may apply our hearts unto wisdom;"
2, our account after death,
  2 Cor. v. 10, "we must all appear before the judgment seat of Christ, that every one may receive the things done in his body, according to that he hath done, whether it be good or bad;"
  Heb. ix. 27, "it is appointed unto men once to die, but after this the judgment;"
3, the terror of hell torments.

III. The examples of God's judgments for sin,

1, upon the whole world which He had made;
2, upon His church, the quintessence of the world, when they sinned in the wilderness;
3, upon His saints, the quintessence of His church; as David His beloved;
4, on the angels in heaven offending;
5, on His Son when He took our sins upon Him, and felt the bitterness of God's justice, of which one saith well, *magna amaritudo peccati quæ tantam amaritudinem peperit*, 'great is the bitterness of sin, which is the cause of such bitterness and woe.'

§ 4. *Of humility.*

After fear comes humility.—Humility was resembled of old by casting dust and ashes on their heads, as not worthy to be above the ground.

True humility is to give all glory to God, and none to ourselves, from whence will follow exaltation, Luke xiv. 11, "he that humbleth himself shall be exalted."

The graces of God are compared to waters, Isa. xii. 3, "with joy shall ye draw water out of the wells of salvation;" Rev. vii. 17, "the Lamb . . shall lead them unto living fountains of waters;" and as waters poured upon hills will not stay, but run down to the lowest places and fill the valleys; so, saith Augustine and Chrysostom, the graces of God descend unto the lowliest and humblest, and abide not with any other.

Humiliation cometh by knowledge of ourselves, what we are, and what we ought to be; which truly to know is the true *γνῶθι σεαυτόν*.

Nature of true humility.

1. To ascribe nothing to our own power; Deut. viii. 17, not to "say in thine heart, my power and the might of mine hand hath gotten me this wealth;"

2. Nothing to our own merit, Deut. ix. 5, "not for thy righteousness, or for the uprightness of thine heart."

Humility teacheth us to deny ourselves; Matt. xvi. 24, "if any man will come after Me, let him deny himself, and take up his cross, and follow Me;" to go *in fundum*, 'into the centre of the earth,' and there to see *nostrum nihil*, 'our nothingness,' we have no good in us; and so resign our reason as not worth obeying, and our will as not worth the following.

Advantages of humility.

1. Humiliation hath this privilege, that he that is thus made low cannot fall; for there is nothing lower than the earth, and so no fear of the threats of cutting or casting down.

2. And it hath also the promise of exaltation: which passeth reason; but God, that made all of nothing, and light out of darkness, hath made humiliation the way to exaltation; the

humble shall be exalted, but *superbus miser indignus misericordiâ*, 'a miserable man that is proud is unworthy of pity.'

Humility comprehendeth three things,

1, *humiliationem cordis*, 'the humility of the heart,' to desire that God may have all the glory;

2, to restrain our appetite from desire of degrees of excellency;

3, submission to our brethren,

Ps. cxxxi. 1, "Lord, my heart is not haughty, nor mine eyes lofty; neither do I exercise myself in great matters, or in things too high for me;"

Phil. ii. 3, "in lowliness of mind let each esteem other better than themselves."

Of pride.

Pride, the contrary to humility, is either { in the subject, or in the object.

In the subject,

in superiors' disdain, as Saul to David in the triumph;

in inferiors' murmurings, as in Chore.

In the object, and that either,

in respect of the gifts, whether they be outward or inward; or,

in respect of something which only seemeth and indeed is not, as Rev. iii. 17, "thou sayest I am rich, and increased with goods, and have need of nothing; and knowest not that thou art wretched, and miserable, and poor, and blind, and naked," Laodicea; worse than the devil, for he had something to be proud of.

Satan saith of himself, Isa. xiv. 14, *ero similis altissimo*, 'I will be like the highest God;' and to our first parents, *eritis sicut dii*, 'ye shall be gods,' Gen. iii. 5. But we must learn, not *similis Deo*, 'like God,' but *humo*, 'to the earth,' that is *humilis*, 'humble.'

Pride is in five things.

1. In thinking we have that which we have not, Rev. iii. 17, Laodicea.

2. In thinking every little good we have, greater than it is, 2 Cor. x. 14, "stretching . . ourselves beyond our measure;"
Ezek. xxviii. 12, "thou sealest up the sum, full of wisdom, and perfect in beauty."

3. To attribute that we have to our own power, as did Nebuchadnezzar; Dan. iv. 30, "is not this great Babylon, that I have built for the house of the kingdom by the might of my power, and for the honour of my majesty?"

4. To make ourselves the end of that we do or of that we have, as did also Nebuchadnezzar, "for the honour of my majesty."

Of these two last there are two signs;

a. if being rebuked for mis-spending God's blessings, we say they are our own, and we may do with our own as we will;

β. if we murmur against God when He taketh away any of His gifts from us; for seeing we have nothing but that God hath lent us, we must be content to pay Him that we owe Him.

5. To give more excellency to ourselves than to others: this was the pharisee's fault; though he did attribute all to God, yet he said he was better than other men; Luke xviii. 11, "God, I thank thee that I am not as other men are."

Means to pride.

1. Because those things which should humble us, puff us up and make us proud.

2. Whereas other sins are in base and vile things, pride is in excellent things; and when all other sins are beaten down and consumed to ashes, even of those ashes ariseth pride; yea we are proud that we are not proud, and so pride cometh even from humility.

Further rules for humility.

There is also forbidden in this commandment constrained humility; such as was in Pharaoh, who was humble for a time, so long as God's hand was upon him, but no longer: such men Bernard[m] calleth *humiliatos non humiles.*

[m] [In Cant. Serm. 34. col. 674 F.]

Neither must we be so humbled as to give back in a good cause, for *detrimentum veritatis non est commendatio humilitatis,* 'to cause detriment to truth, can in no wise be a commendation of humility.'

We must thus think of the evil that is in us, that our evil passeth all men's; of the good that we have, that there is more in others than in us.

Means to humility.

1. To consider the baseness of our metal, that we are but dust and ashes; and this will bring us to that humility that is in the brain.

2. To bring it into our heart, we must consider that we are sinners, bondmen, and slaves to Satan, not having in us one good thought.

3. To consider our afflictions and diseases, the forerunners of death.

4. To consider the examples of humility, and especially Christ, whose birth, preaching, miracles, and death, were all in humility.

Signs of humility.

1. In speech, not to talk of high matters and proud things, Phil. iv. 11, "I have learned in whatsoever state I am therewith to be content;"

2. To set ever before us *bona aliena et mala nostra,* 'what good is in others, and what evil is in ourselves;'

3. To suffer backbiting and shame, Ps. xxxviii.;

4. To be content to be condemned that God may have the glory.

§ 5. *Of hope.*

Now as out of knowledge apprehending God's justice, came fear; so out of the same, apprehending mercy, cometh hope and love.

And as true fear is *timor humilians,* 'joined with humility,' so true humility hath joined with it hope, lest it should drive to despair; as in Judas, Matt. xxvii. 5, "he cast down the pieces of silver in the temple, and departed, and went and hanged himself."

To hope is to look for God's mercy, which is *porta spei*, 'the gate of hope;' whence all good things come.

How related to other graces.

Faith in respect of our weakness bringeth fear, and in respect of God's mercy bringeth hope. Faith believeth the promise, hope looketh for it; for that may be believed that is not hoped for, as hell.

Of faith, hope, and charity, Bernard[x] saith,

fides		*reposita sunt bona,*
spes	*inquit*	*mihi reservantur,*
caritas		*curro ad illa.*

Fear cometh by the faith of the law, and hope by the faith of the gospel.

The use of hope.

The use of hope is twofold;

that we rest in hope in this life;

that we rest not here, but look for a better.

As our life is a sea, hope is compared to an anchor whereby we hold fast; as it is a warfare, our hope is a helmet to save our heads from hurt. As the body liveth *spirando,* so the soul *sperando;* and if it come once *desperare,* then the party is in a miserable case; for *spes vitæ immortalis est vita vitæ mortalis,* 'the blessedness of this life is only the certainty of the life to come.'

Rules for hope.

In hope three things are to be regarded;

1. We must take heed, that as we went out of ourselves by fear, so we do not by hope return to hope in ourselves, but our hope must be in God,

Ps. xxxix. 7, "my hope is in Thee;"

1 Pet. i. 21, "that your faith and hope might be in God."

2. It must be of things to come; for hope that is seen is no hope, Rom. viii. 24.

3. The things we hope for must not be looked for with security, as if it were an easy matter to be attained; but 1 Cor.

[x] [In Ps. Serm. x. col. 538 E.]

ix. 27, we must chasten our bodies and bring them in subjection.

The nature of hope.

In the nature of hope there are,

1. Joy, because we hope for that which is good;

2. Grief, because the good we hope for is delayed; now because *dilatio boni habet rationem mali,* 'the deferring of good is in some kind counted an evil,' therefore our hope cannot be secure. And the remedy of the delay is only patience, as Augustine[y] saith in Ps. xxxvi. *sustine tu ipsum qui sustinuit te; si sustinuit ille te dum corrigeres vitam malam, sustine tu illum dum coronet vitam bonam,* 'be patient towards Him, Who was patient towards thee; if He was patient with thee till thou didst correct the enormity of thy life, be patient at His delay, until He crown thy life godly spent;' and therefore "hold fast," Heb. x. 23.

Basil compareth the gospel to a net, and fear to be the lead which maketh it sink and keepeth it steady, and hope the cork which keepeth always above; without the lead of fear it would be carried hither and thither, and without the cork of hope it would sink down.

For outward things, or God's temporal gifts, there is a desire lawful when God giveth lawful means to come by them; but we must take heed that we do not *malè agendo quærere,* 'seek to get any thing by ill means.'

Extremes to be avoided in hope.

The object of hope is } *bonum* { *possibile, arduum;* good { possible, hard to obtain.

That good we look and hope for, is 'to come,' or else it were no hope; and not only *futurum,* but *arduum,* 'hard to come by;' possible, but hard. And from these two come two extremes of hope, which are here forbidden, Presumption and Desperation.

The first, presumption.

The first extreme is, when we consider it to be possible, but not hard; and so wax idle and fear not, but fall to presumption.

y [vid. vol. iv. col. 267.]

This presumption is,

1. When we presume of ourselves and our own strength, whereas we must know that there is *gratia præveniens*, 'preventing grace,' Ps. lix. 10,—"the God of my mercy shall prevent me,"—before we can do any good; and so also *gratia perficiens*, 'perfecting grace,' to continue in well doing; and to bring it to perfection; so that of ourselves we can do nothing, *nisi gratia præveniat et subsequatur*, 'unless grace prevent and still assist us,' Ps. xxiii. 6, "goodness and mercy follow us all the days of our life."

2. When we presume of others, and hope of help from them; whereas we must know that if God will strike, no man can withstand Him. *Fiduciam homini cum Deo præstat solus Deus homo, id est, Christus;* 'only God-man, that is Christ, can afford and assure us of confidence before God;' for He is the only shield between us and God's axe; Ps. xviii. 30, "the word of the Lord is tried; He is a buckler to all those that trust in Him."

3. When we presume upon God, not grounding ourselves upon His word, which begetteth faith, and faith begetteth hope; and this is a false hope, to presume upon God's mercy without repentance for our sins, or amendment of life.

The second, desperation.

The second extreme is, when we consider this *bonum futurum*, 'good to come,' to be hard, and not possible to be attained; and that is called desperation; and is,

1, that which cometh of sensuality; when this *bonum futurum* hath either no taste unto us, or it is not esteemed by us; this is epicurism, Let us eat and drink, to-morrow we shall die;

2, that which cometh of too great sorrow; when we imagine that there is such a thing in the creature as exceedeth the power of the Creator; which was Cain's error, for God's mercy is greater than our misery; it is above all.

The means to hope.

1. Compare the enduring hope of the faithful with the perishing hope of the wicked; Prov. xi. 7, "the hope of unjust men perisheth."

2. Mark the examples of others that have hoped and were not deceived, Ps. xxii. 4, "our fathers trusted in Thee; they trusted, and Thou didst deliver them;" for this is the devil's craft, to persuade us that our cause is worse than any man's.

3. Remember what experience we have had of God's mercy, 1 Sam. xvii. 37, "the Lord that delivered me out of the paw of the lion and out of the paw of the bear, He will deliver me out of the hand of this Philistine."

4. Consider the faithfulness of Him that hath promised, and that His *dicere est facere*, 'His word and deed are all one.'

The signs of hope.

1. Uprightness of conscience, as in Ezekias,
   2 Kings xx. 3, "I beseech Thee, O Lord, remember now how I have walked before Thee in truth and with a perfect heart, and have done that which is good in Thy sight;" and,
   1 John iii. 3, "every man that hath this hope in him purifieth himself, even as He is pure;"
   custos spei conscientia, 'conscience is the preserver of our hope;'
2. Care to do well;
3. Comfort in trouble,
   Rom. v. 3, 4, "we glory in tribulations also: knowing that tribulation worketh patience; and patience, experience; and experience, hope;"
   Esay xxx. 15, "in quietness and in confidence shall be your strength;" for such as we are in adversity, such we are indeed.

§ 6. *Of Prayer.*

The fruit of hope is prayer. *Interpres mentis oratio; spei operatio oratio; precibus, non passibus, itur ad Deum;* 'prayer is the interpreter of our mind; the operation of our hope is prayer; we go to God by prayers of our minds, not by the paces of our feet;' therefore *ascendat oratio, ut descendat gratia*, 'let thy prayer ascend, that grace may descend.'

By prayer is not only meant open prayer, which is called 'the calves of the lips,' Hos. xiv. 2, (which is not in this first commandment,) but,

PART III.

a. the inward meditation of the heart,
1 Cor. xiv. 15, "praying with the spirit;"
Esay xxxviii. 14, Hezekiah's prayer; Rom. viii. 26, the groaning of the spirit, and

β. private prayer, in private families. Prayer is called *clavis diei,* and *sera noctis,* 'the key to open the day,' and the 'bar to shut in the night.'

Prayer maketh for God's glory.

Prayer maketh much for God's glory; and that two ways;
1, we acknowledge His goodness and power when we become suitors to Him for supply of things needful;
2, when we render thanks to Him for whatsoever we obtain and enjoy.

In Psalm cvii. David sets down five sorts of men who in this kind glorify God;
such as wander out of the way,
they which are troubled,
prisoners,
they which are in tempests,
they which are in danger of the enemy;
all which are delivered by God's goodness and mercy, and David thereupon addeth, "O that men would therefore praise the Lord," &c.

By prayer,
the poor are comforted,—Ps. xxxiv. 2, "my soul shall make her boast in the Lord; the humble shall hear thereof, and be glad;"—
sinners are restored, and
God glorified;
therefore a necessity is imposed on us to use it.

Christ, who never instituted any needless thing, indited a form of prayer for us, Matt. vi.;
And God required morning and evening sacrifice, expounded to be nothing else but morning and evening prayer,
Num. xxviii. 3, "two lambs of the first year without spot day by day, for a continual burnt-offering;"
Ps. cxli. 2, "let my prayer be set forth before Thee as

incense, and the lifting up of my hands as the evening sacrifice;"

Dan. vi. 10, Daniel "kneeled upon his knees three times a day, and prayed, and gave thanks before his God, as he did aforetime."

It worketh miracles in all the elements.

In the air; Elias by prayer shut up the middle region that it could not rain, 1 Kings xvii. 1;

In the fire; 2 Kings i. 10, prayer brought fire from heaven to destroy the captains and their fifties;

In the earth; Ps. cvi. 17, at Moses' prayer the earth opened, and swallowed Corah, Dathan, and Abiram;

In the water; Exod. xiv. 16, the Red sea was divided by prayer;

In the heavens; the sun stood still, as we read, Joshua x. 12;

In earthly things; Exod. xvii. 11, "when Moses held up his hand, Israel prevailed;"

In death; Esay xxxviii. 5, Ezekias' life lengthened;

With God Himself; Exod. xxxii. 10, when Moses prayed, God as though He suffered violence, bade him, "let Me alone."

Encouragement to prayer.

But how may I, miserable man, be bold to pray to the eternal God?

As one saith, *non tua præsumptione, sed divina permissione*, 'not out of presumption, but by divine permission;' for

α. God commandeth it; Ps. l. 15, "call upon Me in the day of trouble;" and,

β. if we pray we shall be delivered out of trouble,

Ps. xci. 15, "he shall call upon Me, and I will answer him; I will be with him in trouble, I will deliver him;"

Acts ii. 21, "whosoever shall call on the name of the Lord shall be saved;" but,

γ. if we do not, we shall be cursed,

Jer. x. 25, "pour out Thy fury upon the heathen that know Thee not, and upon the families that call not on Thy name."

But if we join these two places together,

Matt. vii. 8, *unusquisque qui petit accipiet,* 'every man that asks shall speed,' and

John xvi. 23, *quæcunque petieritis,* 'whatever ye shall ask,'

it will make us pray with great confidence, if *omnis omnia accipiet,* if 'every man shall have granted to him every thing.'

What is contained in prayer.

Invocation is here commanded; wherein is

1, a lifting up of our souls to God with confession of our sins, Ps. xxv. 1—7, "unto Thee, O Lord, do I lift up my soul; O my God, I trust in Thee, let me not be ashamed, let not mine enemies triumph over me; yea, let none that wait on Thee be ashamed; let them be ashamed which transgress without cause. Shew me Thy ways, O Lord, teach me Thy paths; lead me in Thy truth, and teach me; for Thou art the God of my salvation, on Thee do I wait all the day. Remember, O Lord, Thy tender mercies and Thy loving-kindnesses, for they have been ever of old; remember not the sins of my youth, nor my transgressions;"

2, a pouring forth of our hearts to declare our desires, Ps. cxlii. 2, "I poured out my complaint before Him; I shewed before Him my trouble."

Prayer is either
- petition
  - for ourselves
    - deprecation, δέησις,
    - precation, προσευχὴ,
  - for others . . intercession, ἔντευξις,
- . . . . thanksgiving, εὐχαριστία.

First, of deprecation.

Deprecation must be,—as James v. 13, "is any among you afflicted? let him pray;"—in time of affliction, or fear of evil; because *remotio mali habet rationem boni,* 'the taking away of evil is in effect a doing us good,' and so cometh under hope, and so to be prayed for.

Deprecation is in three things;

1, *ut malum avertatur,* 'to prevent an evil before it come;' Dan. ix. 16, "let Thine anger and Thy fury be turned away from Thy city Jerusalem, Thy holy mountain;"

2, *ut malum auferatur*, 'to be delivered out of it;' Ps. xxv. 22, "redeem Israel, O God, out of all his troubles;"

3, *ut minuatur*, that it may be no more than we may be able to bear it; Ps. lxxxv. 4, "turn us, O God of our salvation, and cause Thine anger toward us to cease."

Rules for deprecation.

1. We must not say as commonly we do, I would I were out of the world; but as Christ prayed for His disciples to the Father, John xvii. 15, not that He would take them out of the world, but deliver them from evil; and so doing we have God's promise not to be tempted above our strength, 1 Cor. x. 13, for either our strength shall increase as the cross increaseth, or else our trouble shall diminish.

2. We must stand affected as Jehoshaphat, 2 Chron. xx. 12, and say, "Lord, we know not what to do," our troubles be so great and our enemies so many, "but our eyes are upon Thee;" and as the Three children appointed to the fiery furnace, who said, "we are sure our God can deliver us; but if He will not, we will trust in Him and not serve other strange gods," Dan. iii. And Christ set us a perfect good pattern, saying in His agony, "not My will, but Thy will, O Father, be done!"

Secondly, of precation.

Precation is the desiring of something that is good; and this is very usual in the psalms. It hath three degrees,

to give to them that want,
to stablish and confirm them that have,
to increase it in them that have little.

Here we must observe certain steps;

Unum petii, that is, 'one thing especially,' Ps. xxvii. 4, Luke xi. 13; first pray for the Holy Ghost; and then for temporal things, *secundum voluntatem ejus*, 'according to His good pleasure.' And here *resignatio* is an excellent virtue, to submit and resign all we have, yea even ourselves, into God's hands; 2 Sam. xv. 26, "here am I, let Him do to me as seemeth good in His eyes."

Quest. But doth *omnis omnia accipere?* hath every man granted to him all good?

Answ. Surely many ask and receive not; and then seeing God hath commanded us to ask, and if we do not ask He is offended with us, surely therefore the cause why we receive not, must be in ourselves, and in our asking.

So that in asking, this we hold,

1. That it is not a demonstrative sign of grace and favour always to have our prayers heard and our requests granted, Ps. lxxviii. 29; and that the devils sometimes have their requests;

2. We must know that the denying of our requests is not a sign of reprobation; as we see in Paul, 2 Cor. xii. 8; and that

a. God doth not deny us our just requests, but defer the granting of them, that we might ask more earnestly and esteem them more highly; for *desideria dilatione crescunt, et cito data vilescunt,* 'our desires by being delayed are inflamed, and requests easily granted seem not worth acceptance;'

β. or else God deferreth the granting of our requests to bestow a better thing upon us, as grace to Paul;

γ. or if our requests be not made aright, then they are like children's prayers, that will ask a knife to hurt them, as well as bread to feed them, and those things, *non accipiendo accipimus,* 'we receive, yet receive not.'

Of intercession.

Intercession is to pray for others; (of this Augustine to Ambrose, *Frater, si pro te solum ores, solus pro te oras; si pro omnibus oras, omnes pro te orant,* 'brother, if you pray for yourself only, you pray alone for yourself; if you pray for all men, all men pray for you;')

- for the church, Ps. cxxii. 6, "pray for the peace of Jerusalem;"
- for governors, Rom. xv. 30, "I beseech you, brethren, . . that ye strive together with me in your prayers to God for me;"
- for our natural brethren, 1 John v. 16, "if any man see his brother sin a sin which is not unto death, he shall

ask, and He shall give Him life for them that sin not unto death;"

for our enemies, Matt. v. 44, "pray for them which despitefully use you, and persecute you."

Gregory upon the Evangelists[z], speaking on Jer. xv. 1, where it is said, "though Samuel and Moses," &c. asketh the question, Why these men are mentioned? and answereth, Because they prayed for their enemies; Moses for the Israelites when they would stone him, and Samuel for them when they would depose him from ruling over them.

And these prayers are most effectual; for *qui pro aliis orat, is pro se laborat,* 'he that prayeth for others, he striveth for himself;' for though he profit not them, it shall profit himself, his prayer shall be turned into his own bosom, Ps. xxxv. 13.

Thirdly, of thanksgiving.

Thanksgiving is the last point of prayer.

God's glory is the chiefest end; and therefore, whether we receive before we ask, Esay lxv. 24, or when we ask, Matt. vii. 8, it is reason w[illegible]der, *quid retribuam,* 'what shall I return unto the Lord?' Ps. cxvi. 12.

The heathen could say, *gratus animus est meta benignitatis,* 'a thankful mind is all which a kind and good heart aimeth at.' And it is the condition of the obligation wherein God hath bound Himself by His promise to hear us, Ps. l. 15, "thou shalt glorify Me;" so that if thou dost not glorify Him by thanksgiving, thou breakest the covenant, and art an usurper.

Thanksgiving standeth in four things.

1. Confession, that we have received it from heaven, and not from ourselves; as Austin saith, *ut is qui confitetur habere se quod non habet, est temerarius, sic qui habere se negat quæ habet, ingratus; ideoque utendum est ut datis, non ut innatis, ut alterius, non nostri,* 'as he that confesseth that he hath that which he hath not, is rash; so he that denieth that he hath what he enjoyeth, is unthankful: therefore we must

[z] [Hom. xxvii. § 8, vol. i. col. 1564.]

use what we have as things given us, not as things springing from ourselves, as things that are another's and not our own.'

2. Contentation, when we rest in the gifts of God, and are satisfied with that which we have, Ps. xvi. 6, "the lines are fallen unto me in pleasant places, yea I have a goodly heritage."

3. Annunciation, to tell it to others what God hath done for us; Ps. lxvi. 16, "come and hear, all ye that fear God, and I will declare what He hath done for my soul;"

— in the congregation, Ps. cxi. 1, "I will praise the Lord with my whole heart, in the assembly of the upright, and in the congregation;"

— yea to all nations, Ps. lvii. 9, "I will praise Thee, O Lord, among the people, I will sing unto Thee among the nations;"

— yea to all posterity, Ps. xxii. 31, "they shall come, and shall declare His righteousness unto a people that shall be born, that He hath done this;" not to keep close the graces of God.

4. Exhortation to others to do the like; Ps. xcv. 1, "O come, let us sing unto the Lord, let us make a joyful noise to the Rock of our salvation;" and if there were no men, we should call upon the creatures to praise God, Ps. cxlviii.

Thanks is never truly given to God, but there is a better thing received; as Bernard[a] saith, *ascensus gratiarum est descensus gratiæ*, 'upon the ascending of thanks followeth a descending of grace;' and grace fails when our thanks fail.

The excellency of thanksgiving.

The excellency of thanksgiving is well to be considered.

Chrysostom asking the question, Why David was called a man after God's own heart? answereth, Because David saw thanksgiving most of all pleased God, and therefore used it most of all; he esteemed prayer as an excellent thing, Ps. lv. 17, and appointed certain hours thereunto, yet he preferred the praising of God above all, and therefore used it seven times a day.

[a] [vid. Serm. De dil. Deo, ad fin. et passim.]

And for this cause the christian church, and innumerable angels, yea all the creatures in heaven, earth, and sea, sang praises, saying, "praise, and honour, and glory, and power, be unto Him that sitteth on the throne, and unto the Lamb for evermore," Rev. v. 11, &c.

Hence David counted his tongue exercised in the praises of God the best member which he had; therefore in the church of God every man should speak of his praise.

And this was the reason why the fathers ended with a doxology, "Now to Jesus Christ with the Father and Holy Ghost, be given all honour, praise, glory," &c. "for evermore."

Why it is that we may ask and not receive.

But to speak a little more concerning that question, *quare non omnis omnia accipit quæ p[illegible]?*

For the matter of our petitions;

Right invocation must be,

1. *Animata,* 'our hearts set upon it;' therefore it is that Dav[illegible]geth his soul to praise the Lord; our prayers must be with understanding, or else they are without life; therefore saith Paul, "I will pray with the spirit and with the understanding also," 1 Cor. xiv. 15.

2. Our prayer must be constant, not like the waves of the sea; but seeing prayer is *interpres spei,* and *abbreviarium fidei,* 'the interpreter of our hope, and the brief sum of our faith,' therefore it must be as an anchor to take fast hold, not wavering or slippery;

   James i. 6, "he that wavereth is like a wave of the sea driven with the wind and tossed;"

   Ps. cxlv. 18, "the Lord is nigh unto all them that call upon Him, to all that call upon Him in truth."

3. With humility, or else it is no prayer; a form whereof we have, Dan. ix. 18, "we do not present our supplications before Thee for our righteousnesses, but for Thy great mercies."

4. We must not make absurd prayers, *orationes sine ratione,* 'orisons without reason;' namely, when we do *accedere pro pace sive pro remissione peccatorum, et ipsi peccata*

retinemus, as Tertullian[b] saith, 'pray for peace and remission of our sins, and yet persist in our sins;' how can we say to God, Forgive me, and to our brother, Pay me?

a. We must give therefore if we will receive,

Prov. xxi. 13, "whoso stoppeth his ears at the cry of the poor, he also shall cry himself, but shall not be heard;"

β. and we must forgive, if we will have forgiveness,

Mark xi. 25, "when ye stand praying, forgive, if ye have ought against any, that your Father also which is in heaven may forgive you your trespasses."

5. We must not set days to God, wherein if we be not heard, we will leave prayer and God too; but we must pray continually, without fainting;

1 Thes. v. 17, "pray without ceasing;"

Luke xviii. 1, "men ought always to pray, and not to faint."

Means to prayer.

Prayer is the means of all other graces; therefore it hath no means, yet helps it hath.

1. To consider our own imperfections; to have as it were a table of our wants.

2. To consider God's benefits, to have a register of them. —David made a diligent search after God's benefits, even the least of them; and his course was,

a. first to give thanks for new benefits, Ps. xl. 1, 3, "I waited patiently for the Lord; and He inclined unto me, and heard my cry;—and He hath put a new song in my mouth, even praise unto our God;"

β. if there were no new, then blessed be God for His old loving-kindness; Ps. cxxxix., he thanks God for taking him from his mother's womb.

If thus we would recount God's goodness to us, we should never have any idle time, so great are His mercies, so many first and last, least and most, are His blessings upon us.

3. Fasting, which is as it were the wings of prayer; as

[b] [vid. de Orat., § 10. p. 133.]

Augustine[c] saith, *jejunium orationis robur*, 'fasting adds strength to prayer,' *oratio vis jejunii*, 'prayer gives strength to fasting.'

4. To desire other men's prayers to help us, as one saith, *si oratio tua fulmen sit, ascendat ad cœlum sola et per se; si non, sit grando inter imbrem*; 'if thy prayer be as a thunderbolt, let it be sent up to heaven alone, and by itself; if not, let it be as hail amidst drops of rain,' that is, assume the prayers of the godly.

Signs of thankfulness are,

To have the soul satisfied as with marrow and fatness, Ps. lxiii. 5.

To have a care of God's glory, Ps. lxvi. 8, "O bless our God, ye people, and make the voice of His praise to be heard;"

And a care to please God for His benefits, Ps. liv.—For the joy of the benefit received must not take away our care to be thankful.

We shew our readiness to this duty when we provoke others to it, "Come, let us rejoice," Ps. xxxiv. 3, yea to call all creatures to praise God, Ps. cxlviii., as David did.

§ 7. *Of the Love of God.*

After the obtaining of that which we pray for, followeth love; and whereas we said before that to have a thing was, first to know it, and then to esteem it; this esteeming doth properly appertain to love.

Love is

1, *concupiscentiæ*, 'of concupiscence,' when we love to the end to receive some good thing of him whom we love, called *amor mercenarius*, 'mercenary love;'

2, *benevolentiæ*, 'of good will,' without respect of any good looked for, called *gratuitus*, 'a free love.'

Others divide love to be,

quoniam, 'because' He hath heard our voice;
tametsi, 'though' He kill us, Job xiii. 15.

[c] [vid. Serm. in Quadr. ccvi., sq., vol. v. col. 922, 924.]

We may also distinguish love, as if we should be said to love our { meats, friends.

In the one we love our own good, *quod cupimus,* 'which we have a desire unto;'

In the other, to do them good, *quibus benevolumus,* 'to whom we wish well.'

The Apostle saith, 1 Cor. xv. 46, "that is not first which is spiritual, but that which is carnal;" which Augustine, Basil, Ambrose, and Bernard refer to faith and love, shewing that Cæsar's virtues were in greater account than Cato's; Cæsar's being courtesy, affability, clemency, liberality, &c., Cato's, constancy, faithfulness, justice, &c.; because these reached not to the commodity of others, as the former did. That which is natural will be first, *concupiscentia,* 'a concupiscence,' before it be *cupiditas,* 'a desire;' and because *nemo repente fit summus,* 'no man presently cometh to the highest pitch' of love, we must take this *amor mercenarius,* 'mercenary love,' as the inchoation and mean whereby to attain to the other which is *gratuitus,* 'a free love.'

Love above faith and hope.

Love is the greatest virtue, even above faith, and hope;

1. In breadth, for faith and hope are within the bounds of man's person, but love is to God Himself, and from Him to our friends, yea our enemies; *beatus qui amat te et amicos in te et inimicos propter te,* 'blessed is he, who loveth Thee, and his friends in Thee, and his enemies for Thy sake,' saith Augustine[d].

2. In length; where the other end with life, love is after this life, even in heaven.

And whereas faith and hope are in us, but not in God at all; love is in God; yea, He loved us first; as Bernard saith, *nescio quid amore majus; deduxit Deum de cœlo, hominem invexit in cœlum, Deum homini pacavit, hominem Deo reconciliavit,* 'I know not what is greater than love; it brought God from heaven, it elevated man to heaven, it appeased God's anger towards man, it reconciled man to God.'

[d] [Confess., lib. iv. cap. 9, vol. i. col. 102.]

Why we should love God.

And then seeing *magnes amoris est amor,* 'love is the lodestone attractive of love,' and God hath loved us first; great cause have we to love God again, who hath loved us[e],

1. *Prior,* 'first;' 1 John iv. 19, "we love Him, because He first loved us;" *durus est qui amorem non rependit,* 'he is hard hearted who requites not love with love;'

2. *Tantus,* 'so great;' as Augustine, *non licet conari exprimere quantus,* 'we may not attempt to express how great He is;'

3. *Tantillos,* 'as small as could be;' even before we were, Rom. ix. 11, "the children being not yet born, neither having done any good or evil;"

4. *Tales,* 'so ill conditioned;' Rom. v. 10, "when we were enemies;"

5. *Tantum,* 'so highly;' as we may see in God

α. the Father, His *tantum,* 'so much love,' John iii. 16; *sic,* 'so greatly,' that He spared not His own Son;

β. the Son, His *tantum,* 'so much love,' content to leave heaven and to come down and suffer

ignominy, Matt. xxvii. 63, "that deceiver;"
poverty, Luke ix. 58, "the Son of man hath not where to lay His head;"
sickness, Esay liii. 4, 5, "He hath borne our griefs, and carried our sorrows;"
hatred, John v. 18, "the Jews sought to kill Him;"
death itself, John xv. 13, "greater love hath no man than this, that a man lay down his life for his friends;"

and all for our sakes, for the love He bore us;

γ. the Holy Ghost, His *tantum,* 'so much love,' as to come and dwell with us when Christ left us; Rom. v. 5, "the love of God is shed abroad in our hearts by the Holy Ghost which is given unto us."

So that we may say, What could God do more?

6. *Gratis,* 'freely;' Ps. xvi. 2, "my goodness extendeth not to Thee;" He can receive nothing of us but love; *nihil*

[e] [S. Bern. De amore Dei, cap. 6. col. 1145; De caritate, cap. 31. col. 2359.]

autem decentius quam ut amor amore compensetur, 'nothing doth more beseem us than to return love for love.'

How much we should love God.

Quest. Now how much should we love God again?

Answ. Bernard answereth this question; *quia fecisti me, ideo me tibi debeo; nunc autem cum renovasti, quantum? dicto me fecisti, sed renovasti multis dictis, factis, passis,* 'because Thou hast made me, therefore I owe myself to Thee; but now seeing that Thou hast made me anew, what do I owe Thee? Thou madest me with a word, but Thou hast made me anew with many words, deeds, sufferings.'

And with the second making there came the gift of God himself; *nisi dedisset se pro te, non reddidisset te tibi; si me solum mihi reddidisset, potui me illi denuo; at cum se mihi, quid illi reddam?* 'had not Christ given Himself for thee, He had not restored thee to thyself; had He restored myself only to myself, I could have given myself to Him again; but when as He hath given Himself unto me, what shall I return to Him again?' Yet that which followeth is our comfort, *etenim si non possim quantum debeo amare, ultra quod possum, si possim, velim; et si minus reddo, quia minor sum, quia tamen totâ animâ diligo, nihil deest,* 'surely if I can not love Him so much as I ought, I would go farther than I can, if I could; and if I return less to Him because I am less, yet because I love Him with my whole heart there is nothing defective.'—And so this we must labour to attain unto, to love Him with all our heart and all our soul.

Our love to God may be examined by this, whether we be *contenti lege Domini,* 'content with God's law;' for *qui regem amat, legem amat,* 'he that loveth the king, loveth the law;' and so it is with God and His law.

The contrary to this is { *amor mundi,* 'the love of the world,'
amor sui, 'the love of a man's self.' }

Means of love.

Among many, one means to make us love God, is the consideration of the profit we shall reap by it; He hath given His Son for a price, His Spirit for a pledge, and He reserveth

Himself for a reward; *dedit Filium pretium pro nobis, Spiritum sanctum testem, et seipsum pro nobis servat, daturus coronam,* 'He gave His Son a price to purchase us, the Holy Ghost a witness testifying His truth to us, and He hath reserved Himself for us, when He will give us the crown of glory.'

Signs of love.

1. To think of God with a deep thought, a long thought, and an often thought, *cogitatione profundâ, continuatâ, crebrâ;* for Matt. vi. 21, *ubi thesaurus, ibi animus,* 'where the treasure is, there will the heart be also;'

2. To esteem well of the pledges of God's love, the word and sacraments;

3. *Ubi amor, ibi oculus,* 'where the love is placed, there will the eye be;' as Esau's eye was on the pottage, Gen. xxv. 31;

4. A grief for God's absence from us, Ps. cxx. 5, "woe is me that I sojourn in Mesech, that I dwell in the tents of Kedar!"

5. Not to think the time long that we serve Him, as Jacob because he loved Rachel, thought seven years a short time, Gen. xxix. 20;

6. To be afraid to lose Him; *quod cupis habere, times perdere; cuicunque cupis conjungi, ab eo times separari,* 'that which thou desirest to have, thou art afraid to lose; to whomsoever thou desirest to be united, thou wilt fear to be separated from him;'

7. To be grieved when we think we have lost Him, and feel not our former comfort;

8. To have a care to recover God's love again, Ps. cxxxii. 4, "I will not give sleep to mine eyes, or slumber to mine eyelids," &c.;

9. If we can be content to love God so much the more, if all men beside ourselves should hate Him, as Ps. cxix. 126 sq., "they have made void Thy law, therefore I love Thy commandments above gold, yea above fine gold;"

10. If neither water can quench it, nor fire consume it, but we can forego all for it.

PART III

Effects of love.

Now the two effects of love are, obedience, and patience.

Of obedience Gregory saith, *probatio dilectionis est exhibitio operis,* 'the proof of our love is seen by the promptness of our good works;' obedience then as the active, and patience as the passive, do both depend upon love.

First effect of love, obedience.

Love between equals is called *amicitia,* 'friendship,' but where one party is superior, *reverentia,* 'reverence,' or rather *observantia,* 'observance,' the natural act whereof is obedience; and though Christ be our friend and our brother, yet the apostles call themselves His servants, and Rom. vi. 16, "whom ye obey, his servants ye are."

In the Lord's prayer, in the first petition we desire to glorify God's name, and that is by the kingdom of God coming, and that cometh by doing His will, which is obedience.

Nihil facit bonos vel malos mores, sed boni vel mali amores, 'nothing maketh our carriage good or evil, but our good or evil love,' Augustine.

The causes of all evil, and of the want of obedience are these,

amor malè inflammans, 'love inflaming to evil,'
timor malè humilians, 'fear dejecting us to evil.'

That our obedience may be true, there must be *idem velle,* and *idem nolle,* 'a willing and nilling the same,' betwixt God and us; suffering all our actions and all our wills to be ruled and directed by God's will.

Obedience better than sacrifice.

Though sacrifice be acceptable unto God, yet obedience is better than sacrifice;

1. In obedience *offertur propria voluntas,* 'our own will is offered;' that which is our own, as it is dearer to us, so it is better accepted of God; but in sacrifice we offer strange flesh, and not our own.

2. In obedience we offer up ourselves a living sacrifice; in the other, dead flesh of slain beasts.

3. In sacrifice the things may be our own, but in obedience we offer ourselves; and *obedientia non potest plus dare quam dedit, dedit enim se,* 'obedience cannot give more than it hath given, for it gave itself.'

4. Obedience is *juge sacrificium,* 'a daily sacrifice;' a perpetual mortifying of the will, reason and members, &c. whereas sacrifices are consumed in an hour.

Obedience is a compound word of *ob* and *audio;* and the rule of compounds is, *in compositis et copulativis utrumque faciendum,* 'in compounds and copulatives both parts must concur.'

We have great reason to hear Him, because He heareth us; neither can we hear a better counsellor, and if we hear not Him we shall hear a worse; for *oves qui non audiunt pastorem, incidunt in lupos,* 'they that will not follow the shepherd to the pastures, shall follow the butcher to the shambles.'

And the next thing in obedience is to keep that we hear.

The degrees of disobedience are,

1, *negligentia ubique culpabilis,* 'negligence, which is every where culpable;' Matt. xxii. 12, "friend, how camest thou in hither not having a wedding garment?"

2, *contemptus ubique damnabilis,* 'contempt, which is every where damnable;' Luke xiv. 18, "they all with one consent began to make excuse."

Signs of obedience.

1, If we obey in God's law as well that point which the prince's law doth not take hold of as that which it doth, as namely, the third and fourth commandments;

2, If in those things wherein God seemeth to strive with nature, we follow God, and prefer Him before our parents, our brethren and kindred, as Abraham did.

Second effect of love, patience.

The second proper effect of love is patience; "Charity suffereth long," 1 Cor. xiii. 4; it is a fruit of love. A heathen man said, *non amo quenquam, nisi offendam,* 'I love not any man, unless I offend him,' for so I shall know whether he love me or no, by his forbearing of me; and

Augustine saith, *qui desinit sustinere, desinit amare,* 'he that ceaseth to bear with me, ceaseth to love me.'

Durum pati, 'it is a difficult matter to suffer,' for evil is the object to patience; so that patience is never *propter se, sed propter magis bonum,* 'for itself, but for a greater good.' And this is the reason of christianity, that we suffer wrong and forbear a little pleasure here on earth, that we may have greater joy in heaven; so that *ardor desideriorum facit tolerantiam malorum,* 'vehemency of desire makes us patient of evil.'

We offend against patience, when we are ignorant of the original of affliction, and consider not the cause from whence it cometh, and so separate God from being the author thereof; and

1, if the affliction be within us, we take unto ourselves *terrenas consolationes,* 'earthly comforts,' our pleasures and our friends, and so labour to drive it away;

2, if the affliction be without, ascribe it *humori naturæ, non rationi gratiæ,* 'to the course of nature, not to the course of God's grace;' then we think we have injury, and so look not to God that is the smiter, but unto man that is but God's rod.

Means to patience.

1. To consider that we suffer justly, we deserve it, Luke xxiii. 41, "we receive the due reward of our deeds;"

2. As it is just, so it is of faith in regard of the promise, Ps. lxxxix. 33, sq., that His mercy shall never be taken away; "My loving-kindness will I not utterly take from him, nor suffer My faithfulness to fail; My covenant will I not break, nor alter the thing that is gone out of my lips;"

3. To consider, that continual prosperity in temporal things is not always a sign of God's favour, but rather the contrary.

4. Seeing thou canst not help it, make a virtue of necessity, Acts ix. 5, "it is hard kicking against the pricks;" therefore do it willingly, and suffer patiently.

Of the cause of affliction.

A great mean to patience is to consider the cause of affliction, both the beginning and the end.

Of the beginning of affliction.

For the beginning of affliction, it is from God, Who is indeed not only the sovereign good, but the author, original, and fountain of all good; from Whom it is as impossible that any evil should be derived, as for Himself to be evil. God's smiting us is good and healthful for us; He abhors to hurt and to be hurt, for He is an only and sovereign power doing us good.

Those that do not consider this are like Simon of Cyrene, that carried the cross and was not crucified on it; and such men, if their afflictions be within them, they take *terrenas consolationes*, 'earthly consolations,' to drive them away; if they be without them, they judge them *ex aliorum facto*, 'by others' deeds,' to be injuries; and so *omittentes Deum percussorem homines baculo petunt*, 'passing by God Who smiteth them, they fall upon men with their weapons,' who are but God's instruments.

Whereas they should consider that God's punishments are of two sorts,

a. some mere punishments, which befal plainly without the concurrence of man's intention or hand, as famine, dearth, earthquake, the earth's barrenness, inundations, diseases, death; in all these there is nothing impure, because they flow from a most pure fountain;

β. other punishments are of a mixed nature, because they are inflicted by using men as His instruments; such are tyranny, wars, oppressions, slaughters; in these there is something impure, because they flow and stream along through the impure channel of human affection.

Of men as God's instruments herein.

Quest. But is there any injustice in the execution hereof?

Answ. In regard of men there is often injustice, but in regard of God never any. The instruments are oftentimes as the Sabeans were against Job; look therefore to the author, not to the actor; as David did when Shimei railed on him, 2 Sam. xvi. 10, 12, "the Lord hath said unto him, Curse David; who shall then say, Wherefore hast thou done so?—It may be that the Lord will look on mine affliction, and that the Lord will requite me good for his cursing."

Neither must we curiously enquire why God useth the wicked to punish the godly; *consilia enim Dei miranda sunt, non rimanda, cui uni licet quod libet, et nihil libet nisi quod licet,* 'God's counsels are to be admired, not questioned; because He alone can do what He pleaseth, and He lists to do nothing but what is best.'

Princes deal by inferior magistrates; magistrates have their executioners; parents sometimes punish by their servants; why may not God do the like, and when He pleaseth, to punish by His own hand; and when it seemeth good to Him, to punish by the hand of some other? Nebuchadnezzar is called God's servant; if an angry servant have a mischievous bent, it's no matter; for thy part let him alone, and look to the mind of Him that sets him on work; for thy Father, Who bids him smite thee, stands by, so that the servant shall not multiply one stripe more than thy Father's prescription gives way to. The devil also God sometimes useth to afflict His children, but he is bound within certain limits, Job i.

What point of wisdom is greater than to draw good out of evil, and to turn destruction into salvation? Now the power of God doth especially demonstrate itself, because it not only doth overcome His enemies, but doth also draw them to Him and to His tents and party, that they war for Him. Which thing falls out daily, when God's will is done upon evil men, though it be by evil men; when those things which ill men do against His will, He so moderates, that yet they be not done beside His will.

Of the ends of affliction.

Now for the ends of afflictions; they are three;
to exercise good men;
to chastise such as have slipped;
to punish wicked men.

First, to exercise good men.

First, to exercise the good; and this very profitable, both to confirm themselves and others, and also to try and prove them;

1. To confirm themselves; the seaman is taught by a tempest, the soldier by dangerous enterprises, and a faithful man by afflictions; trees shaken by the winds take deeper root, and good men assaulted by the waves of affliction stick closer to virtue.

2. To confirm others also; the courage and patience of good men in affliction is as it were a torch light to this dark world; and they call others by their examples, as it were chalk out their way where they should go. Paul was killed by Nero, but the axe which killed him animates and secures us boldly to die for the truth. To conclude; so many select injuriously and violently smitten and slain, by the streams of their blood embolden us to persist firm and constant. Now all these things would be buried in obscurity, without the bright shining of affliction.

3. To try and prove them also; how else could any man be assured of his firmness? It was therefore a noble speech of Demetrius, No man seems to me more unhappy than he who never felt adversity.

Secondly, to chastise such as have slipped.

Secondly, to chastise and correct those that are fallen.

Affliction is to us as a whip when we have sinned, as a bridle before we sin to keep us from it; so that,

1, as the Persians, when they would punish a nobleman, took his garments and smote them as the man himself; so God our Father in all our castigations toucheth not us, but our body, riches, lands and outward estate;

2, chastisement also is a bridle, which God opportunely puts into our mouths when He sees us about to sin, as provident physicians sometimes let thee blood, not because thou art sick, but lest thou shouldst be sick; so God by calamities takes those things from us which would be the fuel and bellows kindling vice in us, for He knows the nature and bent of all men which He hath made.

Thirdly, to punish wicked men.

Thirdly, to punish the wicked. Punishment doth properly pertain to evil men; yet is not evil, but good, *α.* first, if you look unto God, the law of Whose justice requires that men's sins should either be amended, or taken quite away; now chastisement takes away those which can be washed off, those which cannot, punishment takes away;

β. secondly, if you regard men, whose society cannot stand if violent and wicked-natured men shall slip away unpunished;

γ. thirdly, if you regard the wicked men themselves running headlong into vice and mischief; they cannot be drawn therefrom without cutting off, therefore God's pleasure is to take them away lest they should ever sin;

δ. fourthly, in respect of justice, for all punishment is good, and all impunity is evil.

And thus much of the first point, that we must have a God.

There remain yet two points,
The second, to have Him for our God, which is Religion;
The third, to have Him alone, which is Sincerity;
and out of the words "before Me," Integrity;
and out of the word "shalt," Perseverance.

§ 8. *Of religion.*

Our affection is evermore bent to some religion;
- either an idol; 1 Cor. viii. 7, "some with conscience of the idol unto this hour eat it as a thing offered unto an idol," &c.;
- or the world; 2 Cor. iv. 4, "the god of this world hath blinded the minds of them which believe not;"
- or our belly; Phil. iii. 19, "whose god is their belly;"
- or money; Eph. v. 5, "covetous man, who is an idolater;"

All these dishonour the true God; and therefore it is not enough to have a god, but we must have a true God.

Chief errors in religion.

In religion there are three usual errors;

1, when we never seek more, but, "in this I was born, and in this will I die," and so religion findeth us, and not we it;

2, when we take unto ourselves a religion upon some offence, and stubbornness to be revenged of some injury;

3, when religion is upon a sudden found out, and as it were stumbled upon, without either ordinary study or ordinary time.

Quest. But if a man be born in time of true religion, what need then any more search?

Answ. I say, yet he must *probare*, 'try and examine' it, whether it be true or no, which is proportionable to the seeking of it.

We must seek it therefore, and that,

1, before all other things, Matt. vi. 33, "seek ye first the kingdom of God;" first of all, for it sanctifieth all other things; we must "seek the Lord while He is near," Isa. lv. 6, lest while we are seeking other things He be gone farther off;

2, with our whole heart, after a serious and earnest and hearty manner; Deut. iv. 29, "thou shalt find Him, if thou seek Him with all thy heart and with [illegible] soul;" Jer. xxix. 13, "ye shall seek Me, and find Me, when ye shall search for Me with all your heart."

Having sought religion, and found it, we must rest in it, "consenting to wholesome words," 1 Tim. vi. 3, and make it our girdle, Eph. vi. 14, our "loins girt about with truth."

Contrary to this resting in true religion, are

schism in things indifferent;
heresy in great matters;
apostasy, denying and falling from all.

Means to true religion.

α. Reading the scriptures; Acts viii. 28, the eunuch;
β. prayer, alms and fasting; Acts x. 10, Cornelius;
γ. to increase our small knowledge; Acts xviii. 24, Apollos.

Signs of true religion.

Augustine in his book *De civitate Dei*, mentioneth four;

the antiquity;
the purging of the soul;

PART III.

the small beginning;
the examples of virtue.

Thus much of religion.

§ 9. *Of sincerity.*

Sincerity is to have God alone for our God, commanded in those words, Matt. iv. 10, "with all thy heart, with all thy soul;" so expounding that word "only," Deut. vi. 13, for He will not give His glory to another.

Our worship of God must be sincere,

1, in respect of the matter, that it be not corrupt, not mingled with falsehood;

2, in respect of the quality or affection, that it be not,
- lukewarm, half hot, half cold, Rev. iii. 16;
- like to them, Isa. xxviii. 15, to whom all things are alike, "we have made a covenant with death, and with hell are we at agreement;"
- double hearted; James iv. 8, "purify your hearts, ye double minded."

Of integrity.

Now for integrity; "before Me."

This commandment is by this addition distinguished from the other three that follow; the other concerning God's outward worship, this His inward.

The Lord fashioned the eye, Ps. xciv. 9, yea He framed the spirit, Zach. xii. 1, and therefore seeth more than the eye or spirit, yea more in us than we do ourselves; and therefore, though *bonum coram homine sit bonum apparens*, 'what is good before man be an apparent good,' yet if it be *revera bonum*, 'good indeed,' it must needs be *bonum coram Deo*, 'good before God,' or, 'in His sight.'

God must have not only the outward but the inward man, the heart, "the inward parts," Ps. li. 6; and in this respect the kingdom of heaven is said to be within us, Luke xvii. 21. God requireth the heart, because from the heart cometh life and all the faculties of soul and body, and without it all the parts are dead.

Job i. 1, *integer et rectus*, 'straight and sound,' are joined together; so we must have these two properties, we must be *recti,* straight, not crooked, and *integri,* sound, not hollow; for so is a good work comely both within and without; Exod. xxv. 11, "thou shalt overlay it with pure gold, within and without thou shalt overlay it."

Means to integrity.

To set God before our eyes continually.

To think upon judgment, and our account.

To consider that eye-service is nothing pleasing to God, Eph. vi. 6.

To consider how Christ gave His heart-blood for us; therefore Bernard saith[f], *justè cor nostrum vendicat, qui suum pro nobis dedit,* 'He justly challengeth our heart, who gave His heart for us.'

Signs of integrity.

If we be not *conscii mali,* 'guilty of evil to ourselves,' and so fear not what men can do unto us, 1 Cor. iv. 3.

If we continue our strength and stedfast mind under the cross, as Ezekiah did, 2 Kings xx. 3, "I beseech Thee, O Lord, remember now how I have walked before Thee in truth and with a perfect heart, and have done that which is good in Thy sight."

If the hatred of sin begin in ourselves, Rom. vii. 24, "O wretched man that I am! who shall deliver me from this death?"

If we can truly say the two last verses of the 139th Psalm, "Try me, O God, and know my heart; prove me and know my thoughts, and consider if there be any way of wickedness in me;" or a milder trial, Ps. vii. 3, "If there be any wickedness in my hands;" or at least, Ps. iv. 4, let us examine our own hearts upon our beds, "Commune with your own heart upon your bed, and be still."

Of perseverance.

Now for perseverance. The answer to *non habebis,* 'thou shalt have no other gods,' is not *non habeo,* 'I have no other,' but *non habebo,* 'I will have no other.' These verbs

[f] [Ep. cxliii. p. 240 b.]

of time, *fui, sum, ero,* may all work in us a fear to see what we have been, what we are, and what we shall be, especially because we know not whether God will forsake us or not.

Perseverance is distinguished from patience, in that the object of patience is *tristitia crucis,* 'the sorrow of bearing the cross,' and the object of perseverance is *tædium diuturnitatis,* 'the tediousness of long delay.'

Here are condemned,

Those that persevere and continue in an evil thing,

"rise early that they may follow strong drink, that continue until night, till wine inflame them," Esay v. 11;

"they that tarry long at the wine," Prov. xxiii. 30;

Those that do at once fall quite away, or if not, yet are wavering and unstedfast, as Pharaoh was.

Means to perseverance.

As in patience, to prepare ourselves against our enemies, Josh. i.;

to set much by religion, for if we set little by it we shall not continue;

to desire not to run in vain;

to consider the continuance of the reward, which shall last for ever.

Signs of perseverance.

1. Not to look back but forward, *nunquam dicere, sufficit;* for *cum desinis esse melior, incipis esse deterior,* 'never to say, it is enough,' for 'when you cease to be better, you begin to be worse;' as they that row against the stream, if they hold still, are carried backward.

2. That which is, Rev. ii. 19, "I know thy works, and charity, and service, and faith, and thy patience, and thy works; and the last to be more than the first;" if our last fruit be more than our first; and if we "grow from strength to strength," Ps. lxxxiv. 7; if our "love may abound yet more and more in knowledge and in all judgment," Phil. i. 9.

Thus much of the first commandment.

THE SECOND COMMANDMENT.

It teacheth the manner of God's outward worship, and hath in it two things;

1, the precept itself, "thou shalt not make to thyself any graven image," &c.;

2, the reason of the precept, "for I am a jealous God, and visit the sins of the fathers," &c. So princes after that they have set down the things which they command in their laws and statutes, add presently, *qui secus faxit punietur*, 'he that transgresseth what here is commanded, shall undergo condign punishment,' and thereby declare how he shall be corrected by law, who would not be directed by the law.

§ 1. *Of the precept.*

The precept prescribeth two things;

1. That for His honour in outward worship, He will have *modum à se præscriptum*, 'the manner prescribed by God;'

2. He will have *reverentiam exhibitam*, 'reverence yielded to that manner.'

Of the general thing here forbidden.

The general thing here forbidden is the making of images. But a further thing is set down, Col. ii. 23, invented worship, for 'to make' in this place signifieth 'to invent.' By the fault here expressed and forbidden we must understand all sins of like nature; for so by a synecdoche in other commandments under one gross sin expressly forbidden, the rest of inferior or equal impiety are forbidden. So that ἐθελοθρησκεία, 'will-worship,' Col. ii. 23, is forbidden; man must not think himself so wise to devise a worship for God, nor must he be so humble as to bow down to any representation of God; this honour is only due to one Lord God.

Testimony of scripture hereupon.

Against the use of images, we have

1. God's express command, "thou shalt not make to thyself," &c.

PART III.

2. We have Moses' commentary on this commandment, Deut. iv. 13—15; in the mount no object was presented to their senses, but "only a voice was heard."

3. We have the interpretation of Christ;

a. God must be worshipped "in spirit;" He is a spirit, and cannot be expressed by an image;

β. God must be worshipped "in truth;" but an image is at the best a counterfeit representation of the truth, and not truth itself; hence it is that the truth is opposed to feigned worship, John iv. 23.

God saith, "thou shalt not make to thyself;" so then, though God the law-maker appointed the representation of cherubim, and of the brasen serpent, yet may not man presume to devise the like; he must take such resemblances as God Himself gave him, and not of his own invention propound any; except God have said to him as to Moses, these and these representations shalt thou make.

Of the general thing here commanded.

The general thing here commanded is, that we should worship God after the order that He hath prescribed; "see that thou make all things to the pattern," Heb. viii. 5, Exod. xxv. 40; for as Chrysostom[g] saith, *non est honor sed dedecus, si vel contra vel præter mandatum fiat,* 'it is not honour but dishonour, if it be done either against or besides God's command.'

This that is here commanded we express by

- "hearing of that one Prophet," namely Christ; Acts iii. 22, "Him shall ye hear;"
- not adding or detracting any thing, Deut. xii. 32, "what thing soever I command you, observe to do it: thou shalt not add thereto, nor diminish from it;"
- not altering any thing, Jer. ii. 11, "My people have changed their glory;"
- nor leaving any thing undone, Deut. v. 32, "ye shall observe to do therefore as the Lord your God hath commanded you: ye shall not turn aside to the right hand or to the left."

[g] [In Matth. Hom. l. § 3. vol. vii. p. 518.]

Herein we have to consider { the eternal substance, the ceremony.

Of the eternal substance.

The eternal substance standeth in four things;

1. Preaching the word, which we see hath been always used;

Before the flood, Noah; 1 Pet. iii. 19, "He went and preached unto the spirits in prison;"

In Moses' time, Deut. xxxiii. 10, "they shall teach Jacob Thy judgments, and Israel Thy law;"

In the prophets' time, Isa. lxi. 1, "the Lord hath anointed me to preach;"

In the time of the second temple, Neh. viii. 2—4, "and Ezra the priest brought the law . . and he read therein, . . and Ezra the scribe stood upon a pulpit of wood," &c.

In Christ's time, Luke iv. 16, "as His custom was, He went into the synagogue on the sabbath day, and stood up for to read;"

In the christian church, Mark xvi. 15, "He said, Go ye into all the world, and preach the gospel to every creature;" 1 Cor. i. 21, "it pleased God by the foolishness of preaching to save them that believe."

2. Invocation, called "the calves of our lips;" which is

a. Petition,

Gen. iv. 26, "then began men to call upon the name of the Lord;"

Gen. xx. 7, "he is a prophet, and he shall pray for thee, and thou shalt live;"

Exod. viii. 8, "intreat the LORD, that He may take away the frogs from me and from my people;"

Numb. x. 35, sq., this was at the beginning of battle, "rise up, O Lord;" and at the ceasing of the battle, "return, O Lord;"

1 Kings viii. 22, Solomon's prayer; and

Luke xi. 1—4, Christ's.

β. Thanksgiving,

commanded, Deut. xxxi. 19, "write ye this song for you, and teach it the children of Israel;"

practised, Gen. xxiv. 27, "blessed be the LORD God of my master Abraham, who hath not left destitute my master of His mercy and His truth;" so also,

Exod. xv. 1, "then sang Moses and the children of Israel this song unto the LORD;"

Ps. xcv. 2, "let us come before His presence with thanksgiving;"

2 Chron. vii. 6, "the priests waited on their offices; the levites also with instruments of music of the LORD, which David the king had made to praise the LORD, because His mercy endureth for ever;"

Ezra iii. 10, "when the builders laid the foundation of the temple of the LORD, they set the priests in their apparel with trumpets, and the levites the sons of Asaph with cymbals, to praise the LORD, after the ordinance of David king of Israel;"

Matt. xxvi. 30, "when they had sung an hymn, they went out into the mount of Olives;"

Eph. v. 19, sq. "speaking to yourselves in psalms and hymns and spiritual songs, singing and making melody in your heart to the Lord; giving thanks always for all things unto God and the Father in the name of our Lord Jesus Christ;"

Col. iii. 16, "let the word of Christ dwell in you richly in all wisdom; teaching and admonishing one another in psalms and hymns and spiritual songs, singing with grace in your hearts to the Lord."

3. Sacraments,

Gen. xvii. 10, circumcision; Matt. xxviii. 19, baptism;
Exod. xii., the passover; Matt. xxvi. 26, the supper.

4. Discipline,

a. commanded, Matt. xviii. 18, "whatsoever ye shall bind on earth shall be bound in heaven, and whatsoever ye shall loose on earth shall be loosed in heaven;" John xx. 23, "whose soever sins ye remit, they are remitted unto them, and whose soever sins ye retain, they are retained;"

β. executed, Acts v. 3—10, by Peter, on Ananias and Sapphira; 1 Cor. v. 3, by Paul, on the incestuous person; "I verily have judged already . . to deliver such an one unto Satan," &c.

Rules for it, 1 Tim. v.

Thus much of the eternal substance.

Of the ceremony.

For the ceremony, we have four things;

1, that the ceremonies be not many, and those necessary, Acts xv. 19, sq., "my sentence is, that we trouble not them which from among the gentiles are turned to God; but that we write unto them, that they abstain from pollutions of idols, and from fornication, and from things strangled, and from blood;"

2, that the ceremony be to edify, not to pull down that which the substance setteth up, 1 Cor. xiv. 26, "let all things be done unto edifying;" Gal. ii. 18, "if I build again the things which I destroyed, I make myself a transgressor;" and this is against prayer in an unknown tongue; 1 Cor. xiv. 4, "he that speaketh in an unknown tongue edifieth himself, but he that prophesieth edifieth the church;"

3, that it be for order, 1 Cor. xiv. 40, "let all things be done decently and in order;" and ver. 33, "for God is not the author of confusion, but of peace, as in all churches of the saints;"

4, that it be for decency; 1 Cor. xi. 13, "judge in yourselves, is it comely that a woman pray unto God uncovered?"

Means to perform this commandment.

1, To keep *volumen utriusque fœderis*, 'the volume of both covenants,' Josh. i. 8; *legendo*, 'by reading,' God's book, not the legend and scholastical fancies; but to keep the *depositum*, 'that which is entrusted to us,' 1 Tim. vi. 20, without adding or detracting;

2, that we keep it without spot, 2 Cor. ii. 17, "not as many, which corrupt the word of God; but as of sincerity, but as of God, in the sight of God speak we in Christ;" 1 Tim. vi. 14, "that thou keep this commandment without spot;" for one spot will mar all; 1 Cor. v. 6, "a little leaven leaveneth the whole lump;" we must take heed that Uriah's altar creep not near the Lord's altar, 2 Kings xvi. 14.

Signs hereof are, when we say or prove nothing in matter of religion but in this manner,

1, as the prophets did, *dictum Jehovæ*, 'the word of the LORD;'

2, as Christ, Matt. xxii. 32, by a syllogism, "the God of Abraham, and the God of Isaac, and the God of Jacob; God is not the God of the dead, but of the living;"

3, as the apostle, 1 Cor. xi. 23, that which we "have received from the Lord."

Now whereas to *non facies*, 'thou shalt not do it,' it might be said, *non facio, sed factum reperio*, 'I do it not, but I find it done;' it is therefore added, "thou shalt not bow down to them," by whomsoever they be made; "thou shalt not worship them."

Of the worship of images.

Whether God will be worshipped with images or no, all the stir between the papists and us, is about εἰκὼν and εἴδωλον· but the word in the original is more than both these, פסל, which cannot be well expressed either in greek or latin, and signifieth any kind of conception or imagination which may arise.

The kinds of images were usually these,

sculptile, 'a thing graven,'
fusile, 'a thing cast,'
ex utrisque conflatum, 'one made of both.'

To take away all images, God made sure work by forbidding all manner of likeness in heaven, earth, waters;

a. In heaven; then,
not of the Deity, Isa. xl. 18, "to whom then will ye liken God? or what likeness will ye compare unto Him?" in defence whereof the papists now are almost weary;
nor of angels; forbidden for special reason, because the philosophers worshipped their *Intelligentias*;
nor of men's souls;

nor of the sun, which they called the queen of heaven, because in hebrew it was in the feminine gender; Jer. xliv. 17, "to burn incense unto the queen of heaven;"

nor of the stars, as Moloch the star of Saturn was worshipped, Acts vii. 43.

β. In earth; the images of men, women, serpents, dragons, worms, plants, &c.

γ. In the water; the images of syrens, water snakes, fishes, &c.

And generally against all images;

1. The Israelites heard only a voice, Deut. iv. 12, "ye heard the voice of the words, but saw no similitude, only ye heard a voice;" but a voice cannot be painted;

2. The nature of faith is not to see what it believeth;

3. The true worship is spiritual; John iv. 24, "God is a Spirit, and they that worship Him must worship Him in spirit and in truth."

Quest. If all images were forbidden, why then were the cherubim?

Answ. They were set in the Holy of holies, where the people came not, and the priest but once a year.

History of image worship.

And to shew the beginning and going on of images;—

Irenæus[h], who lived two hundred years after Christ, and Epiphanius[i], make mention of certain heretics that had images of Christ and His apostles received from Pilate; also of the Cross, whereunto they attributed divers operations.

Also Epiphanius[k] sheweth that the Valentinians had images of the Virgin; and Augustine[l] sheweth that both they and the Manichees had images in policy, to please the gentiles.

Also divers for the love of their friends departed, set marks on their faces and in other places, to remember them; some had their images engraven in a ring, and from their rings they grew to their parlours, and so into their streets, then into the church-yards, and afterwards into churches.

h [Cont. Hær., lib. i. cap. 24. § 5. p. 102; cap. 25. § 6. p. 105.]

i [Hær. xxvii. § 6. vol. i. p. 208.]

k [Hær. lxxix. § 4. vol. i. p. 1061.]

l [Cont. Adim., cap. 13. vol. viii. col. 126.]

The papists' arguments, 1. *From fathers and councils.*

Object. The papists, out of Basil[m], allege that the same honour is due to the abstract which is due to the pattern.

Answ. But we answer, that Basil's meaning is to prove that Christ is equal with God; now if they can shew us any such image of God as Christ is, we will worship it.

Object. Also, say they, Eusebius[n] mentioned that the gentiles set up Christ's image for the miracles that He wrought on the woman of Syrophœnicia.

Answ. An absurd reason, the heathen did so, *ergo,* the christian ought to do so.

To allege counterfeit fathers, as Athanasius, Damasus, &c.; of them we will say no more, but, *noveris oderis,* 'if thou hast known them, hate them.'

Among the councils, they only allege the second council of Nice[o], at the which there were more unlearned and evil disposed men than ever at any. Constantia was their president, an heathen and unnatural woman, who plucked out her son's eye because he loved not images. This council is so absurd, that it hath more than the papists would have it, viz. *unam adorationem et unum honorem Dei et imaginis,* 'one adoration, and one honour of God and the image.'

Other councils directly are against images.

The fathers also against them, as Irenæus[p]; Clemens[q]; Tertullian[r]; Origen[s]; Arnobius[t], who calls them *fabrorum opus,* 'the work of smiths;' Lactantius[u]; Ambrose[x]; Hierome[y] upon Ezek. xvi. 17, *una est imago, Christus imago Dei,* 'there is but one image, Christ the image of God;' Epiphanius[z], who rent down the image of Christ as he spied it upon a wall. Yet after these fathers, about the year six hundred, images

[m] [De Spir. Sanct., c. xviii. vol. iii. p. 38. ἡ τῆς εἰκόνος τιμὴ ἐπὶ τὸ πρωτότυπον διαβαίνει.]

[n] [E. H., lib. vii. cap. 18. p. 343.]

[o] [vol. xii. col. 951 sqq.]

[p] [vid. p. præced.]

[q] [e. g. Strom., lib. v. cap. 5. p. 662; cap. 6. p. 667; lib. vii. cap. 5. p. 845; Cohort. ad Gent., p. 44.]

[r] [vid. Apol., capp. 13—16. pp. 13, sqq. cap. 41. p. 33 B; cap. 47. p. 40 A; De Idol., p. 85 sqq.]

[s] [Cont. Cels., lib. viii. cap. 17. vol. i. p. 754 B.]

[t] [Adv. Gent., lib. vi. cap. 9 sqq. p. 208.]

[u] [Div. Inst., lib. ii. cap. 2. vol. i. p. 116 sqq.]

[x] [De fug. sæc., cap. 5. vol. i. col. 429; Epist. xviii. § 8. vol. ii. col. 835.]

[y] [vol. iii. col. 794.]

[z] [Epist. ad Joan. Episc. Hierosol., vol. ii. p. 317.]

got some hold; about the year seven hundred, more; *anno* eight hundred, very much.

2. *From differences of words.*

The romanists leaving the original of the hebrew, betake themselves to the greek translation.

Object. They profess προσκυνεῖν, 'to fall down to,' but not λατρεύειν, 'to worship with *latria*,' because say they, Matt. iv. 10, μόνος, 'alone,' is not joined with προσκυνεῖν, but with λατρεύειν, so that we may προσκυνεῖν to saints.

Answ. But we say to this, that the devil required no more of our Saviour Christ but προσκυνεῖν, and therefore unless we make προσκυνεῖν proper to God, Christ's answer will not serve nor be sufficient.

As for their distinction of δουλεία, 'service,' and λατρεία, 'worship,' though it hath been long in the schools, yet in none of the fathers but Augustine, of whom, though he were a reverend man, we may say, as he saith of himself, he had no great knowledge in greek or hebrew.

But to distinguish them aright indeed, δοῦλος is a servant of our own, and λάτρις is a hired servant, (and so came *latro*, 'a hired soldier,' of λύτρον, *merces*, and by the abuse of their calling came to that odious name as it is now used;) and the Seventy interpreters used it here, because the Israelites should not be hired for money to dress and adorn the images of the heathen, as it was their use at that time.

3. *That they worship not the image itself.*

Object. But now the learneder sort seeing this distinction fail them, have found out another shift, *non colere et adorare imagines, sed Christum et sanctos per imagines,* 'not to worship and adore images, but Christ and the saints by the images.'

Answ. And this was the very allegation of the heathen, *non idola sed numen aliquod cui idolum ædificatur,* 'not the idol, but some deity to whom the idol was erected,' Lactantius[a] *De orig. error.*, cap. 2; *non simulachra sed Martem et Venerem per simulachra,* 'not the images, but Mars and

[a] [vol. i. p. 116, sqq.]

Venus by the images,' saith Chrysostom, Hom. xviii. in Epist. ad Eph.[b] And indeed it was plainly the error of the Israelites; they would not worship the calf, for they did not think it to be God, but by the calf they would worship God, the calf being used as a representation of God.

4. *That the ignorant need the help of an image.*

Object. And here the Romans fly to a third shift, which is, that the ignorant people must have something to help them to remember God.

Answ. But if the people must be put in mind, of what shall it be?

a. Not of the Deity, for they themselves are weary of that, and Hosius saith, *In Decalog.*, cap. 66, such images crept in, *dormientibus pastoribus*, 'while the pastors slept.'

β. Not of Christ as God, for His attributes are infinite; and that were but to divide Christ, seeing His deity cannot be painted, and so they fall[c] into that anathema, 1 Ephes. Concil.

γ. Not of Christ as man and now glorified, for as Eusebius saith to Constantia[d], His glory is now greater than it was upon the mount, when the disciples could not look upon Him.

δ. Nor as He was man in the flesh, for that were to teach lies, Abac. ii. 18; and it teacheth us to forget His passions, which cannot be painted.

And if they will remember saints by them, we see to them is denied *προσκυνεῖν*, Rev. xxii. 9, "see thou do it not, for I am thy fellow-servant;" and as Augustine[e] saith well, *si audirent angelos, discerent ab illis non adorare angelos*, 'if they would be ruled by the angels, they should learn of the angels not to worship angels;' and we see, Coloss. ii. 18, worshipping of angels condemned.

§ 2. *Of our behaviour in God's worship.*

Now let us see how we ought to behave ourselves in God's worship.

1. As this commandment is for God's outward worship, so if it be in our hearts we must bring it forth; *bono debe-*

[b] [§ 2. vol. xi. col. 129.]

[c] [viz. as dividing Christ, vol. iv.]

[d] [Boivin, in not. ad Niceph. Greg., p. 725.]

[e] [In Ps. xcvi. § 12. vol. iv. col. 1049.]

tur manifestatio, 'it is requisite that what is good should be outwardly manifested;' we must not put our candle under a bushel; *bonum lucis non est ponendum sub malo tenebrarum,* 'light which is good must not be put under the evil of darkness.'

2. *In copulativis utrumque faciendum,* 'in duties conjoined by a copulative both must be done;' and 1 Cor. vi. 20, 'body and spirit;' and the devil knowing that God will be glorified in both, requireth of our Saviour the one, namely, the bowing down of the body, Matt. iv. 9, because he knew if God had not both, he would have neither of both.

3. In the sanctuary, that is, in times and places of religious exercises, *observa utrumque pedem,* 'look to both feet;' have a care of thy lowest members, much more of our eyes, ears, and hearts.

Of the sign of worship.

This outward worship of God is in { *signo,* 'the sign of it,' / *facto,* 'the doing of it.' }

The signs of outward worship are two;

1. To empty ourselves, and *deponere magnificentiam;*

Job. xix. 9, to take our crowns, or our glory, the best things that we have, and to cast it at His feet; Rev. iv. 10, they "cast their crowns before the throne;"

2 Sam. vi. 22, "I will be more vile;"

1 Cor. xi. 4, *nudatio capitis,* 'uncovering the head;' for *pileo donari,* 'to have liberty to put on the hat,' was a sign of honour, and peculiar to freemen.

2. *Humiliari,* 'to make ourselves near the ground,' to bow down; that which the devil desired of Christ; and is a sign of God's worship, 1 Kings xix. 18, "I have left me seven thousand in Israel, all the knees which have not bowed unto Baal;" the contrary is plagued, Esay ii. 9, "the mean man boweth down, and the great man humbleth himself; therefore forgive them not."

Of the act of worship.

The fact itself of worshipping hath two things,

1. To be at command, Matt. viii. 9, "go, and he goeth; come, and he cometh." To come, and to come willingly;

for that *nescio vos*, 'I know you not,' which Christ shall pronounce in His judgment, is either to them which never come to His house, and so He knows them not; or they come of ill-will, and so hear of Him, but know Him not. We must come *maturè et quotidiè*, 'in due time, and daily,' Proverbs viii. 17, "those that seek Me early shall find Me;" wait at His door, verse 34, "blessed is the man that heareth Me, watching daily at My gates, waiting at the posts of My doors."

2. To do His will, "do this, and he doeth it," Matt. viii. 9, and to do it first of all, Luke xvii. 8, as Abraham's servant, Gen. xxiv. 33, would not eat till he had done his master's business.

Of behaviour in the four parts of worship.

To apply these things to the point of God's outward worship, Prayer, Preaching, Sacraments, and Discipline,

We must have the form of our behaviour in them from our fathers the faithful; Jam. v. 10, "take, my brethren, the prophets . . for an example;" 1 Pet. iii. 5, 6, "the holy women . . whose daughters ye are," &c.

First, in coming and going to them.

They never came together without bowing down, neither ever departed without external signs of reverence.

1. For their coming together, it was with coming, kneeling, worshipping, and falling down to the ground; 2 Chron. vi. 13, 14, "Solomon had made a brazen scaffold . . and upon it he stood, and kneeled down upon his knees before all the congregation of Israel, and spread forth his hands toward heaven, and said," &c.

2. For their departure, they bowed themselves and worshipped, 2 Chron. xxix. 29, "when they had made an end of offering, the king and all that were present within bowed themselves, and worshipped."

The first thing then in all these four parts of God's worship, Prayer, Preaching, Sacraments, and Discipline, is, that there be a reverend behaviour *in accessu et recessu*.

Secondly, in our presence at them.

The second thing is, for our presence at them.

Of behaviour in prayer.

I. In prayer; seeing it cometh of humility and hope, we must have outward signs like and answerable to these two.

1. For humility, there must be in our prayer *depositio magnificentiæ,* 'a laying aside of greatness and part;'

1 Cor. xi. 4, with uncovered heads;
Gen. xviii. 2, kneeling down, as Abram did; and
Gen. xxiv. 26, his servant;
Exod. xii. 27, the people;
1 Kings viii. 54, the prophets;
Luke xxii. 41, Christ;
Acts ix. 40, Peter;
Eph. iii. 14, Paul;
Acts xx. 36, the whole church;
Acts xxi. 5, the elders.

But the word in hebrew for kneeling signifieth service; and service may be also standing, as Gehazi stood before Elisha, and Samuel stood and ministered before the Lord. So,

Gen. xviii. 22; xix. 27, "Abraham got up early in the morning to the place where he stood before the Lord;"
Gen. xxiv. 12, 13, Abraham's servant prays standing;
Exod. xxxiii. 10, "all the people rose up and worshipped;"
Numb. xxiii. 18, "rise up, Balak, and hear;"
Ps. cxxxv. 2, "ye that stand in the house of the Lord;"
2 Chron. xxiii. 13, "the king stood at his pillar;"
These are for public prayers.

In private prayer a man may, if he be so affected, prostrate himself before the Lord, as did Moses and Aaron, Numb. xx. 6; Moses at the mount, Deut. ix. 18; Christ, Matt. xxvi. 39.

2. For hope, in our prayer the sign thereof is *oculus elevatus,* 'eyes lift up,' and hands stretched out.

Ps. cxxi. 1, "I will lift up mine eyes unto the hills from whence cometh my help;"
John xi. 41; xvii. 1, "Jesus lifted up His eyes, and said," &c.
Exod. xvii. 11, "when Moses held up his hand, . . Israel prevailed;"

Ps. lxxxviii. 9, "I have stretched out my hands unto Thee;"

1 Tim. ii. 8, "I will that men pray every where, lifting up holy hands."

Oculus elevatus expectat, manus extensa petit, 'the eye lift up expects, the hand stretched out craves.'

Sitting at prayer is not warranted; Balaam willed Balak to stand by his burnt offering, Numb. xxiii. 15, and being set he bid him rise, verse 18.

This is the behaviour that is to be used in petition; but in deprecation our eyes may be cast down, with the publican, Luke xviii. 13.

Of behaviour in preaching.

II. In Preaching, or hearing the word,

a. it is lawful to sit;

Ezek. xxxiii. 31, "they sit before thee as My people, and they hear thy words;"

Mark iii. 32, "the multitude sat about Him;"

Luke v. 17, "as He was teaching, there were pharisees and doctors of the law sitting by;"

Luke x. 39, Mary "sat at Jesus' feet, and heard His word;"

Acts xx. 9, Eutychus sat while Paul was preaching.

β. it is lawful also to stand; Neh. viii. 5, when Ezra opened the book, "all the people stood up."

Of behaviour in sacraments.

III. For the sacraments, the form of them sheweth what our behaviour ought to be in them.

Of behaviour in discipline.

IV. For discipline, it is plain; the judge sitteth, and the accused standeth before him.

Fitting carriage of the body why of use.

The decent and fitting carriage of the body is of use,

1, because we ought to glorify God with our bodies, 1 Cor. vi. 20;

2, that our hearts may learn their duties by the outward gesture of our bodies, and be alike affected, that thereby we may move others to worship God with us; 1 Cor. xiv. 25, "falling down on his face he will worship God, and report that God is in you of a truth."

Here are forbidden the contrary to the former; as to be proud, and not humble; slack, and not diligent in God's service, either in coming or obeying. Of such people Chrysostom speaketh, *ludus vocat, et venis; jubet, et facis: tuba Dei vocat, et non venis, jubet et non facis,* 'pastime calls, and thou goest to it; it commands, and thou obeyest; the trumpet of God calls, and thou goest not; it commands, and thou obeyest not.' Thou mayest judge by the centurion's servant whose servant thou art; even his that saith, Go, and thou goest, Matt. viii. 9.

Rules of behaviour in divine service.

But to come more especially to the point of God's liturgy or public service; we must observe therein these five points,

1. *to observe unity.*

1. Unity, as we may see by that,
 1 Cor. xi. 33, "tarry one for another;" and
 Matt. xxii. 12, he that was not uniform was punished;
 Ps. cxxii. 1, "I rejoiced when they said, We will go to the house of the Lord;"
 Acts ii. 1, they met with one accord;
 Acts iv. 24, with one accord they prayed;
 Acts viii. 6, so they heard; and
 Ps. xxxiv. 3, David exhorteth them to sing so.

The confusion of tongues was a great curse, and it was a blessing that all the earth was *unius labii,* 'of one kind of speech.' In the heavenly Jerusalem there shall be a sweet consent and harmony, as of harpers making pleasing melody, Rev. xiv. 2; and all sing one song, Rev. xv. 3.

2. *not to sleep therein.*

2. We must not slumber nor sleep at it.

For we must serve Him with fear, and sleep is without fear; Jacob fearing his brother Esau, slept not all night.

Of this we have an example, Acts xx. 7; Paul preached, and the people heard till midnight; of which Chrysostom saith, *mediâ nocte vigilabant, ut eos condemnent qui mediâ die dormiunt,* 'they watched at midnight, to condemn them who sleep at mid-day.'

And surely the actions of a natural man being eating, drinking, and sleeping, sleep is by the same reason condemned that the other two are, 1 Cor. xi. 22, namely, because we have houses to sleep in. So 1 Thess. v. 7, "watch, for they that sleep, sleep in the night;" but we may say, they that sleep, sleep in the day. And so where the place of sleeping should be our houses, and the time of sleeping should be the night; we in the day time sleep at church; and we know not whether God will in that sleep utterly forsake us; we see Matt. xxvi. 40, when our Saviour had commanded His disciples to watch and they slept, some of them afterward departed from Him, and some forsware Him.

The two disciples going to Emmaus, had *cor ardens,* 'their heart burning,' when Christ talked with them, Luke xxiv. 32; and that cannot be *sub oculo gravi.*

3. *to be present in heart.*

3. Our hearts must be present, or else our outward watching will not serve the turn;

If we have *cor fatui,* 'a fool's heart,' Eccles. vii. 4, it will be in the house of mirth where sport is;
but a wise heart will sėek for knowledge, Prov. xv. 14;

the fool's eye is in all quarters, wandering here and there, Prov. xvii. 24;
but the wise fasten their eyes, as they did, Luke iv. 20;

it is nothing to hear, unless we be attentive, Luke viii. 18;
as Lydia, Acts xvi. 14;
with a wise ear, Prov. xviii. 15.

4. *not to talk therein.*

4. We must not talk during the time of God's service; it is a sign of reverence to be silent; as if one should turn from us to speak with another while we tell him a message, we

would think he little regarded us; Zeph. i. 7, "be still at the presence of the Lord," who speaketh by His messenger.

And therefore in the primitive church, the first word was *σίγα λαὸς*, 'be still and silent, ye people;' and so Paul beckoned with his hand to this purpose, Acts xiii. 16.

5. *not to depart till it is ended.*

5. Depart not from it till it be ended;
   Exod. xxxiii. 11, Joshua "departed not out of the tabernacle;"
   Tit. ii. 10, "not purloining;"

For as we pray that God should hear us,
   Ps. xxx. 10, "hear, O Lord, and have mercy;"
   Ps. xxxviii. 21, "go not far from us;"

so we should take heed we go not from Him; for that dreadful sentence, "depart from Me," Matt. xxv. 41, shall be a punishment to those that go from Him here.

Preaching is a speaking of God to us, and prayer is our speaking to God; and the law is equal,—Ps. cvii. 11, 12, "because they rebelled," &c.—as we deal with God, so God should deal with us: and if we complain, Lord, why hast Thou forsaken us; the Lord may answer us again, *serve mi, quare dereliquisti me*, 'thou My servant, why hast thou left Me?'

In the primitive church it was excommunication to go out till the end; from the first word *σίγα λαὸς*, 'be still and silent, ye people,' till the last word *λαοῦ ἄφεσις*, 'the dismission of the people,' as appeareth in the fourth council of Carthage.

Quest. But may we not be absent for any cause?
Answ. Yes;

1. If we be sick, and so cannot come;
2. If we offer a sacrifice ourselves, we may be absent from another man's sacrifice; for it is best to be the principal agent in God's service;
3. The necessary visitation of the sick may stay us; for, Matt. ix. 13, "I will have mercy and not sacrifice."

Thus much for the precept.

§ 3. *Of the reason of the precept.*

Now the reason of the precept, which is *pœna et prœmium*, punishment to the offenders, and reward to them that keep the commandment.

First, of the punishment.

Quest. Why is this commandment the first with punishment, as the fifth the first with promise?

Answ. 1. Because the punishment must be proportionable to the fault, Deut. xxv. 2; and the sin against the first commandment is hidden, and therefore left to God; as the knowledge of it, so the punishment: but this is visible, and therefore this punishment is set down, "that others may fear," 1 Tim. v. 20.

2. Because men do commonly inflict punishment upon them that worship God; therefore God to meet with them, because fear of men's punishments should not keep us from worshipping of Him, threateneth a punishment if we worship Him not.

Quest. Where it is said here that God is a jealous God, hence ariseth this question, Whether there falleth the affection of a man into God or no, ἀνθρωποπάθεια?

Answ. We answer, No; but both here and where it is said, God repented Him, and such like, it is only meant that God will do as men do which have the like affections of jealousy and repentance, &c.

Before the punishment there is a censure of the sin, and it standeth in two things;

1. It is called iniquity or perverseness;
2. That those offend herein are said to hate God; for if the case stand betwixt ours and God's for His worship, if we prefer not Him and His will before our own, we hate the Lord.

The punishment itself is called a visitation, and the grievousness of it we measure,

1, by the greatness of it, being in our children, which are as ourselves, 2 Sam. xviii. 33; Luke viii. 41, 42; ix. 38, and a principal part of ourselves, even the seed, as though now there were nothing left in us but the chaff;

2, by the continuance of it, the whole memory of man, a generation; nay more, three or four generations.

Of sins visited on the children.

Quest. But if the punishment be upon our children, May one man be justly punished for another man's offence?

Answ. That which seemeth to stand against it is,

Deut. xxiv. 16, 'the fathers shall not be put to death for the children, nor the children for the fathers;'

Jer. xxxi. 29, 30, "in those days they shall say no more, The fathers have eaten a sour grape, and the children's teeth are set on edge: but every one shall die for his own iniquity; every man that eateth the sour grape, his teeth shall be set on edge;"

Ezek. xviii. 2, 20, "What mean ye, that ye use this proverb concerning the land of Israel, saying, The fathers have eaten sour grapes, and the children's teeth are set on edge?" "The soul that sinneth, it shall die; the son shall not bear the iniquity of the father, neither shall the father bear the iniquity of the son; the righteousness of the righteous shall be upon him, and the wickedness of the wicked shall be upon him;"

2 Cor. v. 10. "we must all appear before the judgment-seat of Christ, that every one may receive the things done in his body, according to that he hath done, whether it be good or bad;

Gal. vi. 5, "every man shall bear his own burden."

How explained by the schoolmen.

To these the schoolmen answer, as to that, Esay xxxviii. 1, 'thou shalt die and not live;' that is, say they, not meaning *quid futurum est, sed quid ex dispositione nostrâ futurum esset*, 'what is to come to pass, but what was to come to pass answerable to our condition and estate;' so here God speaketh not, say they, *quid faciet, sed quid ex dispositione meriti nostri faceret*, 'what He will do, but what should be done according to the condition of our desert.'

But this would breed a neglect of the commandment. More fully therefore to answer it:—

What the true account.

There are three kinds of punishment;

1. Satisfaction; and this must needs be just one for another, as Christ satisfied for us, and as in suretyship. Where one oweth a debt, and another taketh upon him to pay it, this satisfaction is just; for Christ in this manner satisfieth for us; our case was woeful if this satisfaction was unjust.

2. Medicine; and in this also it is just; the head being sick, the arm may be let blood; and for the preservation of a better member, we may put in jeopardy a worse. So to deliver the father from eternal punishment, the son may suffer temporal.

3. Correction; the covenant of blessing being made with us and our seed, if we break the covenant, our seed may also justly be punished; as we read Cant. ii. 15, the church findeth a nest of little foxes, which have not yet destroyed any vineyard, nor worried any lambs; yet "take us the little foxes," saith the church, for if they grow up they will do both; and so because there is a poisonous nature in the cockatrice' eggs, we may tread them under our feet.

The use hereof is double;

1, to breed mutual care in fathers and children, 2 Sam. xii. 15, 16, "the Lord struck the child that Uriah's wife bare unto David, and it was very sick; David therefore besought God for the child, and David fasted, and went in, and lay all night upon the earth;"

2, to acknowledge our corruption, Deut. xxvi. 5, "a Syrian ready to perish was my father;" and with David, Ps. cvi. 6, to confess, "we have sinned with our fathers."

Thus much of the punishment.

Secondly, of the reward.

The reward is mercy, and that to thousands, whereas the punishment was only to four generations; not that His mercy is greater than His justice, but that He is more delighted in the one than the other.

This mercy is to them that love Him; the trial of this love is the keeping of His commandments; and the keeping of this way, the way of God's commandments, is the keeping of our own souls.

And thus much of the second commandment.

THE THIRD COMMANDMENT.

Object and end of this commandment.

The object of this commandment is the Name of God. The thing commanded is praise, and this praise must be to His name; we must "publish the Name of the Lord, and give glory to God," Deut. xxxii. 3.

The end of this commandment is the praise of God. And as the former commandment spake of the external exhibited worship of God *in signis*, 'in the outward signs;' so this speaketh of the same *in verbis*, 'in our words.'

This great work can never be sufficiently done by us; for who can set forth all His praise and glory?

God made all things for His glory, Esay xliii. 7; now if we must be like our Creator, and if He created us for His glory, the glory of God must be

inwardly, the scope that we must aim at; and
outwardly, the matter of our speeches and actions.

Glory and praise

a. is given to God's person, and to His name; Ps. xxix. 2, "give unto the Lord the glory due unto His name;"

β. and is performed by our mouths and tongues; Ps. xxxiv. 1, "His praise shall continually be in my mouth;" the manner of it Moses sheweth, *enunciabo*, Deut. xxxii. 3, "I will publish the Name of the Lord;"

γ. David was not content to praise God, but sayeth, "make His praise glorious," and would have his mouth filled with God's praise, and other ears attend thereunto; Ps. lxvi. 16, "come and hear, all ye that fear God, and I will declare what He hath done for my soul;"

δ. and that continually, Ps. lxxi. 15, "my mouth shall shew forth Thy righteousness, and Thy salvation all the day;"

ϵ. and in the great congregation, Ps. cxl. 1, "His praise in the congregation of saints;" Ps. xl. 9, "I have preached righteousness in the great congregation;"

ζ. this praise David would have to continue as long as the sun endureth, and that all nations blessed in Him should call Him blessed;

Ps. xxii. 27, "all the ends of the world shall remember and turn unto the Lord, and all the kindreds of the nations shall worship before Thee;"

Ps. lxxii. 17, "His name shall endure for ever; His name shall be continued as long as the sun; and men shall be blessed in Him; all nations shall call Him blessed."

What is contained herein.

This commandment hath a Precept, and a Penalty.

First, of the precept.

The precept in these words, "Thou shalt not take the Name of the Lord thy God in vain."

The precept hath in it three things,

I. "The Name of God." The name is that whereby we know a man or a thing, and whereby we are known; and by the name we distinguish a thing from all other things; so whatsoever God is known by, is meant by His name in this place.

God proclaimed His name, Exod. xxxiv. 6, 7. His name there proclaimed is either,

a. pertaining to His essence, as Jehovah; or

β. expresseth His adjuncts, whereof

some are affirmative, as merciful, eternal, omnipotent;

others negative, as invisible, incorporeal, immutable; or,

γ. effects, as Creator, Redeemer, Sanctifier.

All these and the rest whatsoever are reverently to be used; the angel saith his name is fearful, Judg. xiii. 18; much more is God's, Deut. xxviii. 58, "this glorious and fearful Name, The Lord thy God."

II. "Take." The Hebrew word for this hath two uses,

1. *in gloriosis*, 'in things glorious,' to bear up, or lift up, as to lift up a standard, Exod. xvii. 15, as servants do their masters' badges on their shoulders; so they honour their masters.

We do contrary to this,

a. when we strive for our own praise, and think to get us a name: this is to play the giants, as they, Gen. xi. 4, "go to, let us build a city and a tower, whose top may reach unto heaven; and let us make a name, lest we be scattered abroad upon the face of the whole earth;" and

β. when the Name of God is abused to cloak sin; as when Jezebel feigned a religious proceeding in judgment, that she might unjustly destroy Naboth.

2. *in necessariis*, 'in things necessary,' to lift up a burden.

The first of these uses is for those that take God's name upon them, those that are called by His name, as we are called christians by Christ's name, Acts xi. 26.

The second use is for them that swear, for that is a burden and a heavy thing.

III. "In vain."—For the understanding whereof we must note in every action, the End, the Agent, and the Work.

1. For the end; we know that is in vain which hath no end; and therefore we must look *cui bono*, 'to what good end,' our words or actions may tend; and our ends must be,

a. God's glory, or else God will account of us as David did of Nabal, 1 Sam. xxv. 21, all is in vain He hath done for us, and all we do is in vain;

β. our own salvation;

γ. the edifying of our brethren.

2. For the agent; in him his heart must be considered, which is the principal agent; for if that be not stedfast, all is but chaff, fit to be blown about with every blast, and so light and vain, yea "vanity" itself, "tossed to and fro," Prov. xxi. 6; "like the chaff which the wind driveth away," Ps. i. 4.

3. For the work; that must needs be vain, when it is not to some good end and purpose.

When an oath is to be used.

Therefore, an oath is taken necessarily to end strife, which cannot be done before there be a stronger confirmation on the one side than the other; now

a. if this can be effected by reasons and proofs, they are to be used, as Gen. xxxviii. 25, "discern, I pray thee, whose are these, the signet, the bracelets, and staff;"

β. when arguments fail, the matter is to be confirmed by two or three witnesses, Deut. xix. 15, "at the mouth of two witnesses, or at the mouth of three witnesses, shall the matter be established;"

γ. if two witnesses fail, an oath is to be used, and here it is to good purpose and seasonable.

How to be used.

Now for the taking God's name in an oath;

an oath is { *jusjurandum assertorium de facto,* 'an oath affirming something to have been done;'
jusjurandum promissorium de futuro, 'an oath promising something afterward to be done.' }

And these must be,

a. sub Deo teste, 'taking God to witness;' which is called contestation, Judges viii. 19, "as the Lord liveth;" and

β. sub Deo vindice, 'before God the avenger of falsehood;' called execration; *sic faciat mihi Dominus,* 'so and so God do unto me.'

Now when a man hath thus sworn, it is in greek called ὅρκος, 'a hedge' that he hath set about himself, which he may not break through; because he is bound *persistere in dicto et præstare pollicita,* 'to stand to his word and do what he promised.'

And because that the hebrew word שבע, which signifieth 'to swear,' signifieth also 'to satisfy;' he to whom we do swear, must be therewithal contented; as *juro,* 'I swear,' is interpreted *pro jure habeo,* 'I account it law,' as sure as the *jus,* 'law itself,' and so the controversy ended.

How it maketh for God's glory.

Quest. But how maketh this oath for God's glory?

Answ. 1. *Quod confirmatur per certius confirmatur,* 'that which is confirmed must be confirmed by that which is more certain;' then this is God's glory, that His name should be accounted more certain than all things else whatsoever.

2. It sheweth a great faith in us;

a. in the contestation, we shew that we believe that God will bring every thing to light, 1 Cor. iv. 5, "the hidden things of darkness," and "the counsels of the hearts;"

β. in the execration, we shew that we believe the power of God to bring judgments upon us; Rom. xii. 19, "I will repay, saith the Lord."

Is allowed and commanded of God.

God commandeth to swear, Deut. vi. 13, "thou shalt fear the Lord thy God . . and shalt swear by His name;"

and alloweth of an oath rightly taken,

2 Chron. vi. 22, 23, "if a man sin against his neighbour, and an oath be laid upon him to make him swear, and the oath come before Thine altar in this house; then hear Thou from heaven," &c.

Ps. lxiii. 11, "every one that sweareth by Him shall glory."

And used by the saints.

And God's saints have sworn, either,

1, For the glory of God,

2 Chron. xv. 14, "they sware unto the Lord with a loud voice, and with shouting," &c.

Neh. x. 29, they "entered into a curse and into an oath, to walk in God's law;" or,

2, for the help of mankind, as in a league betwixt Abraham and Abimelech, Gen. xxi. 23, 24, "swear unto me here by God that thou wilt not deal falsely with me," &c.; "and Abraham said, I will swear;" or,

3, in mutual conspiring together, as Judges xxi. 1, "the men of Israel had sworn in Mizpeh, saying, There shall not any of us give his daughter unto Benjamin to wife;" or,

4, for union, as Josh. ix. 15, the princes of the congregation to the Gibeonites;

or between a king and his subjects; of a king to God, as 1 Kings i. 29, David concerning Solomon;

of subjects to their king, as 2 Sam. xxi. 17, "the men of David sware unto him, saying, Thou shalt go no more out with us to battle, that thou quench not the light of Israel;" or,

5, for the safeguard of one's life, as Josh. ii. 12, the spies to Rahab; or,

6, for a serious matter, as trust in marriage, Gen. xxiv. 3, Abraham and his servant; or,

7, to decide a matter in doubt where no other means help, as Exod. xxii. 8, 11, he "shall be brought unto the judges, to see whether he hath put his hand unto his neighbour's goods;" "then shall an oath of the Lord be between them both," &c. or

8, in some case of a private man, as

Rom. i. 9, "God is my witness, whom I serve with my spirit in the gospel of His Son, that without ceasing I make mention of you in my prayers;"

2 Cor. i. 23, "I call God for a record upon my soul, that to spare you I came not as yet unto Corinth."

Objection of the anabaptists answered.

Object. The anabaptists object, that we must not swear at all; grounding upon that speech of our Saviour Christ, Matt. v. 34, "swear not at all."

Answ. But we must interpret this speech after the scope of the place, which was to confute the doctrine of the pharisees, who taught that a man might swear and forswear, so he took not in his mouth God's name; and our Saviour

1, forbiddeth them so to swear at all; and

2, teacheth us, when we do swear, that we must swear only by His name;

a. we must not leave out His name, and swear by other things, Amos viii. 14, "by the sin of Samaria, and say, Thy god, O Dan, liveth; and, The manner of Beer-sheba liveth;" for it is called, An oath of Jehovah;

β. we must not add any thing to it; as *vivit Dominus et Moloch*, 'the Lord and Moloch live.'

It appeareth then, that we may swear; and that in swearing we must take the Name of God.

We must not take God's name in vain.

Now that we may not take His name in vain, we must swear, Jer. iv. 2, in truth, in justice, and in judgment.

1. "Truth;" commanded Lev. xix. 12, we must not swear falsely to perjure ourselves,

in assertion, either { *in cognito*, 'when we know;' / *in dubio*, 'when we know not.' }

in promission, when { *aut non statuimus præstare*, 'either we resolve not to perform;' / *aut non præstamus*, 'or do not perform.' }

2. "Justice;" and that requireth that we should swear only *in honestis et possibilibus*, 'in things honest and possible;' for that which is *inhonestum, non est jus*, 'dishonest, is not just;' and *impossibile non est omnino jurandum*, 'an impossible matter is not at all to be sworn unto.'

A thing impossible or dishonest is so, either from the very beginning, or cometh so to be afterwards. Herod's oath was not simply unlawful at the making, but when the damsel asked St. John baptist's head, it was unlawful, and might and ought to have been broken, because by keeping it he added two other sins to the first of rash swearing; those were, unlawful manslaughter; and foolish superstition in performing his oath. So then if we have sworn unjustly, we must take heed that we sin not in performing, as we have done in promising; but *in malis promissis conscinde filum*, 'when any evil thing is promised, cut the thread.' Hence it was that David, having rashly sworn to be revenged on Nabal for his churlish answer, afterward blessed God that he performed not what he had sworn, 1 Sam. xxv. 22, and 32.

3. "Judgment;" and that requireth three things at our hands;

a. that we take an oath reverently, not rashly, Eccles. v. 2, "be not rash with thy mouth, and let not thine heart be hasty to utter any thing before God;"

β. to take it as a holy thing, and therefore not to make it common;

γ. we must account it a matter spiritual; and not to say, *juravi linguâ, mentem injuratam gero,* 'I sware with my tongue, my mind and intention was not sworn;' for God will take that sense that the words carry; *Deus sic accipit ut ille qui dat,* 'God so understands an oath, as he who propounds it.'

Means to keep ourselves from rash swearing.

The means to keep ourselves from rash swearing, are these four;

1. As Augustine[f] saith, *cave facilitatem, nam facilitas affert consuetudinem, et consuetudo blasphemiam,* 'take heed of proneness to swear, for easiness to swear brings on a custom of swearing, and custom leads to blasphemy.' This blasphemy is that horrible sin which in scripture wants a name, and cometh under the name of *berek,* which is 'blessing;' as in Job ii. 9, "bless God and die," meaning thereby blaspheming Him;

2. Leave those imperfect oaths, *per fidem,* 'by my faith,' or 'in good faith,' &c.; which is as much to say, as *obligo fidem meam Deo,* 'I swear by my faith to God,' or 'oblige my faith in God' for the truth of what I speak; which being God's gift may be taken from us;

3. By ridding ourselves of impatiency and vain glory; for in an angry man's mouth nothing is so ready as an oath, and in a vain glory we think it a bravery and a magnificent thing to swear; *ideo leviter existimamus jurare, quia leve existimamus juramentum; et ideo leve existimamus, quia leves sumus æstimatores,* 'we therefore lightly esteem swearing, because we think an oath a slight matter; and therefore we account it slight, because we are slight and unskilful judges of an oath;'

[f] [De mend., cap. xv. § 28. vol. vi. col. 436.]

4. Consider that no precept hath been more visibly punished.

Of vows.

Besides oaths we must also take heed how we take the Name of God in vows.

A vow differeth from an oath thus; an oath is necessary between man and man; a vow is voluntary between God and man: and this vow is, when by the particular consideration of God's graces in us we bind ourselves, either secretly in heart, or openly in word before others, to yield unto Him any duty which of necessity we are not bound unto.

To vow were an easy matter, if that were all: but we must *reddere*, 'pay our vows,' as well as *vovere*, 'vow;' for *non reddere est devovere*, 'not to pay is to devote' and give up ourselves to misery, and to forswear, yea to bring a curse upon ourselves; so that we must have a full purpose to perform.

But with our purpose in all our vows we must have these conditions;

that he that promiseth be *sui juris*, 'at his own government,' and free; neither *servus nec puer*, 'servant, nor a child under age;'

that the thing vowed be in his power;

that it be lawful to be performed;

that it be no frivolous matter, but worthy to be vowed unto the Lord.

Thus much of the precept.

Secondly, of the penalty.

The penalty followeth, "The Lord will not hold him guiltless that taketh His name in vain."

The reason of this penalty is;

1. Because many men, to spare themselves or to save their credit, will take God's name in vain, the Lord telleth them that which they thought to be safe for them shall turn to their destruction; it shall draw down God's curse upon them.

2. The laws of the land punish the abusing of men's names, but we have none that take order for the Name of God that that be not taken in vain; and therefore God himself will look unto it and take order for it.

For the punishment of the breach of this commandment, look

α. Zach. v. 4, the curse of God upon the false swearer and upon his house;

β. Lev. xxiv. 14, the blasphemer shall be stoned; and,

γ. for execration, Numb. v. 27, according to the wish, so shall it come to pass, if the party be guilty; and,

1 Sam. ii. 30, God will honour them that honour Him, but they that despise Him shall be despised.

Thus much of the third commandment.

THE FOURTH COMMANDMENT.

How punctually expressed.

Because *publicorum cura est minor*, 'the care of public matters is less,' therefore God hath set down this commandment in very particular manner.

We see that in the duties of the second table; for four of the commandments are ended in a word, because common honesty, philosophers, politic and civil laws took order for them, and they were usually censured by all tribunals; concerning the fifth commandment, because God saw an humour in men unwilling to be brought under subjection, he thought it necessary to fence it with a reason; in the which commandment, God speaketh fully and particularly, because men are prone to think thought to be free.

But in the first table each commandment hath its reason; and above all, this fourth commandment is most punctually expressed;

1, both negatively and affirmatively;

2, it lays a charge on ourselves, our sons, daughters, servants, strangers, cattle;

3, it cometh in with a *memento*, lest worldliness should make us forget it;

4, here is a pattern set before us; we are to do only what God hath done before us;

5, here are many several reasons given to bind us to our duty, and not one single reason, as in the other three commandments of this table.

Chief parts of the commandment.

The principal parts of this commandment are two,
1, a precept, "remember that thou keep holy," &c.;
2, a reason of the precept, "for in six days," &c.

Of the precept.

'Sabbath;' this word betokeneth a day of rest, signifying a work to go before.

'Sanctify,' or keep holy; this word is twice in this commandment; first, attributed to man; secondly, to God, in the end of the commandment.

Now for such words as are attributed both to God and man, we have this rule; that they are attributed to God, *sub modo destinandi,* 'in respect of God's so appointing them to be,' and to man, *sub modo applicandi,* 'in the way of man's applying them to use.' So Christ took water, bread, and wine; and He took them to destinate them to a holy use: and we take water, bread, and wine, to apply them to that use whereunto they were destinated; the water in baptism, and the bread and wine in the supper of the Lord.

Days, and so likewise bread and wine, are not more holy of themselves, one than another, but because they be separated and set apart for holy uses; so Lev. xx. 26, "and ye shall be holy unto me; for I the Lord am holy, and have severed you from other people that ye should be Mine."

In sanctifying any thing,
1, there is a separation of it to a holy use, as of water for baptism, of bread and wine for the Lord's supper;
2, the blessing thereof, this is God's ordinance and proceeds from Him;

Now because God is pure, all things are pure to Him; and therefore He needs not to sanctify a day to Himself, wherefore He sanctifieth it for us.

God sanctified the sabbath by resting from His works He had made, and destinating it to be kept holy by us;

We must sanctify it by our rest, and keeping it holy; by our obedience,

1, in our judgment, by a reverend esteeming of it, not as a day appointed by man;

2, in our use; set down, Esay lviii. 13; not following our own will, nor doing our own works.

The sabbath not a ceremony.

Quest. But is not the sabbath a ceremony, and so abrogated by Christ?

Answ. Do as Christ did in the cause of divorce, look whether it were so from the beginning; now the beginning of the sabbath was in paradise, before there was any sin, and so before there needed any Saviour, and so before there was any ceremony or figure of a Saviour.

Object. And if they say it prefigured the rest that we shall have from our sins in Christ;

Answ. We grant it, and therefore the day is changed, but yet no 'ceremony' proved.

1. From the Law.

a. By the distinction between the law and a ceremony, Deut. iv. 13, 14; the law came immediately from God, the ceremonies were instituted by Moses.

β. It were not wise to set a ceremony in the midst of moral precepts; there be many amongst the prophets that cannot distinguish.

γ. This is a principle, that the decalogue is the law of nature revived, and the law of nature is the image of God; now in God there can be no ceremony, but all must be eternal; and so in this image, which is the law of nature; and so in the decalogue; whereas a ceremony is, *ἀπὸ τῆς εἰς καιρὸν μόνον*, 'a matter only to endure for a time.'

2. From the gospel, Eph. ii. 14, "hath made both one, and hath broken down the middle wall of partition;" all ceremonies were ended in Christ; but so was not the sabbath, for, Matt. xxiv. 20, Christ biddeth them pray that their visitation

be not on the sabbath day, so that there must needs be a sabbath after Christ's death.

3. Those which were ceremonies were abrogated, and not changed; but those which were not ceremonies were changed; as the ministry, from the levites, to be chosen throughout the world; the seats changed; so here, the day changed from the day of the Jews to the Lord's day, Rev. i. 10.

The commandment taketh order, 1. *for the work.*

There is in this commandment a taking order { for the Work, and
for the Persons.

First, for the work, there is,

1. a double permission,
   - *a.* six days thou shalt labour,
   - *β.* in them do all thy work;
2. a double opposition,
   - *a.* the sabbath is the Lord's,
   - *β.* in it do no work.

Out of these two permissions and oppositions we have two under-reasons of this commandment;

1. Because we ourselves by the right of creation are the Lord's, we could not have been angry if He had given us but one day or no day for ourselves; but seeing He hath given us six days, He is as liberal to us as He was to Adam; giving him all the trees in the garden but one, so to us all days in the week but one. And as the devil there said, May ye not eat of every tree? so he saith to us, May ye not work upon every day? But by this great liberality of God we learn to make the devil a better answer than was there given him, and to say with Joseph, Gen. xxxix. 9, How should we deceive Him in this one, seeing all the rest are ours by His goodness?

2. "But the seventh day is the sabbath of the Lord;" this is the second under-reason. If God had permitted us this day, we might also have wrought in it; but seeing He hath not allowed it us, we cannot without stealth break into it.

Rest, and sanctifying the day, are both commanded, but not equally.

a. Sanctifying is the end, and is chiefly aimed at.

β. Rest is a subordinate end, and conduceth to our sanctifying the Lord's day aright: for a thing is best done when it is alone attended; by doing divers things, men's minds are distracted; Adam could not both dress the garden and observe the sabbath in one day, because of distraction; we have much more need of rest for a remedy.

Thus much of the work.

2. *For the persons.*

Now secondly for the persons. The master of the family, it is thy honour to be first in God's service; of thee more is required, because to thee more is given. Thou must with Joshua say, "I and my house," Josh. xxiv. 15. And by Christ, *exemplum dedi vobis,* 'I have given you example; go you and do likewise.' If thou obeyest not, how shall they of thy household observe this law? "Thou, thy children, thy servants, thy cattle, the stranger that is within thy gates;" i. e. within thy jurisdiction or protection.

Of the reason of the precept.

The main reason of the commandment is, "for in six days the Lord made heaven and earth, and rested the seventh day." It is a rule, that *ratio immutabilis facit præceptum immutabile,* 'a reason which is immutable maketh the precept immutable;' and this reason of the commandment can never be taken away, and therefore the commandment itself must still continue; the day may give place, but sanctification never.

The reason is *ab exemplo;* a fit reason to move all, John xiii. 15, "I have given you an example;" and 1 Cor. xi. 1, "follow me as I follow Christ." God should be obeyed for the keeping the sabbath, even because He gave men His own practice for example, and because they need rest to free them from distraction, and to gain strength to their weary bodies; but much more seeing it would become far more profitable to them for their souls, because God had sanctified and blessed it by His ordinance to that end; we must not resist His ordinance, Rom. xiii. 2.

Augustine findeth no reason why God should be six days

in making the world, seeing He could have made it with a word, but that we should be in a muse when we think of it, and should think on His works in that order that He made them, as David did, Ps. civ.

Of the holy rest of the sabbath.

The sabbath is *sanctum otium,* 'a holy rest,' a returning rest from the works of the week-day; but yet with this canon, *ab eo quod nec antea fieri poterat nec postea poterit, non ita est avertendum,* 'from that which could not be done before nor afterward, we are not to refrain.'

We must so give rest both to our bodies and souls upon this day, that nothing trouble us; remembering that which is Ps. xlvi. 10, *vacate et videte,* 'put off employments, and behold;' of which all that ever wrote, say as the philosopher said, *postulandum secessum ut melius intendamus,* 'we must crave freedom from work, that we be more intentive to the present duty.' And therefore not only worldly cares, but even the works of our calling are forbidden at this day, that so our whole body may be at commandment to serve God; not that the works of our calling are evil, but because they will not suffer us wholly to be occupied in God's service, and *toto hoc die vacandum Domino,* 'the whole day must be employed in God's work.'

Many precepts in scripture concerning it.

Such is the perverseness of our nature, when God saith labour, we rest; when He saith rest, we labour; yea, we will make it a policy to find labour upon that day which He hath denied us to labour in.

And therefore for this rest we have six commandments;—

1. Exod. xvi. 6, "cease from gathering manna for this day;" it is *mercatura animæ,* 'the market day for the soul,' wherein are better things than manna to be gathered, John vi. 58, the "bread which came down from heaven; he that eateth of this bread shall live for ever;" 1 Pet. ii. 2, 3, "desire the sincere milk of the word, that ye may grow thereby; if so be ye have tasted that the Lord is gracious."

2. Neh. xiii. 15, if it be brought us we must not buy it; here fairs and markets are forbidden on this day;

3. Jer. xvii. 22, no burdens or carriage on this day, except we will have God to give us such a burden as the Jews had, of the captivity;

4. no, not in harvest time, when it is most likely to be tolerable, Exod. xxiv. 21, "six days thou shalt work, but on the seventh day thou shalt rest; in earing time and in harvest thou shalt rest;"

5. no journeying on this day; a daily abuse amongst us; Exod. xvi. 29, "tarry every man in his place;"

6. Exod. xxxi. 15, not so much as to build God's house, though there were great use, yea, and great haste of it that it should be builded.

Whether we must observe it as the Jews did.

And here arise certain questions;

Quest. 1. Whether we must observe the sabbath as the Jews did, not to kindle any fire nor to dress any meat on that day?

Answ. We say, no; for this was but ceremonial and belonged only to them. For it is a rule, that every moral duty may be performed of all men; but they under the north pole cannot be without fire one day, and they under the equinoctial cannot keep their meat for heat; and therefore this cannot take place amongst them, and so not general to all, nor perpetual to be observed for ever.

Whether we are absolutely bound to rest.

Quest. 2. Whether all those rests are absolutely to be holden or not?

Answ. We answer, no; for,

1, our rest must be a sanctification; and,

2, that rest may be without sanctification, is amongst us most manifest; and

3, that there is sanctification without rest, we prove thus;—

Sanctification is in the Means, or Practice; and where Rest is not joined with these two, we must leave it. For seeing rest is destinate to sanctification, it is a rule in logic, that *tantum destinati sumendum est quantum ad finem prodest*, 'we must take so much of that which serves for an end as is behoveful to attain that end;' as in medicine; and therefore, where rest leaveth these two, we must leave rest;

a. For the means, that they may be without rest, our Saviour sheweth, Matt. xii. 12, against the Jews, which always urged the outward rest only, and teacheth them, that we must not so rest but that we may do well upon the sabbath day; and the minister's greatest day of labour is the sabbath day, *quando est in opere cultûs Dei,* 'when he is employed in the work of God's worship;' so we read of a sabbath day's journey, Acts i. 12; so that for the means to sanctification we may leave rest upon the sabbath day.

β. For the practice, much more; for the means are less acceptable to God than the practice; Matt. xii. 7, the work of mercy is preferred before sacrifice, which is but the means of sanctifying the sabbath; and so the means must give place to sanctification. As if there should be a fire in the time of sermon, or such like, it is a deed of mercy to leave the means and help to quench the fire. For God will be glorified in the preservation of His creatures; yea, the very least things may not be lost, John vi. 12, "gather up the fragments that remain, that nothing be lost;" much less the life of any thing; as we see Matt. xii. 13, for man's life; Luke xiii. 15, for beasts'; and Matt. xii. 11, for other peril.

But this necessity must be present, not imminent; for *in præsenti necessitate quisque magistratus est, et quisque personam Dei habet, ut potius occidat quam occidatur,* 'in urgent and present necessity every one is a magistrate, and every one representeth the person of God, that he may kill rather than be killed;' but if the danger be not present but imminent; as if one should tell him there is wait laid for him, he must then go to the magistrate.

We must also mark here and take heed, because God seeth the heart, that we be sure that we could not do it before, nor can do it after; for we must not draw necessity upon ourselves.

An idle rest not enough.

Quest. 3. But if we rest, is that enough, *bene vestiri, et nil agere,* 'that we put on our best apparel and do nothing'?

Answ. Surely no; for as bodily labour profiteth little, so bodily rest profiteth as little; and to keep the sabbath on that idle manner, is but *sabbatum boûm et asinorum*, 'the sabbath of oxen and asses.'

The sabbath not for revel or riot.

Besides these idle sabbath keepers, there are two other sorts which are neither idle nor well occupied on the sabbath.

1. Those that Augustine speaketh of, *jucundi, qui vacant nugis, spectaculis, theatris, choreis,* 'merry company, who spend their time in pastimes, shows, stage-plays, dancing;' and Hom. xxv., *venatores,* 'hunters;' and Leo, Serm. iii. *De quadrages.* addeth, *vacantes chartis, rationibus et comessationibus,* 'such as play at cards, look to their reckonings, or revel like good fellows;' this Augustine calleth *sabbatum aurei vituli,* 'the sabbath of the golden calf.'

2. That are drunken and surfeit on the sabbath day; for seeing the works of our calling are not lawful on that day, much less these or any the like sinful actions; for this were a double offence, both against other commandments and this, and therefore may well be called *sabbatum Satanæ,* 'Satan's sabbath.'

What the right sabbath.

The right sabbath is, Esay lviii, 3, *deliciæ Jehovæ,* 'the delight of the Lord,' to leave our own wills, and to follow His; and that both publicly and privately;—

a. publicly, for the whole city; that God may be praised in the great congregation; and that in the assembly all men might be known by one band of obedience, Joel ii. 15; and that the commonwealths might have ὁμοψυχίαν, 'concurrence and accord of hearts and souls,' as the heathen had ὁμοσιτίαν, 'a concurrence and meeting together to eat and drink;'

β. privately, for every particular man; that it may be *mercatura animæ,* 'the merchandise of the soul to him,' to lighten his understanding, and to reform his will.

The sabbath how sanctified.

But how is the sabbath sanctified?

1. God sanctified it, Gen. ii. 3, that is, He separated it from others to be kept holy, Zach. vii. 3, making that applicate unto us, which in God is destinate.

2. We are sanctified by the Holy Ghost, Rom. xv. 16; this was prefigured by the holy oil, Lev. viii., shewing to us the spiritual unction, 1 John ii. 27. The Holy Ghost was resembled by fire; we must prepare matter fit for it, that we quench not this fire; this is done by our being employed in the works of the Lord's day;—

3. Our sanctification of the sabbath standeth in {prayer, the use of the word, thanksgiving.

1. *By prayer.*

Prayer is to be used,

1. Before the sanctification of the sabbath; either
   privately, Ps. cxi. 1. "secretly among the faithful;" Mark vi. 46, "He departed into a mountain to pray;"
   publicly, Acts xvi. 13, "by a river side, where prayer was wont to be made;" 1 Cor. xiv. 16, saying Amen, &c.

2. After the sanctification of the sabbath, Numb. vi. 24, "the Lord bless thee," &c.; for unless He continue His spirit which He hath given us, the enemy will prevail against us; Luke viii. 12, "then cometh the devil, and taketh the word out of their heart, lest they should believe and be saved."

2. *By the use of the word.*

The use of the word, Deut. iv. 10, which is,

1. To read it or hear it read privately, before we come to the public assembly, that so we may the better apprehend it, and gather more fruit by it, when we are publicly taught; as the Jews had their παρασκευὴν, their 'day of preparation.'

2. To hear it publicly;
   a. both the law,
      Acts vii. Stephen's discourse;
         xiii. 15, "after the reading of the law and the prophets," &c.

M

PART III.

27, "the prophets which are read every sabbath day," &c.

xv. 21, "Moses of old time hath in every city them that preach him, being read in the synagogues every sabbath day;"

β. and the gospel,

1 Thess. v. 27, "I charge you by the Lord that this epistle be read unto all the holy brethren."

3. After we have heard it, to search the scriptures, and to examine that which hath been delivered.

4. To ponder in our hearts that we have heard spoken;

Luke ii. 19, "Mary kept all these things, and pondered them in her heart;"

Ps. cxix. 97, "it is my meditation all the day."

5. To confer of it between ourselves and with others also.

And this conference may be,

1. Between the teacher and the hearer; so was the use of the Jews, that the eighth day, which was the last of the sabbath, the doctors sat, and all the people came and were resolved of their doubts;

and thereupon it was that Christ did oppose them, not as a teacher (as some think) but as a learner; Luke ii. 46, "they found Him in the temple, sitting in the midst of the doctors, both hearing them, and asking them questions;"

Luke iii. 10, the people to John the baptist, "what shall we do then?"

Acts ii. 37, they "said unto Peter and to the rest of the apostles, Men and brethren, what shall we do?"

2. Between hearers; and that,

a. either between equals,

Gal. ii. 2, Paul at Jerusalem;

2 Kings ii. 11, Elijah and Elisha;

Luke xxiv. 17, the two disciples going to Emmaus;

Mal. iii. 16, "they that feared the Lord spake often one to another," &c.;

teaching one another, because that doth some much good, which doth nothing move other some;

β. or else between superiors and inferiors, as the master and the servant.

3. *By thanksgiving.*

The giving of thanks is also a duty of the sabbath.

Ps. viii. 1, 2, there is a general use of them; and there is also a particular use, Ps. ix. 11.

Ps. xcii. is a psalm for the sabbath; in this, the works of God's hands are meditated upon, ver. 4; His judgments on the wicked, ver. 7; His mercies, ver. 10, &c.; all these David mentions in his song to the instrument of ten strings, the viol and the harp, and hereby both stirreth up himself to his duty, as also setteth forth the praise of his God.

The want of plentiful thanksgiving is a greater blemish in our church than many of those which are urged. Praise is due to God, because He heareth our prayers, Ps. lxv. 1, 2, "praise waiteth for Thee, O God, in Sion; and unto Thee shall the vow be performed; O Thou that hearest prayer, unto Thee shall all flesh come."

also by sacraments and discipline.

Also besides these three, the sacraments and discipline are for the sabbath day, but not for every sabbath.

and by works of mercy.

And though rest be commanded on the sabbath, and working forbidden; yet, as before we shewed, those good works which tend to the practice of holiness are to be done on the sabbath day, and are also a part of our sanctification of the sabbath; namely, works of mercy, outward and inward.

Of outward mercy.

I. Outward, or in bodily things, Matt. xxv. 35; to feed the hungry, refresh the thirsty, receive strangers, clothe the naked, visit the sick and those that are in prison; as lastly, to bury the dead, as Augustine[g] saith; *ne pateat miseria,* 'to cover our misery, and take it out of our sight.'

[g] [vid. lib. De cur. pro mort., vol. vi. col. 515 sqq.]

Object. To them that say, they know not who needeth,

Answ. We answer, *occurrere est succurrere,* 'to visit them and know their wants is the way to relieve them aright;' and it is necessary they should give, for as Augustine saith, *petit suum pauculum temporarium, da, et recipies magnum æternum,* 'the poor man begs a small temporary kindness, give it him, and thou shalt receive a large eternal benefit.'

Object. To them that say they have little,

Answ. We answer, God doth not *respicere quantum,* 'respect how much,' but *ex quanto,* 'out of how much.' But in our giving we must take heed that we do not take away on other days to give on this day, for that were to give *majorem partem diabolo,* 'the greater part to the devil.'

Of inward mercy.

II. Inward, or in spiritual things; of which Augustine saith, *principalior est interna caritas, quia parti principaliori medetur,* 'inward charity is of greater esteem than outward, because it cureth the more principal part of man.'

And this inward mercy is of seven sorts;—

1. to teach the ignorant, Ps. li. 13, "then will I teach transgressors Thy ways;" Dan. xii. 3, to "turn many to righteousness;"

2. to advertise the doubtful, Prov. xxvii. 9, "by hearty counsel;"

3. to exhort the slack, 2 Cor. xiii. 11, to "be perfect, be of good comfort;"

4. to forgive, Matt. vi. 14, "if you forgive men their trespasses, your heavenly Father will also forgive you;" *qui dat non recipit nisi remittit, qui remittit, recipit, etiamsi non dat,* 'he that giveth receives not a reward unless he forgive; he that forgiveth shall receive, though he gave not.'

5. to forbear, 1 Thes. v. 14, "be patient toward all men;" Gal. vi. 2, "bear ye one another's burdens, and so fulfil the law of Christ;"

6. to pray one for another, James v. 16, "pray one for another;" Luke xxiii. 34, "Father, forgive them, for they know not what they do;"

7. to reconcile others, Matt. v. 9, "blessed are the peacemakers."

Of the sabbath of fast.

Now besides this sabbath, there is also included by the rule of *homogenea*, 'things of like nature' to be alike, another sabbath, Lev. xvi. 31, the day of fast. For as Augustine saith, before the fall there needed but one glorifying of God, namely, by giving of thanks; but since the fall, by reason of our great backsliding, God must also be glorified *sacrificio tribulati spiritûs*, 'with a sacrifice of a troubled spirit,' for the mortifying of our flesh.

Neither is this a matter ceremonial; for Christ saith, Luke v. 35, that we shall fast after His taking; and we see the same accordingly practised,

by the whole church, Acts xiii. 2, 3, "as they ministered to the Lord, and fasted,"—"and when they had fasted and prayed," &c.

by Paul, 2 Cor. xi. 27, "in fastings often."

This sabbath of fast is either public or private;

public, to which the silver trump must be blown,

Joel ii. 15, "blow the trumpet in Zion, sanctify a fast;"

private, that none know of it,

Matt. vi. 17, "but thou when thou fastest," &c.

Of public fast.

The reasons of public fast;

I. For turning away some evil, either *culpæ*, or *pœnæ*, 'of fault, or punishment.'

Both these are either ours, or others'; and first, *pœnæ*;

1. Our own, when God's arrows are upon us;

Josh. vii. 6, Joshua before Ai;

Judges xx. 26, the children of Israel defeated by Benjamin;

1 Sam. vii. 6, the children of Israel at Mizpeh;

Joel ii. 14, "who knoweth if He will return and repent?"

or when they hang over our heads, Esth. iv. 3.

2. Others', as Zech. vii. 5, the fast of the fifth and of the seventh month.

For *malum culpæ*, 'the evil of sin,' seeing we have all offended God, we should all fear His judgments to come upon us, as Ezra, for the people's affinity with strangers, Ezra ix.; x. 6.

II. For the procuring of some good.

Acts xiii. 2, 3, "as they ministered to the Lord, and fasted, the Holy Ghost said, Separate Me Barnabas and Saul for the work whereunto I have called them. And when they had fasted and prayed, and laid their hands on them, they sent them away;"

xiv. 23, "and when they had ordained them elders in every church, and had prayed with fasting, they commended them to the Lord on Whom they believed."

And for all these causes, public fast is necessary, and not to be neglected, as we regard God's judgments.

Of private fast.

Private fast likewise is,

1. *Ob malum pœnæ,*
   - *a.* for ourselves,
     - under His hand, 2 Sam. xii, 16, "David therefore besought God for the child; and David fasted, and went in, and lay all night upon the earth;"
     - near His hand, 1 Kings xxi. 27, "when Ahab heard those words, he rent his clothes, and put sackcloth upon his flesh, and fasted," &c.;
   - *β.* for others, Ps. xxxv. 13, "when they were sick, I humbled my soul with fasting;"

2. *Ob malum culpæ,* i. e. *propter languorem boni,* 'for the evil of sin,' that is, 'for the fainting of goodness,' in us; for without fasting some temptation cannot be avoided, Matt. xvii. 21.

And as the public fast, so also the private fast is not only for turning away of evil, but for procuring some good,

generally, Acts x. 30, Cornelius;

particularly, Matt. iv., Christ; Acts xiv. 23, Paul and Barnabas in ordaining elders.

Each hath an outward and an inward part.

Now as of the other sabbath, so also of this, there are two parts, outward abstinence, and inward sorrow;

1. In the outward fast is required,
   a. that it be wholly all the day,
      Lev. xxiii. 32, the day of atonement;
      Ezra x. 6, Ezra for the strange marriages; and
   β. wakefulness is required, Joel i. 13, "lie all night in sackcloth, ye ministers of God;" and
   γ. to lay off our good apparel, and put on more vile clothes, Exod. xxxiii. 4, Neh. ix. 1; and lastly,
   δ. that there be a separation from all labour that is used on other days than the sabbath; and,
   ε. *quod ventri subtrahitur, illud pauperi detur,* 'what thou sparest from thy belly, give to the poor.'

2. Neither will outward abstinence serve the turn, without inward sorrow, Esay lviii. 3; and herein is
   a. first, an indignation against ourselves, which is an affection mixed with fear, that we have undergone the danger of so great a punishment, and
   β. secondly, sorrow, that we have offended so good a God; and to these must be added,
   γ. a desire of amendment, and a promise to take a more strict order hereafter in our serving of God than we have done.

For indeed both these sabbaths are spiritual, as we may see by that, Esay lviii. 3; we must cease from our own works, yea from our own thoughts, if we will rightly sanctify them.

Means to sanctify the sabbath.

1. A place of sanctification; we must 'reverence His sanctuary,' Lev. xix. 30, and xxvi. 2; Ps. cxxxii. 3—5, "I will not come into the tabernacle of my house, nor go up into my bed; I will not give sleep to mine eyes, or slumber to mine

eyelids, until I find out a place for the Lord, an habitation for the mighty God of Jacob."

And for this place of God's worship the apostles took order that it should not be too pompous, neither yet too homely, but that it be decent, with that *εὐσχημοσύνη*, 'handsomeness and good order,' which though it be not the more weighty point of the law, yet is not to be neglected.

2. Persons fit for all actions excellent; such as are able to do more than read and speak, Lev. xxi. 6, "they shall not profane the Name of their God;" for Prov. xxix. 18, "where there is no vision, the people perish."

So we see in the scriptures, what alteration and destruction had been for the rarity and want of prophecy,

Judges xvii. 7, the story of Micah;

1 Sam. iii. 4, the sons of Eli;

2 Chron. xv. 3, 5, 6, under Asa; "for a long season Israel hath been without the true God, and without a teaching priest and without law: and in those times there was no peace to him that went out, nor to him that came in, but great vexations were upon all the inhabitants of the countries; and nation was destroyed of nation, and city of city: for God did vex them with all adversity;"

2 Kings xvii. 16, Israel under Hosea;

so that Moses wished, Numb. xi. 29, that all might prophesy, and Paul, 1 Cor. xiv. 5; and we see by experience that our enemies would invade us in such places where the people are least taught in the word of God.

3. Maintenance of the places of God's worship, and not only so, but of schools also; so Moses was brought up in all manner of learning, Acts vii. 22; and to this end Josh. xv. 15, there was a city like our universities, *kiriath sepher*, 'a city of letters,' or 'a city of books;' and Acts xix. 9, Paul disputed in the school of one Tyrannus.

4. Maintenance of the person; Neh. x. 37, "the tithes to the levites;" 1 Cor. ix. 14, "they that preach the gospel must live by the gospel."

a. All that labour must have something for their labour,

and much more then they that minister unto us spiritual things must be made partakers of our temporal things; PART III.

β. And that they must not have less than the tenth part, may be thus proved;

first, by the connecting of their ministry to the priesthood of Melchisedek; Lev. xxvii. 32, "the tenth part holy to the Lord;"

secondly, in regard that which Jacob promised was moral, namely, that he would give the tenth of all to God;

thirdly, the reason of it was not peculiar to the Jews, but continueth still to us, and therefore the reason remaining, the thing itself also still continueth.

Thus much of the fourth commandment:

And so of the first table.

THE SECOND TABLE.

PART IV.

The sum of the first table was, "Love the Lord thy God with all thy heart," &c. Matt. xxii. 37; the sum of the second table, "Love thy neighbour as thyself."

And they are well joined together, and this latter dependeth well upon the former, *ut rivus justitiæ ducatur è fonte pietatis*[h], 'that the stream of justice may run along from the well-spring of piety.' For the first table treateth of our duty and piety to God, and the second of our justice towards man; and in this God giveth us a testimony of His love to man, whom He made like to Himself, and for whose good He hath made one table of the law, and that consisting of more precepts than the former table which concerned Himself.

Neither doth it derogate any thing from the love of God, but rather increaseth it; for,

a. if we love our friend, we will love his child, and so 1 John iv. 21, "let him that loveth God, love his brother also;" "for if we love not him whom we see, how shall we love God Whom we never see?" and

β. if we love man which oftentimes doth us hurt, how should we choose but love God who is always doing us good?

[h] [S. Greg. Moral., lib. xix. cap. 23. col. 624 sq.]

The commandments of the second table serve for the uniting of man to man, as the commandments of the first were for the uniting of man to God: God is to be ever a ready help at hand, our defender and upholder; and there is no man who needeth not also the help of his neighbour, whence it followeth that we ought to love one another.

Matter of the second table.

In this second table are generally three things,
the thing commanded, "love;"
the object of love, "our neighbour;"
the manner of it, "as ourselves."

1. *The thing commanded.*

Love is either

amor, 'a natural affection' which extendeth itself to all God's creatures, with a desire that they may remain in that course that God hath set them; or it is

benevolentia, 'good will,' which is in reasonable things only; but rash, and may be with error; or else

dilectio, 'rational choice' of one beloved, which is with consideration, and without error; and this is the love here commanded, for as Augustine[i] saith, *verus amator debet esse verus æstimator*, 'a true lover is one which can truly value things to their worth.'

If we love our brother we must,

1. Rejoice at his welfare, Rom. xii. 15, "rejoice with them that do rejoice;" not be envious to hinder others from the partaking of our good, which was the fault of the servant that hid his talent, Matt. xxv. 26; or if we have not the talent, we must not envy others that have it; which was the devil's fault, and the cause of the first temptation.

Here also is comprised the duty of having peace with all men, Rom. xii. 18, as far as is possible; and if at any time there be a breach of peace, that we should not be peremptory and unappeasable. The angels sang "Glory to God and peace on earth;" and there is nothing more to be desired than concord in all good, nothing more to be shunned than discord

[i] [De doctr. christ., lib. i. cap. 27. vol. iii. col. 13.]

in good. Which sometimes falls out by human frailty, which Christ signified by saying, He came not to send peace on earth, but the sword; yet peace is His gift, and "blessed are the peace-makers" in good; and on the contrary, cursed are the peace-makers in evil.

2. Do no man hurt, by inflicting evil upon him, or by detaining good from him, Lev. xix. 3.

3. If any man do us hurt, recompense him with good; "bless them that persecute you," Rom. xii. 14, "that curse you," Matt. v. 44.

4. Succour the hungry and needy, Prov. xxii. 9, Matt. v. 44, if we have this world's goods; which are defined to be, those which we may depart withal *salvo statu nostro*, 'without prejudice to our estate.'

5. We must pray for him, Rom. xii. 14, Matt. v. 44, for to pray for our neighbours is *radius caritatis*, 'a beam of charity.'

6. We must perform the duties of our calling toward our neighbour, as if one be a lawyer, he must give good counsel; and so of the rest, Luke vi. 27—29.

Thus much of the thing commanded, love.

2. *The object of love.*

The object of our love must be our neighbour.

The pharisees took this word straitly for their friends only, Matt. v. 43, "thou shalt love thy neighbour, and hate thine enemy:" but Christ, Luke x. 37, sheweth that *misericordia, non loci differentia, facit proximum*, 'mercy, and not difference of country, makes one our neighbour;' and if he be a neighbour that sheweth mercy, and *proximus* is *proximo proximus*[k], then he must be also a neighbour that standeth in need of mercy, though he be our enemy. And the law confirmeth the same, Deut. xxii. 1, "if thy brother's ox go astray, thou shalt bring him again to thy brother;" and Exod. xxiii. 4, "if thou meet thine enemy's ox going astray, thou shalt bring it to him again;" the self same law for brother and enemy.

The object of our love is said to be our 'neighbour,' or our 'brother;' we may use both words;

[k] [Aug. ubi sup., cap. 30. vol. iii. col. 15.]

1. if he be our brother, there is *identitas originis*, 'one and the same original' unto us; we are all of one blood; and we see even in beasts identity causeth love, as those of a kind will love one another; and so children like their own faces in a glass;

2. if he be *proximus*, why then in regard of use love him; for one neighbour shall have use of another, and stand in need of him, and society should be *amoris magnes*, 'the lodestone of love.'

Cautions hereupon.

Now in this love to our neighbour, we must consider two things;

1. Take heed we take not the sin of our neighbour for our neighbour; for[l] *omnis peccator, quatenus est peccator, est odio habendus; omnis homo, quatenus est homo, est diligendus: sic homines diligamus, ut non diligamus errores; ob id quod facti sunt, non ob id quod fecerunt*, 'every sinner, as he is a sinner, is to be hated; every man, as he is a man, is to be loved: let us love men so that we love not their sins, and love them for that which God made them, not that which by sin they made themselves.'

2. For degrees, whether *alius alio propinquior*, 'one man is nearer than another.'

It is certain there are degrees; for to omit our duties to our parents is worse than to omit the same duties to a stranger.

Now where there is a greater duty, there must be a greater affection, and so greater love; and the order of our love must be thus,

a. To God, for He is that *bonum*, 'good,' by the participation whereof all other are *bona*, 'good;' and to which all other give place, as in policy to *bonum publicum*, 'the public good.'

β. Our own souls, for we are *unitas*, 'an unity,' or one entire in and with ourselves, and cannot be but united[m] with our brethren.

γ. The souls of our brethren before our own bodies; for

[l] [Aug. De doctr. christ., lib. i. cap. 27. vol. iii. col. 13.]

[m] [i. e. with our brethren we can at most be only *united*.]

any man's soul may directly be partaker of the universal good which is in God, but so can no man's body but by participation with the soul, and therefore the soul is to be preferred.

δ. Our own bodies before other men's.

ε. The bodies of our neighbours; and among them,
first to them that have need; and of those,
first to the household of faith, Gal. vi. 10; and of them,
first to our countrymen, Ps. cxxii. 8, "brethren and companions;" and of these,
first them which are *nostri*, 'our friends and acquaintance;' and of them,
first to our own, and namely, them of our household, 1 Tim. v. 8, and our kindred; and
first the wife, Gen. ii. 24, "they shall be one flesh;" "am not I better to thee than ten sons?" 1 Sam. i. 8.

Thus much of the object, our neighbour.

3. *The manner of our love.*

The manner of our love, 'as ourselves;' *non quantum, sed sicut*, 'not so much as thyself, but after the same manner.' Wherein are four things;

1. The end, *propter quod amas teipsum*, 'for which thou lovest thyself,' that must be, *quia Deum amas, ideoque omnia quæ sunt Dei; ob hanc causam dilige fratrem, quia Deum amat, quia Dei est*, 'because thou lovest God, and therefore all things which are God's; for this cause love thy brother, because he loveth God, because he is God's.'

2. The means to this end, *ad quod teipsum amas*, 'to which end thou lovest thyself:' thy love to thyself should be chiefly in respect of thy soul, so chiefly love the soul of thy neighbour. And therefore as Augustine saith, *aut ama me quia sum Dei, aut ut sum Dei*, 'either love me, because I am God's servant, or as I am God's servant;' and so we must not *consentire ejus voluntati in malo*, 'consent to his will in any evil.'

3. Not for the use of him, or because we hope to have a good turn of him, but *gratuito*, 'freely.'

4. After the order and in the degree before spoken of;

namely, after God, and after thine own soul; and first his soul, and then thine own body, and then his body.

And thus our love must be *ex fonte pietatis*, 'flowing from the spring of piety,' *justus, verus, ordinatus*; 'just, true, and directed to the right end.' So that our love must be toward our neighbour, not as always it is towards ourselves, but as it ought to be; nor as an evil man loveth himself, but as a man's heart well regulated affecteth his own self.

THE FIFTH COMMANDMENT.

Of higher and lower place.

God hath not made all men alike, but hath made some partakers of His excellency, and set them in superior place; others of a meaner degree, and set them in a lower place; that mutual society might be maintained. For this He hath provided in this commandment; here He establisheth the cloth and chair of estate, having given such excellency to some that He styled them gods, Ps. lxxxii. 6; to these, others of inferior rank must submit and shew their observance.

The commandment hath two parts,
the precept, "honour thy father," &c.;
the reason, "that thy days," &c.

First part of the commandment, viz. the precept.

The precept containeth the duties of
- inferiors, to honour;
- superiors, to be father and mother.

Of the words of the commandment.

God dealing seriously with man, delighteth to knit up His speech in a short compass, and therefore in one word expresseth His command. Hence in the negative commandments He maketh choice of the ugliest and loathsomest word of that kind, to terrify us from those words which signify sins not so gross; so in this commandment He maketh choice of the 'father' and 'mother' to beautify the commandment, and sweeten the duty withal.

Now as Chrysostom saith, they must first be fathers, before they be honoured as fathers.

"Thy father:" the hebrew word is אבה, *abba*, which is, 'he that hath a care or desire to do good:' so that he is a father by whom others are in any better estate; for as natural fathers are *causa existendi*, 'cause of our being,' so others are *causa bene existendi*, 'cause of our well being.'

"Honour:" the word כבד, *kabad*, signifieth *aggravare*, 'to increase and aggravate and add,' so that we must add an excellency unto them; we must *addere pretium*, 'add estimation,' and *addere pondus*, 'add weight,' and by translation *honorem*, 'honour;' make it a matter of weight to honour them; and seeing they bear the person of God, they must not be set light by.

Why rulers are appointed.

We see 1 Tim. ii. 2—4, the apostle goeth thus to work: God would have all men saved; that they might be saved, He would have them live in godliness and honesty; that they might so do, He would have them taught the knowledge of God; and that they might intend this, He would have them lead a peaceable and a quiet life; peaceable in regard of outward invasions, and quiet in regard of inward tumults and troubles. Now if the natural father and natural mother could have performed this, they needed no other; but Gen. x. 8, there comes one Nimrod, with a company of hounds at his tail, (that metaphor it pleaseth the Holy Ghost to use,) and he takes upon him to be a hunter, that is, a chaser of men, to disturb and trouble them; and after that God first allowed, and after instituted, that there should be

α. governors, to deliver us from unreasonable and evil men, 1 Tim. ii. 2; and

β. government, both for resisting of outward foes, and for quieting of inward strifes; and to comfort and cherish good men, that love to live quietly, to come to knowledge of God, and of a religious demeanour of themselves.

The magistrate is the minister of God to take vengeance on them who do evil, but a cherisher and comforter of such as do well, Rom. xiii. 4. The benefit received from his vigilancy is well set forth, Dan. iv. 10, under the representation of a great tree, and Esay xxxii. 2, by comparing him to a river in dry places, and the shadow of a great rock in a dry land. Our study must be to give him all due submission and honour, for in his peace we shall have peace, Jer. xxix. 7.

Of the duties common to superiors and inferiors.

"Honour thy father and thy mother."

First of the duties in general.

The duty standeth as well in the action as in the manner of the action, and neither are to be omitted.

There are some duties which are *officia reciproca,* 'mutual duties between the inferior and superior,' due by either of them to the other of them;

1, love, but in a higher degree than that which is due to every one; the name of it is *στοργὴ,* which is a natural affection, either ascending or descending, and that either properly, or by analogy, Phil. ii. 22, as a son to the father.

2, to wish well to him whom we love; and because *christianum votum est oratio,* 'prayer is a Christian's well wishing,' therefore to this wishing well we may add prayer for them.

Duties of the inferior generally: first, honour;

The first is honour, and that, inward, or outward.

Honour, in exact speech, belongeth to God alone; yet He hath pleased to impart some beams thereof to men; He hath made some vessels of honour; He calls them to it, and fits them with gifts; they have *ὑπεροχὴν,* 'excellency;' *ἐξουσίαν,* 'power;' and *ἀρχὴν,* 'a place of authority' to exercise their power.

1. Inward honour is that *honesta opinio,* that 'good opinion' and reputation that one man hath of another, wherein we witness a certain excellency to be in him whom we do thus honour.—The contrary hereof was in Corah and his company, Numb. xvi. 3; this was his thesis, The Lord is among us all, we are all alike holy to the Lord; and therefore Moses

and Aaron should be no more excellent than the rest of the people.

2. Outward honour what it is and after what sort it is to be exhibited, is better known and determined by the manner of the country, than otherwise; because all are not alike, every country hath not the same fashion: for ourselves, we may reduce it to these heads;

α. To rise up, when that person of excellency is in presence, which either by nature, or by analogy and proportion, is our father; Job xxix. 8, "the young men saw me, and hid themselves; and the aged arose, and stood up;" and 1 Kings ii. 19, Solomon to Bathsheba, "the king rose up to meet her;"

β. To uncover the head, in token of our reverence of him; 1 Cor. xi. 4, "every man praying or prophesying having his head covered, dishonoureth his head;"

γ. To bow the knee; Gen. xli. 43, to Joseph, "they cried before him, Bow the knee: and he made him ruler over all the land of Egypt;"

δ. To stand; as Exod. xviii. 13, Moses sat because he was judge, and all the day long the people stood; and 2 Kings v. 25: Gehazi stood before Eliseus, as our servants stand before us.

ε. To be silent when our betters speak, and to give ear unto them; Job xxix. 9, 10, "the princes refrained talking, and laid their hand on their mouth; the nobles held their peace, and their tongue cleaved to the roof of their mouth."

ζ. When we are by necessary occasion to speak, to use words of submission; as Sarah called her husband 'lord' or 'sir,' Gen. xviii. 12; and Joseph's brethren, not knowing it was their brother, "thy servant our father is in good health," Gen. xliii. 28; and Rachel to Laban her father, Gen. xxxi. 35, "let not my lord be grieved that I cannot rise."

η. The last duty of outward honour is in the scriptures comprehended under the name of 'service,' Luke xvii. 8, or 'waiting upon;' it comprehendeth all such duties as are used by servants to their masters.

secondly, fear;

After honour followeth fear; which doth properly belong

to the superior, in regard of his power; and it is an awe or reverent fear, or a standing in awe of them;

Lev. xix. 3, "ye shall fear every man his father and his mother;" and

Eph. vi. 5; we must "with fear and trembling serve our masters according to the flesh," and much more kings, because

Prov. xvi. 14, their "anger is as the messengers of death."

thirdly, obedience.

The next thing due unto them in regard of their government is obedience, expressed 1 Tim. vi. 1, by being "under the yoke;" that is, when they will us to do this or that, we must put our necks under the yoke of their commandment; Prov. xxiii. 22, "obey thy father," and so Eph. vi. 1; as

Isaac obeyed Abram his father, Gen. xxii. 9;
Jacob obeyed Laban his master, Gen. xxxi. 6;
the people promise to obey Joshua, Josh. i. 16.

Wicked therefore was the doctrine of the pharisees, Mark vii. 11, 12, that a man should give to the treasury, and so be freed from honouring his father.

For this cause it is that we pay tribute and custom, to shew that we are not only ready ourselves, but our goods also are at commandment.

Now the manner of our obedience is this,

1, it must be in simplicity and singleness of heart, with a good conscience, Col. iii. 22;

2, it must be *alacriter*, 'with cheerfulness;'

3, we must do it continually, at all times, and in all cases lawful, not contrary to God's commandments.

Reasons for obedience.

And because we are not given to this by nature, therefore six reasons are given to move and induce us to perform this obedience;

1. the very placing of the commandment may move us much, in that God hath put it before our goods, yea before

our life, to shew that obedience to government ought to be dearer to us than our goods, yea than our lives;

2. the names of father and mother which God hath given to governors, which are names of nature, full of love, and the more apt to move obedience;

3. the promise of long life, a thing no less amiable; for death is a thing repugnant to nature;

4. it is a good thing, 1 Tim. ii. 3, it is to God acceptable; yea, it is that which God is specially delighted with, *εὐάρεστον*, Col. iii. 20, and they that are thus obedient, they are *καλοὶ, ἀπόδεκτοι, εὐάρεστοι*, 'good, acceptable, well-pleasing;'

5. it is not only good, but *δίκαιον*, Eph. vi. 1, 'it is right;' we cannot forbear it without injury; and therefore Christ saith, Matt. xxii. 21, "give unto Cæsar that which is Cæsar's;" it is his own, and therefore if you keep it back, you do him wrong and injustice;

6. it standeth us in hand so to do; and the reason is, Heb. xiii. 17, they watch over our souls; so that where honour is detracted, there care of preservation is diminished; and by reason hereof the power, wickedness, and impudency of naughty men is increased, and we the more troubled.

Duties of the superior generally.

Now the duties of superiors in general.

The nearness of the two significations of the word כבד, *kabad*, which signifieth both 'heaviness' and 'honour;' and in the greek *τιμὴ*, 'honour,' and a loss or 'mulct;' in latin, *onero*, 'to burden,' and *honoro*, 'to honour;' sheweth that this honour goeth not without a charge and a burden, and that it is required of them that they should be that which they would be honoured for.

1. They must know that their office is *διὰ τὸν κύριον*, 'in and for God,' and that they be God's ministers, 1 Pet. ii. 13, Rom. xiii. 4; they are God's vicegerents; their judgment is His, and not their own, 2 Chron. xix. 6, "ye judge not for man, but for the Lord."

2. To make their places yet more weighty, 2 Cor. xii. 14, the children are not for the fathers, but the fathers for the

children. Ps. lxxviii. 71, David was taken from the sheepfold to be a king; but why? *ad pascendum Israel,* 'to feed Israel:' and after the same manner it is between those that are fathers and children by nature; God in the beginning saw the want and defect that was in children, and therefore ordained a duty to be shewed unto them before they are able to give honour; and then afterwards for a recompence the children are to give honour to their parents, that have helped them when they could not help themselves. And as God ordained the children to be thus holpen, and their wants to be supplied by their parents; so must those that are in authority nourish and cherish those that are under them, as their own flesh; as Moses, Numb. xi. 12, carried the people in his bosom, as a nurse.

3. Seeing God hath made them fathers and mothers, and those that are under them children, and consequently hath made a difference of high and low, they must take heed that they do not pervert this difference and make them equal, or set those before whom God hath set behind. We see the order that the prophet Nathan used to king David, 1 Kings i. 26, "me thy servant, and Zadok the priest, and Benaiah the son of Jehoiada, and thy servant Solomon;" he cometh last, though he were the king's son, and the prophet Nathan knew well enough in what order to place him. The contrary to this was the fault of Eli, 1 Sam. ii. 29; whereas Eli's sons should have honoured him, he honoureth them, and intreateth them, as an inferior should do his superior, "I hear evil of you, I pray do thus no more;" and it is said there that God would make their seed abjects, because they gave away the honour from themselves.

4. As this order is thus established by God, and must by men be retained, so it must also be practised, and not be a bare and naked resemblance, or dumb idol, but put to use; for, 1 Thes. iv. 11, the superior must see that such as are under him fall to work; and if any break order, then Rom. xiii. 4, he hath not authority in vain, but *propter vindictam malorum,* 'to be avenged of evil men;' but for those that do well, he must encourage them, "well done, good servant and faithful," Matt. xxiv. 23.

Of the manner of their government.

Now for the manner of their government.

1. For himself, David, Ps. ci. 2, speaking how he will govern, beginneth with this, He will "walk uprightly" himself, and so be an example before his people. Gregory[n] maketh the right use of power to be, *ut homo sit potens in seipso, adversus seipsum, pro seipso*; that is, he should be of power in himself against the rebellious affections of his own nature, that so he may do himself good, and bring himself to goodness.

2. Toward others that are under him, Lev. xxv. 43, he must not deal cruelly, but use moderation; not in proud manner to use contumelious words and tyrannous deeds, but, as all christians, Eph. iv. 31, so especially those in high place must be far from anger, bitterness, crying out, and railing, and such like; he must not be *tanquam leo in vi suâ*, 'as a lion in his violence and in his rage;' for so Zeph. iii. 3, a naughty governor is described to be like a roaring lion.

Their duty is further set down at large, Ps. lxxxii. from the second verse to the end of the psalm. In this psalm is set down,

α. how "God standeth in the congregation of princes," and seeth how they use their honour;

β. He observeth whether they oppress or relieve the poor, verses 3 and 4;

γ. He sheweth that if they abuse their power, the foundations shall be shaken, and all will go to wrack;

δ. that though He calls them gods, yet they be but men; they have rule committed to them, but Christ hath power to dispossess and punish them;

ε. that they shall die like men, verse 7; *non siccâ morte*, 'of violent deaths,' as did many of the Israelitish kings afterwards;

ζ. that God was the great Judge, and would arise and judge the earth, ver. 8; because men executed not God's judgments aright, but became evil shepherds, as those spoken of, Ezek. xxxiv. 2, 3.

[n] [The passage is in St. Augustine, De Trin., lib. xiii. cap. 13. vol. viii. col. 939.]

PART IV.

Whether wicked superiors should be honoured.

Quest. 1. Whether inferiors owe any honour to superiors that are evil and wicked?

Answ. Yes, they do; for the wickedness of a man cannot take away the force of God's commandment, nor make void God's ordinance; no more than man's unbelief can frustrate God's promise, as we read, Rom. iii. 3.

1. Though they be froward, we must submit ourselves, 1 Pet. ii. 18; as when Sarah dealt roughly with Hagar, yet the angel willeth her to return back to her mistress and to submit herself unto her: and as in the family, so in the commonwealth; we know Saul dealt very roughly with David, and yet still he acknowledged subjection unto him, so that he would do him no violence when opportunity was offered him in the cave.

2. And not only being froward, but though they be wicked, yet obedience and honour is to be done unto them; for,

a. It is God that set them up, though it were in His wrath, Hos. xiii. 11; and Jer. xxvii. 7, the Lord saith, that He had given Nebuchadnezzar the government that he had, and all nations should serve him; and Esay x. 5, the rod of His wrath, the king of Ashur, was by Him purposely set up.

β. Paul commands to "pray for kings," though they were heathen and wicked, 1 Tim. ii. 2; and Peter bids "honour the king," 1 Pet. ii. 17, when as then Nero ruled. Paul useth the benefit of this wicked prince's power, and appealeth from the deputy to Nero, Acts xxv. 11.

γ. Even the hearts of ungodly rulers are in the hands of God; He turneth them as the rivers of waters, which way He will, Prov. xxi. 1.—Only this distinction may be added; look what honour we give them, we do it not to man, but to God himself, in reverence to His ordinance; not τῷ προσώπῳ, 'to the person,' but τῷ προσωπείῳ, 'to the vizard' that God hath put upon him; as the heathen emblem was, *ὄνος ἄγων μυστήρια,* 'an ass laden with the image of the goddess Isis;' and the people fall down and worship, but the inscription is, *non tibi, sed religioni,* 'not to thee but to religion.'

δ. And again, this we may further say, that be a government never so bad, yet it is better than none at all; an oligarchy when the rule is under a few, is better than an anarchy when there is no ruler at all: and therefore, Hos. xiii. 11, though God gave them a king in His anger, yet He took him away in His wrath and in the fury of His anger; for then their plague was greater, to be without a prince, than to have a bad one.

Wicked rulers not to be absolutely obeyed.

Quest. 2. But to go a degree farther, *utrum malo in malo,* or *ad malum, obediendum,* 'whether we must obey an evil man in an evil thing; or whether we owe (as we call it) absolute obedience to evil magistrates?'

Answ. No, we do not; for absolute obedience is due to God only, and kings are to be obeyed so far as their commandments are not repugnant to God's commandments; for if God command one thing and they another, *Deo potius quam hominibus,* 'better obey God than man,' Acts iv. 19.

No man can serve two masters, Matt. vi. 24; when God and they command all one thing, they are but *unum agens,* and so but one master; and there are not two masters, till man break order, and become a master himself against order.

Our Saviour's rule is, Luke xiv. 26, "he that cometh to Me must hate father and mother and all;" which He expoundeth, Matt. x. 37, "he that loveth father or mother more than Me, is not worthy of Me;" for *bonum quod impedit majus bonum, in eo minus diligendum,* 'that good which hindereth a greater good, is less to be loved.'

Examples of this.

God the Superior of all, the great Superior, took order they should not fall down nor bow to any image; Nebuchadnezzar a prince, a lesser superior, he commands the contrary; he was disobeyed, and the disobedience was no disobedience, for disobedience is not but ἐν τάξει, 'in due place and order,' and he had gone out of order first, Dan. iii. 18.

Darius went out of order, Dan. vi. 9, when he forbad prayer to God, which God had first commanded; Daniel contrary to the king's decree prayeth; Daniel kept his order; the king was out of order, the fault was the king's.

In this commandment God commandeth to honour father and mother; and yet we see, 2 Chron. xv. 16, Asa had given charge that no idol should be erected; and because his mother Maacha did erect an idol, he deposed her, though she were his mother; and yet no breach of this commandment.

So that as we said, it is no disobedience in the inferior, if the superior go out of the line and the inferior keepeth it.

We see 2 Sam. xi. 16, Joab for obeying the king's letter, and putting Uriah but to chance-medley, yet he is condemned for it; and so are the soldiers of Herod, for killing the children and executing his will, Matt. ii. 16.

When our Saviour, being forgotten by his father and mother, was found disputing in the temple, his mother reprehendeth him for putting them in fear; "why hast thou done thus," saith she? and our Saviour, though He were obedient to His father and mother, yet He maketh her this answer, "wot you not that I must go about My Father's business?" as if He should say, I have a father indeed, Joseph; but I have a superior Father in heaven, and I was to go on His business, and so could not wait upon you, Luke ii. 49.

To conclude this point; 1 Pet. ii. 13, this honour must be *propter Deum,* 'for God's sake;' and that is, Eph. vi. 1, *in Deo,* 'in the Lord;' that is, Tit. iii. 1, in every good work. And as Hierome saith, *honorandus generator sed præponendus Creator,* 'our father must be loved, but our Father and Creator must be preferred before him.'

And yet notwithstanding all this, it shall be good and expedient *non μικρολογεῖσθαι,* 'not to carp at every little thing,' but rather obey, if it be in our power,

a. in a thing doubtful, as 2 Sam. xxiv. 4; Joab though he could see no reason to number the people, yet because the king recommended, he obeyed, and yielded unto it;

β. though it be an unjust commandment, yet if it be not directly contrary to God's will, there may be just obedience unto it; Matt. xvii. 27, it was more than Cæsar could require of Christ to pay tribute, because He was a stranger; yet rather than He would break quietness, He gave it.

Particular duties between superior and inferior.

Now the particular duties between superiors and inferiors.

Husband and wife.

First to begin with the husband and the wife;
and first their mutual duties each to other;
and then their several duties.

their mutual duties.

Their mutual duties may be gathered out of the three words that signify marriage;

1. *Conjugium,* the 'fellowship of a yoke,' which is better borne by two than by one alone; so one must help another to bear all burdens: therefore unequal matches, which are hindrances to religion, not bearing all one yoke, are condemned, 1 Cor. vii. 39, not being *in Domino.*

2. *Matrimonium, ut mulier fiat mater,* 'matrimony, that the woman may become a mother;' Gen. i. 28, for propagation; and Mal. ii. 15, for increase of God's church, the holy seed. By God's institution was to be observed the marriage of one man with one woman; "it was so from the beginning," when God would have men multiply on the earth and fill it with a holy progeny.

3. *Nuptiæ,* 'marriage, or covering,' of *nubo,* 'to cover;' as it were coverings after sin, to cover each other's shame.

their several duties.

The several and particular duties of husband and wife.

1. The husbands must live with their wives as men of knowledge, 1 Pet. iii. 7; for she must ask of him at home, and therefore he must be able to answer her asking, and to instruct her.

And here the wife's duty is submission; not to stand upon her own will, but to be subject to her husband; which subjection must be with acknowledgment that the man is the woman's head, 1 Cor. xi. 3; and therefore because the senses of seeing and hearing are in the head, she must see and hear by him. Yet she must not be too much kept under; for as she was not made of his head, so not of his feet, but of his side, that she might be his equal.

2. The husband must also love his wife, and not only with the general duty of love, whereof we spake before, but with an especial love and respect peculiar to her, so as he must forsake father and mother and cleave unto her; and his love must not be fleshy or in outward respects only, but in the spirit, Eph. v. 29; and especially to have this care, that he may present his wife to God as Christ did His church, without spot or wrinkle.

And the wife's duty in this case must be the very same, answerable to her husband's; she must love him with the same love that he is to love her withal. 'Tis also the woman's duty to fear God, so shall she be truly praiseworthy, Prov. xxxi. 29, 30; such a one as Lydia, Acts xvi. 14. Beauty in her without graciousness, is but as a gold ring in a swine's snout, Prov. xi. 22; her chief ornaments are modesty, humility, and inward virtues, 1 Tim. ii. 9.

3. The husband must be the provider for his wife, and so for his children and family, 1 Tim. v. 8.

And the wife must also have a care to look to that which her husband hath provided, 1 Tim. v. 14, that nothing be lost, John vi. 12; and therefore they must keep at home and be good house-wives.

4. There must be in both husband and wife *officia resultantia,* honour and love of their friends mutually; as we see in Moses toward his father-in-law, Exod. xviii. 7, 12, Numb. x. 29; and for the woman, very excellently in Ruth toward her mother-in-law, Ruth i. 16.

Father and son.

The duties between father and son.

1. The first duty of the parents is in the beginning of their children; wherein *non tam generatio spectanda est quam regeneratio,* 'not so much generation and birth, as regeneration and the new birth is to be regarded;' so that this

duty must not be performed with a brutish appetite, but by sanctifying themselves to the propagation of God's church.

This duty the child cannot answer; and therefore his duty herein is, to honour his parents, though they be never so mean and base; yea to do them service; Luke xv. 29, "lo, these many years do I serve thee."

2. The second duty, Eph. vi. 4, is to nourish them when they have begotten them; and not against nature to give them a stone when they ask for bread, Matt. vii. 9. Neither must they only nourish them, but bring them up, laying up for them, and dividing the inheritance; and if there be no inheritance, then to provide them some art, such as every one is most fit for; and the choicest of all, to God's service, as Hannah did, 1 Sam. i. 11.

And to answer this, the son must not falsely purloin or embezzle from his parents, as wicked children do, but maintain them rather, if the parents want, and he be able.

3. They must not only bring up their children, but bring them up in the Lord, that they may be christians, and sons of God, as well as they are their sons; Gen. xviii. 19, "I know him, that he will command his children and his household after him, and they shall keep the way of the Lord, to do justice and judgment;" Deut. iv. 9, "teach these thy sons and thy sons' sons."

4. To all these they must add their own example, and where need is, correction, Prov. xxix. 15; for he that correcteth not his son, hateth him, Prov. xiii. 24. There is a bundle of foolishness in the heart of a child, and the rod of correction will drive it out, Prov. xxii. 15; this must be done while there is hope, without regarding of the child's murmuring, Prov. xix. 18; for protracting of time is dangerous. It is recorded of David as a blemish to him, that he was never displeased with Adonijah, 1 Kings i. 6.

5. The last duty is a particular kind of prayer and blessing, which sanctifieth all the rest, or else all other means are nothing worth, Gen. xlix. 28.

The son's duty answerable hereunto is, to be willing to receive instruction, and not to mock at good counsel, but to be wise, that so he may make his father glad, Prov. x. 1; to imitate his father's good example; and to be subject to correction, Heb. xii. 9.—Here are condemned marriages without consent of parents; for the woman's vow to God, Num. xxx. 4, cannot stand without his consent, much less the vow of marriage; and 1 Cor. vii. 30, the father must give his daughter in marriage.

Master and servant.

The duty of the master and servant.

Mastership and service are lawful; Jacob served twice seven years, Gen. xxix. A man in poverty may serve to get means thereby, Deut. xv. 12; so may an ignorant man to get knowledge and skill thereby, for these two are proportionable: servitude came first into the world for a punishment, when the servant gaineth maintenance and knowledge thereby.

I. The first duty of the master is *ars imperandi,* 'knowledge how to enjoin them their works;' and here must be observed four things;

1, that his commandment be lawful, for else in performing it, he shall displease *κύριον κατὰ πνεῦμα,* "the Master according to the spirit;" and though we have a master according to the flesh, yet the Master according to the spirit is to be preferred; as Joseph preferred God before his mistress, Gen. xxxix. 9;

2, the commandment must not only be lawful but possible; for a thing may be lawful, and yet not possible; and therefore Abram's servant putteth the doubt, Gen. xxiv. 5, "what if she will not come?" and is in that case set free;

3, it must be profitable to some good purpose, for nothing must be done in vain;

4, it must be proportionable to time, place, and person.

The duty of the servant answerable to this is, Matt. xxiv. 45, faithfulness and discretion.

1. For faithfulness, the heathen could say that *servus totus alterius,* 'a servant is wholly another man's to be commanded.' And therefore, Matt. vi. 24, he can serve but one master, because his duty is infinite; he cannot set down any time

when he shall have done, but must work all day, Luke xvii. 7; at night too, until the master set him free; yea, he must spare from his own meat to do his master's business.

Opposite to this faithfulness is,

a. when they will do something beside their master's business, or let something stick on their fingers; Tit. ii. 10, filchers; Luke xvi. 1, wasters;

β. lying, 2 Sam. xvi. 3, Ziba; 2 Kings v. 22, it was the fault of Gehazi;

γ. slothfulness, when he will not give his master all his strength; *non accuratè agere,* 'not do his duty exactly,' as the poet saith, but be *servus glis,* 'a servant of a dormouse nature;' not like Jacob, Gen. xxxi. 40, who could not sleep for his master's business;

δ. Eph. vi. 7, they that do their work unwillingly; or with murmuring, Tit. ii. 9; not like the centurion's servant, that heard but 'go,' and he went;

ε. eye-service, deceitful diligence, only at their own pleasure and before their master's face, Eph. vi. 6, Col. iii. 22; whereas they should do it with singleness of heart, lest the chief Master be displeased.

2. For discretion in servants; they must do for their master as the steward did for himself, Luke xvi., cast for their master in due time and upon all fit occasions to do him good.

II. The second duty of the master is, not to be *asper,* 'sharp and bitter,' Lev. xxv. 43; but Col. iv. 1, "do unto them that which is just and equal," for they are *conservi,* 'fellow servants' also to the chief Master; and *in futuro,* 'in the time to come,' the masters may be servants to men; and therefore *quod tibi fieri vis, hoc fac alteri,* 'do as thou wouldst be done unto.'

III. The third duty is, Prov. xxvii. 27, xxxi. 19—27, to provide them meat, drink, and clothes, or wages agreed upon.

Teacher and hearer.

The duties of the teacher and hearer.

Qualifications of a teacher.

In teachers there should be,

1, χάρισμα, God's 'gift' of gracious and natural parts;

2, education to it, at home and in the schools; 2 Tim. iii. 15, "from a child thou hast known the holy scriptures;"

3, exercise and study, 2 Tim. iii. 14, "continue thou in the things which thou hast learned and hast been assured of;" and

4, they must be called to it by imposition of hands.

In choosing men for this work it is to be observed that they be,

1, *solertes*, 'of an active intelligence;'

2, *dociles*, 'apt to conceive;'

3, *instanter operantes*, 'diligent in their calling,' as was Paul.

But he who shall be a teacher must especially know that the divine light of sacred doctrine is from above, and therefore that he must

1, use prayer, Ps. cxix. 66, "O learn me true understanding and knowledge;" and

2, have a special regard to God's commandments; Ps. xix. 8, "the commandment of the Lord is pure, and giveth light unto the eyes;" and

3, that he must awake and stand up from sin; Eph. v. 14, "awake thou that sleepest, and arise from the dead, and Christ shall give thee light."

In the manner of his teaching he must,

first, clear parables and dark speeches;

secondly, proceed in method and order; Luke xxiv. 27, "beginning at Moses and all the prophets, He expounded unto them in all the scriptures," &c. and

thirdly, teach as his hearers are able to learn; John xvi. 12, "I have yet many things to say unto you, but ye cannot bear them now."

His duties: first, to set forth the truth;

In particular, the first duty of the teacher is, Prov. xxii.

19, 20, to make known to the people the words of truth; which is done,

1, by precept; Ps. cxix. 12, "teach me Thy statutes;"

2, by example; Prov. xxiv. 32; John xiii. 15, "I have given you an example, that ye should do as I have done to you;"

3, by experience;

4, by correction, that *παθήματα*, 'corrections,' may be *μαθήματα*, 'instructions.'

Hence it was that Christ questioned with His disciples, and practised them in baptizing, and casting out of unclean spirits, and curing of bodily diseases by their touch or otherwise, and the errors of men's minds by their doctrines. First Christ set the twelve on work to preach, then the seventy afterward; some laid the foundation, as Paul, others built thereupon, 1 Cor. iii. 10; some were the prime labourers, others came upon their labours; some planted, some watered. And when the disciples had fulfilled their duties, they render a reason thereof to Christ; and Christ encouraged and commended them in some things, in others He reproved and checked them.—I shew every thing in the example of Christ, because His example is most perfect; and because He was the chief Teacher, and made choice of the name of a Teacher; and because others were to learn by His example.

The hearer's duty answerable to this is,

1, to be *φιλήκοος*, 'studious of hearing,' that the word may come *in aurem*, 'into the ear,' and so *ad cor*, 'into the heart;'

2, to be *ζητητικὸς*, 'ready to ask questions;'

Exod. xiii. 14, Deut. vi. 20, "when thy son asketh thee in time to come,"—

John xvi. 17, "then said some of His disciples among themselves, what is this that He saith unto us?"

Matt. xiii. 10, "the disciples came and said unto Him, Why speakest Thou unto them in parables?"

secondly, to be careful of his doings;

The second duty of the teacher is, *vitia morum magis quam verborum vitare; potior enim est bene vivendi quam optimè dicendi facultas*, 'to shun vices in his carriage more carefully than errors in his words, for the art of living well is rather to be desired than the art of speaking well.'

The scholar's duty answerable is, Lam. iii. 27, to 'bear the yoke in his youth;' and to be at direction, and to be humble minded.

thirdly, to protect his scholars.

The third duty of the teachers is, they must be *tutores*, they must *tueri*, 'defend and protect' their scholars; as Christ did His disciples, Matt. ix. 14, xii. 2, for plucking the ears of corn.

The hearer's duty answerable is,

to bring every one his offering; Numb. vi. 14, 15, the Nazarite;

1 Sam. i. 21, Elkanah;

1 Sam. ix. 7, Saul to Samuel;

Luke v. 29, Levi to Christ;

Matt. v. 24, "then come and offer thy gift."

Also to minister unto them,

as Samuel did to Eli, 1 Sam. ii. 11;

and Elisha to Elijah, 1 Kings xix. 21, and 2 Kings iii. 11;

and John's disciples, Matt. xi. 2;

and Christ's, Matt. xxvi. 17.

And lastly, there must be *resultans officium*, 'a duty reciprocal towards their teacher;' as our Saviour charged His disciples with His mother, John xix. 27; and after His death, His disciples buried Him.

More particularly the minister's duty.

The apostle, Heb. v. 1, sheweth that the minister is taken from men, and ordained for men, in things appertaining to God, to deal with God for the church.

Now this being an honour, no man must take it unto him unless he be called. Now God's calling is known by his talents, Matt. xxv. 14, and therefore unless God have given him gifts he is not called by God; but,

a. having this calling, and

β. having in the university where this was taught, his bringing up, and γ. having, 1 Tim. iv. 14, the laying on of hands of the company of eldership;

we come now to his duties; we shall find them, John x. 11, &c. 1 Tim. iii. Tit. i.

Three evil kinds of minister.

There are four sorts mentioned, John x.;

three bad, ... { a thief, a hireling, a wolf,

one good, namely, . . the good shepherd.

They may be distinguished into { a lawful calling, an unlawful calling.

1. If he have not a lawful calling, if he come not in by the door, that is, according to Christ's institution, if he have not his talent, he is an usurper and a thief; as Jer. xxiii. 21, God saith, "they ran and I never sent them, they prophesy and I bade them not, I never spake to them."

And this cometh by wresting the law; which is done two ways, Deut. xvi. 19;

1, *per gratiam*, 'by favour' at the suit of some great man or some friend, by having respect of persons;

2, *per munus*, 'by taking rewards.'

And so the law being perverted *per gratiam* and *per munus*, the ordinance of God is laid aside; and then cometh *cita impositio*, 'a too sudden laying hands on him;' because he hath not the gift of the heart to commend him withal, for the gift of his hand the bishop letteth him go unexamined, and so (contrary to Paul's rule to Timothy, 1 Tim. v. 22.) "layeth hands suddenly" upon him.

And how can God bless the proceedings of those that come not in by the door? *Quæcunque malo inchoantur principio, difficulter bono perficiuntur exitu*, 'whatsoever hath an ill beginning, can hardly be effected with a prosperous issue.'

2. The other sort, hirelings, John x. 13, are they that

have no care of feeding, but their end is to clothe themselves, Ezek. xxxiv. 3, Zech. xi. 15; and as the fathers say, they have not *instrumenta boni pastoris*, 'the implements of a good shepherd,' but only *forcipes* and *mulctram*, 'a pair of shears' for the fleece, and 'a pail' for the milk. And if the flock be in danger, for the danger of the soul they care not, but if there be the least danger of the wool or the milk, they bestir themselves.

3. And if a wolf come, that is, a persecutor or a false teacher, either they fly, John x. 12, or else they become wolves themselves, and do as great harm to the flock as the wolf doth.

One good kind of minister.

4. Now the good shepherd, he it is only that performeth his duty; and the duty of the good shepherd may be reduced to these four heads;—

His duties: first, to be an example in his life;

To go before his sheep, John x. 3, 4, as the manner of the east countries was, not to drive his sheep but to go before them; so the good shepherd must go before his flock by his good example, 1 Tim. iv. 12; he must be τύπος, that is, such a thing as maketh the stamp upon the coin; and it is also used, Tit. ii. 7, and 1 Pet. v. 3. And Moses requireth he should have *thummim*, 'integrity of life,' as well as *urim*, 'light' of learning, Deut. xxxiii. 8. And it is said of our Saviour Christ, our *typus*, Acts i. 1, *cæpit facere et docere*, He 'began to do and teach;' so the minister must do first and teach after; he must be an example unreproveable, 1 Tim. iii. 2, and unblameable, Tit. i. 6.

And this must be in him, and his;

1. In himself, 1 Tim. iii. 2, "without spot;" as Lev. xxi. 21, not misshapen, or having blemish, that is to say, any notorious sin or crime that is outward, to be laid to his charge; and the reason is, 2 Cor. vi. 3, that there may be no offence

given to the weak, or slander to the gospel, by the wicked; but that even the enemies may by his example become christians.

2. In his household, that is, in his charge; those that are committed to him; that is, if he be a prophet, in the church; if a father, in his sons; if a master, in his servants.—And this standeth in these points;

a. those that be under him must be religious and faithful children; Tit. i. 6, "faithful children, not accused of riot, or unruly;"

β. they must be under obedience; 1 Tim. iii. 4, "in subjection;" or else it is a presumption of negligence, faintheartedness, or carelessness in him;

γ. they must use reverence, gravity, modesty, 1 Tim. iii. 4; they must be no rioters, drunkards, or such like.

The duty of the people, answerable to this example of the shepherd, is to follow his example; if he must be *typus gregis*, 'a pattern to his flock,' they must be *ἀντίτυπον pastoris*, as in the print of the coin the iron and the coin are of the same figure.

secondly, to teach by his learning;

As he must be an example and go before them in life, so he must also teach and instruct them by learning; and therefore must be διδακτικὸς, 'able to teach.'

It is well observed that the verb *doceo*, 'to teach,' doth govern two accusative cases, as Esay xxviii. 9, *quem docebit scientiam*, 'whom' he will teach knowledge; they must have *quem*, 'whom' they should teach, and *quid*, 'what' they shall teach, namely, knowledge. Many have *quem*, 'a people to teach,' but have not *quid*, 'knowledge to teach them,' and so they are not teachers sent from God, but thieves and robbers sent by the devil. God himself saith to such unlearned priests, Hos. iv. 6, "because thou hast refused knowledge, I have refused thee that thou shalt be no priest unto Me."

And to enquire what measure of knowledge is needful for him to have, the schoolmen say he must have *competentem*, 'competent,' if not *eminentem scientiam*, 'knowledge in an eminent degree;' and what competent knowledge is, we may see Tit. i. 9, in these three points; he must be able to

a. hold fast the faithful word according to knowledge;

β. exhort and comfort, and that with wholesome doctrine;

γ. improve and confute them that say against it.

thirdly, to have a care of the manner of his doctrine;

As he must be an example in his life, and teach them by his learning, so he must have a care of the manner of his doctrine, in what sort he doth teach.

We read of three faults that fell into the church in the apostle's time;

1, *φιλομυθία*, 2 Tim. iv. 4, 'a desire to hear fables;' when a man is soon full, and cannot abide to hear of a thing often, but will have new; as 2 Cor. xi. 4, they must have *alium Jesum*, 'another Jesus' or Saviour;

2, Tit. iii. 9, they did *κενοφωνεῖν*, they must 'have questions to no profit,' and decidings of high and nice points;

3, they had *pruritum aurium*, 'itching ears,' 2 Tim. iv. 3; a desire to hear an eloquent declamation out of a pulpit; to have a period fall roundly, pleasing the ear, and doing the soul no good.

Against these the apostle setteth down a form for the preacher to follow;

1, that which he teacheth must be wholesome and uncorrupt doctrine, Tit. ii. 1, 7;

2, he must not meddle with things of no profit, but he must intend the people's good by his preaching;

3, for the delivery it must be with learning; as 2 Cor. xi. 6, "though rude in speech, yet not in knowledge;" and he must not only have *vetera*, 'old matters,' but *nova*, 'new;' not new doctrine, but new ways of expressing, and new arguments;

4, and he must also use a plain and perspicuous order, and an orderly delivering of it, which is called *ὀρθοτομία*, 'a dividing of the word aright;'

5, and according to that, Heb. iv. 12, "the word is a two-edged sword," it is a special point in preaching that their words must have two edges, for else the back commonly doth as much hurt as the edge doth good. And that is when they do not meet with both extremes; as when they speak of obedience, they deal as if they would take away all disobedience, and would have a man never to disobey; and when they speak of peace, they do it so as if we should have peace with all men and be at variance with none; whereas with the wicked we must have no peace;

6, and lastly, the minister must deliver the word, Tit. ii. 7, *ἐν ἀδιαφθορίᾳ*, with authority, gravity, and majesty; as knowing that it is not his own word, but the everlasting truth of God.

fourthly, to reprove and confute.

As he must be of good life, and sufficient learning to teach, and must teach them after a right and good order; so with his teaching them that which is good, he must

reprove the offenders, and

improve and confute them that are contrary minded.

1. For the manner of his reproving, he must

1.) first *arguere*, and then *redarguere*, first 'prove' the fault, and then 'reprove' it; and,

2.) in regard of the person offending,

α. if they be only led by a disposition to a fault, then *ἐν πρᾳότητι*, 'in humility,' 2 Tim. ii. 25;

β. if it be done in contempt, then *μετὰ πάσης ἐπιταγῆς*, 'with all authority,' Tit. ii. 15;

γ. if the parties be froward of nature, then *ἀποτόμως*, 'roundly and sharply,' Tit. i. 13;

δ. if it be a public fault, then 1 Tim. v. 20, *ἐνώπιον πάντων*, reprove him 'openly,' that others may fear.

2. For improving or confuting the adversary,

α. if it may be, to stop his mouth, Tit. i. 11;

β. if that cannot be, yet Tit. ii. 8, that he may be confounded;

γ. if not that, yet Tit. iii. 11, that inwardly he may be convinced in his conscience, "condemned of himself;"

δ. if that will not be, yet 2 Tim. iii. 9, that his madness

may be made manifest, and the hearers may see his folly.

The people's duty in respect of all this pains of the minister is, to yield him 'double honour,' as it is, 1 Tim. v. 17;

1, the honour of reverence, Phil. ii. 29, both in judgment and in affection;

2, the honour of maintenance, to make them partakers of all our goods.

Of magistrates.

After the fatherhood of the church, order requireth that we speak of *patres patriæ*, 'the fathers of the country,' magistrates, who are nursing fathers and mothers in God's church and in the commonwealth.

How there came to be magistrates.

It appeareth by three actions of God,

by the judging the angel,
the man, woman, and serpent; and
the punishment of Cain,

that authority first and principally pertaineth to God, which afterwards came to man by God's approbation and appointment.

The power ecclesiastical would have been sufficient to have governed the world, but that Cain building a city, Gen. iv. 17, made the godly first take order for their defence; and so city against city was the occasion of civil government, because some men, like the horse and mule, Ps. xxxii. 9, would still be offering violence and injury if there were not a power to bridle them.

Now seeing they must have government, the main reason why they would be under one man, and give *potestatem vitæ et necis*, 'power of life and death,' to one particular, was, *præstat timere unum quam multos*, ''tis better to fear one than many;' better one wolf than a great many, and so a man's life to be continually in hazard of every man.

After the flood God gave the sword into man's hand, Gen. ix. 6, to shed the blood of him that should shed another man's blood; and then Sem, called Melchizedek king of Salem, took upon him to defend God's people from Nimrod and his fellow-hunters.

Office of a magistrate generally.

The magistrate is called also a shepherd, and he must feed the people as well as the minister, Gen. xlix. 24, Joseph; Ps. lxxviii. 71, David; Numb. xxvii. 17, Joshua; and he must look, Ezek. xxxiv. 18, 21, that the fat sheep do not trample and spoil the grass with their feet, so that the lean can eat nothing; nor trouble the water that they cannot drink; neither strike at them with their horns, but that they may feed quietly without disturbance.

And as they must have a care of them that are in the inside of the fold, to feed the flock within; so to keep away the wolf without; that is to say, to keep and preserve them from foreign invasions; and so to be right nursing fathers and mothers unto them. We have a good example in an evil king, 1 Sam. xi. 5; Saul hearing the people that they were sorrowful and wept, "what aileth this people that they weep?" saith he; a good pattern for all kings, *videre ne quid sit populo quod fleat*, "to have a care that his people be not disquieted, that they may not weep.'

Magistrates are either { βασιλεὺς, 'the king,'
ἡγεμόνες, 'under-officers.'

The reason of the under-officers is, Exod. xviii. 13, because Moses, or one man, cannot hear all; approved by God himself, Numb. xi. 16.

Qualifications of a magistrate.

Now what manner of men should magistrates be? surely such as are called by God; according to that rule, Deut. xvii. 15, *quem Deus elegerit*, 'whom the Lord thy God shall choose;' and he whom God calleth must be thus qualified;

1, he must not be affected to Egypt, which is the nursery of idolatry; not affected to false religion, Deut. xvii. 16;

2, he must not be uxorious, voluptuously given to pleasure, Prov. xxxi. 3, 4; wine and women are not for kings and princes;

3, he must not gather gold and silver, that is, he must

not be covetous, Deut. xvii. 17; it was Solomon's fault, 1 Kings xii. 4.

Duties of a king.

And being thus qualified, and so meet for a kingdom, and set in his seat, his duties are,

first, to acknowledge his power to be from God;

To acknowledge himself to be there not by himself, but by God; *per me reges regnant,* 'by Me kings reign,' saith God. And so their style runneth, *Cæsar Dei gratiâ,* 'Cæsar, or chief governor, by the grace of God;' and that therefore their power is not *arbitraria,* 'arbitrary,' or at their own pleasure, but *delegata,* 'delegate' and put upon him by God; and therefore he must say with the centurion, Matt. viii. 9, "I myself also am under authority;" they are under God, and therefore must so rule as God himself would rule; and how is that? even as His word prescribeth and no otherwise.

The duty of the subject answerable is, to acknowledge him to be God's deputy,—1 Sam. x. 26, "there went with him a band of men whose hearts God had touched"—and to reverence him accordingly.

secondly, not to break into God's right;

The second duty of the prince is,—Seeing God hath been so liberal to Cæsar as to make him king and His deputy, he must not requite Him by breaking into that which is God's peculiar; for we see our Saviour maketh a division, *quæ Cæsaris, quæ Dei,* 'some things to Cæsar, some to God;' as namely the court of conscience; the Lord only keepeth His court there; and therefore the king must not *dominari conscientiæ,* he must command nothing to any man against his conscience; yet those whose consciences are not well instructed, they must labour to rectify them, and if they be obstinate, and will not yield to religion, they must compel them, Luke xiv. 23; and if there be not *intus voluntas,* 'a will within,' there must be *foris necessitas,* 'a necessity laid on them by others;' and therefore let papists come and hear, that they may be caught.

And generally, he must *pascere populum*, 'feed the people,' that is, provide for them,

1, for their souls, that preachers be sent into all places; 2 Chron. xvii. 9, Jehoshaphat;

2, for their bodies, he must

lay up corn against a dearth, and see there be plenty, Gen. xli. 49, Joseph;

send ships abroad, for outward and foreign commodities, 2 Chron. ix. 21, Solomon;

and for inward right to all men at home, provide judges, as Jehoshaphat, 2 Chron. xix. 5;

and to avoid wrongs from abroad, provide soldiers, 2 Chron. xvii. 2.

The people's duty answerable to these is,

1. That they break not into God's right, neither take the sword out of the king's hand; nor be seditious, or disobedient unto him; Prov. xxiv. 21, "fear God and the king, and be not seditious."

2. In regard of their care over us, we must not *dare*, 'give,' but *reddere Cæsari quæ sua sunt*, 'render to Cæsar that which is his due;' that is, because they keep our tillage safe, they must have tribute out of our lands, and because they keep the sea safe, they have *vectigal*, 'custom,' and *censum*, 'subsidy,' out of our goods; and in time of necessity, indiction or tax, as Solomon, 1 Kings xi. 28.

thirdly, to do justice;

The third duty of the king is, in cases of appeal to do justice himself; for that is it that must establish his throne, Prov. xvi. 12; and without it *magna regna*, 'great kingdoms,' are nothing else but *magna latrocinia*, 'great robberies.'

And in his justice he must look,

1, that the righteous may flourish, and that *bonis omnia benè*, 'they which do well may have well,' Prov. xi. 10;

2, to the wicked his looks must be terrible in judgment, Prov. xx. 8, that so he may drive away evil, Deut. xiii. 8; for capital crimes, *non parcat illis oculus tuus*, 'let not thine eye spare them.'

The people's duty herein is, in respect of his justice to fear him, Prov. xvi. 14, "the wrath of a king is as messengers of death, but a wise man will pacify it;" Prov. xx. 2, "the fear of a king is as the roaring of a lion; whoso provoketh him to anger sinneth against his own soul."

fourthly, to be humble and meek in ruling.

The fourth duty of the king is humility and meekness in ruling; to use his power meekly and mildly; not as Pilate, John xix. 10, "I have power to crucify thee, and I have power to loose thee;" but every magistrate should do well to say with Paul, 2 Cor. x. 8, "I have no power to hurt, but to do good; to edification, and not to destruction."

It is the difference that a heathen man maketh between a good king, and a tyrant; a tyrant saith, *ἔξεστί μοι*, "I may do it, and I will do it:" the good king saith, *καθήκει μοι*, "I must do it, it is my duty, I pray you pardon me."

To conclude, *pauciora licent illi, quam ulli, cui licent omnia*, 'he who may do all things, may indeed do less than any man.' And if he will not be mild, but of an austere, cruel behaviour to his people, they may well fear him, but sure they will not love him, and then *φόβος*, 'fear,' may well breed *κολακείαν*, 'flattery,' but not *εὔνοιαν*, true 'good will.'

The people's duty to such a mild king is,

1. (not to fear him, but) to be afraid of him, that is to say, in their love to him to be afraid lest any hurt should come unto him, as the people were afraid of David, 2 Sam. xviii. 3;

2. and another duty of the people is, to bear with the infirmities of this mild king, and to be as meek toward him in covering his uncomeliness if any be, Exod. xxii. 8; unless it be some enormous sin, or that he be a troubler of Israel, 1 Kings xviii. 18.

Thus much of the king's duty.

The under-officers' duty is, to be in all things serviceable, aiding and assisting to the king in the execution of his several duties afore-mentioned, according to their authorities in their several places.

And the people's duty answerable is, to reverence, obey, fear, and love them as deputies of the king himself.

Other kinds of excellency.

From magistrates, we come to those that have in them an excellency above others, though it be separated from the estate of government, yet it maketh them worthy of honour.

And this excellency is in respect of one of these three goods;

of the mind, which they call *excellentiam doni*, 'the excellency of some inward gift;'

of the body, as old age;

of the outward estate, as nobility, wealth, &c.

Excellency of mind.

First, for the gifts of the mind.

Those that have the gift of inventing crafts and sciences, as Jubal did music, Gen. iv. 21, are therefore called fathers. These gifts of the mind are they which the schoolmen call *gratiæ gratis datæ*, *χαρίσματα*, 'free gifts of God;' and wheresoever they fall into any man, he is to be honoured for them; because, though these be not the very fear of God, neither make a man any thing more holy, yet in respect they are for the profit of the whole body, they are to be honoured, and he for them; and much more then is he to be honoured in whom is *gratia gratum faciens*, as they call it, the true fear of God and grace indeed.

What honour we owe to men of great gifts;

Now let us see what is the duty and reverence that we owe unto such men that have those gifts?

first, to acknowledge their gifts;

Acknowledgment of their gifts, and to commend them, and to praise God for bestowing them, and not to think, that *qui auget alienam famam detrahit suæ*, 'he who advanceth another man's fame detracts from his own.' If the prophet Ezekiel had been of that mind, he would not have commended Daniel living in his own time, for fear of impairing his own credit, Ezek. xxviii. 3. So John baptist of Christ, "I am not worthy to unloose His shoe latchet; He must increase, I must decrease," as the morning star doth when the sun is up.

Contrary to this, we, like Saul, cannot abide that any man's thousands should be more than ours, 1 Sam. xviii. 8;

and therefore if we can, we will deny that he hath any such gift in him, or at least not in such measure as is supposed; or else we make light of the gift itself, that it is but a mean and base gift; or if the gift be such as all men see to be a rare and an excellent gift, then we begin to carp at him for some other defect, or else to charge him with the abuse of his gift, or at least, some imperfection in his life, one thing or other is still awry.

Now the duty of him that hath the gift is, 1 Cor. xv. 10, to know Who it is that hath separated him, and that he hath nothing by nature, but that he hath it was given him by God, and therefore he must be humble, Ezek. xxviii. 17; and he may humble himself, either with the defect of other gifts, or at least with the body of sin which he carrieth about him, Rom. vii. 24; that so the grace of God may not be in vain in him; and it may be in vain three ways,

- in respect of doing good in the church;
- in respect of doing himself good thereby;
- in respect of his own salvation, 1 Cor. ix. 27; if he be not humble, he may preach to others, and himself be reprobate.

secondly, to prefer those that have the greatest gifts;

The second duty that we owe to men of gifts is, to prefer those that have the greatest gifts, and to give the greatest gifts the greatest pre-eminence; for as in philosophy *bonum est eligendum, malum fugiendum,* 'good is to be chosen, evil to be shunned,' so *è bonis optimum, è malis minimum,* 'of good things we must choose the best, of evils the least.'

This was the reason of founding of colleges, because men thought if they left their lands to their kindred, they should have *hæredes promiscuos,* 'they knew not whether they should be good or bad,' but in colleges they should have *hæredes ex optimis,* 'heirs of the best choice.'

For this point of choosing the best, see 2 Kings x. 3, of Jehoram's children, *eligite optimum et aptissimum,* 'choose the best and the fittest;' Gen. xli. 39, Pharaoh to Joseph, "because God hath endued thee with the greatest wisdom."

To give some reasons in this case;

1. Whom God chooseth not, He will not bless; and He chooseth none but the best;

2. It is worse to make an Hophni, than not to correct an Hophni: Eli was blamed for not correcting; much greater had his sin been if he had put in an Hophni, whose mind is on the pot;

3. Set an unmeet workman about any thing, and the work will be in danger of marring; so by this means they do *ponere sub periculo*, 'endanger,' the souls of them that are committed to their charge.

Now the duty of the superior that is thus qualified with gifts is,

1. 1 Sam. ix. 21, to think meanest of himself of all others, and to say, 1 Sam. xviii. 18, "what am I, and what is my father's house?"

2. And if he be preferred according to his gifts, he must not think that he is fallen into the pot, that is, into a place of ease and rest, but that his place being higher, he must now do more good there than he could do in a lower place.

thirdly, to make use of their gifts.

The third duty that we owe to men of gifts is, to make use of their gifts, *eo se conferre ubi Deus est*, 'to go to one to enquire with whom God is;' Exod. xviii. 15, the people asked of God when they asked of Moses; and so 1 Sam. ix. 9, they went to the prophet to ask of God.

And the duty of him that hath the gifts is, *utendum præbere*, 'to be ready to have his talents and gifts used and employed;' and to make account, διὰ τοῦτο ζῶ, 'I live to this end, and to this purpose, to be used of others:' so saith Wisdom, Prov. ix. 4, 5, "come hither to Me;" and our Saviour, John i. 39, "come and see."

Thus much for the goods of the mind.

Excellency of body.

Now for the goods of the body, which is old age.

Our duties are,

1. To hold our peace, and give them leave to speak, Job xxxii. 6, 7; and the reason, Job xii. 12, because with the

ancient is wisdom. The contrary was Rehoboam's fault, 1 Kings xii. 6.

The duty of the aged answerable to this is, that they be not, Esay lxv. 20, *pueri centum annorum,* 'children of a hundred years old;' they must have *canum intellectum,* 'a hoary and aged understanding,' as they have *canum caput,* 'a hoary and aged head.'

But if they be not such, yet for their age we must honour them; though for their wisdom they be not worthy *hoc pati,* 'to have the honour done unto them,' yet in respect of their age it is meet for us *hoc agere,* 'to do them this honour.'

2. To rise up before them, Lev. xix. 32; because, Prov. xx. 29, old age is a glory, yea, Prov. xvi. 31, a crown of glory.

The duty of old men answerable is, that which followeth in that place, Prov. xvi. 31, that his age be found in the way of righteousness; and Tit. ii. 2, they must be sober, honest, discreet; sound in the faith, in love, and in patience.

Thus much of the goods of the body.

Excellency of estate.

Now for the outward estate of nobility, wealth, &c.

We see David, 1 Sam. xxv. 8, called Nabal, though wicked, yet because he was wealthy, 'father;' "send I pray thee to thy servant and to thy son David," saith he.

And our duty is,

1. To place them with the elders in the gate, to prefer them that are wealthy; and the reason, because *nervus reipublicæ argentum,* 'money is the sinew of the commonwealth;' there may come much benefit to the commonwealth by them, as Nehemiah had a hundred and fifty Jews at his table, Neh. v. 17.

The duty of rich men answerable is,

a. 1 Tim. vi. 18, to be willing to part with their goods; and if either he be a nobleman himself, or allied, or of acquaintance, let him help forward good causes; and especially provide for the prophets, as the woman of Shunem did, 2 Kings iv. 9, 10, a chamber, a bed, and a table, a stool, and a candlestick.

β. Again, rich men must learn not to be high minded,

nor to put their trust in their riches, 1 Tim. vi. 17, nor to count them their strong city, Prov. xviii. 11; nor to be churlish, as Nabal was to David's servants, 1 Sam. xxv. 10, nor to despise the poor.

2. The second duty of the meaner sort towards these noble or wealthy men is, to account them their fathers, and themselves their sons, as David did Nabal; and to give them honour and reverence accordingly.

Of benefactors.

There is yet one case more wherein honour and reverence is due, and that is when a man bestoweth a benefit upon us.

And in this, as in the former, consider the duties of benefactors, and of those to whom the benefit or good turn is done.

Duties of a benefactor.

The benefactor's duty is thus;

1. No man, though he be rich, is bound to every one in particular, not *in beneficio,* 'in bounty;' *in officio,* every man is bound to do some duty or other to every one, but for benefits they may make their choice. But to some they must give; and in their giving they must have this care, to do it freely; contrary to the course of giving benefits, or benefices, now a days, wherein the givers look not *ubi optimè,* 'where best,' but *ubi quæstuosissimè,* 'where most gainfully;' as if a man should bestow so much bread on his horse because he is to ride upon him, so they bestow upon such a man because they will make use of him.

2. He must give not only freely, but speedily: *bis dat qui cito dat; apage homines quorum lenta sunt beneficia, præcipites injuriæ,* 'he doth a double kindness who doth one quickly and readily; away with those men whose kindnesses are slow paced, and injuries ride in post haste;' as now the manner of men is, *profundere odium, et instillare beneficium,* 'to pour out hatred, to drop in favours, not all at once, but by little and little.'

3. When you have done a man a good turn, forget it, or at least wise upbraid him not with it.

Duties of the receiver of a benefit.

The duty of him that receiveth a benefit is,

1. To acknowledge that man to be the instrument of God in that blessing, and to let his estimation or valuation of the thing be as great after he hath it as it was before he received it.

2. The effusion of this affection upon all fit occasions. If he remember it, I need not, for *exprobratio est satisfactio pro beneficio,* 'an exprobration is a satisfaction for a kindness;' but if he forget it, I must not, but I must speak of it, and that, not extenuating it, but I must be *benignus interpres,* 'a favourable interpreter;' first, that it was a great benefit, or at least a great one to me; or if not, yet he did it with so good an affection that I cannot but think highly well of it.

3. If he ever stand in need we must do him the like good turn, if we be able; not to injure him, and then to make *finem injuriæ beneficium,* 'to think we do him a benefit by making an end of an injury;' nor as they do in policy now a days, *mergere ut extrahatur,* 'first drown them, that they may pull them out again,' and so make them beholden by plucking them out.

The contrary to these is the sin of unthankfulness, which indeed is a great vice, and abhorred even of the heathen.

But we must beware we take not that for unthankfulness which is not; for

1. *Ingratitudo est in rebus gratiæ,* 'ingratitude is seen in matters of favour,' and not *in rebus officii,* 'in matters of duty:' and therefore if he do me a matter of duty or of office, or justice, he cannot for this exact any thankfulness at my hands; but let him come to me *in re gratiæ; in beneficio, quod licet dare aut non dare, facere aut non facere,* 'in a matter of kindness; and in bounty, where he may give or not give, do a kindness or not do it;' and I will be thankful.

2. Again, he hath done me a good turn, he would have me now to follow his appetite to do some unjust thing; I will not, but refuse to consent unto him; is this unthankfulness? no, for the rule is, that the love to myself must be the rule of the love to my neighbour, and so it is not required that I should do any more for my neighbour than I would do for myself; now then, if my own appetite would lead me to any unjust thing, should I consent unto it? no, for so I should hurt myself by consenting to sin against my own soul. And so, for the pleasure he hath done me, he would have me do him a displeasure by consenting to sin by his instigation, and so hurt both his soul and mine own, and do evil for good; and in this case it is no unthankfulness though I deny him; it may be *species injuriæ*, and *species ingratitudinis, quæ sæpe incidit in virum bonum*, 'a kind of injury, a kind of ingratitude, which often may be found in a good man.' But a good man through the midst of all the infamy and reproach of his ingratitude, will *tendere ad officium*, 'be ready to do a good turn.'

Means by which a governor shall rule aright.

1, by carrying himself as he that mindeth to give account; Ps. ci. 2, "O when wilt Thou come unto me?" Jer. xiii. 20, "where is the flock that was given thee, thy beautiful flock?"

2, by first having an eye to the well governing of his own house; so Joshua saith, "I and my house will serve the Lord;"

3, his eyes must be to the faithful of the land, and his bent to choose men of wisdom and uprightness to be in authority with him; Ps. ci. 6, "mine eyes shall be upon the faithful of the land, that they may dwell with me:"

4, to esteem of all under him as citizens of the city of God, and coheirs with him of an heavenly kingdom.

Second part of the commandment, viz. the reason.

We are now come to the reason of the commandment, "that thy days may be prolonged in the land which the Lord thy God giveth thee."

This is the first particular commandment that hath a particular promise, Eph. vi. 2; and the reasons why God addeth a reason to this commandment may be these,

1, because *adorant plures orientem solem quam occidentem,* 'more men adore the sun-rising, than the sun-setting:' and old age when they have one foot in the grave are for the most part despised;

2, because as we have in our birth received the benefit of our life from our parents, as the instruments, so by our parents' blessing it might be also preserved and prolonged.

Whether dutiful children are always long lived.

Object. But our experience sheweth us that obedient and dutiful children often die betimes, and disobedient, stubborn, and contumelious children prosper and live long.

Answ. We answer with Solomon, Eccles. ix. 2, 3, "all things in this world are alike to all men;" and these outward things, as glory, riches, preferment, and long life, they are but the gift of God's left hand, and are common both to good and bad, as well as poverty and adversity; and the reason is,

1. Prosperity and riches are given to the wicked, *ne boni nimis cupidè prosequerentur,* 'lest good men should too eagerly seek after them,' and poverty and adversity is also common to the godly as well as to the wicked, *ne illa turpiter effugiantur,* 'lest in base manner we should fly from them.'

2. And again, adversity is common to both, why? because if God should send adversity to all the wicked and to none of the godly, men would think all the punishment were in this world, and that there were no judgment to come; and if He should send adversity only to His children, men would think there were no profit in serving the Almighty, and that He did not respect His children, neither had any care of them, but did quite forget them, Ps. x. 11: and therefore that He may shew He hath a providence, He will give to some of His children these good things; and that He may shew He hath a judgment to come, He giveth them also to some of the wicked; and

a. not all to the wicked, because they should not sacrifice to their net and their yarn, that is, they should not make the outward means their god, Hab. i. 16;

β. neither all to the godly, because the devil and his instruments should not say that the godly do not serve God for nought, or that they serve Him because of His blessings.

Why long life is promised to dutiful children.

Quest. But how is it then that long life is promised to those that honour their parents?

Answ. 1. We have a good exposition of this place, Deut. v. 16, where it is said, "that thy days may be prolonged, and that it may go well with thee;' so the meaning is, that so long as it may go well with them, and be a benefit unto them, so as they may live prosperously, their days shall be prolonged; but if their life come to be a displeasure to them, then to have their days lengthened will do them no pleasure, nor be any blessing to them; and life may be a displeasure,

a. in regard of the evil days, 2 Kings xxii. 20; Josias a good king taken away, because he should not see the evil days that were to come upon the land;

β. in regard of himself, for fear lest he be corrupted; and therefore, *raptus est à facie malitiæ Enoch,* 'Enoch was taken up to God from the wicked and unworthy world.'

2. When Herod promised the daughter of Herodias the half of his kingdom, Mark vi. 23, if he had given his whole kingdom, certainly it had been no breach of promise; so, if God promise *vitam prolongatam,* 'a long life,' and give *vitam perpetuatam,* 'everlasting life' for it, here is more than half in half; as he that promiseth ten pieces of silver and giveth ten pieces of gold, breaketh not his promise, so here no breach of promise in God, but performance with advantage.

3. The best and most sufficient answer is this; there is no temporal thing of this life that doth *cadere in promissum Dei,* 'come within the compass of God's promise,' but only so far forth, as it shall help and further the next life, the life to

come. This life is but *via ad vitam*, 'the way to life,' and whatsoever He promiseth us in the way, it is but to help us to the end of our journey. And therefore, as all earthly felicity is no felicity unless it dispose us to that felicity that is heavenly, so long life is no life unless it help us in the attaining of life eternal; neither is it any blessing, unless *ita disponatur de minimo, quemadmodum convenit summo*, 'the least thing be so disposed of, as that it conduceth to the greatest,' or at least so as that *periculum non fiat de maximo*, 'hazard of the greatest matter be not incurred.'

Why long life is given to the wicked.

Object. But why doth God give long life to the wicked seeing it is here promised to the godly?

Answ. For divers reasons;

1. To prove if at any time they will be brought to repentance, 2 Tim. ii. 25.

2. God respecteth their progeny; as cutting off wicked Amon, good Josiah succeeded him, 2 Kings xxi. 24; and cutting off Ahaz, good Hezekiah succeeded him, 2 Kings xvi. 20; now that these good kings might come of them, He first suffered those wicked kings to live long before they were cut off.

3. Because He must have rods of His wrath to punish His disobedient children, and for trial of His church; Esay x. 5, "O Assyrian, the rod of Mine anger, and the staff in their hand is Mine indignation."

4. Every one of us may learn an universal document from hence, Rom. ix. 22; if God, to make His wrath and power known, suffer with long patience the vessels of wrath prepared to destruction, we must learn much more to be patient and long-suffering in those injuries that are done to us.

5. To conclude this point, and so to make an end of this commandment; if God do give long life unto the wicked, He will be even with them for it another way; as we may see, Esay lxvi. 24,

a. the godly shall come forth and look upon their condemned carcasses;

β. their worm shall never die; that is, the worm of their conscience shall evermore trouble them; though their life be *longa*, 'long,' it shall not be *læta*, 'joyful;'

γ. their fire shall never be quenched;
their name shall be an abhorring to all flesh;
yea their remembrance shall be cut off, Ps. xxxiv. 16;
and their name shall rot, Prov. x. 7.

And thus much of the fifth commandment.

THE SIXTH COMMANDMENT.

Place of this commandment.

All the duties between man and man in particular pertained unto the fifth commandment; and now follow *officia promiscua*, 'duties general to all,' in the next four commandments,

- the sixth, concerning the life of man and the preservation thereof,
- the seventh, concerning chastity or the preservation of wedlock,
- the eighth, concerning his goods,
- the ninth, concerning his good name.

First, of the sixth, "thou shalt do no murder."

This commandment is put before the others which follow, because life is dearer to us than those things which pertain thereunto, and which are spoken of in the rest of the commandments.—Each man hath a good esteem of his own person; from this desire of excellency in himself, Cain killed Abel, because Abel was better than he. So Joseph's brethren hated him, because he was more made of than they, and should in time rule over them; his eminency would have seemed to darken their appearance, and clouded their splendour.

Words of the commandment.

God hath made choice of one word 'murder' to signify a whole catalogue of sins, for the helping of man's weak memory, and to shew that the under affections comprehended under the name of murder are no less odious to God than is murder itself; which if they had not been expressed in this word, would have seemed light. See Lev. xix. 17, 18, "Thou shalt not hate thy brother in thine heart; thou shalt in any wise rebuke thy neighbour, and not suffer sin upon him. Thou shalt not avenge nor bear any grudge against the children of thy people, but thou shalt love thy neighbour as thyself: I am the Lord;" Matt. v. 22—26.

Of anger in general.

St. John had an eye to this commandment through his whole epistle, but especially and plainly, 1 John iii. 15, saying, "he that hateth his brother is a murderer." And hereby he sheweth that God giveth His law to the heart (the fountain of the affections) and to the affections, as well as to the actions, for which man taketh order.

And here we may consider that the affection of anger is the gate of the devil, whereby, James iii. 16, there is a way made to strife, &c.

Anger, the first motion to murder, is when our desire and appetite is hindered, and then there is naturally *ebullitio sanguinis*, 'a disturbed rising of the blood,' and after that ὀργὴ, a 'desire' of removing that impediment.

Anger is not as some other affections, namely, envy, which doth of itself *sonare malum*, 'is of an evil sound;' as soon as a man hears it, he hates it; but anger is none of these; for it faileth not in the object as they do; but it faileth in one of these,

in the cause of our anger;
in the quantity and measure of it.

The apostle, Eph. iv. 26, hath a distinction between anger and sin, "be angry but sin not;" for indeed anger is no sin of itself, but either when we are angry

α. for no cause,
β. for a light cause, or
γ. if the cause be just, our anger is extreme, we keep no measure in it.

To be moved with indignity is a good thing, and a virtue,

called νέμεσις, when a man seeth a thing done that ought not to be done, either against God's glory, or the good estate of the church or commonwealth; and this is *ira per zelum, ira spiritûs sancti,* 'a zealous anger, and the anger of the Holy Spirit.' It was our Saviour's anger, John ii. 14, against the profaners of the temple.

Of sinful anger.

And the other is called *ira per vitium,* and *ira carnis,* 'a vicious anger,' or 'carnal anger,' when it is either

α. εἰκῆ, 'without a cause,' Matt. v. 22, or

β. not kept *intra modum,* 'within due bounds and measure,' Rom. xii. 19.

When this affection is not *ancilla rationis,* 'at the command of reason,' it becomes *radix amaritudinis,* 'a root of bitterness,' Heb. xii. 15; or if you so please to call it, *venenum serpentis,* 'the poison of the serpent.'

And this sinful wrath is either

α. at the first rising in us, or it is

β. *suppuratio vitii,* 'an impostume or inward rankling of it;' and then, if it be
against a superior, it is called a grudge;
against an equal, rancour;
against an inferior, disdain.

The grudge, if it continue a little longer, will grow
to an impostume of envy;
and the rancour to hatred;
and the disdain to contempt.

And these impostumes commonly break out into issues in the { tongue, countenance, action.

α. That which breaketh out at the tongue, they call *spumam vitii,* 'the foam or froth of it:' which
against our superiors, is *susurrus,* 'whispering and detractions;'
against our equals, ἐριθεία, 'contentious speech,' railing and brawling;
against our inferiors, scoffs, taunts, and reproaches.

β. That which breaketh out in the countenance, is called *icterus vitii,* 'the jaundice of it;' we shall know it,

- if it be to a superior, *per obliquos oculos,* 'by a wry look;'
- to an equal, it will be over all the face, pale eyes, sweating and foaming at the mouth;
- to an inferior, by a high look.

γ. That which cometh into action or execution, is called *lepra peccati,* 'the leprosy of the sin;' for it breaketh out into fighting, wars, and such like; and all these are murder's cousins.

How far this commandment reaches.

Now in this commandment is not only forbidden murder and his kindred, but there is also commanded in general that we should preserve the life of our neighbour. The Hebrews say, we should be to our neighbour *lignum vitæ,* 'a tree of life;' what that is, Prov. xi. 30, "the fruit of the righteous is a tree of life;" to deal justly, and offer no wrong, and so to have *cor sanum,* 'a sound heart;' which is the true *lignum vitæ,* the life of the body, Prov. xiv. 30, and without it our life is but a dying life, *ἄβιος βίος.*

Neither is murder of the body only, but of the soul also; and the murder of the soul is referred to two lives, this life present, and the life to come.

Now as it is accounted murder of the body if the good estate of the body be indamaged, which good estate of the body is called *incolumitas corporis,* 'the good plight and habit of the body,' and is indamaged three ways,

- *in integritate corporis,* 'in the perfectness of each member of the body,' when we are maimed and lose a leg or arm or other member;
- *in incolumitate,* 'in the safety of the body,' when we are hurt or wounded, though not so maimed;
- *in libertate motûs,* 'in freedom of going whither we will,' when we are bound or shut up in prison, and cannot use our body;—

So again, if the incolumity of the soul be indamaged, it is murder of the soul; now the incolumity or good estate of the soul is, *dilectio*, 'love;' against this cometh *odium*, 'hatred,' and all his crew or retinue;

gaudium, 'joy;' against this cometh that, when a man is so dealt withal that he falleth *in ἀκηδίαν*, 'into a slothfulness or sluggishness,' that he is unfit for any thing;

pax, peace and quietness; either,

within himself,

against which is *scandalum*, 'scandal or offence;' or

between him and other,

against which is discord and contention.

Generally therefore, whatsoever is against the life itself, or against the good estate of our life, God hath intended to comprehend in this commandment.

Of destroying life: first of beast;

Particularly to the point of killing.

A man may offend in the killing of man or beast.

The Manichees held that we might not cut down a tree, nor slip a branch of it, because there is life in it; and much less kill a beast. But this is a very fond opinion; for God before the flood gave both herbs and trees to man, Gen. i. 29; and Gen. ix. 3, whatsoever liveth and moveth is meat for man, not only herbs, but beasts also and living things; very plainly, 1 Cor. x. 25, "whatsoever is sold in the shambles, eat it."

And that the killing of beasts cannot be contained in this law, to be here forbidden, it is plain by these two reasons;

1. Where there is not *jus societatis*, 'the law of society,' there is not *societas juris*, 'an agreement in one joint law or right;' now beasts can have no right of society with us, because they want reason;

2. It cannot be sin to use things to the end for which they were ordained; now the less perfect are for the more perfect, as herbs for beasts, and herbs and beasts both for man.

Yet is not the killing of beasts absolutely in our power and liberty: but in these two cases we are forbidden to kill them;

1. When it turneth to the detriment of our neighbour; the killing of the beast of itself is not the sin, but in respect of the hurt and damage that we do therein to our neighbour;

2. We must not kill him in the impatiency of our wrath, exacting that power or understanding from him which is not in him; as Augustine saith, men must not be foolishly bent, but they must have *facilitatem motûs*, 'a more temperate motion in their anger.' If the poor pen do through their negligence or perverseness not write as they would have it, *capiunt et collidunt*, 'they take it and dash it;' so in beasts, if they do not as we would have them, we in our impatiency strike or kill them, which we ought not to do.

secondly, of man.

To come to man-killing, which is the murder here meant.

A man may offend in killing { himself, or / his neighbour.

Of killing one's self.

The heathen, as Lucretia, Seneca, Cato, though they could never have been brought to kill others, yet they durst lay hands on themselves, and are therefore highly accounted of among the heathen; but christian religion telleth us it must not be so, and that no man hath power over his own life.

1. We must remember, that the general rule of this law of the second table is, *sicut teipsum*, 'as thyself;' therefore we must needs understand it thus, *non occides alium, sicut non occides teipsum*, 'thou oughtest not to kill another, as thou killest not thyself.' And the proportion is, between the law of nature and charity: as in nature we love ourselves, so in charity we must love our neighbours; and so here, as in charity we must not kill others, so in nature we must not kill ourselves; for nature first maketh *alimentum individui*, 'sustenance to the individual,' before she give *propaginem speciei*, 'seed for propagating the kind.'

2. No man is his own, but is a part of the society or commonwealth wherein he liveth, and so cannot injure or kill himself but he brings detriment and damage to the whole company.

3. Our life is the gift of God, who "killeth and maketh alive," 1 Sam. ii. 6, and therefore we must not dispose of God's gift without the mind of the Giver: and the rather because, 1 Cor. vii. 23, we "are bought with a price," and then are we His servants that bought us; and then as, Rom. xiv. 4, "who art thou that judgest another man's servant?" so, who art thou that killest another man's servant?

It is worse than beastly to kill or drown or make away with ourselves; for Matt. viii. 32, the very swine would not have run into the sea but that they were carried by the devil.

To conclude this point with Augustine,

No man may kill himself,

a. either that he may *fugere molestias temporales,* 'fly temporal evils,' for by this means *incidit in æternas,* 'he falls into eternal evils;'

β. neither *ut evitet peccatum alienum,* 'to prevent another's sin,' for *incidit in proprium,* 'he falls into his own sin;'

γ. nor *pro suo peccato,* 'for his own sin,' for there is a time of repentance;

δ. neither *ut non peccet,* 'that he may not sin at all,' for *incidit in peccatum certum ut evitet incertum,* 'he falls into an undoubted sin in striving to avoid an uncertain sin.'

Thus much against the killing of a man's self.

Of killing another man;

Come to the next, manslaughter *in alium,* 'the killing of another man.'

The reasons against it are divers,

1. The general reason, *quod tibi fieri non vis alteri non feceris,* 'do as thou wouldest be done unto.'

2. Thou must not deface the image of God which thy neighbour beareth.

3. He is thine own flesh, Esay lviii. 7, and therefore thou must not hate him, much less kill him.

PART IV.

4. By this means thou shalt come to be *filius diaboli,* 'the child of the devil,' who was the first murderer, John viii. 44.

5. Murder is a crying sin, Gen. iv. 10, and will not cease till God take revenge.

6. It is a cursed sin; Gen. iv. 11, *maledictus Cain,* 'cursed was Cain;' and Cain's own confession was, "behold Thou hast cast me out from Thy face;" so it is excommunication, and the depriving of the grace of God.

7. God will require the blood of a man even of a beast that sheddeth it, and much more at man's hand will He require it, Gen. ix. 5.

which is aggravated by circumstances.

The killing of another man is augmented by circumstances, of the person against whom it is; as namely,

1. If it be against a public person, it is a worse and more grievous sin, because it is *peccatum in plures,* 'a sin against a great many;' and he doth what he can to put out the light of Israel, 2 Sam. xxi. 17.

2. If it be against a private man, and no magistrate, then consider, whether he be

a. near unto us in blood, or kindred, or alliance; and it is worse to shed their blood than the blood of a stranger, because *superadditur respectus,* 'there is a double respect,' both as a man, and so *homicidium;* and a father, and so *parricidium;* or a brother, and so *fratricidium;* and such like;

β. a stranger, that is not so near unto us, but removed from us: and they are either of strength to defend themselves; or weak ones, as the fatherless, the widow, and the stranger; it is worse to kill one of these, because they are destitute of power to help themselves, Exod. xxii. 21, 22.

Of those that are able to resist, it is worse to lay hands on a good man and an innocent man, than upon a wicked man: for in killing a good man, we sin, not only against charity, but against justice also, for he is *indignus,* 'unworthy of death,' and against the commonwealth too; for a good man is *κοινὸν ἀγαθὸν,* 'a common good,' and the commonwealth hath need of such; yea, we injure God himself, for Zech. ii. 8, they are as it were the apple of God's eye.

Of the restraint of this commandment.

A magistrate may take the life of his subjects;

Quest. But may not the magistrate put a man to death, notwithstanding it is said, "thou shalt not kill"?

Answ. Certainly, the nature of man is so perverse and crooked, that without *occides,* 'thou shalt kill,' *non occides,* 'thou shalt not kill,' would not be kept; and therefore a deep wound must have a new wound made, *fiat incisio, ut vitetur occisio,* 'the body must be lanced a little that it may not die of a deeper wound.' So God hath given power to magistrates, *ut sanguis fundatur, ne sanguis funderetur,* 'to shed blood, that blood may not be shed.' And as in the natural body, so in the civil body or the commonwealth, if any one part be so corrupt that it endangereth the whole, it is no cruelty to cut it off, for *melius est ut pereat unus quam unitas,* 'better one bad man than all the land perish.' And as in common fires as long as there is hope to quench it, men bring water, but when the fire is so masterful that there is no hope to extinguish it, the whole house is pulled down, and *incendium extinguitur ruinâ,* 'the fire is put out by the ruin of the whole house;' so in the civil body, less sins have less punishments, but God wills that he who killeth should die, that evil might be taken from Israel. For if blood be not satisfied with blood, two evils will follow,

1, God's wrath;

2, impunity will encourage others to do the like;

therefore God addeth the reason, for preventing this inconvenience; namely, the murderer must be punished by death, that other may hear and be afraid to commit the like sin.

Now that this may be lawfully done; it is manifest, Gen. ix. 6, that blood may be shed; and Matt. xxvi. 52, "he that taketh the sword, shall perish by the sword:" but yet every man may not use the sword at his pleasure against him that sheddeth blood, but Rom. xiii. 4, the sword is given to one, namely, the magistrate, who is there called God's minister; and he is not to bear it in vain, but to take vengeance upon evil doers. Now *quod organon est utenti, id minister est jubenti,* 'that which an instrument or weapon is to him who useth it, the same is an officer to him who is the commander;' and therefore it is not the sword, nor the minister, that is, the magistrate, but God who is *jubens,* 'the commander,' that doth shed the blood of the wicked.

And therefore for the magistrate's use of the sword; as the prince's officers, the sheriff and other, must do nothing but *ex præscripto,* 'as is prescribed them,' so the prince himself and all magistrates must have their prescript from God: now God's prescript is only against the wicked; as for the innocent man, his blood must not be shed, Exod. xxiii. 7; if it be, then as in Ahab's case for stoning of Naboth, *rex homicida,* "the king is a murderer," 2 Kings vi. 32; so of Joash for killing Zechariah an innocent prophet: but as for the murderer on the other side, *non miseraberis, non parcet oculus tuus,* 'thou shalt not pity him, thine eye shall not spare him,' Deut. xix. 13; there is an irrevocable writ gone out that every murderer must die.

though under what restriction;

Quest. Then the question is, whether any man that is a murderer may be any way executed?

Answ. And for answer, three points are necessarily to be considered in this matter;

1. It must not be *judicio privato,* 'by a private judgment;' every private man may not take it upon him, but he must be a magistrate;

2. Not *judicio usurpato,* 'by an usurped judgment;' the magistrate must be kept within his limits; Rom. xiv. 4, *quis tu qui judicas alienum servum,* 'who art thou who judgest another man's servant,' other subjects that pertain not unto him. If further than *jus gentium,* 'against the law of arms,' any be put to death, it is usurped.

3. Not *judicio temerario,* 'by rash judgment,' without lawful trial; the matter must be first enquired after and tried out, that he may be *sons damnatus,* 'a guilty man, and justly punishable;'

Acts xxiii. 35, Felix would have Paul's accusers come before he heard him; and

John xviii. 29, wicked Pilate could say, "what accusation bring you against this man?" and

Acts xxv. 16, Festus saith, "it is not the manner of the Romans to condemn any man before his accusers come face to face before him;"

and in this pleading or accusation, God will not have blood to be shed at the witness of one man, but either three, or two at the least.

In regard hereof Christ, who in respect of the godhead knew what Judas would do, yet did not exclude him from His company, because he was not yet convicted, nor his fault manifested according to God's law, so that he appeared guilty.

It is evident in the story of the Bible, that judges rash and precipitate one way will also be faulty the other way: Saul, who spared guilty Agag, put to death the faultless Gibeonites, and would have killed Jonathan upon a slight occasion; so Ahab, who would not kill the man worthy to die, 1 Kings xx. 42, yet would have Naboth, a guiltless man, murdered.

or of the subjects of another.

Object. But may the prince in no case shed the blood of those that are not under his dominion, but are *servi alieni,* 'subjects to another prince'?

Answ. Surely, yes; the magistrate hath not only a sword to see rule kept at home, but *gladium exteriorem,* 'a sword to strike some abroad;' against the wolf and enemy abroad he hath the sword of war. The whole order whereof is set down at large, Deut. xx. from the beginning to the end of the chapter; and John baptist, Luke iii. 14, doth not say to the soldiers, *abjicite arma, deserite militiam,* 'cast away your weapons, leave off your warfare,' but teacheth them their duty in war, and doth not quite take away war; therefore war is lawful.

But in war three things are required.

1. It must be *ex justâ auctoritate,* 'commanded by just authority;' Judg. i. 1, the Israelites would not go out to war

till they had authority from God and a lawful guide; so David would not fight with Goliah till Saul were first acquainted with his enterprise, 1 Sam. xvii. 37.

2. It must be in a just cause, either to defend ourselves, or to rescue others, as Abram did Lot, Gen. xiv. 15, when he had been taken prisoner, and received injury; and in this case, of injury and wrong offered by one nation to another, according to *jus gentium*, 'the law of nations,' one nation may war against another.—But here take heed it be not for every light and small injury, but to revenge some notorious wrong; as in case of religion, as they took it, Josh. xxii. 11, 12, or in weighty matters of the commonwealth, Judg. xx. 23.

3. It must be done with a right end and purpose; not to spoil and prey upon them, as Saul on the Amalekites, 1 Sam. xv. 9; but we must fight as they that fight the battles of the Lord, and let no evil be found amongst us, as David, 1 Sam. xxv. 28.—If herein we err, blood will stick to our girdle and to our shoes, as to Joab's, 1 Kings ii. 5; the thing which chiefly we are to look unto is, that we be valiant for our people and the city of our God, 2 Sam. x. 12.

Whether a private man may take away life.

Quest. But may a private man in no case shed the blood of another private man?

Answ. 1. Necessity hath no law, *necessitas est exlex;* nay more, *necessitas dicit legem legi,* 'necessity giveth law to law;' and therefore in a case of necessity, which we must take *pro impendente necessitate,* 'for a present imminent danger,' and not imminent only, but *pro termino indivisibili,* the pinch of necessity admits no evasion; in that case every man is a magistrate, and that by authority from God; Exod. xxii. 2, if a thief by night break into my house, I may kill him; and much more then to save my life. And for this reason St. Peter had a sword; and as St. Austin saith, by law a man is permitted to wear a sword, that thereby he may terrify them who would offer him violence, and to keep himself from evil and harm if he be necessitated thereunto.

But if the *terminus* be *divisibilis,* admitting a way to avoid the danger, that the necessity hath a latitude, and the danger not present, but as it was with Paul, they swore his death; we must then do as Paul did, Acts xxiii. 17, not presently run upon them, but reveal it to Lysias the chief captain; reveal it to the magistrate.

But the danger being present, I may in my own defence shed his blood that would shed mine; for I must *plus favere vitæ meæ quam alienæ,* 'tender more my own life than another man's;' and it is *inculpata tutela,* 'a defence of myself without blame,' when I cannot otherwise save myself.

2. Again, for this private shedding of blood, he that is slain is either slain of purpose, or without purpose; now as in things natural, there is *per se,* 'a thing effected with intention,' and *per accidens,* 'a thing falling out by accident; and we do not attribute to nature things that are done *per accidens,* 'by accident;' so in moral things, there is *ex intentione,* 'things done of set purpose,' and *præter intentionem,* 'beside our intent and purpose;' and it maketh neither a good nor evil action that is done *præter intentionem,* 'beside our intent.' Yea God himself, Deut. xix. 1, Exod. xxi. 13, appointeth sanctuaries of refuge for those that kill other men *præter intentionem,* 'beside their intent;' now God will allow no sanctuary for vices, and therefore if it be done without intent to hurt, God accounteth it for no sin.

But yet with these two caveats;

1. That when we do thus kill another man, we be *in opere rei licitæ,* 'in a lawful action;' for Exod. xxi. 22, if two men strive and hurt a woman with child, and death follow either of her or her child, they shall pay life for life, though it were not their intention to kill her, yet because they were about an unlawful thing, as fighting was.

2. There must not lack *debita sollicitudo,* 'a good taking heed;' there must be due care and diligence to avoid the hurting of our neighbour; for otherwise, Exod. xxi. 33, if a man dig a pit or a well, and cover it not, and another man's ox or ass fall into it, he shall make it good, because he might have taken heed before and covered the well.

Thus much of the restraint of the commandment, in what cases it is lawful to kill and to shed blood.

Of the extension of the commandment;

Now the extension of the commandment.

in respect of others;

1. Of those that willingly and of purpose commit murder,
   a, some do directly; Numb. xxxv. 16, they that with iron, wood, or stone, or any instrument, kill another; and
   β, some indirectly; by poison, witchcraft, sorcery, killing of children in the womb, taking strong and strange purgations to the end *abigere partum*, 'to hinder childbearing;'

also to be cooperator, accessary to killing, is to kill, as Matt. xx. 49, Judas to the killing of Christ;
and 2 Sam. iii. 27, Joab to Abner; and ch. xx. 9, to Amasa;
also by bringing one into danger, as Saul made David captain to the intent to have him killed, 1 Sam. xviii. 17; so David dealt with Urias, 2 Sam. xi. 15;
so to bear false witness touching life, 1 Kings xxi. 13;
so for magistrates to permit it when they may hinder it, Matt. xxvii. 24, Pilate;
and all these ways we may commit this sin, and kill another man.

and in respect of ourselves.

2. Now we may also be accessaries to our own death,

a. If we put ourselves in danger and need not; *qui amat periculum, peribit in periculo*, 'he that loveth danger, or needlessly runs into danger,' shall perish in the same;

β. Or if we do not use all lawful means to escape danger, as Christ did, Matt. iv. 6; and Paul, Acts xxvii. 31; and for this cause he adviseth Timothy to drink a little wine for his stomach's sake, 1 Tim. v. 23;

γ. In this kind a man may sin in too much care about apparel, 1 Tim. vi. 8, Rom. xiii. 14. Undue exercise, Col. ii. 23; eating the bread of carefulness, Ps. cxxvii. 2; and worldly sorrow, 2 Cor. vii. 10; and a heavy heart will dry the bones, Prov. xvii. 22, and hasten death.

δ. So also we sin when we kill ourselves by surfeiting or

drunkenness, or the undue use of any of those things which the philosophers call *non naturalia*, 'not agreeable to our nature.'

Moreover we are commanded not only to preserve the life of the body, but *incolumitatem corporis*, 'the soundness of the body,' so that no one part must be hurt; for if the least part be hurt, the whole accounteth itself hurt, and saith, *quare me*, 'why dost thou hurt me?' so that if any part be hurt, it is a breach of this commandment, Lev. xxiv. 19; and so is every wound and every stripe, of which we read, Exod. xxi. 25.

It touches soul as well as body.

Neither is the murder and hurt of the body only forbidden, but of the soul also; and this murder of the soul is much more grievous than the other of the body.

And as there are two lives of the soul, so in respect of both those lives the soul may be murdered, both in respect of this life, and of the life to come.

1. There may be a murder of the soul concerning the life thereof in this life: for when a man cometh to loathe the benefit of his life, it may be well said that his soul is killed, Eccl. vi. 3, Col. iii. 21, and he that doth any thing to a man that maketh him thus to loathe his life, that man is a murderer of the other man's soul.

2. Concerning the life of the soul in the life to come the soul may also be murdered, namely, if the soul be set in worse estate concerning the life to come,

a. by him that hath charge of souls,

Rev. ii. 14, "Balaam, who taught Balac to cast a stumbling-block before the children of Israel;"

Mal. ii. 8, "you have made many to fall;"

so also if they lay a stumbling-block before the people, or if they be negligent in their places, Ezek. xxxiii. 6, "if the watchman see the sword come, and blow not the trumpet," &c., the people's blood shall be required at their hands; also

β. one private man may murder the soul of another man,

either by giving counsel, *dicto* or *facto*, 'by word' or 'deed,' as Peter, (Matt. xvi. 22, "Master, pity thyself,") as much as in him lay, to hinder our Saviour Christ in His work of mediatorship, and to hurt His soul and all ours; or by example, Gal. ii. 13, Peter at Antioch;

or any other way giving offence to their weak brother, "one of these little ones," Matt. xviii. 6.

The pharisees thought it was no murder unless blood were shed. But we must know that the commandment is spiritual, and our Saviour telleth them, Matt. v. 22, that what the hand or arm committeth, it cometh by virtue of the motion from the heart; and therefore, Matt. xv. 19, out of the heart proceed murders; and for this cause the killing of a man is not accounted capital, Deut. xix. 6, 11, unless it proceed from hatred, which is an affection settled in the heart.

Means to avoid this sin.

For the avoiding of this sin of murder, which proceedeth of anger, consider these two points, and put them well in practice;

1, if it be our anger conceived against others, resist it; Eph. iv. 27, "give not place to the devil;"

2, if it be others' anger against us, give place unto it; Rom. xii. 19, "give place unto wrath;" as Abigail the wife of Nabal would not tell him his fault in the midst of the feast, but deferred it till the next day, 1 Sam. xxv. 37.

Now that these two may be the better put in practice, consider that anger is compounded of two things,

grief for an indignity offered,

desire to revenge and requite it.

Now if our anger stay at the grief it is well, but we must take heed of revenge; we must not say, Prov. xxiv. 29, "I will do to him as he hath done to me," but we must commit it to God to revenge, Deut. xxxii. 35; and we must be so far from revenging or desiring revenge, that if our enemy fall, we must not rejoice at it, lest God seeing it turn His wrath from him upon us;

Job xxxi. 29, "if I rejoiced at the destruction of him that hated me, or lifted up myself when evil found him;" and more plainly,

Prov. xxiv. 17, 18, "rejoice not when thine enemy falleth, and let not thine heart be glad when he stumbleth, lest the Lord see it, and it displease Him, and He turn away His wrath from him."

Of answering hard language.

Quest. But may we not answer hard and injurious words, and defend ourselves?

Answ. Surely of a fool's word *magnum remedium negligentia,* ''tis a great remedy to neglect them;' and Solomon, Prov. xxvi. 4, would have us at some times not to answer him, lest he become, *è stulto insanus,* 'of a fool a mad man;' when he is among such as himself, answer him, lest he seem wise; if he be among wise men, answer him not, and they will regard rather *quid tu taceas quàm quid ille dicat,* 'what thou art silent of than what he uttereth forth.'

Whether actions at law are allowable.

Quest. What shall we think of actions at law? must we be so far from requiting and revenging that we must not bring men to justice that have done us wrong?

Answ. In some cases we may go to law:

1. We must not be, as the pope said of England, "a good ass to bear all," for if it be a case of God's or the truth's, "strive for the truth to death;"

2. But if it be a case of *meum et tuum,* 'mine and thine,' remember what Abram did to Lot, for quietness he would yield from his own right;

3. But because by departing from our right we pluck upon us a grievouser burden than we are able to bear, and make them offer it the oftener, therefore we are allowed to have recourse to the magistrates for relief and succour; but with these rules;—

a. Not for every trifle, not *quod opus est,* but *quod necesse est,* not every thing that will bear an action, but such as if it be not remedied will breed a further inconvenience, and such as nothing but the law can remedy.

β. Before you bring the matter into *forum civile,* 'the public court of justice,' first put it to neighbours and friends among whom ye live, to end if they can, 1 Cor. vi. 4, 5.

γ. Our Saviour when He was required to deal in dividing the inheritance, Luke xii. 14, "who made Me a judge?" saith He, and presently addeth, "take heed of covetousness," verse 15; so take heed you go not to law with a covetous mind.

δ. Still keep a charitable mind to thine adversary, though the law proceed.

ε. Be advised before you go to law, as Prov. xxv. 8, "go not forth hastily to strive, lest thou know not what to do in the end when thy neighbour hath put thee to shame."

Thus much of the sixth commandment.

THE SEVENTH COMMANDMENT.

This commandment is expounded, Lev. xx. 10; and by Christ, Matt. v. 27; and by the apostle, 1 Cor. vi. 16, and chap. vii. wholly.

Place of this commandment.

The dependence of this commandment with the former is, God therefore especially did forbid murder because man was made in the image of God; now here further we may see the image of God to be in chastity and pureness; (this is so evident, that the heathen poet could say, ἁγνὸς νοῦς θεός ἐστι, *deus purus animus est;*) the pureness of this image Adam and Eve lost, and therefore got fig-leaves to cover their shame, and thereby shewed that the flesh is an enemy to chastity.

Subject of the commandment.

As the other commandment dealt with θυμὸς, 'anger,' so this with ἐπιθυμία, 'concupiscence.'

Not that every concupiscence is evil; Col. iii. 5, it is said, ἐπιθυμία κακὴ, 'an evil concupiscence,' as if there were a concupiscence or desire that is not evil; for it is lawful for every man to desire, first to preserve himself, and then his *species,* his 'kind,' but when our appetite is not kept *intra modum,* 'within due compass,' then it is evil: concupiscence, as Plato saith, hath the lowest place, and is *alligatum ventri,* 'tied to the paunch or belly,' as one would tie a horse or an ass to a manger; now being in a lower place, when the lower is most vehement, then the higher is most hindered; and as Chrysostom saith, *dedit Deus corpus animæ ut illud in cœlum eveheret, non dedit animam corpori ut illam in terram deprimeret,* 'God hath given the body to the soul that it might raise it up to heaven, and not the soul to the body that it should press it down to the earth:' so when our concupiscence is used but only for lawful propagation, to which it was ordained, that is a lawful and good and pure concupiscence; when there is *nihil alieni admixtum,* 'nothing else mixed with it.'

How it is to be here treated of.

1. Now as we see, Gal. v. 19, and by our Saviour Christ's interpretation, Mark vii. 21, that adulteries and all unclean thoughts come from the heart; so first let us consider them as they are in the heart; and that,

either *ipsum venenum,* 'the very poison of our nature,' 1 John ii. 16, "the lust of the flesh;"

or else *suppuratio,* 'an inward festering' of this desire, an inward boiling of the pot with the scum in it.

After these, when it begins to break out, the first thing is,

2. *Subactum solum,* when we make ourselves 'meet and apt ground' to receive this vice; the physicians call it *καχεξία,* when a man is disposed to an evil humour, and will still have a desire to have his body fed with that humour: now this evil humour of wicked lust and concupiscence is fed by two means,

a. by *gula,* 'gluttony,' a surcharging of the stomach, called *crapula* when it is with meat, and *vinolentia,* with drink;

β. by idleness, which is either by excess of sleeping, or defect in labour and exercise.

After this *subactum solum,* 'apt ground,' there is,

3. *Irrigatio concupiscentiæ,* 'a watering of the seed by the sin,' *lascivia, aut immodestia,* 'wantonness, or immodesty,'

and may be called *illecebra concupiscentiæ*, Prov. vii. 23, 'the snare of lust;' and it is either in the body, or from without;

a. In the body is,

πλοκὴ, 'plaiting of the hair,' and *fucus*, 'the colouring of the face;'

or in the apparel, ἔνδυσις ἱματίων;

or in the gesture, either some common gait used generally, or a certain kind of gait or gesture in the gait which they learn peculiarly to this purpose, as dancing and such like:

β. And from without our lust is watered,

either by corrupt company;

or by reading lascivious books wantonly;

or by beholding wanton pictures, or plays and spectacles of love,

or by hearkening to wanton tales, or histories or songs that nourish that humour of lust.

4. For the signs, we will use no other but those before;

a. the jaundice of it is in the eyes too, as the former was,

β. and it hath his foam *in sermone obscœno*, 'in unclean talk,' and suspicious and filthy actions.

5. The act itself, whether it be

instinctu proprio, 'of a man's own inclination,' or } it is all one.
consensu alieno, 'with another person's consent,' }

It is practised either with one or more; with more, if there be a pretext of marriage, it is polygamy, without any such pretext *scortatio;* with one alone, called 'whoredom;' and it is either in wedlock, called *fervor*, 'excess of lust,' (for there is a fault even in matrimony,) or it is out of matrimony; either with a party allied, or a stranger; if allied, called incest; not allied, either married to another, or free; if married or betrothed, it is all one, and called adultery; and is when both are married, and that is worst; or the woman only, and the man single; or the man only, and the woman single; and the second is the less evil than the third, because in the third there is *corruptio prolis*, 'a corrupting of posterity.' If she be free and not married, either we retain one peculiar to ourselves, and then she is not a common strumpet, but a concubine; or else there is not this continual keeping, and then if she be not common, it is *stuprum*, whether she be virgin or widow, especially virgin; if she be common, it is fornication properly.

Besides these, the act is either once committed; or often iterated, and then for distinction's sake, we may call it *luxuria*, and the party a whoremonger, when he sets himself after it;

Or that which is beyond this, *clamor adulterii*, 'the cry of adultery,' when they dare impudently defend it.

And last of all is permission; and that is either
- private, of a particular person for his daughter, or wife, or any of his kindred, called prostitution; or
- public, of a magistrate, in suffering and tolerating stews, as Rome doth.

Reasons against the sin of adultery.

Before we proceed, let us see some reasons against this sin of adultery, to make it odious to man, as it is to God.

1. It is of all sins most brutish, and maketh us come nearest the condition of beasts; and therefore by the prophet Jeremy adulterers are compared to neighing horses, Jer. v. 8, and Prov. vii. 22, to an ox going to the slaughter; and Deut. xxiii. 18, God himself saith, they shall not 'bring the hire of a whore, nor the price of a dog, into the house of God;' putting a whore and a dog together; and according to the mind of the learned, who compare a harlot to a bitch that many dogs follow after.

2. It taketh away the heart, Hos. iv. 11; it quite extinguisheth the light of reason, and from wantonness they grow to all uncleanness, and that with greediness, Eph. iv. 19; and brings into all manner of sin, as it did Solomon to idolatry, and David to murder.

3. It is of all sins most inexcusable; other sins may have some vizard or colour, but God having ordained a remedy for this, which is marriage, 1 Cor. vii. 2, he that will not use the remedy is without excuse.

4. It is against the church; for whereas God made marriage an holy institution, and a resemblance of Christ and His church, it is a contempt of the ordinance of God, by

making it unholy and unclean: and Mal. ii. 15, God made them one, because He sought a godly seed; and therefore they that seek any more but one, do as much as they can to hinder God's purpose, that He shall have no godly seed, no church.

5. It is against the commonwealth; Lev. xviii. 28, "shall not the land spew you out if you defile it?" so the translation of the commonwealth cometh by pollution of the land.

6. It is against the whole state of mankind; for whereas marriage is for increase of mankind, they that commit adultery shall not increase, Hos. iv. 10; and so as much as in them lieth, they destroy all mankind, and are *delinquentes in genus humanum*, 'trespassers against the whole estate of mankind.'

7. (because every man respecteth his own particular)

a. It is against a man's body; first, by defiling it, yea, the very garments are spotted, Jude v. 23; and secondly, by weakening and decaying it, as the physicians say;

β. and it is also against his soul, Prov. vi. 32; he that doth it destroyeth his own soul.

8. It is not only against himself, but against others also; for in other sins he may *perire solus*, 'perish alone;' but in this he must have one to perish with him for company.

9. It is injurious to Christ, and that two ways;

a. Christ having paid a price for him, he dealeth injuriously to alienate that which is not his own;

β. being a christian, and Christ his Head and he a member of Christ, he uniting himself to a harlot doth what he can to bring Christ into the body of a harlot.

10. If all these will not move us, then consider the punishment of it;

a. first, it is a punishment itself for those whom God hateth, Prov. xxii. 14; he with whom the Lord is angry shall fall therein, as a punishment to his name and fame, Prov. vi. 33, his reproach shall never be put away;

β. it wasteth his substance, Prov. xxix. 3; yea it shall be a fire to pursue him and all his increase to destruction, Job xxxi. 12;

γ. and lastly, that which is beyond all these, Rom. i. 24, it is one of the punishments of idolatry, and therefore a greater sin than idolatry is, (for every punishment must exceed that whereof it is a punishment, or else the punishment would be a greater allurement to the sin;) and 1 Cor. vii. 12, if any will dwell with an idolater she may, but not with an adulterer; and v. 14, the children of an idolater may be holy and have place in the congregation, but as for adulterer's children, Deut. xxiii. 2, a bastard shall not enter into the congregation of the Lord, even to his tenth generation he shall not enter.

Particulars of the sin.

And now to return to the particulars of the sin.

1. *The festering.*

To begin with the festering of it, which the apostle 1 Cor. vii. 9, calleth 'burning;' and Hos. vii. 4, 'as an oven heated by the baker, so is an adulterer.'

2. *The prepared ground.*

When it begins to break out, the first thing we do is to make ourselves *subactum solum,* to make the 'soil fit' by feeding the evil humour that lay festering before; which we shewed to be by gluttony, and idleness.

Namely, 1) *by gluttony: whether in Meat;*

Gluttony we shewed to be in meat or drink.

In meat, *crapula,* 'feeding too much.' *Gula vestibulum luxuriæ,* 'the throat' or gluttony is the gallery that lechery goes through, and that by reason the faculties stand so, that *nutritiva est officina generativæ,* 'the nutritive faculty is the shop of the generative;' and that being looked to, there is hope the other may be the better dealt withal. It was one of the sins of Sodom, Ezek. xvi. 49, "fulness of bread;" and *venter bene pastus cito disponit ad libidinem,* 'the belly full fed quickly disposeth a man to lust,' saith Jerome upon that place.

reasons against it;

It is injurious to God in destroying His creatures;

a. Luke xv. 13, the prodigal son's fault; it will bring a man to poverty, Prov. xxiii. 21; it decayeth the health and hasteneth death, and nothing sooner than gluttony and surfeiting; we read, Numb. xi. 34, of "graves of lust;" surfeiting is a grave of lust.

β. In the soul, it maketh sermons and all exercises of godliness unfruitful, Luke viii. 14; for Luke xxi. 34, it oppresseth the heart, and maketh it heavy by the fuming up of the meat and drink: yea, it hardeneth the heart; Amos vi. 6, they had no sorrow for the affliction of Joseph, though they themselves drunk wine in bowls: yea, Deut. xxxii. 15, when "my fatling was well fed," saith Moses, *recalcitravit*, 'it spurned with the heel,' and "forsook God that made him."

how it is to be avoided.

To avoid these mischiefs, take Paul's example, 1 Cor. ix. 27; beat down your own body; and one manner of beating it down is, *per damnum*, 'by hindering it' of some commodity that it would have. The servant who is delicately fed will be checkmate with his master, Prov. xxix. 21; a pampered horse will be hard to rule, Ecclus. xxx. 8: so the flesh being too much cherished will kick against the soul; we must do with it as we do with beasts that we will keep under, take away the provender; so in effect it is temperance. It is *φωνὴ τῆς σαρκὸς*, 'the voice of the flesh,' *μὴ πεινᾷν, μὴ διψᾷν, μὴ ψύχεσθαι*, 'let me not be hungry, let me not be athirst, let me not be cold:' when we grow wanton and will not have it in this dish, or we will not eat unless it be thus drest, then *venter est molestus cliens*, 'the belly is an earnest and impatient suitor;' but if having food and raiment we can be therewithal contented, this is the right temperance. Meat is for the belly; and we be debtors to the flesh, but yet we must not live after the flesh: she must not be accustomed to have what she will call for, and never be broken of her desire and appetite, for thereby we shall never be quiet, because after a little while the bridle of temperance will hardly curb her.

Rules of temperance, both general;

Now temperance consisteth in *modo,* 'measure;' and that *modus, in medio,* 'in the mean or middle;' and that is known *per regulam,* 'by rule;' and the rule therefore of temperance is threefold;

1', *necessitas vitæ,* 'the necessity of our life;' our life necessarily requires but convenient food and raiment, 1 Tim. vi. 8:

2, *necessitas officii,* 'the necessity of our calling;' he that is *athleta,* that proveth masteries, must be abstinent and keep a strait diet, 1 Cor. ix. 25; and so a student, and he that will be contemplative; a husbandman must have more, and so our direction must be for our diet, as our employment is;

3, *voluptas quæ neutrum horum impedit,* 'pleasure which hindereth none of these;' but if it be more than is convenient for the maintenance of our life, or for our necessary duties and employments in our several places, it is sin.

According to these rules wo must temper our desire, and give temperance the bridle, that she may *constringere et relaxare,* 'hold in or let loose' the reins; as Augustine saith, *temperantia frænos gutturis constringit et relaxat,* 'temperance pulls in or lets go the bridle of our appetite.'

and particular;

And that we may govern and temper ourselves the better in our diet, consider these five points;

1. The substance; not every day λαμπρῶς with the rich glutton, 'delicately,' Luke xvi. 19. The Israelites were weary of manna, and must needs have quails, Numb. xi. 6; but Daniel and his companions, pulse served their turn, and yet they looked never the worse, Dan. i. 12; and Elijah's provision was but a cake and a pot of water, 1 Kings xix. 6; and Elisha provided but a great pot of pottage for the children of the prophets, 2 Kings iv. 38.

2. The quantity; they that have taken the measure of our throat and other instruments, say that it is less than in other

creatures of answerable proportion, to teach us temperance, and to beware of superfluity, either

a. by surcharging our nature, Hos. vii. 5, or

β. by exceeding our estate; it was Nabal's fault, 1 Sam. xxv. 36, he was a note too high in his feast, he made a feast like a prince.

3. The quality; beware of exquisiteness, Luke x. 41, Martha's fault; we must not make our belly our God, Phil. iii. 19.

4. Eat not too greedily; for this is *os porci habere,* 'to have the snout of an hog;' and this made the devil make choice of the herd of swine to enter into, because of their greediness; they were like cormorants given to devouring, as he himself is, and so like unto him. It was Esau's fault, saith Augustine, *ardenter comedere,* 'to eat ravenously;' for needs must he fall to his meat roundly, who longed after it so greedily that he would part with his birthright to purchase it.

5. Eat not too often; and for that, we must have recourse to the former rules *vitæ et officii,* 'of our life and our calling;' not so often as to hinder our health, not so often as to hinder our calling; not too early, Eccl. x. 16, not too late, Esay v. 11, "woe to them that rise up early to follow drunkenness, and continue until night till the wine do inflame them."

or in Drink.

The same fault is in excess of drink, as before was in excess of meats; *vinolentia,* 'drunkenness,' as ill as *crapula,* 'gluttony,' Eph. v. 18.

And it is the high way to this sin, of adultery, Prov. xxiii. 31, 33; first he saith, "look not upon the wine when it is red, and sheweth his colour in the cup, or goeth down pleasantly;" and what followeth? "thine eyes shall look upon strange women, and thine heart shall speak lewd things."

And therefore St. Peter doth not only forbid drunkenness, 1 Pet. iv. 3, but drinkings; whether they be such as inflame us, Esay v. 11, or whether by using it we get such a habit that we are strong to do it; for though we be so strong that we can keep ourselves from being drunk, yet there is a woe pronounced against this strength, Esay v. 22, "woe to them that are strong to pour in strong drink."

The inconveniences following thereupon are,

1, these drinkers shall never be wise, Prov. xx. 1;

2, and never rich;

3, they are disposed to sin, sometimes against their will, sometime with it, Gen. xix. 33, Prov. xxiii. 32, 33; and wine makes them as men sleeping in the midst of the sea, and on the top of a mast, in danger and not sensible of it.

For we are not altogether tied from the use of wine; but that we may lawfully drink wine;

1. For the help of a weak stomach and for often infirmities, 1 Tim. v. 23, we may use wine; but it must be "a little wine," take heed of excess.—Here they are to be blamed who lay hold on that the apostle saith, "drink wine," but neglect the rest, "a little wine," and regard not the cause, "for infirmities' sake."

2. To ease the heaviness of the mind; Prov. xxxi. 6, "give wine to them that have grief of heart."

3. In a public benefit, for a public gratulation, we may eat the fat and drink the sweet, Neh. viii. 10.

And to this purpose we may also apply and make use of the five rules of temperance.

Thus much of gluttony.

2) *by idleness.*

The second feeder of lust is idleness, Ezek. xvi. 49. It was one of the sins of Sodom; a sin highly displeasing to God, as well in regard of the breach of the next commandment, as also in respect of the loss of time, and that, either by too much sleeping, or by not being exercised in our callings; as appeared in David, 2 Sam. xi. 2; hence Amos vi. 4, they are blamed who stretched themselves upon their beds.

1. For the first point, too much sleeping; Rom. xiii. 13, "walk honestly, as in the day; not in gluttony and drunkenness, neither in chambering and wantonness;" when he hath been in *κώμοις*, 'gluttony,' and in *μέθαις*, 'drunkenness,' then he comes to *κοίταις*, which we translate 'chambering,' but it is

properly 'lying in bed,' long lying; and there is joined with it ἀσέλγεια, 'wantonness,' the beginning of concupiscence, Amos vi. 4, "they stretch themselves upon their beds." And it is the way also to poverty, to love sleep, Prov. xx. 13.

For the quantity of our sleep, it must not be too long; Prov. vi. 9, "how long wilt thou sleep, O sluggard?" It must not be the sluggard's sleep.

For the manner, it must not be dead sleep, as Jonas' sleep was in time of danger, Jon. i. 5; not *sepultura suffocati*, 'the burial of one suffocated,' but *requies lassi*, 'the rest of a wearied man,' as Jerome saith.

2. For the second point of idleness, not being exercised in our callings, but giving ourselves to ease, it is the way

a. to bring us to "hands hanging down," and to "weak knees," Heb. xii. 12; and

β. to corrupt the body; as water standing still will putrify and breed toads and venomous things, so ease will breed diseases; and therefore, 2 Thess. iii. 11, they are condemned that work not, and are exhorted to work and eat their own bread, as if their bread were not their own if they live idly and work not.

3. *The watering of concupiscence;*

Thus much of *subactum solum*, 'the ground fitted;' now followeth *irrigatio concupiscentiæ*, 'the watering of concupiscence.'

For as we must keep ourselves from being a meet mould, or fit ground, for the devil to cast in this seed of lust or evil concupiscence; so we must also beware of those objects and allurements that do *irrigare concupiscentiam*, 'water concupiscence.'

And those allurements we consider,

as they are in ourselves and our own bodies, or
as they are in others and without us.

by allurements in ourselves;

The allurements in ourselves and about our own bodies are,

1. *Adhibere fucum,* 'use painting;' it was Jezebel's vice, 2 Kings ix. 30, "she painted her face, and tired her head," so Jer. iv. 30, "they painted their faces and eye-brows."

2. To disguise ourselves in apparel, 1 Tim. ii. 9, and 1 Pet. iii. 3; condemned even in women, which are rather to be allowed in it than men, because it is *mundus muliebris,* 'womanish adorning;' but St. Peter hath two reasons against it;

a. "let the hid man of the heart be incorrupt," as if he should say, as Cato said, *magna corporis cura magna mentis incuria,* 'great care of our bodies causeth a great carelessness of the soul;'

β. "the saints in old time" did not thus apparel themselves; follow their example, ver. v.

3. The gesture must be looked unto; Micah ii. 3, a plague is threatened against those that have a proud gait: and the prophet Esay, iii. 16, goes to particulars; they are haughty, they go on tiptoes; they have stretched out necks; rolling eyes; a mincing and a tinkling gait.—*Gestum natura dat,* 'the inward temper of the mind is described by the gesture;' there is a generation whose eyes, saith Agur, are haughty: yet grace can mend the defects of nature, therefore none may be excused who neglect the means of grace.

or by allurements without us.

The allurements without us, or the watering of our lust by those provocations that are without and beside the body, do now follow.

1. David, Ps. l. 18, reckoneth one, that is to say, being partakers, keeping company, with adulterers; for Prov. vii. 22, the young man entering into company and communication with an harlot, followed after, like an ox to the slaughter, and a fool to the stocks. And indeed company is very dangerous in this sin, as we see, 1 Cor. v. 6, " a little leaven leaveneth the whole lump;" it may be applied to any vice, but St. Paul there applieth it particularly to this sin, shewing that this vice hath a special virtue to infect and leaven others. And therefore beware of evil company, and not only evil but suspicious company, and at suspicious times; refrain not only

the evil, but that which hath *speciem mali,* 'any show of evil,' 1 Thes. v. 21, 22.

2. After company may come evil books, that speak broadly of filthy matters. These are of the same nature with ill company: the heathen man called his books his *comites,* 'companions;' he was *solus,* 'alone,' and yet he had his *comites,* a book or two; and so having their company, he was *nunquam minùs solus quàm cùm solus,* 'never less alone than when he was alone.'

Evil books contain many evil words, and 1 Cor. xv. 33, "evil words corrupt good manners:" evil words we call these, "stolen waters are sweet," "hidden bread is pleasant;" and Prov. vii. 18, "let us take our pleasure in dalliance;" and such like.

3. To company and evil books, may be added such things as by the eye and ear work the same impressions in the soul, as namely,

a. pictures; *imagines obscœnæ,* 'wanton pictures,' such as Baal Peor, Num. xxv. 18, to stir up wicked and lustful thoughts; and by analogy thereunto,

β. all wanton dancings, Mark vi. 22, or stage-plays, or things appertaining to them: because, our eyes therein do behold vanity, Ps. cxix. 37; a man cannot take fire in his bosom but his clothes will be burnt, Prov. vi. 27, nor a man cannot touch pitch but he shall be defiled, nor see wanton actions but his affections will be moved.

4. *The signs of concupiscence.*

We come now to the signs.

The signs of this sin are { in the eye, in the speech.

1. For the eye, Matt. v. 28, looking upon a woman to lust after her is adultery before God; and 2 Peter ii. 14, some men have "eyes full of adultery;" Gen. xxxiv. 1, the Egyptians looked upon Abram's wife, and fell into this sin, Gen. xii. 14; and therefore, Prov. vi. 25, "let her not take thee with her eye lids."

2. For the speech, which is the froth or foam of this sin,

it is forbidden, Eph. iv. 29, by the name of σαπρὸς λόγος, 'rotten or corrupt communication;' and if idle words shall be accounted for, Matt. xii. 36, much more wanton and broad speeches of filthy matters; or to speak too plain even of lawful duties of marriage. We see the Holy Ghost useth very modest words that way, and seeketh out choice terms, as Gen. iv. 1, "Adam knew Eve his wife;" and Gen. xviii. 11, it ceased to be with Sarah after the manner of women; and 1 Cor. vii. 3, it is called 'due benevolence' from each of them to the other.

5. *The act of incontinency.*

The sin of incontinency is committed, either with more than one, or with one alone.

1. With more, either without law, or with colour of law.

a. Without all colour of law, is *scortatio*, 'whoring;' Deut. xxiii. 17, forbidden, and in the ver. 18, the whore compared to a bitch, and the whore-keepers to a number of dogs. For the punishment of it, Gen. xxxviii. 24, the law of nature did award it death, to be burned; and God himself, Heb. xiii. 4, will punish it, "whoremongers and adulterers God will judge;" and if the civil punishment of the law take not so severe hold of it, God himself will judge it, both in the world to come, Rev. xxi. 8, and in this life with strange and extraordinary judgments, as *lues gallica*, 'the french pox,' an abominable and filthy disease not heard of in former ages.

β. Under colour of law, or with pretext of marriage, is polygamy; wherewith sundry of the patriarchs were entangled, yielding to the corrupt customs of the country about, not enquiring God's will.

1) The creation is plain, Gen. i. 27; and plainer, Matt. xix. 5, for there the number is set down expressly, "they twain shall be one flesh;" and Mark x. 11, "if a man put away his wife and marry another, he committeth adultery against her."

Object. And whereas they object and allege that it was lawful at the first, for increase of children and propagation of the world;

PART IV.

Answ. We say for answer, that indeed if ever it had been to be allowed, it was in the beginning, but the prophet Malachi, ii. 15, calleth men to that, *non fuit sic ab initio,* 'it was not so from the beginning;' and saith, that God having plenty of spirit, yet He made but one; and wherefore one? because He sought a godly seed; and therefore polygamy unlawful for any age that should come after.

2) The first that the Holy Ghost noteth to have two wives, was wicked Lamech, of Cain's race, Gen. iv. 19; and though Jacob had so also, he learned it in Padan Aram, among the idolaters.

3) The prophets have spoken against it; and Christ himself against it; and the apostle, 1 Cor. vii. 2, let every woman have *ἴδιον ἀνδρὰ,* 'her own husband,' and every husband have *τὴν ἑαυτοῦ γυναῖκα,* 'his own wife;' and therefore whatsoever cavils have been devised to defend it, it is unlawful.

2. With one alone this sin of incontinency is committed; and that,

a) First in wedlock, and causes matrimonial; for we are not left to ourselves in matrimony, to use ourselves or them as we list.—But because here we fall into infinite questions, and not very pertinent to this place, we will therefore here content ourselves only with these few considerations touching marriage;

α. we must have Abram's care, Gen. xxiv. 3, not to match with the Canaanites, with the wicked; but as Paul saith, 1 Cor. vii. 39, *in Domino,* 'in the fear of God,' and His true religion;

β. consent of parents must be had, 2 Sam. xiii. 13;

γ. as God brought Eve to Adam, Gen. ii. 22, so desire she may come by the hand of God;

δ. (which more nearly concerneth this place) in marriage we must so behave ourselves, as 1 Cor. vii. 29, having a wife as if we had her not, and, in the fifth verse, being content to master our lusts so that for duties of christianity we may separate ourselves; and at no time in her disease, *in mensibus,* to approach unto her;

ε. not departing from her or divorcing ourselves, but only in case of adultery, as our Saviour's rule is, Matt. v. 32;

ζ. after we are delivered by the death of one party, 1 Cor. vii. 40, so to abide if we can; or at least not quickly to wax wanton and marry again, 1 Tim. v. 11, but stay ourselves for a time, till the body be resolved to earth from whence it came.

β) Out of matrimony we commit this sin, either with one allied to us, or with a stranger.

1. If she be allied, it is called 'incest,' forbidden, Lev. xviii. 6; punished with death, Lev. xx. 17.—And it is set down as a principle, "thou shalt not discover the shame of thy mother, because she is thy mother; nor of thy sister, because she is thy sister;" as though by the light of nature the very naming of mother or sister were enough. And yet this sin for a time was winked at; but Lev. xx. 23, the land spewed out the Canaanites and the Perizzites for this abomination; and Reuben before the law, for this very sin of incest, forfeited both the right of the kingdom, for it went to Judah, and the right of the priesthood, which went to Levi. And not only in the direct line is this incest, but in the collateral also; Mark vi. 18, Herod might not take his brother's wife; and 1 Cor. v. 1, "that one should have his father's wife," a "fornication not once named among the gentiles;" and Amos ii. 7, "a man and his father go in to a maid, to dishonour My holy Name;" so though for necessity it were tolerated in the beginning, yet of itself it is unlawful.

2. Come we to those that are strangers to us and not allied; and they are either married, or free and unmarried.

a) If married or espoused, (for that is all one,) it is adultery, forbidden, Lev. xviii. 20, and punished with death of both parties, Lev. xx. 10; see also Deut. xxii. 22—24. And though the politic laws of men have not made it so, yet by the judgment of all divines, it is capital. And great reason it should be so; for,

a. it is the perverting of the whole estate of those two families whereof the parties are members; and,

PART IV.

β. if the fault be in the woman, and the husband know not of it, there is notorious theft committed, for the man nourisheth and bringeth up a child that is not his, and layeth up inheritance for him, to the injury of his other children;

γ. in which soever of them the fault be, there is a sin against the rest of the children;

δ. yea, and a sin against one that is not, namely, against him that is so begotten, for he shall be born a bastard, and one that shall not be accounted as one of the congregation of the Lord;

ε. it is also against the state of the commonwealth, for it polluteth the land, Lev. xviii. 27.

β) Of them that are free and unmarried,

1. Either the party continueth with us, and then it is *concubinatus*, 'the keeping of a harlot to ourselves not being common,' and she is called a concubine.—God hath shewed how He disliked it by continual crossing of it; first in Hagar, Gen. xxi. 10, "cast out the bond-woman and her son;" Gen. xxxv. 22, in Jacob, by Reuben's incest with Bilhah; Judg. xix. 2, a Levite took a concubine out of Beth-lehem Judah, and as soon as he had taken her, she began to play the whore; 2 Sam. iii. 7, Saul was punished in his concubine Rizpah, to whom Abner went in; 2 Sam. xvi. 22, David was punished in his concubines by his son Absalom in the sight of all Israel.

2. Of those that do not keep a concubine continually to themselves, the deed is done either once only, or often;

1) once only, called 'deflowering,' Deut. xxii. 23, death appointed for it;

2) the deed often done is called 'fornication;' which word, though it be often used for the general sin, yet it is indeed properly called *vaga libido*, 'a wandering lust,' or *vagus concubitus*, 'a wandering and loose use of women;' Prov. ii. 19, they that enter into it hardly return again; Prov. v. 12, in his latter end he shall wonder at himself and say, How was I deceived?

Permission of it.

After the act followeth the permission of it.

The permission of the act is either

1. of private men, Lev. xix. 29, for a man to prostitute his daughter, sister, or kinswoman; or
2. of public persons, Ezek. xvi. 24; they built stews, or brothel houses, called there 'high places,' in every street; which as the prophet there detesteth, so godly princes have been studious to remove them, as Asa was, 1 Kings xv. 12.

Defending of it.

And the last pitch of all is to defend it.

To defend the sin, maketh it a crying sin, Gen. xviii. 21; the Sodomites, Gen. xix. 9, cried out upon Lot when he reproved them, "Away hence," say they, "thou art but a stranger, and shalt thou judge, and rule?" and Prov. xxx. 20, "the adulterous woman saith, I have not committed iniquity:" of these the apostle saith, Phil. iii. 19, they "glory in their shame."

Thus much of the seventh commandment.

THE EIGHTH COMMANDMENT.

Place of this commandment.

In the former commandment the lusts of the flesh are forbidden; in this the lust of the eyes, 1 John ii. 16.

It dependeth well upon the other two commandments. For in the two former commandments order hath been taken, for preservation of life, and generation of children. Now because for the preserving of life we need food and raiment, 1 Tim. vi. 8, and when we have children we must also provide for them, 1 Tim. v. 8, and so by consequent every man is to labour and care in this world, and that either, Eccl. vi. 7, *propter os*, 'for his mouth,' or 2 Cor. xii. 14, to lay up for his children; from hence cometh that worldly concupiscence, which is the object of this commandment. And the end of the commandment is to moderate that concupiscence; which of itself is no sin, as we shewed before in the former commandment; but first to desire that which is sufficient, and then to double that, and to desire matter of superfluity, yea of vanity and pleasure, and from thence to double again, and to have unlawful desires of that which is another man's, this is that that maketh it sinful.

Now it is not the hand only or civil theft, and stealing another man's goods, which God forbiddeth, but also dealeth with the heart; as the heart may be adulterous though the body be not, so there is not only *manus furis*, 'a theft of the hand,' but *καρδία κλέπτης*, 'a thievish heart,' as the heathen said; to this thievery also this commandment reacheth.

Of right and propriety.

Before we come to the things commanded and forbidden, we must first deal

1. with right and propriety, and
2. with alienation;

because *res aliena et nostra*, the distinction of what is another man's and what is ours, the unjust taking and detaining, is the matter of this commandment, comprehended in the word steal; and the object of the concupiscence here moderated is, *meum et tuum*, 'mine and thine.'

The civil lawyers define *furtum*, 'theft,' or *furari*, 'to steal,' to be *rem alienam contrectare*, 'to lay hands on that which is another man's;'
our divines, *consentire contrectationi rei alienæ*, 'to consent to the laying hands on that which is another man's;'
but even *concupiscere rem alienam* is *furari*, to 'covet another man's goods' is 'to steal.'

Quest. 1. But how cometh it to pass that there is *res mea et aliena*, 'mine and thine,' 'his, and his?'

Answ. Surely, Ps. xxiv. 1, "the earth is the Lord's;" and Ps. cxv. 16, He "hath given it to the sons of men," and not only to fill it and make use of it, but to subdue it and rule over it, and over the creatures that are therein; as God gave power to Adam, Gen. i. 28.

Quest. 2. But how came the division and appropriating to particular men? for without that there is not *meum et tuum.*

Answ. Cain first built a city, and called it by the name of his son Enoch, Gen. iv. 17, and so appropriated that to him and his; and that made Seth and his family gather to themselves also private possessions.

After the flood, whether by allotment of Noah, or by their own choice, his three sons had the chief parts of the earth; Ham had Africa, Shem had Asia, and Japheth had Europe. Also afterward, by consent and agreement, things became proper to certain particular persons, as Gen. xiii. 5—12, Abraham and Lot agreed to part the country between them.

Again, we come to have things proper to ourselves *jure primæ occupationis,* 'by the right of first seizing upon them,' as Deut. xi. 24, "all the places whereon the soles of your feet shall tread, shall be yours;" so when we seize upon a country never inhabited; or if it be *terra derelicta,* 'a land forsaken of her inhabitants,' *primus occupator,* 'the first taker of possession in it,' hath *jus,* 'right' and true title in it.

There is also *jus proprium jure belli,* 'a proper right by the law of war;' because the magistrate hath *gladium exteriorem,* 'the outward sword;' and may punish any foreign enemy, even by casting him out, if he and his territories cannot otherwise be in safety from him and his people.

Now this right of propriety or having a thing thus proper to a man's self, includeth four things;

1, he hath not only *dominium,* 'the lordship and rule' of it, but *usum,* 'the use,' as he may use his horse to ride on, and such like;

2, he hath *fructum,* 'the benefit,' whatsoever cometh of that horse;

3, he hath *consumptionem,* 'the wearing it out,' he may spend or kill it;

4, he hath *alienationem,* 'power to confer his right on another,' he may sell or give it.

According to these four rights cometh in *jus proprium,* 'the proper and private right.'

Of alienation.

Now for alienation, it is either
liberal and free, or
illiberal, as to hire, sell, or let it go for debt.
And this alienation is
either a translation of the whole, both the thing, the property, use and all; or of the use only;
and either for a time, or for ever.

To alienate the property, use, and all,
for ever, is *donatio*, a 'giving' it to another;
if but for a time, it is
mutuum, 'a borrowing and lending,' when it is of the whole property;
when but of the use, *commodatum*, 'a permission to use the thing lent.'

Illiberal alienation is that that is done upon some consideration; and it is of three sorts usual with us now a days,
do ut des, as letting a farm at a rent;
do ut facias, as giving for homage or service;
facio ut des, I do a thing for my pay and hire; as all civil contracts.

At first, when men grow weary of liberality, the first brood was *permutatio*, 'changing;' which
α. if it be money for money, is called *cambium*, 'exchange;'
β. if any other thing one for another, and not money, it is 'bartering;'
γ. if it be *pecuniæ pro re*, 'of money for any thing,' it is *emptio*, 'buying;'
δ. if *rei pro pecuniâ*, 'a thing for money,' *venditio*, 'selling;'
and that is either
negotiatio, 'merchandising,' whole sale, or
by parcels, called 'retailing.'

Beside this alienation of the thing itself, there is also alienation of the use only, and not of the property; and that, if it be *usus rei pro pecuniâ*, 'the use of a thing for money,' it is 'letting;' if it be *pecuniæ pro usu rei*, 'money for the use of a thing,' it is 'hiring.'

And out of this, by reason of our distrust, because sometimes we will let one have the use when we dare not trust him with the property, there ariseth therefore from hence, the contracts of words, writings, pawns, pledges and suretiship.

If he have but his bare word, it is
- in him that requireth it, *stipulatio*, 'a requiring of a promise and assurance;'
- in the giver of his word, *sponsio*, 'engagement by word,' a promise.

If it be by writing, which are *proles humanæ perfidiæ*, 'the children of human perfidiousness,'
if his own alone, *chirographum*, 'an hand writing;'
if with others, *syngrapha*, 'a joint evidence of men together.'

Pawns, if they be *rei*, 'real,' they are either
- in regard of some oath, *cautio*, 'cautionary;' or
- for the recovery of some thing received;
  and then it is either
  - moveable, *pignus*, 'a pledge;' or
  - immoveable, as land, *ὑποθῆκαι*, 'a mortgage.'

If the pawn be personal, it is either
- in war, *obsides*, 'hostages;' or
- in peace, in matter of action, called *vades*, 'sureties.'

Of desire, lawful,

Now that we see what the right and property of things is, and how it groweth, let us now consider how far our desire of this property, to make things ours that are not, may extend; and we may take the measure of it after this order;

1. Remember that which is 1 Tim. vi. 8, "having food and raiment, be contented;" if God bestow no more upon us, let us be content with that; because God, as he had plenty of spirit, so He had plenty of wealth, and could have made all rich if He would; and it was in His wisdom that He made some poor, that as the rich might have *præmium benignitatis*,

'the reward of his kindness,' so the poor might have *mercedem patientiæ*, 'the recompence of his patience.'

2. Though we must be contented with our estate, yet it is lawful to gather in summer, Prov. xxx. 25; to provide at one time for the time that is to come, by all honest means, and with a sober mind.

3. As a man seeth his household increase, so his provision may be the more; for he must travail for his household, Gen. xxx. 30, that so he and they may drink out of their own cisterns, Prov. v. 15, and not be chargeable to others, 2 Cor. xii. 13.

4. A man may travail for himself and his, Gen. xxx. 30, but his desire must always be limited according to the conditions above. Every man may labour that his cisterns be full, Prov. v. 15, that is, as the apostle saith, and as Solomon addeth, that he may not be chargeable to others, and yet he have sufficient for himself; therefore he may desire to have, not only for him and his, but Exod. xxx. 12, some offering to the Lord, to help the church; and Matt. xxii. 21, to pay tribute to the king, to help the commonwealth; and 2 Cor. viii. 12, to have to give the poor saints; and Eph. iv. 28, that he may give to him that needeth, whosoever he be.

and unlawful.

Thus far our desire may go, and yet still within compass; but if we go beyond these four, we offend in our desire, and our desire is out of measure, and will come in the end

- *a.* to a murmuring and envying of others in better estate than ourselves;
- *β.* secondly, to an unquiet overcare and taking thought what we shall eat and what we shall do, Matt. vi. 31, Luke xii. 17;
- *γ.* and thirdly, to breed a nest of horse leeches, which are worms, that have *linguam bisulcam*, 'a cloven' or 'a forked tongue,' and cry, 'bring, bring;' *unde habeas nihil refert, sed oportet habere,*' 'no matter whence you get it, have it you must;'

and this is that which we may call *suppurationem concupiscentiæ*, 'an inward rankling of concupiscence.'

Now for the making of *subactum solum*, 'the soil fit,' the way is, to bear a bigger sail than we are able to carry, and so come to have need, and so to unlawful practice; and then he is a fit soil for the devil to cast in his seed; and the devil perceiving man to be thus fitted, moveth him to stealth.

Of what is forbidden in this commandment.

§ 1. *In outward act.*

For the act itself forbidden in this commandment by the name of stealth, it is,

in the attaining and getting of a thing;
in the use of that we have gotten.

In the getting there must be a respect of justice;
in the use a respect both of justice and charity.

Of getting; first, of wrong getting.

We must get our estates justly,

a. that there be no oppression, exaction, fraud, robbery or spoil of our neighbour, or

β. that we consent not thereunto; for it is all one to hold the sack, and to fill it; to do it himself, or to consent unto it.

Of idleness.

a. The apostle, Eph. iv. 28, setting down the affirmative part of this commandment, saith, "let every man labour with his hands the thing that is good;" so that if he have no calling, or any unlawful calling, and so do not labour the thing that is good, he offendeth against this commandment.

β. These idle people, they are against the state of mankind, in paradise, and out of paradise. In paradise, God placed them in the garden, that they might dress it, Gen. ii. 15, and when they were driven out, Gen. iii. 19, in the sweat of their brows they were to eat their bread.

γ. There is no member of the body idle, but each bone and sinew doth his office and service, no one is idle and useless.

δ. And as the Lord at first appointed that man should labour, so when He giveth His reward, Matt. xx. 8, He will say to

His steward, "call the labourers, and give them their hire:" but Matt. xxv. 30, when He cometh to punish, He will not only punish *servum flagitiosum*, 'the wicked servant,' but *servum inutilem*, 'the idle and unprofitable servant,' cast him into utter darkness, as a creature superfluous; for God putteth no difference between *nequam et nequaquam*, 'that which is wicked and that which is not at all;' so an idle servant and no servant, an evil calling and no calling, is all one before God.

Of dealings, 1. *unlawful;*

And as we must not be idle, so we must not be evil occupied to get wealth; for to get wealth by evil means is no better than stealth,

I. Whether it be in unlawful or unjust buying and selling, as namely, when that is sold that cannot be sold; of which nature are,

1, the grace of God: Simon Magus's fault; he would have bought the grace of God for money, Acts viii. 20; called ever since, 'simony;'

2, justice and judgment: *quid dabis mihi ut faciam justitiam*, 'what will you give me to do you justice?' is all one with *quid dabis mihi ut vendam tibi Deum*, 'what will you give me to sell God unto you?' Ambrose and Augustine.

3, benefits and good turns: which should be done freely, and not looking for reward again, as the usurers sell their money: for as *donatio* 'giving,' is *liberalis alienatio sine omni mercede in æternum*, 'a free alienation of our right to a thing for ever without any recompence;' so *mutuatio*, 'lending,' is *liberalis alienatio sine omni mercede ad tempus*, 'a free alienation of a thing for ever without any recompence;' both lending and giving must be free; for he who doth *inscribere pretium liberalitati*, 'set a price of his liberality,' corrupteth the virtue.

2. *Unjust; whether with contract;*

II. Or again, in things that may be sold or contracted for, there may be a fault in the evil manner of contracting, and so a theft.

1. For contracts therefore;—two things are required in every

contract, *labor et merces,* 'the labour and the hire;' *res appretiata, et pretium,* 'the thing valued, and the price;' *cura et stipendium,* 'the charge undertaken, and the wages for it;' *quid pro quo,* 'one thing for another.' If either of these be wanting, it is no better than theft; Ezek. xxxiv. 3, if they "eat the fat, and clothe them with the wool, and kill them that are fed, and feed not the sheep," they are no better than thieves and robbers; and so on the other side, if he do labour, give him his hire, Deut. xxiv. 15; neither defraud him wholly, nor pinch him in it.

2. And now for the substance of contracts,
   there must be no corrupt measure;
   there must be no false weights;
   the matter sold or contracted for must be good; not the refuse of the wheat, Amos viii. 6; nor wine mixed with water, Isa. i. 22; but the ware must be sound and good.

3. For the manner of uttering our wares, we must beware we do not over-reach our neighbour, nor take any advantage of his ignorance or oversight; this is *stellionatus,* 'cozening.'

4. For the price, we must not think when we come to buying and selling that we come to a spoil; and therefore we must avoid that fault which is set down, Prov. xx. 14, 'it is naught, it is naught, saith the buyer,' and when we are gone, boast of our pennyworths.

or without contract.

III. Now of thefts that are without contract,

1. In the family, is *furtum domesticum,* 'thievery in a man's own house;' Tit. ii. 10, pickery in servants, beguiling their masters; to this we may add *servum fugitivum,* 'a fugitive or runagate servant,' because he detracteth himself out of his master's possession, and defraudeth his master of his service; so also the wasters of their master's goods are herein comprehended, Luke xii. 45.

2. Without the family there is a double theft,

a. of things consecrated, and that is 'sacrilege;' Lev. v. 15, there is a law for it; Rom. ii. 22, he matcheth it with idolatry, where he saith, "thou that abhorrest idols, committest thou sacrilege?" which is, to convert to his own use, or to divert a thing from the sacred use to a profane;

β. of things profane, and they are public or private.

1) Public, when a thing is stolen that is the king's, being a public person; or the common-wealth's, called *peculatus*, thievery to the state: and the thieves are called *balnearii fures*, 'thieves at the baths,' because they were about baths and such common places: such are they also that receive common wages and convert it to their own use.

2) Private things are of two sorts,

1. Personal, having life: personal theft is

a. of men, called *plagium*, 'men-stealing;' and the thieves, *plagiarii*, 'men-stealers;' Exod. xxi. 16, punished with death if he steal him and sell him; 1 Tim. i. 10: to this may be added Judas's sin, the betraying for money, Matt. xxvi. 15, though it be not an outright selling of him: and it is also

β. of beasts, and then they are called *abgregarii*, 'stealers of flocks or herds,' as the Sabeans and Chaldeans, Job i.

2. Real theft is of things not having life, as of money, raiment, or other goods; Exod. xxii., order is taken for these thefts particularly.

Aggravation of the guilt.

Now all thefts are aggravated and made more grievous by circumstances of the persons against whom they are committed; as if they be done against the widow, fatherless, strangers, or poor, Exod. xxii. 21—25; and Prov. xxiii. 10, "enter not into the fields of the fatherless, for He that redeemeth them is mighty, and will defend their cause against thee."

And here is condemned the inclosure of commons, for *cùm primùm occuparentur religione*, 'when religion took place at first,' there was always a consideration had that there should always be poor people, and therefore to them was left a division of lands in common to live upon, set out by marks; Deut. xix. 14, these marks must not be removed; and Deut.

xxvii. 17, the whole congregation curseth them that do it, and Hos. v. 10, see the detestation of it, Job xxiv. 2.

Thus much of the unjust getting of a thing, and of the theft therein committed; which may be drawn to these two, which Nazianzen calleth

ἐπιβολὴ, or *manus injecta*, 'rapine,' or 'violence;' and
ἐπιβουλὴ, 'a crafty way of compassing.'

Secondly, of right getting;

Now the virtue opposite to this is, just getting; Prov. xvi. 8, "a little with righteousness is better than great possessions without equity;" and 1 Tim. vi. 5, not to "think that gain is godliness," but that "godliness is great gain;" and to be able to say with Jacob in every thing they get, when they are asked how they came by it, Gen. xxx. 33, "my righteousness shall answer for me."

and of restitution.

But because the world is full of evil, and men have also *mentem malam*, 'an evil mind;' therefore if a man have overshot himself, there is a restitution appointed for the personal thefts before spoken of, save only for men-stealing; and so also for all real thefts restitution is allowed, unless the manner of the theft, as breaking a house in the night time or such like, alter the case; Num. v. 7; Job xx. 18; Neh. v. 11; Luke xix. 8.

Yea, and not only in things gotten by stealth, but in things gotten by lawful contract, there may be restitution required;

1, that which we call *depositum*, 'a thing committed to one's trust,' Exod. xxii. 7, 10.

2, those things that come *sub ratione inventi*, 'under the nature of things found;' strays, or things lost, Exod. xxiii. 4, Deut. xxii. 2; and so also, Lev. vi. 4.

3, things lent us for a time must be restored; for as Augustine saith, *tametsi benignè dimittitur, tamen non injustè repetitur*, 'though it be parted with in courtesy, yet it is not unjustly called for again,' Exod. xxii. 14.

PART IV.

4, things hired must also be restored, Exod. xxii. 15.

5, things taken in pledge must be restored again to the debtor, Ezek. xviii. 7; and if it be raiment, which they cannot want, it must be restored before the sun go down, Exod. xxii. 26.

Thus much of stealth in getting.

Of using;

Now for the use of that we have gotten,

1, upon ourselves; sufficiency for our own need;

2, upon others; liberality to them that want.

These are the two uses of riches; both set down, Prov. v. 15, 16, "drink the water of thine own cistern, and let thy fountains flow forth;" so first for our own use, and then for the use of others.

first, upon ourselves.

First, for sufficiency for our own need; which is the first use.

It hath two extremes;

1. Niggardliness, or too much sparing. For as a man may *inferre cædem sibi,* or be unclean in himself, as we shewed in the former commandment; so by too much sparing or niggardliness, a man may commit *furtum in se,* 'theft towards himself.' And so Eccl. iv. 8, there is a covetous man alone by himself, that gathereth riches, and never saith, *quare defraudo animam meam,* 'why do I defraud my own self?' so too much niggardliness is a defrauding or theft against a man's self; and not only against himself, but against others also, as Ambrose upon James v. 3, saith, *esurientium est cibus qui apud te mucescit, et sitientium est potus qui apud te acescit,* 'it is the bread of the hungry which mouldeth in thy cupboard, and the drink of the thirsty which soureth in thy barrel.'

And if their sparing be that they may say, as Luke xii. 19, "eat, drink, take thy pastime," God will disappoint them, ver. 20, and suddenly take away their soul; if they spare that they may be kept when they are sick, they shall spend their money upon physicians, as the woman with the bloody issue did, and be never the better; if it be to leave enough to their children, Job xx. 10, their children shall be beggars, and for the most part a prodigal son is the heir of a niggardly father.

2. Prodigality, or too much wasting, is the second extreme in the first use of those things we have gotten; it was the fault of the prodigal son, Luke xv. 13, he "wasted his goods with riotous living." And this riotous waster also is a thief to himself, for with being profuse and lavish, ἐφ' ἃ μὴ δεῖ, 'when he needeth not so to do,' he stealeth from himself ἃ δεῖ, 'the things which he may need;' because he wasteth superfluously, he wanteth things necessary.

Object. And howbeit it be true, that they say, that whatsoever they spend,

1, they do it of their own, and

2, they have enough, and are able to maintain it;

Answ. Yet for all that, it ought not so to be;

1, though they be rich, they must not fare delicately every day, Luke xvi. 19; and

2, for having enough, the heathen man could say, If you should allow your cook store of salt, and he should put too much in the pot, and when you found fault with him should answer you, he had enough, it were a foolish answer, and you would not like it at his hands; no more will God like this action, or think well of this answer at your hands.

This prodigal or wasteful spending is,

1. when they do it παρὰ καιρὸν, 'unseasonably,' daily, oftener than needeth; or else,
2. when they do it in too great a measure, and that is,

a. either above their ability, more than they can maintain,

β. or above their estate and calling.

1) For keeping within compass of their ability, Luke xiv. 29, he that layeth a foundation and is not able to perform it, they that behold it will mock him.

2) For their calling, 1 Sam. xxv. 36, though Nabal be rich, yet he must not make a feast like a king; and much less may mean men exceed.

And he that offendeth herein, his table will be a snare unto him;
to his soul, by offending God in misspending his creatures;
to his body, by breeding diseases; and
to his goods, by wasting and consuming his estate;
and so every way a snare to catch him, Ps. lxix. 22.

secondly, upon others.

To come to the second use, liberality to them that want. We must let our fountains run abroad, something must be given to the poor; Acts xx. 35, "it is a more blessed thing to give than to receive;" those that are rich themselves must be also rich in liberality, 2 Cor. ix. 11; "rich in good works," 1 Tim. vi. 18.

For this matter therefore we must enquire,
how we have our riches given us;
what we are to think of the poor.

How we have our riches given us.

I. How God committeth riches to men we shall see, Deut. xxvi. 5; every man must do God homage for the riches that He hath given him. We see there every man cometh with his basket, and bringeth his rent or offering, and the priest setteth down his basket before the Lord; and then the party,

a. first, acknowledgeth that there is nothing in him or his progenitors, that God should deal so liberally with him or with them, and therefore he is come to do Him homage;

β. secondly, I have brought this out of my substance, and have given it
ad usus ecclesiasticos, 'to ecclesiastical uses,' the use of God's priests, to the levite; and
ad usus civiles, 'for a civil use,' to the strangers, fatherless, and widow; and

γ. thirdly, I have not done this of mine own accord, but by necessity of duty; I have done it 'according to thy commandment.'

So all rich men must confess,

a. That which I have, I have it of the free gift and mercy of God;

β. I have it not for myself only, but there is a rent to be paid, both to the church, and to the poor brethren;

γ. I may not detain this rent, but I am tied unto it of duty by God's command.

What we are to think of the poor.

II. What we are to think of the poor, we shall see, Ps. xli. 1; we must judge wisely of the poor, and not, as our common fancy is, that they concern us not.

Deut. xv. 11, God hath said, "there shall be ever some poor in the land," and therefore hath given commandment that we open our hands to the needy and to the poor.

And they are called in that place, 'thy' poor, and 'thy' needy; so there are some poor that are made *nostri*, 'our own;' we may not shake them off, but are bound unto them; and therefore ver. 7, "thou shalt not have a hard heart, nor a close hand to them," nor ver. 9, "it shall not grieve thee to look upon them."

And thus we see what we ought not do to the poor; and if we do thus, and the poor cry unto the Lord against us, it will be sin unto us, and the reward of sin we know is death.

Now what must we do to the poor? surely, ver. 8, "lend him sufficient for his need;" and if lending will do him no good, "thou shalt give him," ver. 10. Our Saviour Christ hath joined them both together, Matt. v. 42, "give to him that asketh, and from him that would borrow of thee turn not away."

There is in divinity a threefold necessity that we must have a care to relieve,

1, *necessitas naturæ*, 'necessity of nature;' every man is bound to provide for himself, for the sustentation of nature, both inwardly, meat and drink convenient; and outwardly, apparel and house-room;

2, *necessitas personæ*, 1 Tim. v. 8, 'necessity of a person' in want; those that are ours, we must provide for them, and namely for them of our household, or else we are worse than infidels;

3, *necessitas statûs*, or *conditionis*, 'necessity of a man's state or condition,' that every man may have to live according to his estate and condition. We must not say, as Augustine sheweth it to be the common manner of men to say, If a man have three hundred pounds, he hath no more than will serve him; and if he have three thousand pounds, he hath no more than will serve him. But our Saviour teacheth us, Luke xi. 41, *πλὴν τὰ ἐνόντα δότε ἐλεημοσύνην*, 'to give alms of such things as we have,' and to purge our hearts inwardly, and all things shall be clean unto us.

After the two first necessities are served, then give alms of those things that are within; for during those two particular necessities, we are not bound to give; except it be for the common good of the church, 2 Cor. viii. 3, and in that case even those that were in extreme poverty, yet to their power, yea and beyond their power, they were liberal.

So that to conclude this point; we must think of the poor; and thus know, that poor we must always have, and those poor we must relieve, according to their necessities and our abilities.

Giving to the poor is as the sowing of seed.

And the rather to move us, let us know that our liberality to the poor is as the sowing of seed, and our benevolence that we give to the poor, it is indeed seed; now

Gal. vi. 7, "that we sow, we shall reap;" and

Hos. x. 12, "sow righteousness, and reap mercy;" and

2 Cor. ix. 6, "sow sparingly, and reap sparingly; sow liberally, and reap liberally."

Seed we know, if a man love it so well that he keep it still in his barn, worms will breed in it and consume it, and so he shall *amando perdere*, 'lose it by loving it;' and therefore a man must so love his seed that he do *projicere semen*, 'cast his seed,' and that is indeed *amare semen*, the true 'loving of his seed.'

And so the temporal blessings of God being seed, there must be a casting and a scattering of them; and this scattering is not a casting away of the seed, but as when a man hath sown an acre of ground, and one ask whose this seed is, we do not say it is the ground's, but his that sowed it; so riches, wheresoever they are bestowed, being seed, they are *serentis non recipientis*, 'the sower's, and not the receiver's.'

And therefore as the husbandman doth *credere illud quod non videt*, 'believe that which he seeth not,' and so casteth in his corn, and believeth that albeit it rot, and showers and snow fall upon it, yet at last an autumn and harvest will come, and he shall reap an ear for a corn; so if God enlighten our hearts, and give us faith *credendi id quod non videmus*, 'to believe that we see not,' the fruit of our faith in the end will be *videre quod credimus*, 'to see that which we now believe;' and we shall see and feel, that the seed we sow is still *serentis*, it is still our own, and will bring us a hundred fold increase in the end.

Thus much of the things commanded and forbidden in this commandment.

§. 2. *In the heart.*

Now this commandment, as the other, is also spiritual, and therefore striketh not only at the outward actions, but at the heart also; for our Saviour telleth us, Matt. xv. 19, that out of the heart come thefts, and therefore the fountain of them must be dammed up.

For if a man come once to that, 1 Tim. vi. 9, that he "will be rich;" why then, *quod volumus valde volumus*, 'what we will, we eagerly will and desire,' insomuch as Prov. xxi. 26, even the man that is "slothful," yet he "coveteth greedily;" if he have a desire to be rich, he will needs be rich quickly; and then Prov. xxviii. 20, "he that maketh haste to be rich shall not be innocent," but 1 Tim. vi. 9, "come to be drowned in perdition and destruction;" and Prov. xx. 21, an heritage hastily gotten cannot be blessed in the end, because this excessive desire of riches is no better than theft in the heart of him that is infected with it.

How to avoid theft in the heart.

And therefore to avoid this theft of the heart,

1. We must place instead thereof a contented mind; Heb. xiii. 5, "content yourselves with that you have;" and "be not careful what to eat, or what to drink, or what to put upon you," Matt. vi. 25; that is to say, be not so careful as to dis-

trust God's providence, but 1 Pet. v. 7, "cast all your care upon the Lord, and He will care for you:" and if thou be in want, "cast thy burden upon the Lord, and He will nourish thee," Ps. lv. 22; yea, "the lions shall lack and suffer hunger, but they that seek the Lord shall want nothing that is good," Ps. xxxiv. 10. And let this be thy resolution; if God will have me to be rich, He will so bless me in my lawful endeavours that I shall be enriched thereby; if not, say as David said in the case of a kingdom, 2 Sam. xv. 26, "here I am, let Him do with me as it pleaseth Him;" and with St. Paul, Phil. iv. 11, 12, learn to abound and to want, and in all things to be contented in what estate soever thou art.

2. Another thing is, that as we must be content with our estate, so we must have a care to set down and reckon what we are able to reach unto with that estate we have; and to look that *condus* be *fortior promo,* and *promus debilior condo,* 'our receiver and bursar be above our market man,' and 'the market man beneath our cash-keeper;' our comings in must be more than our layings out: or else if *condus,* 'our receiver and cash-keeper,' be the weaker, it will go out the faster, and so a man shall not *sufficere rebus suis,* 'have sufficient for his occasion,' nor *res ejus sufficere ei,* 'his wealth be sufficient for himself;' and then his heart will be set on work to make justice pay for it; rather to use unlawful and unjust means, than not continue as he hath begun.

So these are the two means to avoid the theft of the heart:
to be contented with that we have; and
not to spend above our measure;
and the heart being thus rectified, it is to be hoped that we shall avoid the outward thefts before mentioned, which proceed from the heart, as from the root.

Thus much of the eighth commandment.

THE NINTH COMMANDMENT.

The exposition of this commandment is,
Lev. xix. 11, "thou shalt not lie to thy brother;" and
ver. 16, "thou shalt carry no tales;" and

Zech. viii. 16, 17, "speak every man the truth to his neighbour, and love no false oath;" and

Eph. iv. 25, "cast off lying, and speak every man truth to his neighbour," and

ver. 15, "let us follow the truth in love."

Words of this commandment.

The words of the commandment in hebrew are thus, *non respondebis testimonium falsum super vicinum tuum*, 'thou shalt not answer a false witness upon thy neighbour,' or 'touching thy neighbour.'

1. The word 'answering' there used must be understood according to the hebrew phrase; as the evangelists often use to begin thus, "and He answered and said," where no man speaketh to Him or demandeth any thing of Him: so that by the word of 'answering,' being so understood, it is meant that we should not only speak the truth when we are demanded, but even when we speak of ourselves without any demand of any other, we should speak truly.

2. For the next word, 'witness;' it is of four sorts,

a. The great and chief Witness, even God himself; Job xvi. 19, "behold, my witness is in heaven;" and 1 John v. 7, "there are Three which bear record in heaven, the Father, the Word, and the Holy Ghost:" these are they that bear witness unto all truth. And therefore howsoever wicked men may have the applause and commendation of other men, yet that indeed is the true praise which is not of men but of God, Rom. ii. 29; and therefore we must not stand so much upon the opinion that men have of us, but we must say every one of us, as Paul doth, 1 Cor. iv. 4, "He that judgeth me is the Lord."

β. After this great witness, in the second place is the witness that St. Paul speaketh of, Rom. ii. 15, "their conscience bearing witness:" which though it be a thousand witnesses, yet God is greater than our consciences, 1 John iii. 20; and though we know nothing by ourselves, yet are we not thereby justified, 1 Cor. iv. 4, for when we come to have the matter right up *coram magno teste,* 'before the great Witness,' we may be found to be wrong.

γ. Because God will not speak from heaven, and men's consciences may be seared so as they will deny the truth, therefore the third witness is that of one man to another; Josh. xxiv. 22, "ye are witnesses that you have chosen the Lord to serve Him, and they said, We are witnesses:" and of this kind of witness is this commandment, and the end of it is to establish the truth by witnesses, "by the mouth of two or three witnesses every matter must be confirmed," Matt. xviii. 16.

δ. There is also a witness of dumb creatures, as of a stone, Josh. xxiv. 27; and Abac. ii. 11, "the stone of the wall shall cry out, and the beam out of the timber shall make answer, and testify against them;" and James v. 3, "the rust of your gold and silver shall be a witness against you:" and this to shew that man is unfaithful in his testimonies, in that there must be a refuge to other creatures to witness against him.

3. Now for the third word, 'false;' it signifieth in the original three things:

falsum, to speak 'that which is not so;' *aliter quam res se habet; sermo non adæquatus rebus;* when our words and the matter do not agree;

mendacium, 'a lie;' whereof the common derivation is that *mentiri* is *contra mentem ire,* 'to speak one thing and think another;'

vanitas, 'vanity;' because the speech of man was ordained for two necessary uses, namely, the building up of faith in respect of God, and charity in respect of our brethren, what speech soever hath not one of these ends, it is *signum mendax,* 'a lying sign,' because it hath no *signatum,* 'thing indeed signified;' and therefore all vain and frivolous idle talk is here forbidden.

4. *Quest.* But seeing it is said "thou shalt not bear false witness 'against' thy neighbour," what say you to *officiosum mendacium,* when we may by a lie help him, and save either his life or goods?

Answ. It is altogether unlawful: and indeed the words of

the commandment will not bear it; for the word is ברעך, *bereg-neka,* which is best translated, *super proximum tuum,* which may be either 'for' him, or 'against' him; so the law is, that in any matter concerning thy neighbour thou shalt not speak an untruth, whether it be for him, or against him; the word in the text will bear both, and may be rendered either 'for' or 'against,' and therefore is best interpreted in as broad a signification as may be.

Place and purpose of this commandment.

For the coherence with the former commandments, it is thus:

When God had established authority in the fifth commandment, He took order for promiscual duties in the three next, the sixth, seventh, and eighth commandments; and then if it fell out that those three commandments could not keep all well, but that there were some breach of them or of some of them, then they must come *ad judices,* 'to the judges,' Exod. xxii. 8; and before these judges there must be proofs; and those proofs must be by witnesses, which this commandment taketh order for, that they may witness truly. And so for the rectifying of whatsoever is done amiss against the other three, this commandment was instituted and ordained.

The scope and purpose of God the law-giver in this commandment is, that God, as He is truth itself, so He would have the truth preferred among men; which truth, as John xviii. 37, Christ saith of Himself, so we may all say, we are born and came into the world to this purpose, to bear witness to the truth.

First, of what leads to the offence.

1) *The evil inclination;*

For the offence itself, it cometh from the heart, Matt. xv. 19: false testimonies and slanders proceed from the heart, and from an inclination of nature that we all have, *grassari ad famam,* 'violently to surprise another man's good name;' and therefore we think if we can keep down the credit and estimation of another, we ourselves shall be the better thought of; and so, either from an aspiring desire of our own good, or an envious and malicious mind to our neighbour's hurt, or from some such like corrupt inclination, we are moved to this sin.

2) *The festering of the same.*

And the *suppuratio*, the 'festering' or 'rankling' of it is,

a. When we begin to imagine some device against our neighbour, and to say, "come, let us smite him with the tongue," as they did to Jeremy, Jer. xviii. 18; when we come to those evil surmises, 1 Tim. vi. 4; and from surmises and suspicions, to judging of our neighbours, Jam. iv. 12; yea and to condemning, Rom. xiv. 4; (whereas our judgments and conclusions should not be so hasty, but should be made according to signs *præcedentia et consequentia*, 'precedent and consequent,' and not suddenly, as they dealt with Paul, Acts xxviii. 4, no sooner a viper on his hand, but presently they said he was a murderer;)

β. And not only surmise, and judge, and condemn, but (whereas God's will is that *ubi malum contingit, ibi moriatur*, 'where sin befel, there let it die;' if it be private, let it have private admonition, and there die, and go no further,) Prov. xi. 13, "he that is a slanderer discovereth secrets." Joseph was of another mind, and was very careful therein, Matt. i. 19; because Mary's being with child was secret, and the fact might have been done by one that had a precontract, *in simplici actu fornicationis*, 'in the simple act of fornication,' he would not make her a public example.

γ. And if it be a fault to report secret faults, though they be true, then much more do they offend against this commandment, that report more than is true; as 2 Sam. xiii. 30, false tidings were brought to David that Absalom had slain all the king's sons.

δ. They also offend who mis-interpret men's actions, as Christ's eating, and John baptist's abstinence, Matt. xi. 18.

ε. So do they also who will not suspend their judgment concerning what a man may be hereafter, for a wicked man by God's grace may in time see his folly, 2 Tim. ii. 25.

3) *The prepared ground.*

Come we now as in the former to *subactum solum,* 'the fit soil.' We are made a fit mould for this sin by that which we call *pruritus aurium,* 'itching ears;' if there were no willing hearers of lies, there would not be so many tellers, Ps. xv. 3: we must not only not slander our neighbour, but not receive an evil and false report against him; as Augustine saith well, *discet non libenter dicere, cum didicit non libenter audire,* 'a man will learn not willingly to speak, when he has learned not willingly to hear.'

4) *The watering thereof.*

The next point is *irrigatio concupiscentiæ,* 'the watering and cherishing of this sin.' This is that which St. Peter calls ἀλλοτριοεπισκοπεῖν, 1 Pet. iv. 15, 'to take care of another man's diocese,' to be a curious searcher of other men's doings; such people go about from house to house, and are prattlers, and busy bodies, 1 Tim. v. 13; they are of the mind of Ahimaaz, 2 Sam. xviii. 19, when Absalom was slain, he sued to be the tidings-carrier to the king; every body is ready to be the reporter of an ill matter. It was the fault of the Athenians, Acts xvii. 21, they "gave themselves to nothing else but either to tell or to hear some news." So now a days, we are all of Peter's mind, John xxi. 21, 'what shall John do?' what shall this man do, and what shall that man do? But we must remember Christ's answer, "what is that to thee? follow thou Me:" Peter must not meddle in John's diocese, nor one of us in another man's business, but every man meddle with his own matters, 1 Thes. iv. 11; and if we look well to our own, we shall have no leisure to deal with other men's.

Secondly, of the offence itself.

Now we come to the outward actions. The actual sin against this commandment it is in words especially; and those either vain and idle, or principally false and untrue; either disagreeing from the truth and essence of the things we speak of, or from our mind and meaning.

And these false speeches either concern ourselves, or our brethren; for if it be hurtful to ourselves or our neighbours, it is condemned, because it is against charity; but if it do no hurt, yet if it be false, it is evil, because it is against the truth of God.—And therefore here is condemned falsehood in doctrine, though not as in the third commandment, as it toucheth God's glory, but in this commandment as it hurteth our brethren.

Of lies in general.

Now for false speaking between man and man, and not in matter of doctrine; we may divide it into

I. Lies in general; and for them,

seeing, John viii. 44, the devil was a liar from the beginning, and is the father of lies, and they that speak lies are his children, and seeing it is the property of the wicked to speak lies, Ps. lviii. 3,

and not a light matter, but a fault that bringeth destruction, Ps. v. 6, "the Lord will destroy them that speak lies;" and Rev. xxii. 15, out of heaven, in the place of torments, shall be "those that love and make lies;"

therefore whatsoever it be that is false, is condemned, and not to be uttered, whether it do concern ourselves or others.

Of false witness in judgment;

II. False witness; and that is in judgment, or out of judgment.

For false witness in judgment, Solomon hath a good comparison, Prov. xxv. 18, "a man that beareth false witness against his neighbour, is like a hammer, and a sword, and a sharp arrow;" and how is this? Bernard answereth it, that there are three parties smitten with one and the self-same tongue; namely, the judge, the party that hired him, and he against whom he cometh;

judici est malleus, 'to the judge he is a hammer,' that is to say, he doth astonish the judge, as if he had a blow given on the head, that he knoweth not how to determine or judge the matter;

to him that hired him, he is a sword, to fight for him and his cause; but withal a sword to kill his soul, because he is his instrument against the truth;

to him against whom he witnesseth, he is an arrow, and the wound that he maketh sticketh in him, either in his goods, or life, or good name.

which may be in six different persons;

Neither is this false-witness-bearing to be referred to the witness alone, but to all the parties that have to do in judgment;

The accuser may be a false witness by his untrue accusation;

the defendant, by his untrue defence;

the judge, by the wrong determination;

the notary or registrar, by entering the sentence amiss;

and the advocate by informing amiss;

for every one of these is an actor in judgment.

in the judge;

Of every one of these particularly.

1. The judge: it is most perilous on his side; for Deut. i. 17, the judgment is God's; and therefore what judge soever giveth a wrong sentence, *facit Deum mendacem,* he 'maketh God to speak a lie,' and doth what he can to change God the author of truth into the devil the father of lies.—And seeing the apostle hath said it, 1 Cor. vi. 7, that it is a fault for one man to go to law with another; meaning, that they are to blame that begin suits and quarrels, because both parties cannot be true, being absolute contradictions, and so by the means much untruth must needs be uttered in the place of judgment, and that is derogatory to God, Josh. vii. 19; therefore it were good there were a diminishing of suits, as much as might be; and that men might not go to law for every trifle, but only hard and difficult matters might be brought in to judgment, Exod. xviii.; and that for dispatch of matters there be more seats of judgment than one, as helpers to the higher places, Exod. xviii. 22, to judge the smaller causes.

PART IV.

in the notary or registrar;

2. The notary or registrar: he may also be a false witness, if he enter amiss, and so make false records. There is a memory of such registrars, Ezra iv. 19; Artaxerxes' notaries could find records that the Jews had been a rebellious people, and went about the building of the temple without Cyrus's decree; but when Darius a good king came to bear rule, he could find in a coffer that Cyrus had made such a decree, and so that the other were false records. So in the matter of judgment, not only those that decree wicked things are condemned, but those also that write grievous things, Esay x. 1; that is, when the record is more grievous than the decree, if the notary or registrar go not directly to the sentence, it is a false record: and *quando justitia revertetur ad judicium,* Ps. xciv. 15, 'when Christ the true righteousness shall come to judgment,' they shall answer for it.

in the plaintiff or accuser.

3. The plaintiff or accuser may be also a false witness, and that three manner of ways;

a. when he doth *calumniari,* 'falsely accuse' a man, as Haman did the Jews, Esther iii. 8, that they had laws diverse from all other laws, and were not observers of the king's laws;

β. when he accuseth a man upon uncertainty, and matters that he cannot prove, as the people dealt with Paul, Acts xxv. 7;

γ. when he doth *prævaricari,* which is a metaphor taken from *vari,* 'those that have their knees out of joint,' and the convulsion is inward, so that both touch above and the feet are far asunder, and so in old time when they wore long garments a man might easily have been deceived, thinking them to be as broad at the knees as at the feet: so they that strive together, being friends privily, are called *prævaricatores;* that make a mockery of the place of judgment; such also are they that betray the cause with weak proofs, or taking upon them the defence of one part, take bribes and are corrupted by the contrary.

in the defendant.

4. The defendant may also be a false witness, and that in these three cases;

a. If being demanded according to form of law, he do *versare se ad agitandas actiones aut ad cogitandas excusationes,* 'betake himself to plead he hath done well, or to devise excuses;' as Adam did, Gen. iii.; he put it off to the woman. Job did otherwise, Job xxxi. 33, "if I made a fault, I confessed it."

But we are not bound to accuse ourselves, unless it be before the seat of judgment where a lawful course is taken; as John xviii. 20, Christ saith, "if any can accuse Me, let him come forth;" and so to Pilate, John xix. 9, because they did not proceed *ex publicâ infamiâ nec ex semiplenâ probatione,* 'from a public fame nor upon an half proof,' but only questioned with Him to see if he would accuse Himself, He gave no answer at all.

Or if it be a truth, and stand upon two points or more, we may answer one part and not the other; and so as Paul did, Acts xxiii. 6, *occultare partem veritatis,* 'conceal part of the truth;' the council being divided, some sadducees, some pharisees, the sadducees holding that there was no resurrection nor angels, and the pharisees confessing both, he said he was a pharisee, and was judged and accused of the hope and resurrection of the dead; though indeed it was not for that alone. So if a man have divers ways to defend himself, he may choose which he liketh best.

β. Though for a remedy for those that are oppressed, appeals be allowed, yet if the defendant in an evil cause will delay more than needeth, he is a false witness.

γ. When sentence is given, if he do not submit unto it, he is also a false witness, and resisteth the ordinance of God, and so God himself, Rom. xiii. 2.

in the advocate or lawyer;

5. The advocate or lawyer may be also a false witness, and that in these three respects;

PART IV.

a. If he take evil causes in hand, knowing them to be evil;

1) Exod. xxiii. 2, we must not agree in a controversy to overthrow the truth,

2) and then not put to our hand, nor help him in his plea; 2 Chron. xix. 2, Jehu saith to Jehoshaphat, "wilt thou help the wicked, and love them that hate God?" and Rom. i. 32, they are not only condemned that "do wicked things themselves," but those also that "favour those that do them."

β. If he take too many causes in hand, more than he is able to look well unto; for though they be good causes, yet he must take no more upon him than he is able to perform.

γ. If he do in any cause take a bribe or a gift out of the bosom, that is, secretly, to wrest the ways of judgment, Prov. xvii. 23, or by wrong means seek to bolster out any matter.

in the witness.

6. The witness himself, of whom we spoke in the beginning, may be a false witness, if he do fail in any of these three;

a. Being lawfully demanded by a magistrate to speak his knowledge, if it be not in matters beside the question, he is bound to tell what he hath seen and heard, Lev. v. 1.

β. Though it be not by the magistrate demanded, yet if it be for the delivery of the innocent, he must witness his knowledge, Prov. xxiv. 11. But if the magistrate require it not, or if it be beside the question, he need not answer, unless in case of deliverance.

γ. When he doth swear or testify in any matter, he must speak truly; not according to the greek proverb, *da mihi mutuum jusjurandum,* 'lend me an oath,' do it for me now, and I will do as much for thee another time. But Solomon telleth us, Prov. xi. 21, "though the wicked join hand in hand," and so happily escape the hands of men, "yet they shall not go unpunished" at God's hands.

Thus much for false witness in judgment.

Of false witness out of judgment;

Now for that kind of false witness, which is out of judgment.

Though a man be from the judgment seat, yet he must not say, Ps. xii. 4, *ego sum dominus linguæ*, 'my tongue is my own,' for *nemo est dominus sui nisi ad licita*, 'no man is lord over himself,' neither ought to dispose of himself, 'but to lawful actions.'

which may be in four ways.

There are four ways wherein a man's tongue may offend out of judgment,
and four ways may we be hurt by the tongue,
according to the four good things that a man hath;—

1, favour and credit, against which they commonly oppose *contumelia*, 'disgrace,' when a man is present;

2, good report, name and fame, against which is opposed *obtrectatio*, 'the depraving of a man behind his back:' Plato calleth such a depraver, *mus nominis*, 'a mouse gnawing at a man's good name;' but Paul, 2 Tim. iii. 3, calleth him *diabolus*, 'a devil;'

3, friends and well willers; against this do offend those *susurrones*, 'tale carriers,' of whom Prov. xvi. 28, "he soweth dissension among princes," he is able to set whole realms together by the ears;

4, a man's estate and condition; against this is opposed *subsannatio*, 'scoffing and flouting;' 2 Sam. xvi. 5, Shimei's sin.

Other ways of offending against this commandment.

And not only in words may we offend against this commandment, but by writings also; if we write that which is untrue, as Neh. vi. 6, Sanballat sent a letter to Nehemiah, as full of untruths as it could hold.

And not untruths only are forbidden, but because, 1 Cor.

xiii. 6, "love delighteth in the truth," and Eph. iv. 15, "the truth must be followed in love;" we may offend therefore even in reporting a truth, if our truth have not love joined with it; as 1 Sam. xxii. 9, Doeg told the truth to Saul, that "David went to Nob to Ahimelech, and he asked counsel of the Lord for him, and gave him victuals and the sword of Goliah;" yet though all this were true, David, Ps. lii. 2, saith, "his tongue was like a sharp razor that cutteth deceitfully."

Against this commandment also offend all they that speak fair and mean mischievously; all false brethren, that have their lips swim with butter and oil, and in their hearts carry a sword to stab a man. Matt. xxii. 16, the disciples of the pharisees and the herodians come unto Christ to entangle Him, and they begin smoothly, "Master," say they, there is the butter, saith Chrysostom; "we know that thou teachest truly," there is the oil; but the sword follows, "shall we pay tribute to Cæsar or no?" If he answer 'yea,' all the people will hate Him; if he say 'no,' off goes His head for treason against Cæsar.

The commandment bids us rebuke where need is.

Another thing in this commandment is, that as we must not slander our neighbours and report worse of them than they deserve, so on the other side if they do ill, we must *adhibere fraternam correptionem,* we must 'brotherly rebuke them,' and not suffer them to sin, if it lie in us to hinder it.

1 Thess. v. 14, "admonish them that are unruly;" if it be an ordinary fault not aggravated by circumstances, it must be with the spirit of meekness, Gal. vi. 1; if otherwise, it must be roundly and sharply, Tit. i. 13: if it be an open fault, they must be rebuked openly, 1 Tim. v. 20; if secret, Matt. xviii. 15, secretly and privately in the ear; unless it tend to another man's hurt, and then it must be declared to him, as Acts xxiii. 16, Paul's sister's son told him when there was wait laid for him.

And so as Augustine saith well, there is,
veritas dulcis quæ fovet, 'a pleasing truth which encourag-

eth;' when we are doing well, we must be commended;

veritas amara quæ curat, 'a bitter truth which cureth;' when we do ill we must be rebuked, and this is the way to bring us to repentance and so to amendment, 2 Cor. vii. 8, 9.

Of the vice opposed to this, viz. flattery.

The vice opposed to this virtue of rebuking, is flattery, a common vice among us, because rebukes are odious, Amos v. 10. Albeit indeed *vulnera diligentis,* 'the wounds given by a friend,' are better than *oscula blandientis,* 'the kisses of a flatterer;' as in physic *amarum sanum,* 'a bitter pill which cures,' is better than *perniciosum dulce,* 'a sweet potion which is poisonous:' yet such is our nature, that because we are led by *φιλαυτία,* 'self-love,' we love ourselves, and think well of ourselves, therefore he that will speak well of us and think well of that we do, him we love; and so on the contrary if he mislike us or our actions and speak against any thing we do, presently we hate him; and this maketh flattery so common a vice now-a-days, because as rebukes are odious, so flattery giveth content. Of this mind were they, Esay xxx. 10, that said unto the seers, "prophesy unto us no true things, but speak flattering things unto us."

This vice of flattery is of two sorts.

1. In uncertain things, to commend a man before we know whether he be worthy of it or no. This may be called the hasty commendation, at the first beginning and at first sight to commend a man so highly, that we make the party think he hath done enough and hath answered all expectation; whereas perhaps the greatest matter is still behind, as 1 Kings xx. 11, it is not the putting on of harness, but the putting of it off, that is worthy of commendation; not the beginning, but the end of the race is worthy praise. Such were they of whom we read in Herodotus, which answered Cambyses, that indeed they found it unlawful which he would have done (incestuous marriage), but against that they found that a king might do what he would.

2. In certain things, and them either good, or evil.

a. To commend a man for an evil thing is plainly condemned; *laudatur malè qui laudatur ob malum aut de malo,* 'he is not well praised who is commended for or concerning any evil;' to say to the wicked, "thou art righteous," Prov. xxiv. 24; to call darkness light, and to speak good of evil, Esay v. 20. They may well be called *cæmentarii diaboli,* 'the devil's daubers,' Ezek. xiii. 10; and his upholsters too, for they sew pillows under men's elbows, ver. 18; where the prophet importeth thus much, that the wicked are asleep in sin, and he would have them sleep with as much disease and unrest as might be, without any pillows, or such matters of ease.

β. In good things a man may be too much commended: to praise him above measure for a good action, is no better than flattery, 2 Cor. xii. 6; it makes men think above that they see or hear. To praise with a loud voice is reproved, Prov. xxvii. 14; and David, Ps. xii. 3, prayeth to God to "cut off all flattering lips."

Of committing these same faults against ourselves.

And this vice of flattery may not only be used to others, but may also reflect upon ourselves,

when we suppress the truth in our consciences, Rom. i. 18;

when we glory and boast of ourselves, 2 Cor. xii. 1; whereas we should 'let another man's mouth praise us, and not our own lips,' Prov. xxvii. 2.

And as we must not flatter ourselves, in speaking better of ourselves than there is cause; so again on the other side we must not take upon us a fault that we have not done; as where 1 Sam. xxxi. 4, Saul killeth himself, 2 Sam. i. 10, one cometh and saith he killed Saul, in hope of reward at David's hands; but he was deceived, for David caused him to be slain for killing the Lord's anointed by his own confession.

Neither must we deny any thing of ourselves that is true, whether it be good or evil.

a. If it be good, some think it modesty and humility to deny that they can do so well as they can; but as Jerome saith, *mendax humilitas incauta humilitas,* 'humility telling a lie is an unadvised humility;' and saith he, *non ita caveatur arrogantia ut caveatur aut evitetur veritas,* 'let no man so shun arrogancy that withal he shun and let go truth.'

β. If it be evil that we are charged withal, though we need not voluntarily tell our faults, yet being asked, we must not deny a truth; as Sarah offended in denying she laughed, when indeed she did laugh, Gen. xviii. 15.

And so to conclude, we must

neither affirm any untruth, { of ourselves,
nor deny any truth, { nor of any other.

Question concerning a harmless lie.

There is question concerning *mendacium innocuum,* 'an harmless lie,' of which cometh no loss, as they say.

But saith Augustine, those that say so are not *innocui,* 'harmless,' for though they account no loss but of goods, name, or life, &c. yet there is an error, for there is a loss beyond all these, the loss of the truth. This is in three things;

1. *contrà quàm se res habet,* when the speech is 'contrary to the things spoken of,' though he be persuaded of it in his mind; Augustine, *hic temeritatis non mendacii accusandus est,* here 'the speaker is to be blamed for rashness and not for lying;' such are they, that have not learned their tongue to say *nescio,* 'I know not,' but speak things which they know not;

2. *contrà quàm se animus habet,* 'what the mind knoweth to be false;' the midwives' lie, Exod. i. 19; Michal for David, 1 Sam. xix. 14; the woman of Bahurim, 2 Sam. xvii. 20;

3. *jocosum mendacium,* 'the jester's lie;' Hos. vii. 3, to make the king merry; Gal. i. 10, please none out of truth.

Object. If a man be sick, and I know that his son is dead, and if I tell him it will kill him, what shall I then answer if he ask?

Answ. Augustine answereth as Paul doth, *nihil contra veritatem possumus,* 'we can do nothing against the truth,' 2 Cor. xiii. 8; *perdes omnes qui loquuntur mendacia,* 'Thou wilt confound all them who tell lies,' Ps. v. 6; and so he concludeth that neither for body nor life we may depart from the truth.

Of seeming exceptions.

As for the midwives' lie, no doubt the women of the Hebrews were stronger than the Egyptians, and had done as they said; and so they said true, and told not a lie, but part of the truth.

Rahab's lie, Josh. ii. 4, 5, may better be called *occultatio veritatis,* 'an hiding of the truth;' there is only allowed in her a good disposition.

Quest. Judg. ix. 8, "the trees went forth to anoint a king," was that true?

Answ. It is *vox ficta,* 'a figurative speech,' as Christ often used the like.

Gen. xx. 12, "she is my sister," Abram keepeth back part of the truth.

1 Sam. xvi. 2, when Samuel feared to go to anoint David king, God bade him take an heifer with him, and say he went to do sacrifice.

If a question be moved that hath two meanings, the answer may be made to the one, so it be true; so Christ answered the truth, of another kingdom than Pilate asked, John xviii. 36.

So Jacob was in one sense Isaac's eldest son, because he had bought his eldest brother's birth-right, Gen. xxvii. 19.

So John is Eliah, "in the power of Elias," Matt. xi. 14.

When the thing is changed in circumstance, the performance may be otherwise than was spoken of: the angels would not have come in, had not Lot changed their minds by his importunity, Gen. xix. 2; Peter would not let Christ wash his feet, till he was otherwise persuaded, John xiii. 8: Paul had come to Corinth had not Satan hindered him, 2 Cor. i. 17; so none of these are against the truth.

Now since truth is *æquitas,* this 'equity' is between,

1, the thing and the thought;

2, the thought and the sign of it; and that is *verbo aut facto; factum*, 'a deed,' is a sign of our thoughts, as well as our words are; Matt. vii. 20, "ye shall know them by their fruits."

Miscellaneous rules.

We must take heed of judging another man's heart, God hath only to deal with that, 2 Chron. vi. 30; men's meanings must not be sought after, as Chrysostom saith, "my heart is not your servant, and therefore judge it not."

We must not be too severe in judging: especially for the time to come; leave that also to God; we must not think if one once sleep in sin, that he will never wake; they may return to God; Augustine, *multi sunt intus fures et multæ oves foris; sic multi inserti sunt refringendi et multi infracti inserendi*, 'many within the church are thieves, and many without will in time be sheep; so many graffed in are to be cut off, and many broken off shall be graffed in again.'

If we have offended in a thing unknown, that none can prove ought, *non retegendum peccatum nisi sine peccato celari non potest*, 'the sin is not to be revealed unless it cannot be concealed without sin;' but with David, say to God, *tibi soli peccavi*, 'against Thee only have I sinned,' Ps. li. 4.

If ever we have said to God as they did, Judg. x. 15, "hear us but this once, and we will serve Thee," or in our sickness promised more obedience after health restored, Hos. vii. 14, we must not lie to God, but have a care to perform it, or else the vineyard will lie to us.

THE TENTH COMMANDMENT.

Of the form, exposition, and place of this commandment.

The papists make this commandment two commandments. Which cannot be; our reasons are these:

1, because there is but one period;

2, because then there should be a law of particulars, which is least of all in God's laws;

3, because, Rom. vii. 7, the apostle setteth it down in brief, *non concupisces*, 'thou shalt not lust;'

4, the consent of the Hebrews before Christ, and the fathers since Christ.

The exposition of this commandment we have,

Deut. v. 21, "thou shalt not covet, no nor desire that which is thy neighbour's;"

Esay lv. 7, we must forsake our own imaginations; which are also condemned, Jer. xviii. 12;

Mark vii. 14, that which defileth a man is within him;

Rom. vii. 7, "thou shalt not lust:"

Eph. ii. 3, mention is made of the lusts of our flesh.

The dependence is this; that having taken order in the former commandments both for our actions, and the consenting to those actions, be they good or bad; now He dealeth with the first motions and thoughts of the heart. Prov. iv. 53, "out of the heart cometh life;" and as life, so good and evil life come from the heart.

End of this commandment.

The end of the commandment is,

1. That God might shew himself to look further than man doth, and His law to reach further than man's laws; for though man's law do bind the hands and stop the mouth, yet it saith, *cogitationis pœnam nemo patiatur*, 'let no man be punished by man for his evil thought;' but God's law taketh hold of our very thoughts, and therefore, Acts viii. 22, we must pray that the thoughts of our hearts may be forgiven.

2. To stop the mouths of all proud pharisees that should dare to boast of their performance of God's laws; for though in the other commandments we might flatter ourselves, yet this will make us appear to be most wretched, Rom. vii. 24. In the other commandments the act, yea and the consent to the act, is forbidden; but in this, the thought, which in respect of the consent is called *partus imperfectus*, 'an im-

perfect birth:' in the other, *intentio etsi non consequaris*, 'the intention though not executed;' in this, *cogitatio etsi non sequaris*, 'the thought though not performed.' As Augustine saith, *magnum fecit qui non sequitur malum, sed non sic perfecit, nam cogitare prohibetur*, 'he hath done much who pursueth not evil; but he hath not yet done fully well, because he should not think evil.'

Of the two sorts of concupiscence.

Concupiscence is of two sorts, good, and evil.

1. The good concupiscence is also twofold,

a. the lust or concupiscence of the spirit against the flesh, Gal. v. 17;

β. the concupiscence or desire of nature, or our natural desires and appetites of meat, drink, and such like, are not evil; they were in our Saviour Christ; Matt. iv. 2, He was hungry, and desired to eat; John iv. 6, He was weary, and desired to rest.

2. The evil concupiscence is, when it is not a hand to the understanding, as it ought to be, but choketh and corrupteth it; and it is also of two sorts;

a. foolish concupiscence, which is set upon earthly things, and not upon things that are above, Col. iii. 1; when our natural affection, which of itself is not evil, goeth beyond his bounds, so that we seek wholly these things, and set our hearts upon them;

β. hurtful concupiscence, which is the lust of the flesh against the spirit, Gal. v. 17.

This is that *præputium*, Acts vii. 51, that uncircumcision, that hindereth the ears and heart from that which is good, and corrupteth our understanding in good things: and in evil things it will bring us *per malum aut ad malum*, 'through evil, or to evil;' if our end be good, then *per malum*, to use evil means; or if we use good means, then the end shall be evil. It is called,

the old man, Eph. iv. 22, Col. iii. 9.
sin dwelling in us, Rom. vii. 5.
the sting of death, 1 Cor. xv. 56.
the prick, 2 Cor. xii. 7.

Of the working of evil concupiscence.

The manner of working of this concupiscence is after these six ways:—

1. When sin began, Gen. iii. 6, the fruit was holden out by Satan and presented to our first parents, with these three commendations,

> it was profitable, good for meat;
> it was pleasant to the eye;
> it was to be desired in regard of the knowledge, and so of the preferment, that should come by it; *eritis sicut dii*, 'ye shall be as gods;'

so the first working of the concupiscence is, to hearken to Satan's temptation; 1 Tim. v. 15, to turn back after Satan.

2. The entertaining of the temptation, and retaining it in our hearts, and consenting to it: this is that which Job speaketh of, Job xx. 13, 14, when a man favoureth wickedness, and will not forsake it, but keepeth it close; though it be sweet in his mouth, yet it is poison to him; the gall of asps is in the midst of him. But Satan's suggestions, ever sinful in him, yet are not so in us, if we reject them and never yield to them: occasions of temptations we ought to avoid, but temptations we cannot; nor is it a sin to be tempted, for the devil suffered not Christ to be free from temptation; if we resist them, pray against them, fly unto God for help, they may be trials to us, but God will deliver us from the evil of them.

3. The retaining of the seed of wickedness in our hearts with consent, bringeth forth delight; and this delight is *conceptio peccati*, 'the conceiving of sin.'

4. To stay and continue in this delight, *morosa delectatio;* and this may be called *articulatio fœtûs*, 'the forming and fashioning of the joints' of sin, an evil brat.

5. *Aberratio cordis in peccato*, 'the searching up and down of the heart about a sin;' the reasoning of it, and after it is once lost, to call it back again; and to make a contrary covenant to Job's; he made a covenant with his eyes not to look upon a maid, Job xxxi. 1, and we make covenants still to

look upon sin, and to set all the imaginations of our thoughts upon it; and this is *vita peccati*, 'the very life of sin,' for now it lives and moves.

6. The birth itself, and bringing it forth into action and execution in the course and practice of our lives.

And these six are in every sin, though many men have not the Spirit of God in that measure that they are able to watch them all; and besides, *iniquitas sæpe mentitur sibi*, 'sin often lies to itself.'

The apostle St. James, chap. i. ver. 14, goeth by degrees;
first, saith he, a man is tempted;
and when is he tempted? when he is drawn away by his own concupiscence, and is enticed;
and what followeth of that? then lust conceiveth;
and what doth it bring forth? sin;
and what doth sin bring forth? death.

Of the bait and the hook;

So that our lust becometh sinful two ways;
by the bait and allurement we are enticed, as St. James saith; so the first thing is *esca*, 'the bait;'
by the hook, whereby we are drawn away as it were by force and violence; *uncus*, 'the hook.'

in ourselves;

For Satan taketh advantage of our weakness and corruption; and

1, he offereth us matter of pleasure, or profit, or preferment, all which we take delight in, to see if he can that way allure us, and entice us to that which is evil;

2, if that way prevail not, then he useth force and violence to draw us unto it:

And for the working of sin in our own corrupt nature,
first, we take hold of pleasure,
pleasure breedeth lust,
lust grows to delight,
delight breeds custom, and
custom breeds necessity;

PART IV.

for after once we have taken delight in a thing and used it at any long time, we grow to a necessity of using it still, we cannot abide to leave it; and so that which at first was a bait to allure us, becometh at last a hook to draw us.

from the devil;

And for Satan's working,

1. For his allurements, we know from the beginning how he enticed and deceived our first parents Adam and Eve; he hath *methodum decipiendi,* 'a method of deceiving,' many fetches and devices, as appeareth 2 Cor. ii. 11, "take heed lest Satan circumvent us, we know his enterprises;"

2. If baits and allurements will not serve, then he useth the hook of force and violence to draw us;

1 Pet. v. 8, he is a "roaring lion;"
Matt. viii. 32, the swine were carried headlong into the sea by the devil, there was violence;
2 Cor. vii. 5, fighting without, and terrors within;
1 Thess. ii. 18, Paul saith, he would have come unto them, but that Satan hindered him.

and from the world.

Yea, and the world also hath these two means to prick us on to sin,

baits to allure us, profit, pleasure, and preferment;
hooks to draw us; if baits will not serve, it will be violent with threatening us, by loss, grief, and reproach;

and so as Augustine saith, *aut amor erit mali inflammans, aut timor mali humilians,* 'either love to the bait will entice us to evil, or fear of the hook will draw us, or at least keep us from doing of good.'

And thus { in ourselves, / and from the devil, / and from the world, }
there are these two means,
baits to allure us,
force to draw us into sin.

And thus much of the tenth and last, and so of all the ten commandments.

BISHOP ANDREWES'

JUDGMENT OF THE LAMBETH ARTICLES.

BISHOP ANDREWES'

JUDGMENT OF THE LAMBETH ARTICLES.

[The following account of the 'Lambeth Articles' may be acceptable to the reader.

Whitaker, regius professor of divinity in Cambridge, having imbibed strong calvinistic notions, denounced the Margaret professor as a Pelagian; and having represented to archbishop Whitgift that the orthodoxy of the university was in danger, unless a series of theses, nine in number, which he had framed, should be sent down to Cambridge stamped with the authority of some of the heads of the church, prevailed upon the primate to call a meeting of bishops and others of the clergy at Lambeth for that purpose, and managed to get his theses accepted in the main, though the emendations with which they were sent back were sufficient to shew how little the general tenor of them was really approved by the theologians who had sat in judgment on them. Whitgift was censured afterwards by queen Elizabeth for the whole proceeding, and promised to write to Cambridge that the articles might be suppressed. They are here given, with their emendations;

Articuli Lambethæ propositi prout à cl. v. D. Whitakero in ipsius autographo concepti episcopis aliisque theologis Lambethæ proponebantur.

Articuli Lambethæ propositi prout ab episcopis reliquisque theologis concepti sunt, et de sensu quo admissi sunt.

I.

Deus ab æterno prædestinavit quosdam ad vitam, et quosdam ad mortem reprobavit.

I.

Admissus est hic articulus totidem verbis. Nam si per primum 'quosdam' intelligantur 'credentes,' per secundum 'quosdam,' 'increduli;' lis hìc non intenditur, sed est verissimus articulus.

II.

Caussa efficiens prædestinationis non est prævisio fidei, aut perseverantiæ, aut bonorum operum, aut ullius rei quæ insit personis prædestinatis, sed sola et absoluta et simplex voluntas Dei.

II.

Caussa movens aut efficiens prædestinationis 'ad vitam' non est 'prævisio' fidei aut perseverantiæ, aut bonorum operum aut alîus rei, quæ insit personis prædestinatis, sed sola 'voluntas beneplaciti Dei.' Additur in hoc secundo articulo à Lambethanis 1° 'movens;' 2° 'ad vitam;' 3° mutatur 'sola absoluta et simplex voluntas Dei' in 'sola voluntas beneplaciti Dei;' idque non sine justâ ratione. Caussa enim movens prædestinationis 'ad vitam,' non est 'fides,' sed meritum Christi, cùm Deus servandis salutem destinavit non propter 'fidem,' sed propter Christum. 'Moventis' vocabulum propriè 'merito' convenit; 'meritum' autem est in obedientiâ Christi, non in fide nostrâ. Additur, 'ad vitam,' quia licèt prædestinationis 'ad mortem' caussa sit 'prævisio' infidelitatis et impœnitentiæ, adeòque alicujus rei quæ insit personis prædestinatis 'ad mortem;' tamen nulla est caussa prædestinationis 'ad vitam,' nisi sola 'voluntas beneplaciti Dei;' juxta illud Augustini, 'Prædestinationis caussa quæritur et non invenitur; reprobationis verò caussa quæritur et invenitur.' 'Absoluta et simplex voluntas Dei' majus quiddam dicit, quàm 'sola voluntas beneplaciti,' nam et conditionalis voluntas est beneplaciti, et vult Deus nos rectè facere, si nos velimus ejus gratiæ non deesse; et placuit Deo servare singulos homines, si crederent.

III.

Prædestinatorum præfinitus

III.

In hoc articulo nihil mu-

et certus est numerus, qui nec augeri nec minui potest.

tatur; verissimus enim est si de præscientiâ Dei intelligatur quæ nunquam fallitur, non enim plures vel pauciores servantur quàm Deus præsciverit.

IV.

Qui non sunt prædestinati ad salutem, necessariò propter peccata condemnabuntur.

IV.

In hoc articulo nihil mutatur; verissimus enim est; quia statuit Deus non remittere peccata nisi credentibus. Quòd si ita hanc thesin et priorem interpreteris, ut et 'peccata' et 'damnationem' necessitate quâdam ex ipsâ prædestinatione deducas atque ex eâ fluere existimes, apertè Augustino, Prospero, Fulgentio, &c. contradicis, et cum Manichæis Deum peccati auctorem necesse est facias.

V.

Vera, viva et justificans fides et Spiritus Dei sanctificans non exstinguitur, non excidit, non evanescit, in iis qui semel ejus participes fuerunt, aut totaliter aut finaliter.

V.

Vera, viva et justificans fides et Spiritus Dei sanctificans non exstinguitur, non excidit, non evanescit, in 'electis,' aut 'totaliter' aut 'finaliter.' In autographo Whitakeri verba erant, 'in iis qui semel ejus participes fuerunt,' pro quibus à Lambethanis substituta sunt, 'in electis,' sensu planè alio et ad mentem Augustini; cùm in autographo sint ad mentem Calvini. Augustinus enim opinatus est 'veram fidem quæ per dilectionem operatur, per quam contingit adoptio, justificatio et sanctificatio, posse et intercidi et amitti; fidem verò esse commune donum electis et reprobis, sed perseverantiam electis propriam:' Calvinus autem, 'veram et justificantem fidem solis salvandis et electis contingere.' Et cl. v. D. Overal defendit et in academiâ et in conventu Hamptoniensi, 'justificatum, si incidat in graviora peccata, antequam pœnitentiam agat, in statu esse damnationis;' ibique contraria sententia quæ statuit 'justificatum, etiamsi in peccata graviora incidat, justificatum tamen manere,' à regiâ majestate damnata est. Ita in hoc articulo nihil minùs quàm Whitakeri sententia probata est.

VI.	VI.
Homo verè fidelis, id est, fide justificante prædictus, certus est, certitudine fidei, de remissione peccatorum suorum et salute sempiternâ suâ per Christum.	'Homo verè fidelis, id est fide justificante prædictus,' certus est 'plerophoriâ fidei' de 'remissione' peccatorum suorum et salute sempiternâ suâ per Christum. Nihil hìc mutatur, nisi quòd pro 'cer-

titudine' substituitur vox græca 'plerophoriâ.' Quidam autem ex theologis voluerunt pro 'fidei plerophoriâ' reponi 'spei plerophoriam;' verùm eorum absentia cùm transigeretur negotium, effecit ut maneret vox 'fidei' quam scripserat Whitakerus. Voce autem 'plerophoriæ' usi sunt, quia non designat 'plenam' et 'absolutam certitudinem,' qualis est 'scientiæ vel principiorum fidei,' (cùm fides sit talium rerum quarum est evidentia vel certa scientia,) sed minorem quendam certitudinis gradum, quippe cùm etiam in judiciariis et forensibus probationibus usurpetur.

Verissimus est hic articulus, si de certitudine præsentis statûs intelligatur, aut etiam futuri, sed conditionatâ. Credit enim fidelis se credere, et credit credentem servatum iri; credit etiam perseveraturum se; sed non unâ omninò et eâdem certitudine; quia certitudo hæc partim nititur Dei promissionibus, qui nos tentari ultra vires non patitur; partim pii propositi sinceritate, quâ pro tempore futuro nos Deo obedientiam præstituros sanctè in nos recipimus.

Alioqui si hic sensus affingitur assertioni, hominem certitudine eâdem, quâ Christum credit mortuum et esse mundi salvatorem, credere debere se esse servandum sive electum, repugnaret hæc assertio Confessioni regis Edvardi, in quâ legitur, 'Decretum prædestinationis incognitum est;' et Augustino[a], 'Prædestinatio apud nos, dum in præsentis vitæ periculis versamur, incerta est.' *De civit. Dei*, lib. xi. cap. 12[b], et alibi; 'Justi, licèt de suæ perseverantiæ præmio certi sint, de ipsâ tamen perseverantiâ suâ reperiuntur incerti.'

[a] [vid. De corrept. et grat. cap. 13. vol. x. col. 772. De dono persev. init. col. 821. et cap. 13. col. 838.]

[b] [vol. vii. col. 282.]

VII.

Gratia sufficiens ad salutem non tribuitur, non communicatur, non conceditur universis hominibus, quâ servari possint, si velint.

VII.

Gratia 'salutaris' non tribuitur, non communicatur, non conceditur universis hominibus, quâ servari possint, si velint. Pro 'gratiâ sufficienti ad salutem,' quod erat in Whitakeri autographo, substituerunt Lambethani 'gratiam salutarem,' ut planè appareat loqui eos de eâ gratiâ quæ est actu ultimo salutaris, sive actu efficax, seu quæ per se, non additâ novâ gratiâ, salutem operatur. Hæc quidem non conceditur, sed ne offertur universis, cùm sint plurimi (utpote Pagani &c.) quibus evangelium nec internâ nec externâ voce prædicetur. Ergo illa verba, 'quâ servari possint si velint,' intelligenda sunt de potentiâ proximâ et immediatâ. Nam si de potentiâ remotiore intellexissent, frustrà induxissent vocem 'gratiæ sufficientis,' quæ 'sufficiens' appellari solet, non quòd sit efficax, vel per se actu operetur salutem, sed quòd sufficiens sit ad salutem ducere, modò homo non ponat obicem. Et hæc Augustini et Prosperi fuit sententia, qui gratiam saltem parciorem occultioremque omnibus datam aiunt, et talem quidem quæ ad remedium sufficeret. Unde Fulgentius, 'Quòd non adjuvantur quidam à gratiâ Dei, in ipsis caussa est, non à Deo.'

VIII.

Nemo potest venire ad Christum nisi datum ei fuerit et nisi Pater eum traxerit; et omnes homines non trahuntur à Patre ut veniant ad Filium.

VIII.

In hoc articulo nihil mutatum; non omnes trahuntur tractu ultimo. Sed qui negat omnes trahi tractu remotiore tollit opitulationem illam generalem, sive commune auxilium quo omnium hominum corda pulsari dicit Prosper. 'Tractum' autem theologi Lambethani non intellexerunt (cum Whitakero) determinationem physicam irresistibilem; sed divinam operationem, prout communiter in conversione hominis operatur, quæ naturam voluntatis liberam non tollit, sed ad bonum spirituale idoneam primò facit, deinde et ipsam bonam facit.

IX.	IX.
Non est positum in arbitrio aut potestate uniuscujusque hominis servari.	In hoc quoque nihil mutatum; verissimum enim est salutem nostram esse primariò non in nobis, sed à

gratiâ præveniente, excitante, concomitante et subsequente in omni opere bono; secundariò ab arbitrio et voluntate hominis consentiente atque acceptante. Nulla potestas est arbitrii ad bonum spirituale, nisi gratia non modò tollat impedimenta, sed et vires suppeditet. Non est ergo positum in arbitrio primitus et potissimùm; imo nullo modo in arbitrio est positum, ut homo quilibet quolibet momento ad salutem possit pervenire. At verò esse aliquam aliquando in arbitrio potestatem gratiæ subordinatam et gratiæ consentientem, nemo inficias iverit qui Augustinum audiverit; 'Dum tempus est,' inquit, 'dum in nostrâ potestate est opera bona facere;' et alibi, de pœnis inferni loquens, 'Majus est,' inquit, 'quod timere debes, et in potestate habes ne eveniat tibi.']

Reverendissimi τοῦ πάνυ *doctissimique patris* LANCELOTI WINTONIENSIS (*qui ipse ejusdem pars magna fuit*) *de Synodo oblatis à* D. WHITAKERO *articulis judicium.*

QUATUOR priores articuli de Prædestinatione sunt et Reprobatione; quarum illa ab apostolo dicitur, *ὦ βάθος!* hæc à prophetâ, abyssus multa; Rom. xi. 33, Ps. xxxvi. 6.

Ego certè (ingenuè fateor) sequutus sum Augustini consilium: mysteria hæc quæ aperire non possum, clausa miratus sum, et proinde, per hos sedecim annos, ex quo presbyter sum factus, me neque publicè neque privatim vel disputâsse de eis, vel pro concione tractâsse; etiam nunc quoque malle de eis audire quàm dicere. Et quidem cùm lubricus locus sit, et habeat utrinque periculosa præcipitia, cùmque loci Paulini unde ferè eruitur inter *δυσνόητα* illa, de quibus Petrus, semper sint habiti; cùmque nec multi in clero sint qui ea dextrè expedire, et perpauci in populo qui idonei illius auditores esse possint; suaderem, si fieri possit, ut indiceretur utrinque silentium, nec ita passim et crudè proponerentur à quibusque ut assolet. Certè multo magis expedire arbitror ut doceatur populus noster salutem suam quærere in manifestis vitæ sanctæ et fideliter institutæ (quod et Petrus suadet), quàm in occultis consilii divini; cujus curiosa nimis inspectio vertigines et scotomata generare potest et solet, ædificationem certè in angustis ingeniis vix solet. Sed tamen rogatus sententiam meam de his articulis, idque à dominatione tuâ cui non parere religio fuit, sic paucis respondeo.

AD 1. QUO ASSERITUR PRÆDESTINATIO.

Esse apud Deum in æternâ illâ suâ sive præscientiâ dicere libeat sive scientiâ, quâ videt quæ non sunt tanquam ea quæ sunt, prædestinatos quosdam, quosdam reprobos, extra controversiam esse arbitror. Scripturæ verba sunt, *πρὸ καταβολῆς κόσμου*, id est ab æterno scilicet, elegisse Deum nos; et cùm elegisset, prædestinâsse, Eph. i. 4, 5; elegisse autem *ἐκ τοῦ κόσμου*, 'de mundo,' Joan. xv. 19; quare non omnes in mundo elegisse, sed quosdam, alioqui enim electio non foret. Quos verò non elegit et eligendo approbavit, (ut electionis natura fert) reprobâsse; et Scriptura verbis utitur *ἀπωθεῖν*, 'rejiciendi,' Rom. xi. 2, *ἀποδοκιμάζειν*, 'reprobandi,' Heb. xii. 15. Tantùm ne utrobique par ratio videatur, et eadem prædestinandi ratio, eadem reprobandi; si hoc plenè non constet, cuperem addi, aliter prædestinatos illos, nempe per Christum, Eph. i. 5, aliter hos reprobatos, nempe propter peccatum.

AD 2. QUO PRÆDESTINATIONIS CAUSSA EXPLICATUR.

Verissimum Dei per prophetam verbum est, 'Tantummodo in me auxilium tuum,' id est, nec à quoquam auxilium nisi à me, nec à me quicquam nisi auxilium: verissimum et apostoli, 'Quis discernit?' id est, à Deo solo habere nos quo à reliquis discernimur.

Sed tamen de particulâ illâ ['sola voluntas beneplaciti'] quæri potest,

Primo, includatne Christum, an secludat; id est, sitne actus prædestinandi actus absolutus, an relatus?

Quod ad me, existimo relatum esse: nec ullam esse Dei *εὐδοκίαν ἐν ἀνθρώποις*, id est, 'voluntatem quâ beneplacitum sit ei in hominibus,' nisi in Filio in quo *εὐδόκησε*, nec vel ante vel sine intuitu Christi prædestinari quenquam; sed (ut habent sacræ scripturæ) Christum primò *προεγνωσμένον*, 'præscitum,' 1 Pet. i. 2, deinde in eo nos, Rom. viii. 29; Christum primò *ὁρισθέντα*, 'prædestinatum,' Rom. i. 4, deinde per eum nos, Eph. i. 5; non autem priore loco nos (uti nonnullis videtur), posteriore illum, et propter nos: neque enim prædestinari posse nos *εἰς υἱοθεσίαν*, 'ad adoptionem filiorum,' nisi in Filio naturali, neque prædestinari nos posse ut conformes simus imagini Filii, nisi Filius primò statuatur cujus imagini conformemur. Quare et huic quoque articulo cuperem addi, 'beneplacitum Dei in Christo.'

Deinde quæri potest secundò, includatne præscientiam Dei voluntas hæc sola beneplaciti, an excludat? Ego certè nullo modo existimo divellenda hæc, nempe præscire et prædestinare, sed (quod apostoli faciunt) conjungenda. Neque hìc vero audeo præcipitare sententiam meam, aut damnare patres, qui ferè omnes secundùm prævisam fidem et eligi et prædestinari nos asserunt. Id quod vel Beza[c] ipse fatetur in xi. ad Rom. 2. (edit. 2[a]) 'patres hìc nullo modo audiendi, qui ad prævisionem hoc referunt.' In quo tamen (ut mihi videri solet) potiùs de serie et ordine quo utitur Deus in actu prædestinandi loquuntur, quam de caussâ prædestinationis. Quam seriem alii aliter ad suum quisque captum solent texere patres in eâ mihi sententiâ videntur fuisse; electionem nullam fore nisi ita texatur; Deum primò, diligere Christum, dein nos in Christo; quod apostolus dicit, 'gratificare nos in dilecto,' Eph. i. 6; secundò, gratificatos sic gratiâ donare et fide; tertiò, sic donatos atque ita a reliquis discretos eligere; quartò, electos prædestinare.

Certè electionis hoc natura postulat, quæ nullâ omnino existente differentiâ inter eum qui eligitur et eum qui rejicitur, nec esse nec cogitari potest: sic Œcumenius ex Græcorum sententiâ, p. 323.[d] *εἰπὼν κατὰ ἐκλογὴν, ἔδειξεν ὅτι καὶ διέφερον ἀλλήλων· οὐδεὶς γὰρ ἐκλέγεται ἕτερον ἀφ' ἑτέρου εἰ μή τι αὐτοῦ διαλλάσσοι.* Sic Augustinus[e] *ad Simpl.* i. 2, 'non tamen electio præcedit justificationem' (scil. prævisam), 'sed electionem justificatio: nemo enim eligitur nisi jam distans ab illo qui rejicitur; unde quod dictum est, Quia elegit nos

[c] [vid. ad Rom. i. 1. p. 433. Ad viii. 29. fin. p. 481, et passim.]

[d] [in init.]

[e] [vol. vi. col. 92.]

Deus ante mundi constitutionem, non video quomodo sit dicendum nisi præscientiâ.'

Neque secus scholastici. Thom. *Primâ*, Q. 23. Art. 4,[f] 'prædestinatio præsupponit electionem, et electio dilectionem;' nempe primò fecit eligendos, dein elegit; dilexit ut daret, elegit quæ dedit. Nec alia mihi mens videtur reverendissimi Eboracensis[g]; sic enim ille, 'Quid in Jacobo dilexit Deus ab æterno, cùm nihil boni fecisset? certè quod suum, quod ipse erat illi daturus.'

Certè apostolus ipse non veretur in negotio hoc conjungere *ἰδίαν πρόθεσιν* et *δοθεῖσαν χάριν*, atque hoc *πρὸ χρόνων αἰωνίων*, cùm sc. *δοθεῖσα* illa *χάρις* non nisi in præscientiâ esse potuit; cum æterno scilicet proposito Dei, ipsam quoque gratiam quam se daturum prævidit ante tempora secularia. Neque incommodum inde ullum (ut mihi videtur) si Deus ut coronat in nobis dona sua, sic eligat in nobis dona sua; nempe quæ primò diligendo dedit, quò pòst sic data eligeret: atque ita cùm dilectio, quæ est actus gratiæ quâ Deus discernit, tùm electio, quæ est actus judicii quâ sic discretos seligit, utraque conservantur. Atque hoc modo manebit electio: recentiorum enim series illa omnem plane electionem tollit; quâ Deus ponitur homines nec in ullâ massâ existentes, nec ullo modo per sua dona discretos, primo actu et eo absoluto, simul et semel, hos quidem addicere saluti, illos verò perditioni sempiternæ; post quam addictionem quis electioni locus esse possit non intelligo, aut quomodo illa ipsa addictio electio dici possit.—Sed hæc tota quæstio (uti dixi) de ordine potiùs est quo procedit Deus, ad captum nostrum qui ex parte cognoscimus, quàm de caussâ quoad actum ipsum, qui unus est in Deo et simplicissimus; vel si de caussâ, non de primi actûs caussâ intelligi debet, sed de caussâ quoad integrum effectum (ut loquuntur) in prædestinando.

Quæritur, sitne actus integralis (conceptu nostro) ex variis actibus constans, an primus ille solus? et si plures et varii, quis ordo, quæ series actuum?

'Prædestinatio, quæ sine præscientiâ non potest esse, non est nisi bonorum operum,' Aug.[h] *De prædest. sanctorum*, cap. x.

[f] [vol. x. p. 94. b.]

[g] [sc. Matth. Hutton, S.T.P., archiep. Ebor., "De elect. et reprobat." p. 15. Hardrov. 8vo. 1613.

[h] [vid. vol. x. col. 803.]

'Electi sunt ante mundi constitutionem, eâ prædestinatione in quâ Deus sua futura facta præscivit,' Idem.[i] *ibid.* cap. xvii.

'An quisquam dicere audebit Deum non præscîsse quibus esset daturus ut crederent?' *De dono perseverantiæ*, xiv.[k]

'Ista igitur sua dona quibuscunque Deus donat, proculdubio donaturum se esse præscivit, et in suâ præscientiâ præparavit,' cap. xvii.[l]

'Si nulla est prædestinatio quam defendimus, non præsciuntur a Deo; præsciuntur autem,' *ibid.*[m]

'Hæc igitur (dona) quæ poscit a Domino, et semper ex quo esse cœpit poposcit ecclesia, ita Deus vocatis suis daturum se esse præscivit, ut in ipsâ prædestinatione jam dederit,' xxiii.[n]

AD 3. DE NUMERO CERTO.

Sunt ipsa Augustini[o] verba initio cap. xiii. *De cor. et gra.*, 'Eorum qui prædestinati sunt ita certus est numerus, ut nec addatur iis quisquam, nec minuatur.'

Et Ambrosius[p] *De voc.* l. 2. c. ult., 'De plenitudine membrorum corporis Christi præscientia Dei, quæ falli non potest, nihil perdit, et nullo detrimento minui potest summa præcognita atque in Christo ante secula æterna præelecta.' Certissimum enim est scientiam divinam certissimam esse nec falli posse, novisse autem Dominum qui sunt ejus.

AD 4.

'Qui non est inventus scriptus in libro vitæ' (i. e. prædestinatus) 'missus est in lacum ignis,' Apoc. xx. v. ult. id est, damnatus est; damnatus autem proculdubio propter peccata sua; quis enim hoc negabit? atque id necessariò, si sic loqui placeat; sed necessitate ex hypothesi, non absolutâ; id est, (ut articulus ipse se explicat,) propter peccata, ideòque quia peccarunt, non autem ideò quia non sunt prædestinati.—Quanquam ego (quod et patres et scholastici sedulò faciunt) terminis his ['necessitatis'] et ['necessario'] abstinendum censerem, et pro iis ['certo'] vel ['sine dubio'] substituenda; vitandas enim, quoad ejus fieri potest, *καινοφωνίας*.

i [ut sup. col. 813.]
k [ut sup. col. 839.]
l [ut sup. col. 844.]
m [ut sup. col. 847.]
n [ut sup. col. 856.]
o [vol. x. col. 772.]
p [vol. ii. p. 46. ed. Froben, fol. Basil. 1526. Ben. ut spurium omittit.]

AD 5. DE AMISSIONE FIDEI ET SPIRITUS.

Certè nemo unquam dixerit (credo) 'fidem in electis finaliter excidere:' illa verò non excidit; sed quòd non excidat, hoc habere existimo à naturâ subjecti sui, non suâ; ex privilegio personæ, non rei. Atque hoc propter apostatas, quibus vitio dari non debet quòd excidant à fide, quæ vera et viva nunquam fuit.

An vero Spiritus Sanctus ad tempus auferri aut extingui possit, existimo quæri adhuc posse; fateor hærere me.

De fide;—'Tu stas fide, noli altum sapere, sed time: alioquin excideris et tu;' quomodo non irrisorium præceptum, si non possit excidere?

1. 'Cavete ne errore abducti excidatis propriâ firmitate,' &c.
2. 'Videte ne quis deficiat à gratiâ Dei; excidistis gratiâ, qui in lege,' Gal. v. 4.
3. 'Spiritum Sanctum tuum ne auferas a me,' Ps. li. 13.
4. 'Spiritum nolite extinguere.'

Quomodo non irrisoriæ præceptiones et orationes hæ, si nullo modo excidere à firmitate fidei aut deficere à gratiâ possimus, si nullo modo Spiritus auferri aut extingui possit?

Etsi non sum nescius et hoc ipsum ['non posse amitti totaliter'] exponi posse sic, ut in totum prorsùs vel penitùs amitti nequeat etsi tota amittatur, id est, ita amitti ut non sit locus revertendi unde exciderunt.

AD 6. DE CERTITUDINE SALUTIS.

Existimo quâ certitudine certus quis est, se verè fidelem esse, aut se fide justificante præditum, eâdem certum esse de salute suâ per Christum. Puto autem eam potius esse *πληροφορίαν* spei (de quâ ad Heb. vi. 11.) quàm fidei, et (si unâ voce exprimendum sit) *πεποίθησιν* potiùs quàm *πίστιν*. Non enim eandem certitudinem haberi posse de eis enuntiatis quæ conditionem in se continent quam nos præstare oportet ut veræ sint, ut, 'qui credit, invocat,' vel, 'si credas, invoces,' quam de iis quæ non sunt conditionatæ, sed merè categoricæ, ut, 'Deus est omnipotens,' sed minorem; quæ tamen non hæsitet, sed assensum suum ad alteram partem contradictionis determinet.

AD 7. DE COLLATIONE GRATIÆ.

Gratiam salutarem non existimo conferri omnibus; sed offerri tamen omnibus, hoc ipso quod præviæ quædam ad eam dispositiones non solùm offerantur, sed etiam conferantur omnibus; quibus illi nisi deessent, ipsa quoque salutaris gratia illis conferretur. 'Tribui,' 'communicari,' 'concedi,' si relativæ voces sunt, et acceptionem implicent, verum est; sed si relationem non includant, sed ex parte Dei offerri, vel Deum paratum esse vel præstò ut concedat ac communicet, sic existimo omnibus tribui; offerri itaque, et præstò esse Deum ut conferatur, per homines autem ipsos stare quòd oblata non conferatur, non enim gratiam nobis, sed nos illi deesse. Aug. *De Gen. cont. Manich.* lib. i.[q] 'Istud lumen non irrationabilium animalium oculos pascit, sed pura corda eorum qui Deo credunt, et ab amore visibilium rerum et temporalium se ad ejus præcepta servanda convertunt. Quod omnes homines possunt si velint, quia illud lumen omnium hominum,' &c.

AD 8.

Verè dicitur 'neminem venire ad Filium, nisi trahatur;' et 'omnes non trahi ut veniant ad Filium,' id est, ita trahi ut veniant; sed et illud addendum, 'quod vel non trahantur omnes, vel non sic trahantur, caussam esse dissolutam ipsorum hominum voluntatem, non absolutam voluntatem Dei.'

AD 9.

Non est positum aut in libero arbitrio cujusquam nisi per Filium liberato, aut in potestate ullius nisi datâ illi desuper, servari.

Materia hujus litis futura est: quisque ut affectus est, utque animum habet, voculam aliquam pertrahet ad opinionem suam; si desit, supplebit de sensu suo: ego quod ab initio suasi etiamnum suadeo, fidele utrinque silentium.

Atque hæc de Prædestinatione et Reprobatione. Sed ita tamen, ut sententiam et hâc in re et de ipsis articulis meque ipsum per omnia Gr. Pr. censuræ submissum velim.

[q] [cap. iii. vol. i. col. 648.]

CENSURA

CENSURÆ D. BARRETI[r]

DE CERTITUDINE SALUTIS.

'NEMINEM tantâ firmitate suffultum,' &c. 'ut de salute suâ debeat esse securus.' Ita Ds Barret: jubetur retractare sic, 'Fide justificatos,' &c. 'debere de salute suâ certos esse et securos.'

1. 'Certos' non debuit addi; non enim negaverat ille, nec quisquam (credo) sani cerebri: sanè retractare non debuit quod non asseruit, nec verbum interponi cujus in articulo nulla mentio.

2. 'Securum esse debere quemquam de salute,' minùs commodè dictum. Certè verba illa concionatoris censuram effugere poterant; leviter enim immutata, verba sunt Leonis, sic enim ille (dicente namque Paulo, 'Qui stat, videat ne cadat'), 'Nemo est tantâ firmitate suffultus ut de stabilitate suâ debeat esse securus,' Serm. v. *De quadr.* Sanè parcendum [p. 39.] fuerat, si non illi, saltem Leoni.

Sententiam verò cur minùs probem faciunt hæc.

1. Locus in censurâ citatus nihil ad rem, nempe 'debere justificatos securos esse.' Locus est, Rom. v. 1, 'Fide justificati pacem habemus erga Deum.' Certè; pacato igitur animo licet esse nobis, at non securo. Quippe nec pax ipsa secura est: nam et nobis prima cura incumbit, pax hæc ut vera sit; 'multi enim sanant contritionem filiæ meæ dicentes, Pax, pax, et non est pax,' dicit Deus, Jer. vi. 14, et Ezek. xiii. 10. Deinde si vera sit, secunda cura incumbit, ne per violatas à nobis conditiones pacis auferatur à nobis denuo,

r [vid. "Strype's Life of Whitgift," vol. ii. p. 229. sqq. 8vo. Oxon. 1822.]

Deo ipso dicente, Jer. xvi. 15, 'Abstuli pacem meam à populo isto, nempe misericordiam meam,' &c.

Atque ut securis nobis esse non licet, quia pacem habemus; ita neque quia stamus in gratiâ, sive per fidem. Stanti enim in gratiâ curandum quod dicit apostolus, Heb. xii. 15, 'Videte ne quis vestrûm deficiat à gratiâ Dei.' Stanti autem per fidem, curandum quod idem dicit, Rom. xi. 20, 'Tu fide' sive, per fidem, 'stas; noli altum sapere, sed time;' et quod alibi, 1 Cor. x. 12, 'Qui stare se putat, videat ne cadat;' quæ verba apostoli ab Augustino et Bernardo usurpantur contra securitatem. Aug.[s] *De dono persever.* cap. 8. Bern.[t] Serm. i. *de Septuages.*

2. Sacræ literæ nusquam securitatem suadent: quin potiùs eam vocem malam in partem accipiunt; quasi enim ab eâ abstinendum sit, notantur ab apostolo qui eam usurpant; 'Cùm dicent homines, Pax et securitas, superveniet iis repentinus interitus,' 1 Thess. v. 3; quare tanquam mali ominis declinandam censeo.

3. Neque vocis ratio magis favet. 'Securus' enim excludit curam et non hæsitationem tantùm; reverà enim curæ opponitur securitas: atqui jubemur a Spiritu Sancto omnem curam subinferre; et cupere se dicit apostolus, Heb. vi. 11, 'ut unusquisque nostrûm eandem solicitudinem ad finem usque ostendat.'

4. Rei vero ipsi (nempe securitati) repugnare videtur conditio tum vitæ christianæ, quæ militia est; tum vitæ humanæ, quæ tentatio est super terram: quarum neutra securitatem fert, quin perpetuam potiùs curam et solicitudinem, tum orandi ne in tentationem inducamur, tum considerandi nos ipsos ne et nos tentemur; idque etiam iis qui spirituales sunt, Gal. vi. 1.

5. Perpetuæ illæ Christi et apostolorum voces, 'vigilate,' 'attendite,' 'cavete,' 'tentate vos,' 'probate vos,' &c. excutiendæ securitati sunt omnes, non ingenerandæ; quid enim aliud sonant voces hæ, quàm, 'ne sitis securi?' Nec voces modò sed etiam sententiæ; Paulus, 'Cum timore et tremore operamini salutem vestram,' Phil. ii. 12. Petrus, 'In timore incolatûs

[s] [vol. x. col. 830.] [t] [col. 104.]

vestri tempore conversamini,' 1 Pet. i. 17. Joannes, 'Tene quod habes, ne alius accipiat coronam tuam,' Apoc. iii. 20. Quæ omnes id agunt ut cum fide retineatur et timor, ne certitudo degeneret in securitatem.

6. Certè D. Petrus cùm jubet, 'Satagite ut certam reddatis electionem vestram,' ut nos eniti vult ad certitudinem, ita statuere videtur satagere quemque rerum suarum ut eò tandem perveniat; quasi is summus sit gradus in vitâ hâc, et satis sit, imò præclarè nobiscum actum sit, si eò aspirare liceat.

7. Neque verò quoad certitudinis gradum planè æquandus videtur præsentis vitæ status cum statu futuræ, sed distinctio aliqua retinenda, cùm ultra securitatem nihil sit. Quare sit hoc ipsum, 'securitate frui,' peculiare iis qui defuncti jam sunt, et ἐπινίκιον illud apostoli cantârunt, 'absorpta est mors in victoriam;' nos verò hìc in terris militantes, contenti certitudine, cedamus gradu hoc summo securitatis, et relinquamus eum ecclesiæ in cœlis triumphanti, quæ sola secura est.

8. Malè autem semper successit iis qui ita se certos autumabant ut etiam securi fuerint; Davidi suum 'non movebor,' Ps. xxx. 6, Petro suum 'etsi omnes, non ego.' Meliùs multo iis, qui ita certi ut tamen soliciti: Jobo, 'scio quòd Redemptor meus vivit,' &c. cap. xix. 25, et, 'hæc mihi spes reposita est in sinu meo;' et, 'tamen verebar omnia opera mea,' cap. ix. 28. Paulo, 'certus sum quòd neque mors,' &c. Rom. viii. 38; et, 'tamen castigo corpus meum, ne quo modo cùm aliis prædicavero ipse reprobus efficiar,' 1 Cor. ix. 27.

9. Tametsi quod affertur de 'carnali et spirituali securitate,' frigidum planè sit, cùm pari ratione et de præsumptione et de superbiâ loqui liceat, nempe per κατάχρησιν, abusivè scilicet; tamen etiamsi sic mollire liceat, etiam atque etiam videndum est quid seculi nostri et populi indoles postulet istâ de re doceri; et an expediat, his præsertim moribus atque his temporibus, frigescenti hominum curæ atque conatui benè operandi, per istiusmodi theses frigidam suffundere, et quasi certitudo parum sit, securitatem inculcare; cùm (ut rectè Gregorius) securitas sit mater negligentiæ; cùmque non solùm ex trepidatione nimiâ (ut in Caino) sed sæpe etiam (ut in Saulo) ex nimiâ spe desperatio.

10. Ultimò; à recepto in ecclesiâ loquendi genere non censeo recedendum; qui ferè (cum Leone suprà citato) sentiunt, Nec posse nos nec debere de salute securos esse.

a. Augustinus[u], *Confess.* x. c. 32, 'Et nemo securus esse debet in istâ vitâ, quæ tota tentatio nominatur, utrùm qui fieri potuerit ex deteriore melior non fiat etiam ex meliore deterior.'

De dono persev.[x] cap. viii. 'Deus autem melius judicavit miscere quosdam non perseveraturos certo numero sanctorum suorum, ut quibus non expedit in hujus vitæ tentatione securitas, non possint esse securi.'

Ibid. cap. xxii.[y] 'quoniam de vitâ æternâ quam filiis promissionis promisit non mendax Deus ante tempora æterna, nemo potest esse securus, nisi cùm consummata fuerit ista vita quæ tentatio est super terram; sed faciet nos perseverare in se usque in ejus vitæ finem, cui quotidie dicimus, Ne nos inferas in tentationem.' Sic concionari docet Augustinus.

Ep. cxxx. *ad Prob.*[z] 'Unde mirum videri potest, cùm sis secundùm hoc seculum nobilis, dives, tantæ familiæ mater, et ideo licet vidua non tamen desolata, quomodo occupaverit cor tuum præcipuèque vendicaverit orandi cura; nisi quia prudenter intelligis, quòd in hoc mundo et in hâc vitâ nulla anima possit esse secura:' et paulo post, 'nam etsi sibi quisque, nemo alteri notus est; tamen nec sibi quisque ita notus est, ut sit de suâ crastinâ conversatione securus.'

β. Chrysostomus[a], Hom. xi. in Ep. ad Philip., in verba, 'Si quo modo apprehendam,' 'Dixi me in ipsum credidisse et potentiam resurrectionis ejus, et consortem passionum ejus factum esse, et conformatum morti ejus, veruntamen post ista omnia nondum securus sum:' et paulo pòst, 'Si ergo qui tanta passus est, si qui persecutionem tulit, si qui mortificationem habebat, nondum securus fuit, quid dicemus nos?'

γ. Ambrosius[b] in Psal. xxxvii., 'Nisi forte sic intelligamus, quod etsi innocens quisque sit, securus esse non possit, cui sint adversùs gravissimos hostes quotidiana certamina.'

δ. Hilarius[c] in Psal. cxxxvii., 'Nullum diem justus quisque

[u] [vol. i. col. 187.]
[x] [vol. x. col. 830.]
[y] [ut sup. col. 855.]
[z] [vol. ii. col. 383.]
[a] [vol. xi. col. 287.]
[b] [vol. i. col. 832. § 38.]
[c] [col. 559. § 11.]

sine metu transigit, neque anxia semper erga se fides securi temporis otium recipit; scit enim omnes dies insidiarum sibi plenos,' &c.

ε. Gregorius[d], Epist. xxv. *ad Gregoriam*, 'Inutilem rem postulâsti, quia secura de peccatis tuis fieri non debes, nisi cùm jam in die vitæ tuæ ultimo plangere eadem peccata minimè valebis.'

ζ. Bernardus[e], Epist. cvii. *ad Thom. Beverl.*, 'De quâ tamen jam perceptâ suimet ex parte notitiâ, interim quidem glorietur in spe, nondum tamen in securitate;' Bernardo enim securitas in excessu est, et opponitur timori in defectu. Vide Serm. in Cantic. xi.[f]

η. Fideles de prædestinatione perseverantiâque suâ incertos esse per omnem vitam, probat Augustinus,

In *De corrept. et gratiâ*, cap. xiii.[g] initio ferè.

Contra articulos sibi falsò impositos[h], Artic. 12.

In *Epistolâ* ccxvii.[i]

In *De dono perseverantiæ*, cap. xiii.[k] haud longè ab initio.

In *De civitate Dei*, lib. xi. c. 12.[l]

[d] [vol. ii. col. 869.]
[e] [col. 1493 F.]
[f] [col. 585 sqq.]
[g] [vol. x. col. 772.]
[h] [Al. Prosper. Aquit. pro Aug. doctr. respons. ad object. Vincent. in opp. S. Aug., vol. x. Append. col. 211.]
[i] [vol. ii. col. 799.]
[k] [vol. x. col. 838.]
[l] [vol. vii. col. 282.]

BISHOP ANDREWES'

FORM OF CONSECRATION

OF A

CHURCH AND CHURCHYARD.

CONSECRATIO

CAPELLÆ JESU, ET CŒMETERII,

PER

LANCELOTUM EPISCOPUM WINTON.

JUXTA Southamptoniensem villam ecclesia Beatæ Mariæ collapsa cernitur, solis cancellis ad sacros usus superstitibus: paucæ aliquot ædes ibi in propinquâ parte numerantur; cætera parochianorum multitudo hinc inde sparsim inhabitant in villis, tum loci longinquo intervallo, tum æstuario longe periculoso divisi ab ecclesiâ. Ex eâ accedendi difficultate non profanæ modo plebeculæ animos facile invasit misera negligentia atque dispretio divini cultûs, sed et viri probi sedulique pietatis cultores remoram in trajectu sæpe experti sunt, haud ipso quidem capitum discrimine eluctabilem; consortem hujus infortunii cùm se factum sentiret (dum ibi loci familiam poneret) vir strenuus Ricardus Smith, armiger, heroicos planè animos gestans, atque inspiratos de cœlo, commune hoc religionis dispendium privatis quingentarum aliquot librarum expensis (aut plus eo) redemit, et capellam egregiam, quam Deo divinisque officiis dicari supplex vovet, in alterâ parte fluminis magnificè extruit.

Spectato probatoque capellæ hujus Jesu omni adparatu, adest tandem reverendissimus in Christo pater, honorandissimus Lancelotus episcopus Wintoniensis, Septembris 17, *anno* 1620, *horâ octavâ matutinâ aut circiter; erat autem dies dominicus: episcopus capellam statim ingressus induit se pontificalibus, quem secuti itidem (qui ipsi à sacris domesticis aderant) Matthæus et Christophorus Wren, SS. Theol. Bacc., sacerdotalibus induuntur; egressus dein cum illis episcopus, convenarum magnâ stipante catervâ, fundatorem affari orditur in hæc ferè verba:—*

CAPTAIN SMITH, you have been an often and earnest suitor to me, that I would come hither to you; now that we are come hither to you, what have you to say to us?

Tum ille præfatâ humillimè reverentiâ schedulam porrigit, quam suo nomine recitari cupit per Willielm. Cole, qui episcopo à registris erat; eam ille, ad nutum episcopi, clarâ voce sic perlegit;—

"IN the name of Richard Smith, of Peer-tree in the county of Southampton, esquire, right reverend father in God, I present unto you the state of the village of Weston, and the hamlets, Itchin, Wolston, Ridgeway, and the part of Bittern Manor, (being all of the parish of St. Mary's, near Southampton, in the diocese of Winton,) as well in his own as in the name of the inhabitants of the said village, hamlets, &c., wherein are many households, and much people of all sorts, who not only dwell far from the church, but are also divided from the same by the great river of Itchin, where the passage is very broad, and often dangerous, and very many times on the days appointed for common prayer and that service of God, so tempestuous, as the river cannot be passed; and so the people go not over at all, or if any do, yet they both go and return back in great danger, and sometimes not the same day. Besides, in the fairest weather, at their return from church they press so thick into the boat for haste home, that often it proves dangerous, and ever fearful, especially to women with child, old, impotent, sickly people, and to young children; many times also they are forced to baptize their children in private houses, the water not being passable; and when they lie sick, they are without comfort to their souls, and die without any ghostly advice or counsel; their own minister not being able to visit them, by reason of the roughness of the water, and other ministers being some miles off remote from them.

"And thus much formerly having been presented to your predecessor, he favourably gave leave to the said Richard Smith to erect a chapel on the east side of the said river, at the only proper cost and charges of him the said Richard Smith; which chapel being now finished, with intent and purpose that it may be dedicated to the worship of God, and that His holy and blessed name might there be honoured and called upon by the said Richard Smith, his family, and the inhabitants aforesaid, who cannot without great danger pass over unto their parish church; I, in the name of the said Richard Smith, and in the name of them all, do promise hereafter to refuse and renounce to put this chapel, or any part of it, to any profane or common use whatsoever; and desire it may be dedicated and consecrated wholly and only to religious uses, for the glory of God, and the salvation of our souls.

"In which respect he humbly beseecheth God to accept of this his sincere intent and purpose, and he and they are together humble suitors unto your lordship, as God's minister, the bishop and ordinary of this diocese, in God's stead to accept of this his free-will offering; and to decree this chapel to be severed from all common and profane uses, and so to sever it; as also by the word of God and prayer, and other spiritual and religious duties, to dedicate and consecrate it to the sacred name of God, and to His service and worship only; promising that we will ever hold it as an holy place, even as God's house, and use it accordingly; and that we will from time to time, and ever hereafter as need shall be, see it conveniently repaired, and decently furnished in such sort as a chapel ought to be; and that we will procure us some sufficient clerk, being in the holy order of priesthood, by your lordship, as ordinary of that place, and by your successors to be allowed and licensed, and unto him to yield competent maintenance, to the end that he may take upon him the cure of the said chapel; and duly say divine service in the same at times appointed, and perform all other such offices and duties, as by the canons of that church, and the laws of the realm, every curate is bound to perform."

Post hæc episcopus.

Captain Smith, is this the desire of you and your neighbours?

Quo affirmato, ille :—

In the name of God let us begin.

Orditur igitur à psalmo xxiv.

"The earth is the Lord's, and all that is therein," &c.

Alterni vero respondent uterque sacellanus, et sic deinceps ad finem psalmi; dictâ autem δοξολογίᾳ, *paulatim se promovet episcopus ad portam capellæ, atque recitat è psalmo* cxxii.

"I was glad when they said unto me, We will go into the house of the Lord; our feet shall stand in thy gates, O Jerusalem."

Substitit itaque præ foribus universa multitudo, intrante episcopo et fundatore cum sacellanis, qui genua statim flectunt ubi spectari commodè audirique possint à plebe; atque episcopus infit.

Let us dedicate and offer up unto God this place with the same prayer that king David did dedicate and offer up his, 1 Chron. xxix. 10;

"Blessed be Thou, O Lord our God, and the God of our fathers, for ever and ever," &c., *usque ad finem ver.* 18, *paucis mutatis; deinde*

Most glorious God, the heaven is Thy throne, and the earth is Thy footstool; what house then can be built for Thee, or what place is there that Thou canst rest in? Howbeit we are taught by Thy holy word, that Thy will is not to dwell in the dark cloud, but that Thy delight hath been ever with the sons of men; so that in any place whatsoever, where two or three are gathered together in Thy name, Thou art in the midst of them; but specially in such places as are set apart and sanctified to Thy name, and to the memory of it, there Thou hast said Thou wilt vouchsafe Thy gracious presence after a more special manner, and come to us and bless us.

Wherefore in all ages of the world Thy servants have separated certain places from all profane and common uses, and hallowed unto Thy divine worship and service, either by inspiration of Thy blessed Spirit, or by express commandment from Thine own mouth.

By inspiration of Thy Holy Spirit; so didst Thou put into the heart of Thy holy patriarch Jacob, to erect a stone in Bethel to be an house to Thee, which act of his Thou didst call for, and highly allow of.

By express commandment from Thine own mouth; so did Moses make Thee the tabernacle of the congregation in the desert, which Thou didst honour by covering it with a cloud, and filling it with Thy glory.

And after, when it came into the heart of Thy servant David to think it was in no wise fitting that himself should dwell in an house of cedar, and the ark of God remain but in a tabernacle, Thou didst testify with Thine own mouth, that in that David was so minded to build a house to Thy name, it was well done of him to be so minded, though he built it not.

The material furniture for which house though his father plentifully prepared, yet Solomon his son built it and brought it to perfection. To which house Thou wert pleased visibly to send fire from heaven to consume the sacrifice, and to fill it with the glory of Thy presence, before all the people.

And after, when for the sins of Thy people that temple was destroyed, Thou didst by Thy prophets, Aggai and Zachary, (by shewing how inconvenient it was that they should dwell in ceiled houses, and let Thy house lie waste,) stir up the spirit of Zorobabel to build Thee the second temple anew; which second house likewise by the fulness of the glory of Thy presence Thou didst shew Thyself to like and allow of.

Neither only wert Thou well pleased with such as did build Thee these temples, but even with such of the people afterwards as, being moved with zeal, added unto their temple, their mother church, lesser places of prayer, by the names of synagogues, in every town throughout the land; for the tribes to ascend up to worship Thee, to learn Thy holy will, and to do it. Which very act of the centurion, to build Thy people a synagogue, Thou didst well approve and commend in the gospel.

And by the bodily presence of Thy Son our Saviour at the feast of the dedication, testified by St. John, didst really well allow of and do honour to such devout religious services as we are now about to perform.

Which also by Thy holy word hast taught us, that Thine apostles themselves, and the christians in their time, as they had houses to eat and drink in, so had they also where the whole congregation of the faithful came together in one place, which they expressly called God's church, and would not have it despised, nor abused, nor eaten nor drunken in, but had in great reverence, being the very place of their holy assemblies.

By whose godly examples the christians in all ages successively have erected and consecrated sundry godly houses for the celebration of divine service and worship, monuments of their piety and devotion, as our eyes see this day.

We then, as fellow-citizens with the saints and of the household of God, being built upon the foundation of the apostles and prophets, Jesus Christ himself being the head corner-stone; walking in the steps of their most holy faith, and ensuing the examples of these Thy patriarchs, prophets, and apostles, have together with them done the same work, I say, in building and dedicating this house, as an habitation for Thee, and a place for us to assemble and meet together for the observation of Thy divine worship, invocation of Thy name, reading, preaching, and hearing Thy most holy word, administering Thy most holy sacraments; and above all in Thy most holy place, the very gate of heaven upon earth, as Jacob named it, to do the work of heaven; to set forth Thy most worthy praise, to laud and magnify Thy most glorious Majesty, for all Thy goodness to all men; especially to us of the household of faith. Accept, therefore, we beseech Thee, most gracious Father, of this our bounden duty and service; accept this for Thine house; and because Thine holiness becomes Thine house for ever, sanctify this house with Thy gracious presence, which is erected to the honour of Thy most glorious name.

Now therefore, arise, O Lord, and come into this place of Thy rest, Thou and the ark of Thy strength; let Thine eye be open towards this house day and night; let Thine ears be ready towards the prayers of Thy children which they shall make unto Thee in this place, and let Thine heart delight to dwell here perpetually: and whensoever Thy servants shall make to Thee their petitions in this house, either to bestow Thy good graces and blessings upon them, or to remove Thy punishments and judgments from them; hear them from heaven Thy dwelling-place, the throne of the glory of Thy kingdom, and when Thou hearest, have mercy; and grant, O Lord, we beseech Thee, that here and elsewhere Thy priests may be clothed with righteousness, and Thy saints rejoice in Thy salvation.

And whereas both in the Old and New testament Thou hast consecrated the measuring out and building of a material church to such an excellent mystery, that in it is signified and presented the fruition of the joy of Thy heavenly kingdom, we beseech Thee that in this material temple made with hands we may so serve and please Thee in all holy exercises of godliness and christian religion, that in the end we may come to that Thy temple on high, even to the holy places made without hands, whose builder and maker is God; so as when we shall cease to pray to Thee on earth, we may with all those that have in the like manner erected such places to Thy name, and with all Thy saints eternally praise Thee in the highest heavens, for all Thy goodness vouchsafed us for a time here on earth, and laid up for us there in Thy kingdom for ever and ever; and that for Thy dear Son's sake, our blessed Saviour, Jesus Christ, to whom, &c.

Blessed Father, who hast promised in Thy holy law that in every place where the remembrance of Thy name shall be put, Thou wilt come unto us and bless us; according to that Thy promise, come unto us and bless us, who put now upon this place the memorial of Thy name, by dedicating it wholly and only to Thy service and worship.

Blessed Saviour, who in the gospel with Thy bodily presence didst honour and adorn the feast of the dedication of the temple; at this dedication of this temple unto Thee, be present also, and accept, good Lord, and prosper the work of our hands.

Blessed Spirit, without whom nothing is holy, no person or place is sanctified aright, send down upon this place Thy sanctifying power and grace, hallow it, and make it to Thee an holy habitation for ever.

Blessed and glorious Trinity, by whose power, wisdom, and

love, all things are purged, lightened, and made perfect; enable us with Thy power, enlighten us with Thy truth, perfect us with Thy grace, that both here and elsewhere, acknowledging the glory of Thy eternal Trinity, and in the power of Thy divine majesty worshipping the Unity, we may obtain to the fruition of the glorious godhead, Trinity in Unity, and Unity in Trinity, to be adored for ever.

God the Father, God the Son, and God the Holy Ghost, accept, sanctify, and bless this place to the end whereunto, according to His own ordinance, we have ordained it; to be a sanctuary to the Most high, and a church for the living God. The Lord with His favour ever mercifully behold it, and so send upon it His spiritual benediction and grace, that it may be the house of God to Him, and the gate of heaven to us. Amen.

Hæc precatus episcopus baptisterium adit, atque impositâ manu ait,

Regard, O Lord, the supplications of Thy servants, and grant that those children that shall be baptized in this laver of the new birth may be sanctified and washed with the Holy Ghost, delivered from Thy wrath, received into the ark of Christ's church, receive herein the fulness of grace, and ever remain in the number of Thy faithful and elect children.

Suggestum dein;

Grant that Thy holy word, which from this place shall be preached, may be the savour of life unto life, and as good seed take root and fructify in the hearts of all that shall hear it.

'Αναλογεῖον quoque;

Grant that by Thy holy word, which from this place shall be read, the hearers may both perceive and know what things they ought to do, and also may have grace and power to fulfil the same.

Sacram etiam mensam;

Grant that all they that shall at any time partake at this table the highest blessing of all, Thy holy communion, may be fulfilled with Thy grace and heavenly benediction, and may to their great and endless comfort obtain remission of their sins, and all other benefits of Thy passion.

Locum nuptiarum;

Grant that such persons as shall be here joined together in the holy estate of matrimony by the covenant of God, may live together in holy love unto their lives' end.

Universum denique pavimentum.

Grant to such bodies as shall be here interred, that they with us, and we with them, may have our perfect consummation and bliss, both in body and soul, in Thine everlasting kingdom.

Tum flexis genibus ante sacram mensam pergit porro.

Grant that this place, which is here dedicated to Thee by our office and ministry, may also be hallowed by the sanctifying power of Thy holy Spirit, and so for ever continue through Thy mercy, O blessed Lord God, who dost live and govern all things, world without end.

Grant as this chapel is separated from all other common and profane uses, and dedicated to those that be sacred only, so may all those be that enter into it.

Grant that all wandering thoughts, all carnal and worldly imaginations, may be far from them, and all godly and spiritual cogitations may come in their place, and may be daily renewed and grow in them.

Grant that those Thy servants that shall come into this Thy holy temple, may themselves be made the temples of the Holy Ghost, eschewing all things contrary to their profession, and following all such things as are agreeable to the same.

When they pray, that their prayers may ascend up into heaven into Thy presence, as the incense; and the lifting up of their hands be as the morning sacrifice; purify their hearts, and grant them their hearts' desire, sanctify their spirits, and fulfil all their minds, that what they faithfully ask, they may effectually obtain the same.

When they offer, that their oblation and alms may come up

as a memorial before Thee, and they find and feel that with such sacrifices Thou art well pleased.

When they sing, that their souls may be satisfied as with marrow and fatness, when their mouth praiseth Thee with joyful lips.

When they hear, that they hear not as the word of man, but as indeed it is, the word of God, and not be idle hearers, but doers of the same.

Populus interea tacitè ingressus in imis substitit, dùm hæc in cancellis agerentur; quibus finitis, sedes quisque suas jussi capessunt, atque ad solennem liturgiam sacellani se parant.

Alter sacellanorum coram sacrâ mensâ venerans sic incipit:

If we say we have no sin, we deceive ourselves, and the truth, &c.

Confessionem, absolutionem, dominicam προσευχὴν *recitant, &c.—Psalmos canunt pro tempore accommodos, ps.* lxxxiv. cxxii. *et* cxxxii., *alternis respondente populo quibus facultas erat et libri.—Lectio prima definitur è Gen.* xxviii. *à versu primo ad finem.—Hymn.*, Te Deum, *&c.—Lectio secunda ex secundo capite S. Joan. à versu* 13 *ad finem.—Hymn., Ps.* c.

"I believe in God the Father almighty, Maker of heaven and earth," &c.

Et post usitatas collectas hanc specialem addidit episcopus:

O Lord God, mighty and glorious, and of incomprehensible majesty, Thou fillest heaven and earth with the glory of Thy presence, and canst not be contained within any the largest compass, much less within the narrow walls of this room; yet forasmuch as Thou hast been pleased to command in Thy holy law that we should put the remembrance of Thy name upon places, and in every such place Thou wilt come to us and bless us, we are here now assembled to put Thy name upon this place and the memorial of it, to make it Thy house, to devote and dedicate it for ever unto Thee, utterly separating it from all worldly uses, and wholly and only consecrate it to the invocation of Thy glorious name: wherein supplications and intercessions may be made for all men; Thy sacred word may be read, preached, and heard; the holy sacraments (the laver of regeneration, and the commemoration of the precious death of Thy dear Son) may be administered; Thy praise celebrated and sounded forth; Thy people blessed by putting Thy name upon them. We, poor and miserable creatures as we are, be altogether unfit and utterly unworthy to appoint any earthly thing to so great a God; and I the least of all Thy servants, no ways meet to appear before Thee in so honourable a service; yet being Thou hast oft heretofore been pleased to accept such poor offerings from sinful men, most humbly we beseech Thee, forgiving our manifold sins, and making us worthy by counting us so, to vouchsafe to be present here among us in this religious action, and what we sincerely offer, graciously to accept at our hands; to receive the prayers of us, and all others who either now or hereafter entering into this place, by us hallowed, shall call upon Thee; and give us all grace when we shall come into the house of God, that we may look to our feet, knowing that the place we stand on is holy ground, bringing hither clean thoughts and undefiled bodies, that we may wash both our hearts and hands in innocency, and so compass Thine altar.

Jam alter sacellanus denuo exiens, et venerans ante sacram mensam, incipit litaniam; in fine cujus recitavit hoc ipse episcopus:—

O Lord God, who dwellest not in temples made with hands (as saith the prophet), yet hast ever vouchsafed to accept the devout endeavours of Thy poor servants, allotting special places for Thy divine worship, promising even there to hear and grant their requests; I humbly beseech Thee to accept of this day's duty and service of dedicating this chapel to Thy great and glorious name; fulfil, O Lord, I pray Thee, Thy gracious promises, that whatsoever prayer in this sacred place shall be made according to Thy will, may be accepted by Thy gracious favour, and returned with their desired success to Thy glory and our comfort. Amen.

Post benedictionem populi cantatur psalm. cxxxii., *conscenditque suggestum M. Robinson, Theol. Bac., fundatoris summo rogatu; episcopus hoc ei tandem concessit; (geminas sorores ille atque fundator in uxores duxerant, sed utrâque defunctâ, jam tertiis gaudebat thalamis concionator;) thema ejus desumptum è Gen. cap.* xxviii. *ver.* 16, 17; *inter cætera doctè egit de omnipræsentiâ divinâ, ubivis locorum, tùm speciatim (pro beneplacito suo) in ecclesiâ, deque reverentiâ et veneratione ibi debitâ.—Pergitur in liturgiâ, quâ mulier quædam paupercula purificanda ad limen cancellorum accedens, genua flectit, gratiasque post partum, solenni ecclesiæ ritu, agit; baptizandus autem vel matrimonio jungendus, nullus aderat.—Itur dein ad cœnæ dominicæ administrationem, sacellanorum altero ad australem, altero ad septentrionalem partem sacræ mensæ genu flectente et dicente:—*

"Our Father, which art in heaven, hallowed be Thy name," &c.

Ante epistolæ lectionem hanc specialem collectam, unà cum collectâ solitâ pro rege, recitat sacellanorum alter:—

Most blessed Saviour, who by Thy bodily presence at the feast of dedication didst honour and approve such devout and religious services as we have now in hand, be Thou present also at this time with us, and consecrate us into an holy temple unto Thyself, that Thou dwelling in our hearts by faith, we may be cleansed from all carnal affections, and devoutly given to serve Thee in all good works. Amen.

Epistolam secundus sacellanus, ante sacram mensam stans, legit ex 1 *Cor. cap.* iii. *à ver.* 16 *ad finem.—SS. evangelium prior sacellanus ibidem stans recitat è cap.* x. *S. Joannis à ver.* 22 *ad finem.—Dein symbolum Nicænum, omnibus etiam stantibus.*

Post illa episcopus, sede suâ egressus, coram sacrâ mensâ sese provolvit atque ait:—

Let us pray the prayer of king Solomon, which he prayed in the day of the dedication of his temple, the first temple that ever was, 2 Chron. vi. *ab initio ver.* 18 *ad ver.* 40, *quo finito ait:—*

Thus prayed king Solomon, and the Lord appeared unto

him, and answered and said unto him, I have heard thy prayer, and have chosen this place for Myself, to be an house of sacrifice, 2 Chron. vii. 12.

Thus did God answer; we have prayed with Solomon, answer us, O Lord, and our prayer, as Thou didst him and his; behold the face of Thine anointed, even Christ our Saviour, and for His sake grant our requests.

Dein in cathedram ibidem se collocat, assidentibus Thomâ Ridley cancellario episcopi à dextris, à sinistris verò doctore Barlo archidiacono Winton., actumque consecrationis, pileo tectus, promulgat in hanc formam:—

In nomine Domini Amen. Cum strenuus vir Ricardus Smith de Peer-tree in comitatu Southampt. armiger, piâ et religiosâ devotione ductus, capellam hanc in quodam solo vasto vocato Ridgway-heath, juxta ædes suas communiter nuncupatas Peer-tree, infra parochiam ecclesiæ paroch. Beatæ Mariæ juxta villam Southampt. dioceseos et jurisdictionis nostræ, continentem intra muros ejusdem in longitudine ab Oriente ad Occidentem quinquaginta pedes et dimid. aut circiter, in latitudine verò ab Aquilone ad Austrum viginti pedes et dimid. aut circiter, propriis suis sumptibus ædificaverit, erexerit, et construxerit; eandemque capellam cancellis ligneis distinxerit; sacrâ mensâ decenter instructâ, baptisterio, pulpito, sedibus convenientibus, tam infra super solum quàm supra in modum galeriæ, campanâ etiam aliisque necessariis ad divinum cultum sufficienter et decenter ornaverit; nobisque supplicaverit tam suo nomine quàm aliorum inhabitantium in villâ de Weston, ac hamlettis de Itchin, Ridgway, ac quorundam etiam inhabitantium in manerio nostro de Bitterne, de parochiâ prædictâ, quatenus nos auctoritate nostrâ ordinariâ et episcopali pro nobis et successoribus nostris dictam capellam ab usibus pristinis communibus et profanis quibuscunque separare, et in usus sacros et divinos consecrare et dedicare dignaremur.

Nos Lancelotus permissione divinâ Winton. episcopus, pio et religioso tam ipsius quàm aliorum in villâ et hamlettis prædictis habitantium desiderio in hâc parte favorabiliter annuentes, ad consecrationem capellæ hujus de novo propriis sumptibus dicti strenui viri Ricardi Smith, sic ut præfertur erectæ et ornatæ, auctoritate nostrâ ordinariâ et episcopali procedentes, eandem capellam ab omni communi et profano usu in perpetuum separamus, et soli divino cultui ac divinorum celebrationi in perpetuum addicimus, dicamus, dedicamus: ac insuper eâdem auctoritate nostrâ ordinariâ et episcopali, pro nobis et successoribus nostris licentiam pariter et facultatem in Domino concedimus, ad rem divinam ibidem faciendam, nempe preces publicas et sacram ecclesiæ liturgiam recitandam, ac verbum Dei sincerè proponendum et prædicandum, sacramenta sacræ eucharistiæ et baptismatis in eâdem ministranda, matrimonia solemnizanda, mulieres post puerperium ad gratiarum actionem publicam recipiendas et adjuvandas, mortuos sepeliendos, cæteraque quæcunque peragenda, quæ in aliis capellis licitè fieri possunt et solent. Ac tam presbytero in capellâ prædictâ deservituro preces divinas dicendi, cæteraque præmissa faciendi, quàm domino Ricardo Smith, et familiæ ejus, reliquisque in dictis locis habitantibus, preces divinas audiendi, cæteraque præmissa percipiendi, plenam in Domino potestatem concedimus. Eandemque capellam ad levamen (anglicè, 'a chapel of ease') sub dictâ ecclesiâ parochiali B. Mariæ juxta villam Southampt. tanquam matrice ecclesiâ suâ, quantum in nobis est, et de jure divino, canonibus ecclesiæ et statutis hujus regni Angliæ possumus, in honorem Dei et sacros inhabitantium usus, nunc et in futurum consecramus, per nomen capellæ Jesu in parochiâ sanctæ Mariæ juxta villam Southampt., et sic consecratam fuisse, et esse, et in futuris perpetuis temporibus remanere debere, palam et publicè pronunciamus, decernimus, et declaramus; et per nomen capellæ Jesu nominamus et appellamus, et sic perpetuis futuris temporibus nominandam et appellandam fore decernimus: privilegiis insuper omnibus et singulis in capite usitatis, et capellis ab antiquo fundatis competentibus, capellam hanc Jesu prædictam ad omnem juris effectum munitam et stabilitam esse volumus; et quantum in nobis est, et de jure divino possumus, sic munimus et stabilimus per præsentes; absque præjudicio tamen ullo, et salvo semper jure et interesse ecclesiæ parochialis sanctæ Mariæ juxta villam Southampt. tanquam matricis ecclesiæ; et rectoris, guardianorum, aliorumque ministrorum ejusdem pro tempore existentium (in cujus parochiâ dicta capella Jesu notoriè sita et situata est) in omnibus et singulis decimis, oblationibus, obventionibus, vadiis, feudis, proficuis, privilegiis, juribus et emolumentis quibuscunque ordinariis et extraordinariis eisdem respectivè debitis vel consuetis, ac infra præcinctum seu limites capellæ Jesu prædictæ orientibus et provenientibus, et ad dictam ecclesiam matricem sanctæ Mariæ, rectori, guardianis vel aliis ministris ejusdem de jure vel consuetudine quoquo modo spectantibus vel pertinentibus, in tam amplis modo et formâ prout eisdem debebantur aut solvi solebant ante hanc nostram consecrationem hujus capellæ prædictæ.

Proviso, quod prædictus strenuus vir Ricardus Smith, ac ejus hæredes et assignati, aliique in dictâ villâ et hamlettis, &c. habitantes, non solùm dictam capellam, quoties opus fuerit, impensis suis propriis reficere et reparare, sed etiam ad reparationes prædictæ matricis ecclesiæ sanctæ Mariæ juxta villam Southampt., et cœmeterii ejusdem ecclesiæ, ac ad omnia alia onera ad quæ cæteri parochiani dictæ matricis ecclesiæ teneantur.

Proviso etiam, quòd tam dictus strenuus vir Ricardus Smith, hæredes et assignati ejus, quàm reliqui omnes in dictis villis et hamlettis, &c. habitantes, in signum subjectionis capellæ hujus sub ecclesiâ matrice beatæ Mariæ juxta Southampt. ac senioritatis ejusdem ecclesiæ supra dictam capellam, singulis annis de tempore ad tempus ad festum paschatis, vel ad festum pentecostes, ad dictam ecclesiam matricem venire, et in dictâ matrice ecclesiâ tantùm, non in dictâ capellâ, (si tutò ad ecclesiam parochialem venire possint,) preces audire, et sacramentum eucharistiæ ibidem percipere; vel si tempestate aut alio impedimento detineantur quo minus tunc venire possint, tum die dominico, quo tutò venire possunt, subsequente, venire et eucharistiam accipere omninò teneantur, absque speciali licentiâ nostrâ seu vicarii nostri generalis in hâc parte obtentâ.

Proviso etiam, quòd in dictâ capellâ sacramentum baptismatis non ministretur, nec matrimonia solemnizentur, neque verbum Dei prædicetur, neque sacramenta vel sacramentalia aliquibus profanis conferantur, præterquàm solis inhabitantibus seu degentibus in villâ, hamlettis, &c. prædictis, nec etiam reliquis dictæ matricis ecclesiæ parochianis in occidentali parte ripæ inhabitantibus, inscio vel invito rectore ecclesiæ matricis sanctæ Mariæ juxta villam Southampt. prædictam, seu absque assensu, consensu et licentiâ ejusdem priùs habitâ et obtentâ.

Et ulteriùs, dicto strenuo Ricardo Smith, hæredibus et assignatis suis, liberam et plenam potestatem in Domino concedimus per præsentes, idoneum presbyterum de tempore in tempus nominandi ad deserviendum et divina officia in dictâ capellâ exequenda, à nobis et successoribus nostris de tempore in tempus approbandum et licentiandum: ad quod dictus strenuus vir R. Smith, hæredes et assignati sui, et reliqui in dictis villâ et hamlettis, &c. inhabitantes de tempore in tempus in futurum propriis suis sumptibus dictum presbyterum sive curatum in eâdem capellâ deservientem, et auctoritate nostrâ vel successorum nostrorum ut præfertur approbatum et licentiatum, alent et sustinebunt, ac annuale stipendium viginti marcarum ad minimum eidem presbytero vel curato præstabunt, et solvent ad quatuor festa, Nativitatis Christi, Annunciationis, Nativitatis sancti Johannis baptistæ, et sancti Michaelis, per æquales portiones, sine ullâ tamen diminutione vel defalcatione juris ecclesiastici, decimarum, oblationum, vel obventionum quarumcunque ad dictam ecclesiam parochialem sanctæ Mariæ, seu ad rectorem ejus pro tempore existentem, quo modo de jure vel consuetudine spectantium seu pertinentium.

Et ulteriùs, quòd pro sepulturis in capellâ prædictâ, et in choro seu navi ejusdem, omnibusque aliis in dictâ capellâ vel extra gerendis, vadia, quoad defunctos tam in domo dicti strenui viri R. Smith, hæredum et assignatorum suorum, quàm in dictâ villâ, hamlettis, &c., rectori dictæ ecclesiæ matricis pro tempore existenti, et successoribus suis, et guardianis respectivè, et clerico, cæterisque ministris dictæ ecclesiæ parochialis debitè solvantur, in tam amplis modo et formâ prout pro sepulturis in choro seu intra cancellos seu etiam in navi dictæ ecclesiæ matricis solvi consuetum fuit, et prout solvi solet et deberet si personæ prædictæ intra cancellos seu navim dictæ matricis ecclesiæ sepultæ fuissent.

Quòd si autem aliquando defuerit in dictâ capellâ presbyter, curatus legitimè per nos aut successores nostros licentiatus et approbatus, tunc prædictus strenuus vir R. Smith, hæredes et assignati sui ac reliqui in dictâ villâ, et hamlettis, &c. inhabitantes, ad matricem ecclesiam convenire, aut ibidem precibus interesse teneantur, prout antè solebant, donec dicta capella de legitimo curato ad ibidem divina celebranda idoneè provideatur et idem admittatur. Quòd si autem aliquo tempore in posterum (quod Deus avertat) per continuos sex menses per culpam aut negligentiam parochianorum defuerit idoneus curatus in dictâ capellâ qui ibidem divina celebret, aut si curatus sit qui per sex menses continuos non celebret, tunc nobis et successoribus nostris potestatem reservamus pro eâ vice tantùm idoneum curatum ad dictam capellam nominandi, ad supplendam negligentiam dictorum R. Smith, hæredum et assignatorum suorum. Quòd si autem dicta capella decenter non fuerit reparata vel instructa libris aliisque ad cultum divinum necessariis, per tempus prædictum, (nisi ex legitimâ in eâ parte causâ per episcopum approbandâ hoc contigerit,) tunc in perpetuum post dictos sex menses continuos sic elapsos, teneantur omnes infra præcinctum seu limites dictæ capellæ inhabitantes ad matricem ecclesiam convenire, pro divinis audiendis, prout ante hanc nostram consecrationem tenebantur; aliquâ in hâc concessione seu consecratione nostrâ in contrarium non obstante, ac perinde ac si hæc concessio seu consecratio facta nunquam fuisset.

Postremò reservamus nobis et successoribus nostris, episcopis Winton., potestatem visitandi dictam capellam, prout alias capellas infra nostram diocesin situatas, communiter nuncupatas peculiares, ut nobis eisque constet an decenter in reparationibus aliisque conservetur, et an omnia ibidem decenter et secundum ordinem fiant. Quæ omnia et singula sic reservamus; quoad cætera verò præmissa, quatenus in nobis est, et de jure possumus, pro nobis et successoribus nostris decernimus et stabilimus per præsentes.

Actu demum recitato veneratur denuo, atque infit.

Blessed be Thy name, O Lord God, for that it pleased Thee to have Thy habitation among the sons of men, and to dwell in the midst of the assembly of Thy saints upon earth; bless, we beseech Thee, this day's action unto Thy people; prosper Thou the work of our hands unto us, yea, prosper Thou our handy-work.

Finitis precationibus istis dominus episcopus sedem separatim capessit ubi prius, populusque universus non communicaturus dimittitur, et porta clauditur.—Prior sacellanus pergit legendo sententias illas hortatorias ad eleemosynas, interea dum alter sacellanus singulos communicaturos adit, atque in patinam argenteam oblationes colligit; collecta est summa 4*l.* 12*s.* 2*d. quam dominus episcopus convertendam in calicem huic capellæ donandum decernit.*

Cæteris rebus ordine gestis, demum episcopus sacram mensam redit, (sacellanis utrisque ad aliquantulum recedentibus,) lotisque manibus, pane fracto, vino in calicem effuso, et aquâ admistâ, stans ait,

Almighty God our heavenly Father, who of His great mercy hath, &c.

Eucharistiam ipse primo loco accipit sub utrâque specie; proximo loco tradit fundatori, (quem jam coram sacrâ mensâ in genua supplicem collocârant,) dein utrique sacellano; ad cæteros vero pergentem episcopum atque panem iis tradentem, prior sacellanus subsequitur, et calicem ordine porrigit. Cùm vinum, quod priùs effuderat, non sufficeret, episcopus de novo in calicem ex poculo quod in sacrâ mensâ stabat effundit, admistâque aquâ, recitat clarè verba illa consecratoria.

Finitâ tandem exhibitione dominus episcopus ad sacræ mensæ septentrionem in genibus, recitante quoque populo, ait:—

Our Father, which art in heaven, hallowed be Thy name, &c.

O Lord our heavenly Father, we Thy humble servants entirely desire, &c.

Glory be to God on high, and in earth peace, goodwill towards men.

Concludit denique cum hâc precatione.

Blessed be Thy name, O Lord, that it hath pleased Thee to put into the heart of this Thy servant to erect an house to

Thy worship and service, by whose pains, care, and cost, this work was begun and finished. Bless, O Lord, his substance and accept the work of his hands; remember him, O our God, concerning this; wipe not out this kindness of his that he hath shewed for the house of his God and the offices thereof; and make them truly thankful to Thee, that shall enjoy the benefit thereof, and the ease of it; and what is by him well intended, make them rightly to use it, which will be the best fruit, and to God most acceptable.

Post hæc vota populum stans dimittit cum benedictione hâc.

The peace of God, which passeth all understanding, keep your hearts and minds in the knowledge and love of God, and of His Son Jesus Christ our Lord; and the blessing of God almighty, the Father, the Son, and the Holy Ghost, be amongst you, and remain with you always. *Amen.*

CONSECRATIO CŒMETERII.

STATIM à prandio (quod in ædibus suis vicinis fundator capellæ satis lautè apparârat domino episcopo atque convenarum magnæ frequentiæ) ad rem divinam reversis, alter sacellanorum præit.

Our Father, which art in heaven, hallowed be Thy name; Thy kingdom come; Thy will be done in earth, as it is in heaven; give us this day our daily bread; and forgive us our trespasses, as we forgive them that trespass against us; and lead us not into temptation, but deliver us from evil; for Thine is the kingdom, the power, and the glory, for ever and ever. Amen.

Post responsas, psalmus XC. *recitatur alternis.*

Post psalmum episcopus cum universâ multitudine egreditur capellâ, atque ad orientalem cœmeterii partem stans, denuo sciscitatur.

Captain Smith, for what have you called us hither again?

Ille schedulam, ut priùs, humillimè porrigit, quam præfatus à registris recitat in hæc verba.

"In the name of Richard Smith, of Peer-tree in the county of Southampton, esquire, right reverend father in God, I present unto you the state of the village of Weston," &c. [*ut prius, usque ad*] "the river cannot be passed, whereby it often cometh to pass that they have been constrained to bury their dead in the open fields, the water not being passable, or if they durst venture over, yet the dead body was followed with so little company as was no way seemly.

"And thus much formerly having been presented to your predecessor, the right reverend father in God, James, late bishop of Winton, and petition to him made to give and to grant leave unto the said Richard Smith to enclose a piece of ground for a burial place on the east side of the said river, he favourably gave license and granted power unto the said Richard Smith so to do, as may appear by an instrument under his episcopal seal, bearing date the twenty-third of February, in the year of our Lord God, according to the computation of the church of England, 1617.

"Which place of burial being now enclosed with a decent rail of timber, at the only proper cost and charges of him the said Richard Smith, with intent and purpose that it might be dedicated and consecrated only and wholly for christian burial, for him the said Richard Smith, and his family, and the said inhabitants, and none other; in which respect I beseech God to accept of this sincere intent and purpose, and both he and they are together humble suitors to your lordship, as God's minister, the bishop and ordinary of this diocese, in God's stead to accept this his free-will offering, and to decree this ground severed from all former common and profane uses, and to sever it, as by the word of God and prayer, and other special religious duties, to dedicate and consecrate it to be a cemetery or place of christian burial, as aforesaid; wherein their bodies may be laid up until the day of the general resurrection; promising that they will ever so hold it for holy ground, and use it accordingly, applying it to no other use but that only, and that they will from time to time, and ever hereafter as need shall be, see it conveniently repaired and fenced in such sort as a cemetery or burying place ought to be."

Hoc ipsum verò, ab episcopo paucis interrogatis, vivâ voce confirmant fundator, et qui è viciniâ.—Lectio prima desumitur è Gen. xxiii.—*Secunda lectio destinabatur è primâ epist. ad Cor. cap.* xv. *à ver.* 15. *ad finem, propter angustias temporis omissa.*

Tum dominus episcopus in genua ibi submissus precatur.

O Lord God, Thou hast been pleased to teach us in Thy holy word, as to put a difference between the soul of a beast and the spirit of a man, for the soul of a beast goes down to the earth from whence it came, and the spirit of a man returneth unto God that gave it; so to make diverse accompts of the bodies of mankind and the bodies of other living creatures, in so much as the body of Adam was resolved on, and afterwards the workmanship of Thine own hands, and endued with a soul from Thine own breath; but much more since the second Adam, Thy blessed Son, by taking upon Him our nature, exalted this flesh of ours to be flesh of His flesh whose flesh Thou sufferedst not to see corruption; so that the body returns to the earth, and the soul to Him that gave it; it shall from thence return again, it is but a rest, and a rest in hope (saith the psalmist), for it is a righteous thing with God that the body, which was partaker with the soul both in doing and suffering, should be raised again from the earth to be partaker also, with the soul, of the reward or punishment which God in mercy or justice shall reward, not to one of them alone, but jointly to them both: there being then so great difference, it is not Thy will, O Lord, that our bodies should be cast out as the bodies of beasts to become dung for the earth, or our bones lie scattered abroad to the sight of the sun; but when Thy servants are gathered to their fathers, their bodies should be decently and seemly laid up in the bosom of the earth from whence they were taken. Neither is it Thy pleasure, O Lord, that they should be buried as an ass in the open fields, but in a place chosen and set apart for that purpose: for even so from the beginning we find the holy patriarch Abraham, the father of the faithful, would not bury his dead in the common fields, nay, nor amongst the bodies of Hethites who were heathen men, but purchased a burial place for himself in the plain of Mamre, which became as it were the churchyard of the patriarchs, wherein they laid the dead bodies of Sarah his wife, of himself, his son Isaac and Rebecca his wife; after them Jacob and Leah were buried there. After this manner did the patriarchs in old time, who trusted in God, sever themselves places for burial; whose children we are so long as we do their works, and walk in the steps of their most holy faith.

Ensuing then the steps of the faith of our father Abraham, we for the same purpose have made choice of the very same place wherein we now are, that it may be as the cave of Mamre, even God's storehouse for the bodies of such our brethren and sisters to be laid up in as He shall ordain there to be interred, there to rest in the sleep of peace till the last trump shall awake them; for they shall awake and rise up that sleep in the dust; for Thy dew shall be as the dew of herbs, and the earth shall yield forth her dead.

We beseech Thee, good Lord, to accept this work of ours in shewing mercy to the dead; and mercifully grant that they whose bodies shall be here bestowed, and we all, may never forget the day of putting off the tabernacle of this flesh, but that living we may think upon death, and dying we may apprehend life; and rising from the death of sin to the life of righteousness, which is the first rising of grace, we may have our parts in the second, which is rising to glory by Thy mercy, O most gracious Lord God, who dost live and govern all things, world without end.

Priorem dein formulam per omnia secutus, in cathedram ibi se collocat, atque actum consecrationis promulgat.

In Dei nomine Amen. Nos Lancelotus permissione divinâ Winton. episcopus hunc locum jacentem in vasto solo vulgò nuncupatum Ridgway-heath, infra parochiam ecclesiæ parochialis sanctæ Mariæ, &c., et jam propriis sumptibus strenui viri Ricardi Smith de Peer-tree armigeri in circuitu capellæ noviter ab eo quoque propriis sumptibus suis constitutæ, palis inclusum et arboribus consitum; continentem in longitudine

148 pedes aut circiter, in latitudine 124 pedes aut circiter, in toto verò circuitu 435 pedes aut circiter; à pristinis aliisque quibuscunque communibus usibus et profanis in usus sacros separandum fore decernimus, et sic separamus; ac eundem inhabitantibus vel degentibus in familiâ R. Smith, in villâ de Weston, hamlettis de Itchin, Wolston, Ridgway, et in parte manerii de Bitterne, quæ est de parochiâ sanctæ Mariæ juxta Southampt. in cœmeterium sive locum sepulturæ pro corporibus inibi decedentium christiano ritu humandis, quantum in nobis est, ac de jure et canonibus ecclesiasticis, ac de statutis hujus regni Angliæ possumus, auctoritate nostrâ ordinariâ et episcopali assignamus; ac per nomen Cœmeterii Capellæ Jesu designamus, dedicamus, et in usum prædictum consecramus; ac sic assignatum, dedicatum, et consecratum fuisse et esse et in futurum perpetuis temporibus remanere debere palàm ac publicè declaramus; ac Cœmeterium Capellæ Jesu deinceps in perpetuum nuncupandum decernimus: privilegiis insuper omnibus et singulis cœmeteriis et locis sepulturæ ab antiquo consecratis et dedicatis competentibus cœmeterium prædictum sive locum sepulturæ ad omnem juris effectum munitum esse volumus, et quantum in nobis est et de jure possumus sic munimus et stabilimus per præsentes.

Proviso tamen quòd prædictus Ricardus, hæredes et assignati sui, ac reliqui in dictâ villâ, hamlettis, &c., inhabitantes, propriis suis sumptibus dictum cœmeterium de tempore in tempus in decenti statu conservabunt, et clausuras ejus quoties opus fuerit sufficienter et convenienter reparabunt. Salvis etiam et omninò reservatis rectori ecclesiæ parochialis sanctæ Mariæ prædictæ, ac guardianis aliisque ministris dictæ ecclesiæ pro tempore existentibus in perpetuum, omnibus et singulis oblationibus, mortuariis, feudis et vadiis, pro omnibus et singulis sepulturis mortuorum in hoc cœmeterio aut ratione eorundem de jure sive consuetudine debitis, et in tam amplis modo et formâ ac si personæ prædictæ sepultæ fuissent in cœmeterio matricis ecclesiæ prædictæ. Quas quidem oblationes et mortuaria, feuda et vadia omnia et singula sic de jure ac consuetudine debita rectori, guardianis et ministris dictæ matricis ecclesiæ pro tempore existentibus in perpetuum solvenda, quantum in nobis est et jura patiuntur, reservamus per præsentes; salvâ item nobis et successoribus nostris, tanquam loci ordinariis, potestate visitandi dictum cœmeterium de tempore in tempus, et inquirendi an sufficienter reparatum fuerit in clausuris; et an omnia ibi decenter et secundùm ordinem fiant; et, si minùs fiant, per censuras ecclesiasticas corrigendi.

His finitis precatur denuo.

Lord God of Abraham, Isaac, and Jacob, who because Thou art the God, not of the dead, but of the living, shewest hereby that they are living and not dead, and that with Thee do live the spirits of all them that die in the Lord, and in whom the souls of them that are elect, after they be delivered from the burden of this flesh, be in joy and felicity; Thou hast said Thou wilt turn men into small dust, and after that wilt say, Return again you children of men: Thou art the God of truth, and hast said it; Thou art the God of power and might, and wilt do it; by that power whereby Thou art able to subdue all things unto Thyself, and bring to pass whatsoever pleaseth Thee in heaven and earth, with whom nothing is impossible.

Lord Jesu Christ, who art the resurrection and the life, in whom if we believe, though we be dead yet shall we live; who by Thy death hast overcome death, and by Thy rising again hast opened to us the gate of everlasting life; who shalt send Thine angels, and gather the bodies of Thine elect from all the ends of the earth, and especially those who by a mystical union are flesh of Thy flesh, and in whose hearts Thou hast dwelt by faith: we humbly beseech Thee for them, whose bodies shall in this place be gathered to their fathers, that they may rest in this hope of resurrection to eternal life through Thee, O blessed Lord God, who shalt change their vile bodies that they may be like Thy glorious body, according to the mighty working whereby Thou art able to bring all things, even death and all, into subjection to Thyself.

Holy and blessed Spirit, the Lord and Giver of life, whose temples the bodies of Thy servants are by Thy sanctifying grace dwelling in them; we verily trust that their bodies that have been Thy temples, and those hearts in which Christ hath dwelt by faith, shall not ever dwell in corruption, but that as by Thy sending forth Thy breath at first we received our being, motion, and life in the beginning of the creation, so at the last by the same Spirit sending forth the same breath in the end of the consummation, life, being, and moving shall be restored us again; so that after our dissolution, as Thou didst shew Thy holy prophet, the dry bones shall come together again, bone to his bone, and sinews and flesh shall come upon them, and Thou shalt cause Thy breath to enter into them, and we shall live; and this corruption shall put on incorruption, and this mortal shall put on immortality.

God the Father, God the Son, and God the Holy Ghost, accept, sanctify and bless this place to that end whereunto according to Thine own ordinance we have ordained it, even to bestow the bodies of Thy servants in, till the number of Thine elect being accomplished, they with us, and we with them, and with all other departed in the true faith of Thy holy Name, shall have our consummation and bliss both in body and soul, in Thy eternal and everlasting glory.

Blessed Saviour, that didst for this end die and rise again, that Thou mightest be Lord both of the living and the dead, whether we live or die Thou art our Lord, and we are Thine; living or dying we commend ourselves unto Thee, have mercy upon us, and keep us Thine for evermore.

Reintrantes igitur capellam cantant priorem partem psal. xvi. —*Conscendit suggestum magister Matthæus Wren; thema ei posterior pars ver.* 17. *cap.* ii. *S. Joan.*, Zelus domûs tuæ, &c.; *agit de affectibus in Christo, zelo inter cæteros; nec illo falso, sed pro Deo; nec cæco, sed secundùm scientiam, pro domo, pro cultu Dei; de præsentiâ Dei, præcipuè in templis, magno non morum solummodò nostrorum sed spei quoque et fidei incremento fulcimentoque; Deum locorum distinctione gaudere confirmat, tum exemplo mirifico Jacobi tantopere distinguentis Bethel, tum maximo omnium miraculo quo Christus mercatores è templo ejecit. Enarratis Christi per hoc factum devotionibus concludit in debitam à nobis templorum reverentiam, atque istius fundatoris encomium meritissimum.—Cantatur pars reliqua; et vespertinæ precationes (incipiendo jam à symbolo apostolico) secundùm communem ecclesiæ formulam finiuntur.*

A SUMMARY VIEW

OF

THE GOVERNMENT

BOTH OF THE

OLD AND NEW TESTAMENT:

WHEREBY

THE EPISCOPAL GOVERNMENT OF CHRIST'S CHURCH IS VINDICATED.

OUT OF THE RUDE DRAUGHTS

OF

LANCELOT ANDREWES,

LATE BISHOP OF WINCHESTER.

A SUMMARY VIEW,

&c.

THE FORM OF GOVERNMENT IN THE OLD TESTAMENT.

AND FIRST, UNDER MOSES.

THE commonwealth of Israel was considered either as
personal, containing all the whole people, not a man left, or
representative, in the estate, tribes, cities: whose daughters the towns adjacent are called.

I. The estate had ever one gŏvernor; Moses;—Joshua;—Judges;—Kings;—Tirshathas [or viceroys, Ezra ii. 63][a]; with whom were joined the seventy elders.

II. The tribes had every one their prince, נשיא, *phylarcha,* Numb. ii., with whom were joined the chief of the families, ראשי אבות, *patriarchæ,* Numb. i. 4.[b]

III. The cities had each likewise their ruler, Judges ix. 30, 1 Kings xxii. 26, 2 Kings xxiii. 8, with whom were joined the elders or ancients, Ruth iv. 2, Ezra x. 14; these last, not before they came into Canaan [and were settled in their cities].

It appeareth that Moses sometime consulted only with ראשי אבות, the 'heads of the tribes,' and then one trumpet only sounded, Numb. x. 4; in some other causes with the עדה, the 'congregation,' and then both trumpets called, Numb. x. 3.

The highest bench or judgment, for causes of greatest difficulty, was that of the seventy, who at the first were the fathers

a "Whatsoever is included within these marks [ ] hath been added, to supply the imperfection of the written copy." Ed. of 1641.

b [Exod. vi. 25.]

of each family that came down to Egypt, Gen. xlvi., which number did after that remain, Exod. xxiv. 1, 9, and was at last by God himself so appointed, Numb. xi. 16; see 2 Chron. xix. 8.

The inferior benches, for matters of less importance, were erected by Jethro's advice, of rulers of thousands, hundreds, fifties, and tithings, Exod. xviii. 21, 25, and after established by God's approbation, Deut. xvi. 18.

In every city, as Josephus[c] saith, were seven judges; and for each judge, two Levites; which made together the bench of each city.

THE FORM OF THE ECCLESIASTICAL GOVERNMENT UNDER MOSES.

The priesthood was settled in the tribe of Levi by God.

Levi had three sons, Cohath, Gershon, and Merari; of these, the line of Cohath was preferred before the rest.

From him descended four families, Amram, Izhar, Hebron, and Uzziel; of these the stock of Amram was made chief.

He had two sons, Aaron and Moses; Aaron was by God appointed high-priest.

So that there came to be four distinctions of Levites:
Aaron, as chief; Cohath; Gershon; Merari.

The commonwealth of Israel was at the beginning in the desert, a camp, in the midst whereof the ark and tabernacle were pitched, and according to the four coasts whereof they quartered themselves, on every side three tribes.

On the east, . .	Judah, Issachar, Zabulon, . .	Numb. ii. 3.
south, .	Reuben, Simeon, Gad, ...	ver. 10.
west, .	Ephraim, Manasses, Benjamin, . .	ver. 18.
north, .	Dan, Aser, Napthali, ...	ver. 25.

These same quarters were committed to those four divisions of Levites:

The east quarter	to Aaron and his family, . .	Numb. iii. 38.
south . . .	to the Cohathites, ...	ver. 29.
west	to the Gershonites, ...	ver. 23.
north . . .	to the Merarites, ...	ver. 35.

[c] Antiq., lib. iv. cap. 8. [§ 14. vol. i. p. 163.]

who lodged among them, and took charge of them, as of their several wards.

But there was not a parity in these four, for
Aaron's family, which bare the ark itself, was chief;
Cohath's, which bare the tabernacle and vessels, next;
Gershon's, which bare the veil and hangings of the court, third;
Merari's, which bare the pillars and posts, last.

Neither were all the Levites of each of these several houses equal, but God ordained a superiority among them:

Over the priests, ...	Eleazar, ...	
Cohathites, . . .	Elizaphan, ...	Numb. iii. 30.
Gershonites, . .	Eliasaph,.	ver. 24.
Merarites, . . .	Zuriel,.	ver. 35.

whom he termed 'nesiim,' that is, prelates or superiors.

No more did He permit these four to be equals among themselves, but appointed
Ithamar, Exod. xxxviii. 21, to command over
Eliasaph, with his Gershonites, Numb. iv. 28;
Zuriel, with his Merarites, Numb. iv. 33.
Eleazar, Numb. iv. 16, to have jurisdiction over
his own family;
Elizaphan, with his Cohathites.

Yea, he maketh not Eleazar and Ithamar to be absolute equals, but giveth Eleazar preeminence over Ithamar, and therefore termeth him 'nasi nesiim,' *princeps principum*, or *prælatus prælatorum*, Numb. iii. 32.
And all these under Aaron the high-priest.

So that,
α. Aaron was the high-priest;
β. under him Eleazar; who, as he had his peculiar charge to look unto, so was he generally to rule both Ithamar's jurisdiction and his own;
γ. under him Ithamar, over two families;
δ. under him the three prelates;
ε. under each of them, their several chief fathers, ראשי אבות, as they are termed, Exod. vi. 25; under Eliza-

phan four, under Eliasaph two, under Zuriel two, Numb. iii. 18, &c.;

ζ. under these, the several persons of their kindreds.

This is here worth the noting, that albeit it be granted that Aaron was the type of Christ, and so we forbear to take any argument from him; yet Eleazar, who was no type, nor ever so deemed by any writer, will serve sufficiently to shew such superiority as is pleaded for; that is, a personal jurisdiction in one man resiant over the heads or rulers of divers charges.

THE FORM OF GOVERNMENT UNDER JOSHUA.

The commonwealth being changed from the ambulatory form into a settled estate in the cities of Canaan; as before the Levites were divided according to the several quarters of the camp, so now were they sorted into the several territories of the tribes; so God commanded, Numb. xxxv. 2, 8.

The lot fell so, that the four partitions of the twelve tribes were not the same as when they camped before together, but after another sort; for the tribes of

1. Judah, Simeon, and Benjamin, made the first quarter;
2. Ephraim, Dan, and half of Manasses, the second;
3. Issachar, Asher, Napthali, and the other half of Manasseh, the third;
4. Zebulon, Reuben, and Gad, the fourth.

Now in these four,

1. The charge or oversight of the first was committed to Aaron and his family, and they had therein assigned to them thirteen cities; in Judah and Simeon nine, and in Benjamin four; Josh. xxi. 9, 10, &c.

2. Of the second, the care was committed to the family of the Cohathites, and they had assigned to them ten cities; in Ephraim four, in Dan four, and in the half of Manasseh two; Josh. xxi. 20.

3. The third was committed to the family of Gershon, and they had therein assigned to them thirteen cities; in Issachar four, in Asher four, in Napthali three, in the other half of Manasseh two; Josh. xxi. 27.

4. The oversight of the fourth partition was committed to

the Merarites, and they had therein assigned to them twelve cities; in Zebulon four, in Reuben four, in Gad four; Josh. xxi. 34.

These were in all forty-eight cities; whereof the chief, as may appear, were cities set on hills, and all so situate, in such proportion and distance, as that they most equally parted their tribe among them, to perform unto them their duties of attendance and instruction.

Further, there were in Joshua's time added, by the decree of the princes, the *nethinims* of the people of Gibeon, for the lowest ministries, and for the service of the levites, Josh. ix. 27.—So that now the order was thus;

1, Eleazar;
2, Phineas;
3, Abisua;
4, the three *nesiims;*
5, the *rase aboth,* or heads of the families;
6, the Levites;
7, the *nethinims.*

If this power and superiority was necessary when all the people and priests were within one trench, even within the view of Aaron's eye; much more in Canaan, when they were scattered abroad in divers cities far distant, was the retaining of it more than necessary.

THE FORM OF GOVERNMENT UNDER DAVID.

Albeit in Saul's government small regard was had to the church, yet David found at his coming a superiority amongst them; for besides the priests, he found six princes or rulers over six families of the Levites, 1 Chron. xv. 5, 6, &c.

Uriel . . . over . . . Cohath.
Asajah . . . . Merari.
Joel . . . . Gershon.
Shemajah . . . . . . Elizaphan.
Eliel . . . . Hebron.
Amminadab . . . . . Uzziel.

Likewise between the two priests an inequality: one Abiathar, attending the ark at Jerusalem, the higher function; the other Zadok, the tabernacle at Gibeon, 2 Sam. xx. 25, 1 Chron. xvi. 37, 39.

But after the ark was brought back, he set a most exquisite order among the Levites, and that by Samuel's direction, 1 Chron. ix. 22, so that he is there reckoned as a new founder; of them he made six orders, 1 Chron. xxiii.,

priests, כהנים, ministers of priests,	24,000,	verse 4.
judges, שפטים officers, שטרים,	6,000,	verse 4.
singers, מהללים,	4,000,	verse 5.
porters, שערים,	4,000,	

I. Of priests, Zadok was the chief, of the family of Eleazar, and Abimelech the second, of the family of Ithamar, 1 Chron. xxiv. 3.

Under these were twenty-four other courses,

of the posterity of { Eleazar, sixteen, / Ithamar, eight. } 1 Chron. xxiv. 4.

Which twenty-four are called, in the fifth verse, rulers of the sanctuary, and rulers of the house of God; and to whom the learned interpreters think the twenty-four elders, Apoc. iv. 4, have relation.

II. Of levites that ministered to the priests in their function, likewise twenty-four courses, out of the three families, the heads of whom are set down in 1 Chron. xxiii. 6, and xxiv. 20; over all which Jehdeiah was chief.

III. Of judges that sat for causes as well of God as the king, there were appointed

on this side Jordan, upwards toward the river, Ashabiah the Hebronite, 1 Chron. xxvi. 30;

on this side Jordan, downwards towards the sea, Chenaniah the Izharite, 1 Chron. xxvi. 29;

beyond Jordan, over the two tribes and the half, Jerijah the chief of the Hebronites, 1 Chron. xxvi. 31.

IV. Of officers,

scribes, { Shemaiah, 1 Chron. xxiv. 6;
Seraiah, 2 Sam. viii. 17;
Shevah, 2 Sam. xx. 25.

scribes of the { Levites, 1 Chron. xxiv. 6;
temple, 2 Kings xxii. 3, Jer. xxxvi. 10;
people, Matt. ii. 4;
king, 2 Kings xii. 10. }

V. Of the singers likewise he set twenty-four courses, over which he placed three chief, out of the three families, 1 Chron. xv. 17, and xxv. 2—4; out of

Cohath, ... Heman, Samuel's nephew, 1 Chron. vi. 33;
Gershon, ... Asaph, 1 Chron. vi. 39;
Merari, ... Ethan or Jeduthun, 1 Chron. vi. 44;
of these Heman was the chief, 1 Chron. xxv. 5;
under these were divers others, 1 Chron. xv. 18.

VI. Of porters, who were divided into the

1. Keepers of the watch of the temple, Matt. xxvii. 65, Ps. cxxxiv. 1, who were placed on each quarter of the tabernacle, 1 Chron. xxvi. 13, 14, &c.; on the
east side six, over whom was Shelemiah;
south, four, for the tabernacle two, and two for *asuppim*, over whom was Obed;
west, four, over whom was Hosa;
north, four, over whom was Zechariah;
over all these it seemeth Benaiah, the son of Jehoiada the priest, was the chief, 1 Chron. xxvii. 5.

2. Treasurers for the
a. revenues of the house of God, 1 Chron. xxvi. 20, for
Cohath, Shebuel of Moses' offspring;
Gershon, Jehiel;
Merari, Ahiah.
β. things dedicated by vow,
Shelomith, 1 Chron. xxvi. 26.

Over all the porters was Chenaniah, 1 Chron. xxvi. 29, and xv. 22, 27.

It is to be remembered that, beside Zadok the high-priest and Ahimelech, the second, we find mention of Hashabiah, the son of Kemuel, chief of the whole tribe of Levi, 1 Chron. xxvii. 17. So that there was

one over the ark, ... Zadok.
the second over the tabernacle, . Ahimelech.
the third over the tribe, ... Hashabiah.

As over the

Levites' ministers, ... Jehdeiah.
judges, ... Chasabiah.
officers, ... Shemaiah.
singers, ... Heman.
porters, ... Chenaniah, or Benaiah.

Agreeable to this form we read

That under Josias there were three, that is, Hilkiah, Zachariah, and Jehiel, 2 Chron. xxxv. 8, and that the Levites had six over them, 2 Chron. xxxv. 9.

Again under Zedekiah, that there were carried into captivity Seraiah, the chief priest, and Zephaniah, the second priest, 2 Kings xxv. 18.

Likewise under Hezekiah, at the provision for the levites' portions, there were ten of the levites; over whom was Cononiah and Shimei; and so Kore over the voluntary offerings, and six levites under him, 2 Chron. xxxi. 12, 13, &c.

THE FORM OF GOVERNMENT UNDER NEHEMIAH.

Of whom and Esdras it is recorded, that they did all according to Moses' institution, Ezra vi. 18; Nehem. x. 34, 36.

There was then { Eliashib, Neh. iii. 1, / Seraiah, ... xi. 11, / Zabdiel, ... xi. 14; }

the courses were then but twenty-two, Neh. xii. 12.

There was then { Uzzi, ... Neh. xi. 22; / Jezrahiah, Neh. xii. 42; / Shallum, . 1 Chron. ix. 17. }

under Zabdiel, at his hand, { Adaiah, ... / Amasai, ... } Neh. xi. 12, 13.

under Uzzi { Shemaiah, . / Shabbethai, / Jozabad, .. } Neh. xi. 15, 16.

under Jezrahiah { Mattaniah, / Bakbukiah, / Abda, ... } Neh. xi. 17.

under Shallum { Akkub, . . . } 1 Chron. ix. 17.
{ Talmon, . . } Neh. xi. 19.

So that there was

1, the high-priest,
2, the second and third, overseers of the priests,
3, the princes of the priests,
4, the priests,
5, the overseer of the levites,
6, the princes of the levites,
7, the levites,
8, the heads of the *nethinims,*
9, the *nethinims,* of { the Gibeonites,
Solomon's servants.

[A BRIEF RECAPITULATION OF THE DEGREES OBSERVED UNDER THE GOVERNMENT OF THE OLD TESTAMENT: WITH AN ACCOMMODATION THEREOF UNTO THE NEW.]

Out of these we gather this form to have been;

1. Moses, [in whom was] the supreme jurisdiction, to visit Aaron, Num. iii. 10.
2. Aaron, the
   high-priest, Lev. xxi. 21, Num. xxxv. 28, Neh. iii. 1;
   head, 2 Chron. xix. 11;
   prince of the house of God, 1 Chron. ix. 11.
3. Eleazar, the second, 2 Kings xxv. 18;
   prelate of prelates, Num. iii. 32,
   chief overseer, or bishop, Jer. xx. 1;
   at his hand, Ithamar.
4. Prince of the tribe, 1 Chron. xxvii. 17.
5. Elizaphan, Eliasaph, Zuriel,
   prelates, Num. iii. 24, &c.
   overseers or bishops, Neh. xi. 14, 22.
6. [In] the twenty-four courses set by David;
   the princes of the priests, Ezra viii. 29,
   of God, ... } 1 Chron. xxiv. 5;
   of the sanctuary, }
   elders of the priests, Jer. xix. 1, 2 Kings xix. 2;
   heads of the families, ראשי אבות, Neh. xii. 12;
   chief priests, Acts xix. 14.

7. The priests themselves; whether at Jerusalem, or in the country towns, 2 Chron. xxxi. 19.
8. The overseer of the levites, Neh. xi. 22.
9. The princes of the levites, 1 Chron. xv. 5, 2 Chron. xxxv. 9, Neh. xii. 22.
10. The head of the levites' officers,
    the scribe;
    the singers, 1 Chron. xvi. 5, Neh. xii. 42;
    the porters, 1 Chron. ix. 17, and xv. 23;
    the treasurers, 1 Chron. xxvi. 24, 2 Chron. xxxi. 12.

[11. The levites themselves.]

12. The chief of the *nethinims*, Neh. xi. 21.
13. The *nethinims*, of
    the Gibeonites, Josh. ix. 21.
    Solomon's servants, 1 Kings ix. 21, Neh. vii. 60.

It is not only requisite that things be done, and that they be diligently done (against sloth), but that they be done continually, and constantly.

To this end it is, that God appoints overseers,

α. to urge others, if they be slack, 2 Chron. xxiv. 5, and xxxiv. 13;

β. to keep them in course, if they be well, 2 Chron. xxix. 5, and xxxi. 12, and xxxiv. 12, 13;

γ. to punish, if any be defective, Jer. xxix. 26.

For which,

α. A power of commanding was in the high-priest, 2 Chron. xxiii. 8, 18, and xxiv. 6, and xxxi. 13; a power judicial, if they transgressed, Deut. xvii. 9, Zach. iii. 7, Ezek. xliv. 24; under pain of death, Deut. xvii. 12; punishment in prison, and in the stocks, Jer. xxix. 26; in the gate of Benjamin, Jer. xx. 2.

β. Officers to cite and arrest, John vii. 32; Acts v. 18.

This corporal.

To suspend from the function, Ezra ii. 62.

To excommunicate, Ezra x. 8, John ix. 22, and xii. 42, and xvi. 2.

[This spiritual.]

Why may not the like be [for the government of the

church], there is alleged one only stop; that the high priest was a figure of Christ; who being now come in the flesh, the figure ceaseth, and no argument thence to be drawn.

[For answer whereunto, we are to consider that]

1. This is the anabaptists' only shift; that we are to have no wars, for the wars of the Jews were but figures of our spiritual battle; no magistrate, for their magistrates were but figures of our ministers, pastors, and doctors, and all by Christ's coming abolished.

2. Christ being as well King as Priest, was as well fore-resembled by the kings then as by the high priest; so that if His coming take away the one type, it must also the other. If it be said, there was in the king somewhat else beside the representation, the like is and may be truly said of the high priest; and that some such thing there was, it is plain by St. Paul, who yielded his obedience to the high priest, appearing before him, and acknowledging him a governor of the people, Acts xxiii. 5, and that after the type was expired; which had been merely unlawful, if there had not remained in him somewhat besides the figure.

3. There is no necessity we should press Aaron; for Eleazar being *princeps principum*, that is, having a superior authority over the superiors of the Levites [in Aaron's life-time], was never by any [in this point] reputed a type of Christ; so that though Aaron be accounted such, yet Eleazar will serve our purpose. As also 2 Chron. xxxv. 8, we read of three at once, one only of which was the high-priest, and a type of Christ; the rest were not: let them answer then to the other twain, who were rulers or chief over the house of God.

Why it may be,

1. Out of *dic ecclesiæ*, [the new reformers] tell us, we are to fetch our pattern from the Jews; and therefore it seems they are of opinion that one form may serve both us and them.

2. Except there should be such a fashion of government consisting of inequality, I see not in the New testament how any could perish in that contradiction of Core which

St. Jude affirmeth; for his plea was for equality, and against the preferring of Aaron above the rest.

3. The ancient fathers seem to be of mind that the same form should serve both.

So thinketh St. Cyprian[d], lib. iii. ep. 9. *Ad Rogatianum.*

So St. Hierome[e], ep. 85. *ad Evagrium*, 'Traditiones apostolicæ sumptæ sunt de Veteri testamento;' et *ad Nepotianum, De vitâ clericorum.*

So St. Leo, 'Ita veteris testamenti sacramenta distinxit, ut quædam ex iis, sicut erant condita, evangelicæ eruditioni profutura decerperet; ut quæ dudum fuerant consuetudines judaicæ, fierent observantiæ christianæ.'

So Rabanus[f], *De institutione clericorum*, lib. i. c. 6.

They ground this their opinion upon that they see,

1. That the synagogue is called a type or shadow, and the church the very image of the thing, Heb. x. 1.

2. That God himself saith of the christian church under the gentiles, that He will take of the gentiles, and make them priests and levites to Himself, Esay lxvi. 21, there calling our presbyters and deacons by those legal names.

3. That there is an agreement in the

numbers, { twelve, Num. i. 16, and Luke ix. 1.
seventy, Num. xi. 16, and Luke x. 1.

names, angel, Mal. ii. 7, and Rev. i. 20.

And their often interchange and indifferent using of priest or presbyter, levite or deacon, sheweth they presumed a correspondence and agreement between them.

[Thus then]

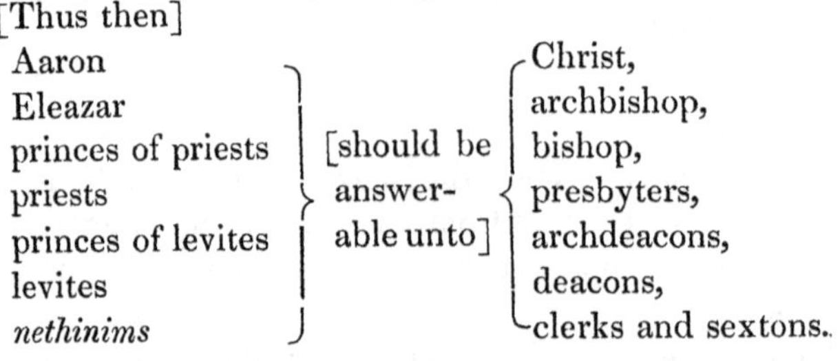

Aaron	[should be answerable unto]	Christ,
Eleazar		archbishop,
princes of priests		bishop,
priests		presbyters,
princes of levites		archdeacons,
levites		deacons,
nethinims		clerks and sextons.

[d] [Ep. iii. p. 5.]

[e] [Ep. ci. "ad Evangelum," ed. Ben., et Ep. xxxiv. vol. iv. par. 2. coll. 803, et 257 sqq.]

[f] [vol. vi. p. 5.]

THE FORM OF CHURCH GOVERNMENT IN THE NEW TESTAMENT.

AND FIRST IN THE DAYS OF OUR SAVIOUR CHRIST.

1. THE whole ministry of the New testament was at the first invested in Christ alone.

He is termed our Apostle, Heb. iii. 1,
Prophet, Deut. xviii. 15, Acts iii. 22,
Evangelist, Esay xli. 27,
Bishop, 1 Pet. ii. 25,
Doctor, Matt. xxiii. 10,
Diaconus, Rom. xv. 8.

II. When the harvest was great, Matt. ix. 38, that His personal presence could not attend all, He took unto Him twelve apostles; as the twelve patriarchs, or twelve fountains (as St. Jerome), or the twelve princes of the tribes, Num. i.;
gathering His disciples, Matt. x. 1;
choosing out of them, Luke vi. 13;
whom He would, Mark iii. 13;
called them to Him, Luke vi. 13;
made them, Mark iii. 13,
named them, apostles, Luke vi. 13.
These He began to send, Mark vi. 7;
gave them in charge, Matt. x. 1, and xi. 1,
to preach the gospel, Luke ix. 2;
to heal, Matt. x. 1, Luke ix. 2;
to cast out devils, Matt. x. 1.
gave them power, Matt. x. 1, Luke ix. 1,
to take maintenance, Matt. x. 10;
to shake off the dust for a witness, Matt. x. 14;
so He sent them, Matt. x. 5, Luke ix. 2;
they went and preached, Luke ix. 6;
they returned, and made relation
what they had {done, taught.} Mark vi. 30.

III. After this, when the harvest grew so great as that the twelve sufficed not all, Luke x. 1, 2, He took unto Him other seventy, as the seventy palm trees, Num. xxxiii. 9; the fathers of families, Gen. xlvi; the elders, Num. xi.

These He
declared, Luke x. 1;
sent by two and two into every city and place, whither He himself would come, *ib.*
gave them power, as to the apostles, to
take maintenance, Luke x. 7;
shake off the dust, Luke x. 11;
heal the sick, } Luke x. 9;
preach, . . . }
tread upon serpents and scorpions, and over all the power of the enemy, Luke x. 19.

These two orders (as me thinketh) St. Paul, Eph. iii. 5, doth comprehend under the name of apostles and prophets; by the seventy, understanding prophets; as usually next to the apostles he placeth prophets ever, 1 Cor. xii. 28, Eph. iv. 11. None of the fathers ever doubted that these two were two several orders or sorts, nor that the apostles were superior to the seventy. It appeareth also, that [the apostles] had in them power to forbid to preach, Luke ix. 49; and that Matthias was exalted from the other order to the apostleship.

This was then the order while Christ was upon the earth,
Christ himself;
the twelve, whose successors were bishops;
the seventy, whose successors were priests;
the faithful people or disciples, of whom five hundred and more are mentioned in 1 Cor. xv. 6, and one hundred and twenty in Acts i. 15.

THE FORM OF GOVERNMENT USED IN THE TIME OF THE APOSTLES.

Albeit Christ saith the people were as sheep without a shepherd, Matt. ix. 38, yet He termeth His apostles harvest-men, not shepherds; for while He was in person on earth, Himself only was the shepherd, and they but *arietes gregis;* but at His departure He maketh them shepherds, John xxi. 15, as they likewise at theirs, 1 Pet. v. 2, Acts xx. 28.

OF THE APOSTLES THEMSELVES.

And first, of their name.

Shelicha, which is the Syrian name, was the title of certain legates or commissioners sent from the high priest to visit the Jews and their synagogues which were dispersed in other countries, with authority to redress things amiss.

ἀπόστολοι, among the Greeks, were officers of great credit, as by Herodotus[g] and Demosthenes[h] appeareth.

Secondly, of their form, what it is.

not to have been with Christ all His time, Acts i. 21; so were others more;
not to be sent immediately of Christ, Gal. i. 1; so were the seventy, Luke x.;
not to be limited to no one place, Matt. xxviii. 19; so were others, Luke xxiv. 33, 50; and St. James went no whither;
not to be inspired of God, so that they did not err; so were Mark and Luke;
not to plant churches; so did Philip the evangelist, Acts viii. 5;
not to work signs and miracles; so did Stephen, Acts vi. 8, and Philip, Acts viii. 6;

But over and above these, and with these, that eminent authority or jurisdiction which they had over all, not only jointly together but every one by himself,

1) of imposing hands in { ordination, Acts vi. 6, confirmation, Acts viii. 17, 18 };
2) of commanding, (the word of the bench, Acts iv. 18, and v. 28,) 1 Thess. iv. 11, 2 Thess. iii. 6, 12, Philem. 8, Col. iv. 10, 1 Cor. xiv. 37, 2 Pet. iii. 2, Titus i. 5, 1 Cor. vii. 6, 17, and xi. 34, and xvi. 1;
3) of countermanding, Luke ix. 49, Acts xv. 24, 1 Tim. ii. 12;
4) of censuring, 1 Cor. iv. 21, 2 Cor. xiii. 10, Gal. v. 12, 1 Tim. i. 20, 1 Cor. v. 5, 11, 2 Thess. iii. 14, Matt. xvi. 19, with xviii. 18, and John xx. 23.

In this power it is, that the bishops succeed the apostles, Iren.[i] lib. iii. cap. 3; Tertul. *De præscript.*[k]; Cyprian.[l] *Ad Florent.* iii. 9; Epiphan.[m] *Hæres.* xxvii., ‘Romæ fuerunt primi

[g] [Clio 21, Terps. 38.]
[h] [De Cor. vol. i. p. 262. Cont. Everg. et Mnesib. vol. ii. p. 1146.]
[i] [p. 175.]
[k] [cap. xxxii. p. 213.]
[l] [Ep. lxvi. p. 165 sqq.]
[m] [Adv. Hær. lib. i. tom. 2. p. 107.]

Petrus et Paulus, apostoli iidem ac episcopi;' Chrysost.[n] in Act. Hom. iii., 'Jacobus episcopus Hierosolymitanus;' Hieron.[o] Epist. 85, et 54, *Ad Marcellam*, et *De scriptor. ecclesiast.*[p] in Petro et Jacobo; Ambros.[q] in 1 Cor. xii. 28, de angelis, et in Eph. iv.[r], 'apostoli angeli sunt.'

OF DEACONS.

At the beginning, the whole weight of the church's affairs lay upon the apostles,

the distribution as well of the sacrament, Acts ii. 42, as of the oblations, Acts iv. 35;

the ordination, Acts vi. 6;

the government, Acts v. 3.

[But] upon occasion of the Greeks' complaint, whose widows were not duly regarded in the daily ministration, (which was as well of the sacrament as of the oblations, otherwise the apostles would not have left out [the mention of] the sacrament in Acts vi. 4,) they transferred that part upon the seven [deacons], whom they had ordained for distribution [of the sacrament], not for consecration, Acts vi., 1 Tim. iii. 12, 13.

Justin. *Apol.* i.[s]; Ignatius[t], *Ad Heronem*; Tertul.[u] *De Baptismo*; Cyprian.[x] *De lapsis*, et lib. iii. epist. 9; Chrysost.[y] Hom. 83 in Matth. Hieron.[z] ep. 48, *ad Sabinianum*, et *contra Lucifer.* Ambros.[a] Offic. lib. i. cap. 41; Gregor.[b] iv. 88; Concil. Nicæn.[c] i. can. 14.

OF EVANGELISTS.

They grew upon occasion of the scattering of the disciples by means of the persecution after the death of St. Stephen,

n [vol. ix. p. 26.]

o [Ep. ci. "ad Evangelum," ed. Ben., et ep. xxvii. vol. iv. par. 2. coll. 803 et 65.]

p [ut sup. col. 101.]

q [vol. ii. append. col. 153.]

r [vid. ibid. col. 241.]

s [§ 65 sqq. p. 83.]

t [vol. ii. p. 108 sqq.]

u [p. 230. cap. xvii.]

x [p. 132, et ep. iii. ad Rogatian. p. 5.]

y [vol. vii. p. 789.]

z [Ep. xciii. vol. iv. par. 2. col. 760, et 299—303.]

a [vol. ii. col. 54 F.]

b [vid. append. ad Gregor. Epist. vol. ii. col. 1288.]

c [vol. ii. col. 690.]

Acts xi. 19; of which number St. Philip is reckoned, Acts xxi. 8, and divers others, Acts xi. 19, of whom Eusebius[d] maketh mention, lib. iii. cap. 37, and lib. v. cap. 10. Upon these was transferred that part of the apostles' function which consisted in preaching from place to place.

OF PRIESTS.

When the churches were in some sort planted by the preaching of the apostles, prophets, and evangelists, that they might be continually watered, and have a standing attendance, the apostles ordained priests by imposition of hands in every church, Acts xiv. 23, and xi. 30, and xxi. 18.

And they made choice of the word *πρέσβυς*, rather than of the word *γέρων* more in use with the Greeks, because it includeth an embassy, and that chiefly of reconciliation, which is the *πρεσβεία* expressed by St. Paul, in 2 Cor. v. 20, with Luke xiv. 32.

OF BISHOPS.

Last of all, that the churches thus planted and watered might so continue, the apostles ordained overseers to have a general care over the churches instead of themselves who first had the same; which is called *ἐπίσκεψις*, Acts xv. 36, and containeth in it, as a strengthening or establishing that which is already well, Acts xiv. 22, and xv. 41, Rev. iii. 2; so a rectifying or redressing if ought be defective or amiss, Tit. i. 5. These are called, Acts xx. 28, אפיסקופא in the Syrian, that is, *episcopi;* by St. John, Rev. i. 20, the 'angels of the churches.' [These were set over others, both to rule and teach,] 1 Tim. v. 17, 1 Pet. v. 2. Upon these was transferred the chief part of the apostolic function, the oversight of the church; and power of commanding, correcting, and ordaining.

The occasion which caused the apostles to appoint bishops [besides the pattern in the time of the law] seemeth to have been schisms, such as were in the churches of

Rome, Rom. xvi. 17,
Corinth, 1 Cor. i. 11, [and iii. 3, 4,]

[d] [H. E., pp. 133, 223.]

Galatia, Gal. v. 12,
Ephesus, Eph. iv. 2, 3,
Philippi, Phil. iv. 2,
Colossæ, Coloss. iii. 13,
Thessalonica, 2 Thess. iii. 11,
The Hebrews, Heb. xiii. 9, James iii. 1;

for which St. Cyprian[e], St. Hierome[f], and all the fathers take the respect to one governor to be an especial remedy; [for which also see] Calvin[g], *Instit.* lib. iv. cap. 4. § 2.

This power even in the apostles' time was necessary: for God chargeth not His church with superfluous burdens; yet had they such graces (as power of healing, doing signs, sundry languages, &c.,) that they of all other might seem best able to want it, for by these graces they purchased both admiration and terror sufficient for crediting their bare word in the whole church. If necessary then in their times that were so furnished, much more in the ages ensuing, when all those graces ceased, and no means but it to keep things in order; so that were it not apparent to have been in the apostles', yet the necessity of the times following, destitute of these helps, might enforce it.

Seeing then God hath no less care for the propagation and continuance of His church than for the first settling or planting of it, Eph. iv. 13, it must needs follow that this power was not personal in the apostles, as tied to them only, but a power given to the church; and in them for their times resident, but not ending with them, as temporary, but common to the ages after and continuing, to whom it was more needful than to them, to repress schism and to remedy other abuses.

So that the very same power at this day remaineth in the church, and shall to the world's end.

OF THE PERSONS [THAT EXECUTED THESE OFFICES.]

1. Albeit the commission were general over all nations which was given to the twelve, yet was that generality only by permission, not express mandatory; else should they have sinned that went not through all nations. Therefore howso-

[e] [Ep. iii. lxvi. pp. 6, 167.]
[f] [Ep. ci. ad Evang., vol. iv. par. 2. col. 802 sq.]
[g] [p. 286.]

ever the commission was to all nations, yet was it left to their discretion how and in what sort they would dispose themselves, as the Holy Ghost should direct them: so that the partition, Gal. ii. 9, betwixt St. Peter and St. Paul, was lawful and good, and no ways derogatory to *Ite, prædicate,* ['go, teach all nations.']

Further, the ecclesiastical history doth testify that they parted the coasts and countries of the world among them by common advice, and so severed themselves,

Peter, to Pontus, Galatia, Cappadocia;
John, to Asia, Parthia;
Andrew, to Scythia, [Pontus] Euxinus, and Byzantium;
Philip, to upper Asia, and to Hierapolis;
Thomas, to India, Persia, and the magi;
Bartholomew, to Armenia, Lycaonia, India citerior;
Matthew, to Ethiopia;
Simeon, to Mesopotamia, Persia, Egypt, Africa, Britany;
Thaddæus, to Arabia, Idumea, Mesopotamia;
Matthias, to Ethiopia.

2. Again, albeit their preaching was for the most ambulatory, yet do the same histories witness that, having settled religion, and brought the church to some stay, toward their end they betook themselves to residence in some one place, divers of them, as,

St. James at Jerusalem, Euseb.[h] lib. ii. cap. 1; Epiphan.[i] *Hær.* lxvi. Hierome[k].

St. John at Ephesus, Euseb.[l] lib. iii. cap. 23; Tertullian[m], lib. iv. *contra Marcion.* Hierome[n].

St. Peter, first at Antioch, and after at Rome.

Which places were more especially accounted their sees, and the churches themselves after a more especial manner were called apostolic, *sedes apostolorum,* Aug.[o] Epist. xlii, *ecclesiæ apostolicæ,* Tertullian[p].

3. Thirdly, it is also plain that the apostles chose unto them as helpers (*συνέργους*) divers who were companions

h [H. E., p. 44.]
i [vol. i. p. 636.]
k [vol. iv. par. 2. col. 101.]
l [H. E., p. 112.]
m [p. 415 D.]
n [vol. iv. par. 2. col. 105.]
o [Ep. ccxxxii. vol. ii. col. 843.]
p [vid. De præscr. hær., cap. xx, sq.]

with them in their journeys, ministered unto them, and supplied their absence in divers churches when they themselves were occasioned to depart; such were,

Apollos, Acts xix. 1, 1 Cor. iii. 6.
Aquila, Rom. xvi. 3.
Archippus, Philem. 2, Col. iv. 17.
Aristarchus, Acts xx. 4.
Clemens, Phil. iv. 3.
Crescens, 2 Tim. iv. 10.
Demetrius, 3 John 12.
Epaphras, Col. iv. 12. i. 7, Philem. 24.
Epaphroditus, Phil. ii. 23.
Epænetus, Rom. xvi. 5.
Erastus, Acts xix. 22.
Gaius, Acts xx. 4.
Jesus Justus, Col. iv. 11.
John Mark, Acts xiii. 5, xv. 37, Philem. 24.
Lucas, Philem. 24, Col. iv. 14.
Secundus, Acts xx. 4.
Silvanus, 1 Pet. v. 12, 1 Thess. i. 1, 2 Thess. i. 1.
Sopater, Acts xx. 4.
Sosthenes, 1 Cor. i. 1.
Stephanas, 1 Cor. xvi. 15.
Timotheus, Acts xix. 22, and xx. 4.
Titus, 2 Cor. viii. 23.
Trophimus, Acts xx. 4.
Tychicus, Acts xx. 4.
Urbanus, Rom. xvi. 9.

Of whom, Eusebius[q], *Hist.* lib. iii. cap. 4; Euthymius, *in tertium Joannis;* Isidorus[r], *De patrib.* and Dorothei[s] *Synopsis.*

To two of these, Timothy and Titus, the one at Ephesus, the other at Crete (Euseb.[t] lib. iii. cap. 4.), the apostles imparted their own commission while they yet lived, even the chief authority they had;

to appoint priests, Tit. i. 5, and Hieron.[u] *in eum locum;*
to ordain them by imposition of hands, 1 Tim. v. 22, 2 Tim. ii. 2;
to keep safe and preserve the *depositum*, 1 Tim. vi. 14, 20, 2 Tim. i. 14;
to command not to teach other things, 1 Tim. i. 3, Tit. iii. 9, 2 Tim. ii. 16;
to receive accusations, 1 Tim. v. 19, 21;
to redress or correct things amiss, Tit. i. 5;

q [p. 90 sqq.]
r [vol. v. p. 187 sqq.]
s [p. 148 b sqq.]
t [p. 91.]
u [vol. iv. col. 412.]

to reject young widows, 1 Tim. v. 11;
[to censure heretics and disordered persons, Tit. i. 11, and] iii. 10, 1 Tim vi. 5, 2 Tim. iii. 5.

And these, after the apostles deceased, succeeded them in their charge of government which was ordinary, successive and perpetual, (their extraordinary gifts of miracles and tongues ceasing with them;) [so] Irenæus[x], lib. iii. cap. 3, *quos et successores relinquebant, suum ipsorum locum magisterii tradentes.*

[OF THE PROMISCUOUS USE OF THEIR NAMES.]

These were they whom posterity called bishops; but in the beginning regard was not had to distinction of names; the authority and power was ever distinct, the name not restrained, either in this, or other.

1. The apostles were called
   priests or seniors, 1 Pet. v. 1;
   deacons or ministers, 1 Cor. iii. 5;
   teachers or doctors, 1 Tim. ii. 7;
   bishops or overseers, Acts i. 20;
   prophets, Acts xiii. 1, Rev. xxii. 9;
   evangelists, 1 Cor. ix. 16.

The name of apostle was enlarged, and made common to more than the twelve;
to Barnabas, Acts xiv. 4, 14;
Andronicus, Rom. xvi. 7;
Epaphroditus, Phil. ii. 25;
Titus and others, 2 Cor. viii. 23;
Timothy, Hieron. *in Cant.* Euseb. *Chron.*

2. The priests were called
   prophets, 1 Cor. xiv. 32;
   bishops, Phil. i. 1, Tit. i. 7;
   so Chrysostom[y], in Phil. Hom. i. [*Quid hoc? an unius civitatis multi erant episcopi? nequaquam, sed presbyteros isto nomine appellavit; tunc enim nomina adhuc erant communia.*]

x [p. 175.]

y [vol. xi. p. 195.]

Hierome[z], *Hic episcopos presbyteros intelligimus, non enim in unâ urbe plures episcopi esse potuissent.*

Theodoret[a], *Non fieri quidem poterat ut multi episcopi essent unius civitatis pastores, quo fit ut essent presbyteri quos vocavit episcopos;* and in 1 Tim. iii.[b], *Eosdem olim vocabant episcopos et presbyteros; eos autem qui nunc vocantur episcopi, nominabant apostolos.*

Œcumenius[c], *Non quod in unâ civitate multi essent episcopi, &c.;*

for in the apostles' absence in churches new planted, the oversight was in them, till the apostles ordained and sent them a bishop, either by reason of some schism or for other causes.

3. The bishops, as the ecclesiastical history recounteth them, were called

apostles, Phil. ii. 25;
evangelists, 2 Tim. iv. 5;
diaconi, 1 Tim. iv. 6;
priests, 1 Tim. v. 17;

[for it is plain by the epistle of Irenæus to Victor, in] Eusebius[d], lib. v. cap. 20, that they at the beginning were called priests, that in very truth and propriety of speech were bishops; and by Theodoret[e], in 1 Tim. iii., that they which were bishops were at the first called apostles.

The name ἐπίσκοποι, saith Suidas[f], was given [by the Athenians to them which were sent to oversee the cities that were under their jurisdiction, *οἱ παρ' Ἀθηναίων εἰς τὰς ὑπηκόους πόλεις ἐπισκέψασθαι τὰ παρ' ἑκάστοις πεμπόμενοι, ἐπίσκοποι καὶ φύλακες ἐκαλοῦντο.* Suid. in ἐπίσκοπος.]

The name 'episcopus' was given among the Romans to him, *qui præerat pani et venalibus ad victum quotidianum,* ff.[g] *De munerib. et honorib.* Cicero[h], *ad Atticum,* lib. vii. epist. 11. *Vult me Pompeius esse, quem tota hæc Campania et maritima ora habeat episcopum.*

[z] [vid. in Tit. i. 5. vol. iv. p. 413.]
[a] [In Phil. i. init., vol. iii. col. 445.]
[b] [Ibid. col. 652.]
[c] [In Phil. i. 1.]
[d] [H. E., p. 238.]
[e] [vol. iii. p. 652.]
[f] [col. 1390.]
[g] [Corp. jur. civ. Digest., lib. l. tit. 4. cap. 18. § 7. col. 1795.]
[h] [vol. viii. p. 304.]

The name in hebrew פקדים, Gen. xli. 34, seemeth to have relation to the second use, for they were such as had charge of the grain laying up and selling under Joseph.

[THE NECESSARY USE OF THE BISHOP'S OFFICE, AND THE CHARGE COMMITTED TO HIM.]

The party, who in the New testament is called 'episcopus,' is in the Old called פקוד, Ps. cix. 8, with Acts i. 20.

In a house or family it is first affirmed of Joseph, Gen. xxxix. 4, who had the oversight and government of the rest of the servants; in a house there may be many servants, which have places of charge, but there is one that hath the charge of all, that is, *œconomus*, 'the steward.' So do the apostles term themselves, 1 Cor. iv. 1, and their office, 1 Cor. ix. 17, and their successors the bishops, Tit. i. 7. Vid. Hilar.[i] in Matt. xxiv. 45.

In a flock, the pastor, Joh. xxi. 15, Acts xx. 28, Matt. xxv. 32, 1 Pet. v. 2, Eph. iv. 11.

In a camp, the captain, Matt. ii. 6, Heb. xiii. 7, 17, 24.

In a ship, the governour, 1 Cor. xi. 28, under whom others, Acts xiii. 5.

In the commonwealth, they be such as are set over officers, to hasten them forward and see they do their duties, as in 2 Chron. xxxiv. 12. xxxi. 13; Neh. xi. 22. xii. 42.

So that, what a steward is in a house,
a pastor in a flock,
a captain in a camp,
a master in a ship,
a surveyor in an office:
that is a bishop in the ministry.

Upon him lieth
[to take care of the churches under him], 2 Cor. xi. 28, Phil. ii. 20, 1 Pet. v. 2, Concil. Antioch.[j], can. 9;
[and for that end to visit them,] Acts ix. 32. xv. 36;
[and to be observant] of that which is well and orderly,
[to confirm it,] Acts xv. 41, Rev. iii. 2; otherwise,
[to redress it,] Tit. i. 5.

[i] [col. 734.]

[j] [A.D. 341. vol. ii. col. 1312.]

To him was committed;

1. Authority of ordaining, Tit. i. 5, and so of begetting fathers, Epiph. *Hæres.* lxxv.[k]; see Ambrose[l], Theodoret[m], and Œcumenius[n] in 1 Tim. iii.; Damasus[o], ep. iii.; Hierome[p], ep. lxxxv, *Ad Evagr.;* Leo[q], ep. lxxxviii; Concil. Ancyran. can. 12 (al. 13).[r] For though St. Paul should mention a company with him at the ordaining of Timothy, 1 Tim. iv. 14, yet it followeth not but that he only was the ordainer; no more than that Christ is the only judge, although the twelve shall sit with him on thrones, Luke xxii. 30.

2. Authority of enjoining or forbidding, 1 Tim. i. 3; Ignat. *Ad Magnesian.*[s]; Cyprian[t], ep. iii. 9.

3. Authority of holding courts and receiving accusations, 1 Tim. v. 19, 1 Cor. v. 12, Rev. ii. 2. Aug.[u] *De opere monachor.*, cap. 29.

4. Authority of correcting, 1 Tim. i. 3, Tit. i. 5; Hieron.[x] *Contra Lucifer.* cap. iv. et ep. liii, *Ad Riparium.* Cyprian.[y] ep. xxxviii. 3. *Ad Rogatianum.*

5. Authority of appointing fasts, Tertullian[z] *Adv. psychicos.*

[k] [§ 4. p. 908.]
[l] [vol. ii. append. col. 295.]
[m] [vid. sup., p. 360.]
[n] [vol. ii. p. 224 sqq.]
[o] [p. 111.]
[p] [Ep. ci. ad Evang., vol. iv. par. 2. col. 802 sq.]
[q] [p. 158.]
[r] [A.D. 314. vol. ii. col. 518.]
[s] [capp. 2—7. vol. ii. p. 17 sqq.]
[t] [Epp. 3, et 55 et 75. pp. 5, 110, 225; et passim.]
[u] [vol. vi. col. 499.]
[x] [vol. iv. par. 2. col. 292. ep. xxxvii. ibid. col. 279.]
[y] [p. 5 sq.]
[z] [De jejun., cap. 13. p. 551.]

A DISCOURSE OF CEREMONIES

RETAINED AND USED IN CHRISTIAN CHURCHES,

WRITTEN BY THE RIGHT REV. FATHER IN GOD

LANCELOT ANDREWES,

LATE BISHOP OF WINCHESTER,

A LITTLE BEFORE HIS DEATH:

AT THE REQUEST OF AN EMINENT PERSON, THAT DESIRED SATISFACTION THEREIN.

PRINTED BY THE ORIGINAL COPY
WRITTEN WITH HIS OWN HAND.

Ex pede Hercules.

A DISCOURSE[a]

SHEWING THAT MANY PAYNIM CEREMONIES WERE RETAINED IN ENGLAND AFTER CHRISTIANITY WAS RECEIVED.

SURELY as darkness was before light, (for 'the evening and the morning,' saith the text, 'made the first day,') and as out of chaos, that *rudis indigestaque moles,* were made all the clear firmaments, even *cœlum crystallinum;* so evident it is that paganism covered all the face of the world, except the little land of Jewry, afore christianity was admitted. And after the admission of christian religion in the western part of the world by the christian emperors, the northern people together with the empires almost every where abolished christian religion: but yet, as Augustinus Curio[b] notes, at length every one of these northern and heathen nations embraced christian religion, saving only the Saracens. My conceit and purpose to shew you is, that of the ecclesiastical government and policy observed in the british and english ancient pagans, as formerly having their commonwealth in frame and beautified with our common laws, they being converted unto christianity, many of the paganish ceremonies and usages, not contrary to the scripture, were still retained in their christian policy; by means whereof tranquillity and peace was observed, and the alteration in the state less dangerous or sensible. For as in general Arnobius[c] is true, writing, nothing was innovated for christian religion *in rerum naturâ;* and as the heathen oracle of Apollo Pythius answereth, the Athe-

a [Printed from an edition bearing date 1653, with a preface by Edward Leigh, informing us concerning the treatise, "that upon speech between bishop Andrewes and a gentleman his near neighbour about the ceremonies, the bishop awhile after, and a quarter of a year before his death, delivered this to him as a collection of his own about that subject, which he had not time, he said, to polish and lick over. Had the author," he proceeds, "intended it to be published, it would no doubt have been more perfect, but I thought it worthy in regard of the author and argument, which few have so generally handled, to be published;" &c.]

b [Hist. Saracen.]

c [Adv. gent., lib. i. capp. 1, 2.]

nians asking him what religion was principally to be embraced, namely, that which was by descent delivered as a custom of their ancestors; so in particular well writeth Dionysius Halicarnasseus, the least ceremonial points of the divine worship a nation, unless necessity compel them, will hardly alter. He instanceth it in the Egyptians, the Moors, the Gauls, the Scythians, the Indians; nay, sir Thomas Smith in his Commonwealth[d] expresseth that our ancestors being heathens, when they agreed to receive christian religion, that which was established before, and concerned external policy, they held and kept still with that which was brought of new by their christian apostles and doctors.

Because I remember Tully's[e] cognizance, namely, that it is a badge of a negligent and dissolute person not to regard what the most sort of the people may conceive of him, and that conceit is worthily the most heinous which may note any to plant by writing, or water by speaking, the cursed roots or seeds of self-springing paganism, I will first prove that this kind of birth of our ceremonies can be no disgrace to our ecclesiastical ceremonies.

Secondly, I will insinuate three observations to be remembered out of the particular proposition proved.

Thirdly, I will point at some of the superfluous and wicked popish ceremonies drawn from the heathens.

Fourthly and lastly, I will instance in many ecclesiastical ceremonies of the heathens, which are or may be used in ours, or in any other christian state.

I. In the first place, allowing much of our ecclesiastical discipline used in the time of our primitive church was borrowed from the heathen, yet that it can be no disparagement unto it, must needs be granted; for otherwise to imagine is the direct opinion of the heretics Manichæi, whose error in this point is solemnly refuted by St. Augustine writing against Faustus[f], and by St. Jerome[g] writing against Vigilantius.

That I may not threaten but persuade,—By the judicial law

[d] [Book iii. ch. 11. p. 278.]
[e] [De off., i. 28.]
[f] [e. g. lib. xx. vol. viii. col. 333 sqq.]
[g] [vol. iv. part ii. col. 284.]

of Moses expressed in Deut. xxi., "If a strange woman be taken in battle, if her beauty please thee, her nails and hair being pared and shaven, and her garment of captivity being taken away, thou mayest lawfully take her to wife," by the moral of this law severally write Isidore[h] and Peter Blesensis[i], the ceremonies of the gentiles, the deformities thereof being taken away, may lawfully be used amongst the christians. Isidore[k] then expounding Deut. xvi., "thou shalt not plant trees near unto the altar," his meaning is, one must not imitate the devotion nor the ceremonies of the gentiles. For the Israelites even by the direction of God made holy vessels, and placed them in the temple of God, of the gold and silver they robbed the Egyptians of.—And it is vulgarly known that the sayings of the heathen poets are used by the Holy Ghost in the New testament.—Again, we may see in Acts xvii. how St. Paul himself, when he was at Athens, the very altar of superstition which was dedicated unto an unknown god, and unto which bloody sacrifices were slain, by as much dexterity and wisdom as that time would permit, did make use thereof, and seem to transpose it to the worship of the true God.—And which is more, it is expressed by St. Paul, it is lawful for a christian, so it be without scandal, to eat those things which are consecrated unto idols. Honestly then writes Mr. Hooker[l], that which hath been ordained impiously at the first, may wear out that impiety by tract of time, as the names of our heathen months and days used throughout all christendom without any scandal. And if the Spaniards well may glory of their Alphonsus[m], king of Arragon, *qui per cloacam ingressus subter muros*, won Naples, and from thence expelled Renate, duke of Anjou, reasonably then out of former rags of the gentiles the glorious and fair garment of christianity in times may be woven. And as Ephraim Syrus[n], a father that lived in St. Basil's time, writeth, if the money be taken out of the purse, yet the purse is not to be cast away; so although the sacrifice and service of the gentiles be taken away, the outward ceremonies may remain.

h [In Deut., cap. xviii. vol. v. p. 472.]
i [Epist. viii. p. 10 sq.]
k [In Deut., cap. iii. vol. v. p. 461.]
l [E. P., Book iv. ch. xii. § 4. vol. i. p. 591.]
m [Becchatellus Panormita, "De dictis" &c. "Alphonsi," 4to. Witeb. 1585. p. 15.]
n [De Pœnit., Serm. ii. vol. i. p. 123 D.]

To conclude; this pedigree of our ceremonies staineth not our christian policy, for that all the good orders of the heathens came by tradition, or reading or seeing the ceremonies that God commanded among the Jews in the land of promise; as it appeareth by Josephus against Appion[o], that the sect of the Pythagorean philosophers translated much of the Jews' laws into their own sect. And as by Eusebius[p], Augustine[q], Theodoret[r], Justin Martyr[s], and others, Plato copied much out of Moses' writings, (for Moses' writings were long afore the empire of the Persians,) so verily if it were for this place, it may be exemplified that the succeeding ceremonies of the heathen were derived from the Jews' ceremonies; and no man can justly deny but that we may use the ceremonies of the Jews, *non ex vi, sed ex analogiâ mosaicæ legis.* And if this point fancy any man, let him read Alcuinus, *De officiis divinis*[t]; Amalarius, *De officiis ecclesiasticis*[u]; Gratian, *De con.*[x]; but especially Mutius Pansa, in his *Osculum christianæ et ethnicæ philosophiæ;* (I can commend Nicholaus Mount-Georgius[y] in his book *De mosaico jure enucleando,* only for his endeavours.) You may observe out of Josephus[z] in the latter time of the Jews' government, that Herod their first king brought much of the roman-heathenish discipline into their policy, and in this respect that many of our christian ceremonies were formerly heathen, and afore that used in the commonwealth of Jewry, wherein God was the lawgiver: they resemble the seventeen vessels which the heathen king Cyrus gave unto the Jews at the building of the temple of Jerusalem, after the captivity of Babylon, among which, as Esdras writes, there were vials of gold twenty-nine, of silver two thousand four hundred and ten; for these were in the last use sacred, being formerly heathen and profane, but most anciently holy and sanctified.

II. The first of the three observations that I am to insinuate

o [vid. lib. ii. capp. 16, 39. vol. ii. pp. 1377, 89.]

p [Constant. orat. apud Euseb., cap. 9.]

q [De doctr. Christ., lib. ii. cap. 28. vol. iii. par. 1. col. 36.]

r [Græc. affect. curat., Disp. ii. prop. fin. vol. iv. p. 758.]

s [passim. e. g. Ad Græc. cohort., capp. 25—33. pp. 25—31. Apol. i., capp. 44, 59, 60. pp. 70 A. 78 C. 79 B.]

t [passim. col. 1009 sqq.]

u [passim. col. 305 sqq.]

x [i. e. De consecratione, Dist. i. cap. 2. col. 2049.]

y [vid. "List of edd." &c. end of this vol.]

z [Ant. Jud., lib. xv. cap. 8. vol. i. p. 687.]

upon the particular to be proved, is the ampleness of the common law, admitting no common law within their land but as parcel and incorporated into the general laws and policies of this land, seeing most of our ecclesiastical law was before there was any popish canon laws observed by the inhabitants, as the civil ordinance of the magistrate in the ages most remote; but of these hereafter in particular.

Secondly, note, if much of the christian policy and discipline was in practice when the state of this land was heathen, the lay catholics are much mistaken in their petition, where they write, we have all our feasts and ceremonies from Augustine the monk. And let them not play Suffenus's[a] part, in delivering there is not the least ceremony or circumstance which hath been added to the solemnization or majesty of God's service, but the year is known when, and the pope by whom it was ordained; but these forget what their father Bellarmine[b] confesseth, that all christian ceremonies were not invented by the pope.

Thirdly, this will sufficiently convict the opinion of them whom Nazianzen[c] ingeniously calls new pharisees, to be but ceremonious, that will not conform themselves to any ceremonies used in the time of popery, seeing we must and ought to obey the ecclesiastical discipline established by the laws of the land, for coming to church, for having prayers, or preaching, or music in our churches, or such like, although (as shall be proved) these ceremonies and customs were used in the time of pagans, and at their sacrifices. Genebrard, by whom it is verified that much learning and railing may be accidents in one subject, writes, that in the year 1560 in England arose a new sect of puritans, so called because they will not pray in the churches that were the catholics', nor wear a surplice; (sure I am that many that wear the liveries of this name are otherwise minded.) And I learn out of Dubravius[d], that the Thaborites of Prague held that the clergy should not be doctors of divinity, or quote the fathers in their sermons, or wear any other than their ordinary garments; but yet for them all, *o quam honestâ voluntate miseri errant.* It is confessed cere-

a [Catull., Carm. xxii.]

b [De Sacram. in gen., lib. ii. cap. 29 sqq. vol. iii. col. 251 sqq.]

c [Orat. xxxvii. cap. 9. vol. i. p. 651.]

d [Hist. Boiem., lib. xxvi. init.]

monies of themselves are things indifferent, as being neither expressly commanded or forbidden by the word of God; and although among the Jews their kings would not permit liberties in ceremonies to the subjects, christian kings may: but yet when they are enacted in a christian state, and made the laws of the land, they must be obeyed of necessity as unto a thing not indifferent. For well write the canonists, an act indifferent, when it is commanded is a necessary act, otherwise idle is the command; and it appeareth by Josephus that the Athenians made a severe law against those that spake against the outward ceremonies established by law or custom; this also may appear out of Livy, and out of Dion. Who knoweth not that the king, the Cæsar of the country, must obey the law of the land? what a presumption is it then for a private man to exempt and privilege himself from obeying the laws of the land! Truly writes a learned common lawyer[e], the laws of men not contrary to the law of God ought to be kept even of the clergy in the law of the soul. And Mutius[f] notes, that Charles the great in Saxony gave equal authority to his magistrates (*scabinis*) to put to death those which contemned and derided the ceremonies ecclesiastical, as those which sacrificed to heathen gods: for Lodovicus Sotomajor well writes in his comment upon the Canticles, godliness being as the soul, yet ceremonies are as the body of christian religion.

III. But I am to point at some of the superfluous and wicked ceremonies of the papists borrowed from the heathen.

Of so large and near affinity is the divine worship of the heathens and papists in the temples, that Lodovicus Vives[g] confesseth there cannot any difference be shewn, unless the papists have changed the names and titles; so that (with Chemnitius[h]) to the followers of the see of Rome we may object what Faustus[i] did to the christians, "ye turn idols into martyrs and saints, whom ye worship with correspondent vows." And I can hardly imagine how plentiful the tears of Petrus Chrysologus and

e [St. Germain, Salem and Byzance, additions, cap. 2.]

f [lib. vii. p. 59.]

g [vid. Chemnit. in not. seq.]

h [Examen. Concil. Trident. in cap. "De imaginibus." p. 676. col. 2.]

i [Aug. cont. Faust. Man.]

Silvanus would run, if they were alive and viewed the antichristian see; for that in their times some of the superfluous heathen ceremonies began to abound in the christian churches, whereupon they complained, although the gentiles' *circensia* were celebrated in the honour of Christ, yet the church being out of that cradle, the particular usage of the gentiles in this kind was not to be imitated. I commend therefore the intent of that emperor, who for reverence of the sign caused (as Sozomenus[i] reporteth) *furcam* to be erected *loco crucis;* and I reverence the opinion of the makers of an ancient statute in Henry the third's time[j], namely that *De pistoribus,* which punisheth a butcher that buyeth flesh of Jews to sell the same to christians. And generally, that the heathen thought their ceremonies would drive away the christians, Abbas Urspergensis[k], a German, and Didacus Covarruvias[l], a Spaniard, wrote that Helena, a Briton, and mother of Constantine, the first christian emperor, born in this island, going to Jerusalem, found in the place where Christ was crucified the idol of Venus placed.

But to instance; the popish purgatory in scope and being agreeth with the heathen purgatory, mentioned in Plato[m] and Virgil[n].—The papistical manner of consecrating churches and church-yards fully imitateth the ceremonies of the pagans when they consecrated their temples and temple-courts or yards, described by Alexander ab Alexandro[o]; in Spain, by Gregorius Lopus, at the beginning of the consecration of a church they must make three crosses in the last part thereof; their sprinkling of holy water is mentioned in the sixth satire of Juvenal[p], and Sozomenus calleth it a heathenish ceremony; in particular, that it was always used at the sanctifying of the capitol, appeareth by Alexander ab Alexandro.—Their having of nuns and women for societies or colleges was used amongst the heathen, as I gather out of Plutarch[q]; and that the whole swarm of friars or monks was first fledged amongst the heathen, at large appeareth by

i [H. E., lib. i. cap. 8. p. 20.]
j [51 Hen. III., stat. vi.]
k [p. 79.]
l [Var. resol., lib. iv. cap. 16. vol. i. p. 436. col. 2.]
m [e. g. De rep., lib. x. Phæd.]
n [Æn. vi. 736 sqq.]
o [Gen. dies., lib. vi. cap. 14. p. 594.]
p [lin. 528.]
q [In tract. "An seni sit gerenda resp.," vol. ix. p. 176.]

learned Hospinian[r].—The papists' placing of images in their temples, and every image to have his several priest; their priests to have shaven crowns, to be unmarried; to have frankincense offerings, fasts and feasts, to have candles in them, and to carry them up and down, in every respect is heathenish; and to do no wrong, Chemnitius[s] in particular proveth this by variety of authors.—The placing of lights in churches at some time is not altogether an heathenish ceremony (although it appear by Seneca the gentiles[t] had it; Suidas[u], in the word λαμπὰς, thinketh they were first used in Athenian temples), for the ancient fathers used a kind of light in the primitive church, which made St. Augustine to write, "they promise to the churches, one oil, another way to solace themselves for the night-light;" but their burning of tapers in their churches at noon-day is altogether a pagan custom, as Rhenanus[v] well observes in his comment upon Tertullian. And I take it their burning of torches at funerals is merely a superfluous ceremony of the gentiles, as appeareth by Virgil[w] and his commentator Servius writing upon the funeral of Pallans,

lucet via longo
Ordine flammarum, et late discriminat agros.

Jerome[x] writing of the death of Blesilla describeth the funeral pomp of the christians.—The papists' kissing of their hands as a kind of worship in their churches agreeth in intent with the heathenish custom (although Prudentius and Optatus make mention of kissing of hands in the primitive church), and this Cælius Rhodiginus (11,) notes out of Pliny[y] and Apuleius[z]. Lucian[a] calls the worshipping by laying the finger to the mouth to be the sacrifice of poor men, as having nothing else to offer.—The learned chief justice of France, Brissonius[b], whom one calls *Varro Galliæ*, particularly writeth why the papists purposely imitate the heathens in turning on the left hand at their right sacrifices.—M. Perkins noteth out

r [De monach., lib. i. cap. 10—12. pp. 20—27.]

s [Examen Concil. Trident. in cap. "De imaginibus," p. 676.]

t [vid. Hieron. in Esai., lib. xvi. cap. 57. vol. iii. col. 418. Lactant., lib. vi. cap. 2. Ammian. Marcell., lib. xxii. cap. 13.]

u [col. 2264.]

v [In lib. v. adv. Marcion., p. 105 b.]

w [Æn. xi. 143.]

x [Ep. xxii. ad Paulam., vol. iv. par. 2. col. 54.]

y [Lib. xi. cap. 103. vol. ii. p. 445.]

z [Metam., lib. iv. p. 132.]

a [De sacrif., cap. xii. vol. iii. p. 85. cf. De salt., cap. xvii. vol. v. p. 130. et Demosth. encom., cap. xlix. vol. ix. p. 167.]

b [p. 37.]

of Ruffinus that *pro thoracibus Serapidis* Constantine caused the sign of the cross to be erected in pillars and houses. Sozomenus[c] writeth, Constantine *pro laboro posuit signum crucis;* and hence he would have this a superfluous ceremony of this kind, but unto this I cannot as yet subscribe.—Likewise where Julius Pacius wittily notes that the whole corps of the canon law or ecclesiastical discipline imitateth the feature and structure of the corps of the civil laws, generally being heathen; for the common law-book called Decretum answereth the Pandects, the Decretal the Codex; for as in the Codex there are the imperial, so in the Decretals there are the pontifical constitutions; and as the answers of wise men, that is, lawyers, are reported in the Digest, so the sentences of the authors are registered in their Decretum; all this I condemn not as an idle correspondence: but to leave this point of our divines, I spare to prove out of Calvin their prayer for the dead as an idle imitation of the heathen; that their worshipping the relics of their saints and martyrs is mere gentilism, the ancient bait of Satan. And therefore generally to conclude, I conceive the Jesuits, (the golden staves and mattocks of the see of Rome, whose name answereth Heraclitus's[d] greek name for a bow, *τὸ μὲν ὄνομα βιὸς, τὸ δὲ ἔργον θάνατος*, that is, "thy name," saith Heraclitus, "a bow, is life, but thy work is death,") in office resemble the heathen priests of the Indians, called brachmans, mentioned by Osorius[e]; he saith, "these heathen clergy-priests also study philosophy and the mathematical arts, insomuch that by their learning and counterfeit holiness they continue all their life-time the singular contrivers of all fraud and villany;" for my warrant I appeal to the catastrophe of many houses of nobility of this realm, acted by the Jesuits.

IV. Now according to my main design I have to instance in many ecclesiastical ceremonies of the heathen which are or may be lawfully used in ours or any other christian state.

For the general, in the civil law-book called Digests, which contains the writings of the old lawyers which were heathens, you may read many precepts, superstitious rather than reli-

c [H. E., lib. i. cap. 4. p. 13.]

d [Eustath. in Hom. (Il. A. 49) p. 31. lin. 6.]

e [De reb. gest. Emm. reg. Lusit., lib. ii. init. vol. i. col. 616.]

gious, of their heathen sacrifices and church discipline; and yet when the emperors of Rome began after to be christians, you may perceive by the civil law-books called Codex how in many points the emperors retain them; but further to exemplify this is a matter fruitless, I stand not hereupon.

But more particularly; the ceremonies on this behalf to be recited I shall refer unto the heathen churches,—the heathen *flamines* or ministers,—the heathen people.

1. That the heathens afore the christians had their temples to resort unto, where they were to worship their paynim gods, no man will deny, (though Diogenes in his cynic mood held temples unnecessary, by affirming the whole world was the godly and holy temple of the gods, where he would pray; and this was also the opinion of Zenon[f], and also of our ancestors the Saxons, as appeareth by Abbas Urspergensis[g]; the Scythians, by Herodotus[h], erected temples or churches to none of the gods but only unto Mars.) But although Clemens Alexandrinus[i] note that in the beginning superstition was the parent of all pagan temples, they being formerly, saith he, the sepulchres for men; yet Isidore[j] well notes out of Tranquillus, that when the people heathen began to be civil, their temples were built, and altered fairer both within and without.—Moreover the very name of the heathen assemblies among the Athenians and the cities of Asia, was *ecclesia*, which retaineth the name of the churches among the christians at this day; Onuphrius Panvinius[k] writeth, the church, *ecclesia*, signifieth a congregation; and it is called *basilicon*, or temple, after the manner of the gentiles.—And as we have bells in our churches, so had the pagans in theirs; by Suetonius, the emperor Octavius Augustus was the first who in the highest place of the temple of Jupiter capitoline hanged bells. That at the ringing of their bells the heathens were wont to meet at their assemblies, as at baths and otherwise, is plain by Martial[l], who writeth,

Redde pilam, sonat æs thermarum, ludere pergis?

[f] [Lil. Gyrald., Synt. xvii. vol. i. p. 452.]

[g] [p. 193.]

[h] [Melp. iv. 59. vol. ii. p. 493.]

[i] [Cohort. ad gent., vol. i. p. 39.]

[j] [vid. Lil. Gyrald., Synt. xvii. vol. i. p. 452.]

[k] [p. 113.]

[l] [Epigr., lib. xiv. 163.]

But yet you may see by a part of the canon law called the Clementines[m], that the Saracens in their steeples have no bells.—For the fabric or structure of the temples, whether the christian temples were square, and the heathens all round, with Dr. Humphrey, as no diversity, I leave it to be enquired of the curious: only I note out of Socrates[n], the ancient and apostolical churches of the christians in Antiochia in Syria, were built round; and out of Gyraldus[o], that the temple of Vesta was like unto a ball, the temple of the Sun and Bacchus is round; and that Stukius in his comment upon Arrianus[p], notes, the temple of Mercury was square, and of cubic figure.—As we have no images in our temples, so likewise was it used of many heathens: among the Romans, their holy and ancient king Numa by a law banished images or idols out of their temples; Tacitus[q] reports the Germans likewise would not represent the gods by images; and Strabo[r] and Herodotus[s] shew how the Persians for their gods neither made altars nor images; and Eusebius[t] writes, the people called Seres by a special law forbad the worshipping of images.

To wade a little further; the gentiles having their temples and churches for their poetical gods, christianity being received by consent of the emperors and civil magistrates, it is to be seen whether those ethnic churches were all demolished, and new ones built of the christians. That many of the heathen churches were utterly ruinated, many historians and fathers witness; among others, St. Jerome[u], writing against Jovinian, telleth of the destruction of the famous temples of Jupiter capitoline; and in his comment upon the Galatians his words are these, *vacua idolorum templa quatiuntur;* and in the Theodosian codex[v] you may see a particular rescript made by the emperor Theodosius the younger, that the paynim temples in the east should be plucked down, they

[m] [Corpus juris canon., vol. ii. col. 1085.]

[n] [vid. H. E., lib. v. cap. 22. p. 297. cf. Euseb. vit. Const., lib. iii. cap. 50. Walafrid Strabo, De reb. eccl., cap. 4.]

[o] [Hist. deor., Synt. iv. vol. i. p. 147.]

[p] [p. 75.]

[q] [Germ., cap. ix.]

[r] [Lib. xv. prop. fin. vol. ii. p. 1064.]

[s] [Clio, cap. 131. vol. i. p. 112.]

[t] [Præp. evang., lib. vi. cap. 10. p. 274 D.]

[u] [vol. iv. par. 2. col. 228 fin.]

[v] [vid. lib. xvi. tit. x. cap. 11. Socr. H. E., lib. v. cap. 16. p. 281. cum locc. parall. in Sozom. et Theodoret.]

being fit to be the dens of devils or unclean spirits; and their subversion of the idol's temples is the reason that by the canon and common law[w] *jus ædificationis* is a special cause that giveth the patronage or advowson of the church unto a lay patron. But yet without controversy, when kingdoms and states turned from idolatry or paganism to christianity, and that in short time (so powerful was the Holy Ghost), many of the heathen temples were not overthrown, but of necessity, after some ceremonies accomplished, were used for christian prayers and assemblies; by means whereof the alteration in the state was not so great, the temporal world with Democritus being not to be new made *ex atomis*, and men sooner and easier embraced public christian religion: and this is the reason that by the common law of England a man may be said to be patron of a christian church although he never built it, if he only endow the church with revenues. And as in foreign countries the emperor Honorius[x] about the year 400 made a law[y] restraining the heat of the christians against the walls and stones of the gentiles' temples (the words of the rescript are, "as we forbid their sacrifices, so we will the ornament of their public works be kept"), and the first christian emperor Constantine[z] made a law against them which pluck down the tombs and monuments of the superstitious heathens, and those laws methinks in foreign countries gave some warrant for retaining heathen ceremonies; so in our country of England it is notorious by the epistles of pope Gregory[a] himself, who sent our Augustine the monk, that although pope Gregory in his epistle to the king of England wrote, that ancient pagan temples in England might wholly be destroyed, yet afterwards the same pope better advising, that somewhat was to be yielded unto them that were weak in faith, as the apostles did, he writeth a peculiar epistle to Mellitus, one of the first apostles or bishops of the Englishmen, and expressly willeth that the temples of the idols in England be not destroyed, but that they be hallowed and sanctified, and turned into oratories for christians. And as in general for

w [Corpus jur. canon. in Decret. Greg., lib. iii. tit. 38. cap. 25. vol. ii. col. 580.]

x [Cod. Theod., lib. xvi. tit. x. cap. 15. vol. vi. par. 1. p. 311.]

y [See other references in Bingham, lib. viii. cap. 2. § 4.]

z [ut in not. x. cap. 3. et comment.]

a [Epp., lib. xi. cf. epp. 66 et 76. vol. ii. coll. 1164, 1176.]

other countries this appeareth by Theodoret[b], so now it is a work of some difficulty to shew you in particular what christian church at this day standing was anciently the temple of such an heathen god. In Rome by full ample authority it is plain, as by Beda in his several books, by Ado[c], by Paulus Diaconus[d], and others, that Pantheon, the temple in Rome for all the heathen gods, was given by Phocas the emperor, about the fifth year of his reign, unto pope Boniface the fourth, and by the said pope dedicated to the honour of Our lady, and of all martyrs; it is now called the round church of Our lady, and the shape and antiquity thereof is portrayed lively in the first inscription of Janus Gruterus's[e] Ancient Inscriptions, whose works may please a man that delighteth in this point: Dion[f] writes, in the reign of the emperor Titus, when Rome burnt by the space of three days, that the temple Pantheon was burnt; but Eusebius[g] saith, In the thirteenth year of Trajan, Pantheon was burnt with a thunderbolt, howsoever it was re-edified by the heathen emperors. It is evident by Beda[h] that we had a pantheon in England; it stood in a town in Yorkshire, now called Godmanham; this temple among our ancestors, the pagan Saxons, was called Godmandingham, and was totally burnt by the people of Northumberland, when at the preaching of Paulinus king Edwin of an idolater became a christian; Beda writes, the heathen person, or *flamen* Coifi was the first *qui injecta lanceâ profanavit et cum omnibus septis suis succendit,* 'burnt,' the very walls of the church-yard. Pope Gregory writeth in his Dialogues[i] that pope Benedict translated the church of Apollo into the oratory of St. Martin's; and cardinal Bellarmine[j] sheweth that at this day the church of St. Cosmo and Damiano in Rome was the material heathen temples of Castor and Pollux; and Ado[k] writeth, In the year 425, pope Sixtus turned the temple of god Bacchus in Rome into the church of Our lady. But for England, (to omit out of Xiphilin[l] the

[b] [Græc. affect. curat. Diss. viii, ad fin. vol. iv. p. 923.]

[c] [Chron. æt. vi. p. 800 b.]

[d] [De gest. Langob., lib. iv. cap. 37. p. 1160.]

[e] [p. 1.]

[f] [Hist. rom., lib. lxvi. p. 756.]

[g] [vid. Præp. evang., lib. vi. capp. 2—4. pp. 238 sqq.]

[h] [H. E., lib. ii. cap. 13. p. 103.]

[i] [Lib. ii. cap. 8. col. 230.]

[j] [De sanct. beat., lib. i. cap. 20. vol. ii. col. 913.]

[k] [Chron. æt. vi. p. 796 b.]

[l] [p. 162 fin.]

abridger that anciently the Britons worshipped commonly in the church of god Victory,) as many learned men[m] have reason to conjecture St. Paul's church in London to have been the heathen temple of Diana, for that the adjacent and skirt-buildings unto the church are called the chambers of Diana, as also that in Edward the first's time (as our chroniclers report) in Paul's church-yard were digged up an innumerable number of ox-heads, which the learned know were anciently the sacrifices unto Diana: so certain I am that St. Peter's church, now called Westminster abbey, was anciently the temple of Apollo; for so it appeareth by one of the charters[n] of king Edgar made to Westminster abbey, and this is also recited in Sulcardus's book, an author that lived near William the conqueror's time. And in the leger book of St. Alban's[o], it is written in the life of St. Eadmerus, the ninth abbot of St. Alban's, who lived in the time of our king Edward the martyr, that in digging for a foundation about St. Alban's abbey was found a book written in the british tongue, and of that the first part discoursed of St. Alban, the second part treated of the idolatry of the citizens of St. Alban's, *Verulamii*, unto the Sun and unto Mercury; hence I conceive probably the ancient churches of St. Alban's were dedicated to the service of the Sun and Mercury their gods.

To proceed, as lawfully the civil and supreme magistrates gave the temples of the heathens to the christians, as well St. Augustine[p] notes in one epistle, that the christian emperors did pass over to the true catholics the churches and revenues which were given by donatists to error and schism; yet before the heathen temples were consecrated and purged, the christians would not use any christian service in them: and this well appeareth out of Nicephorus, lib. vii. cap. 46[q], who reports Constantine the great, the first christian emperor, that in the wars he might have a christian church to say a christian service in, he built him a church that might be carried up and down after his camp, *μεταφορητὴν ἐκκλησίαν, ecclesiam portabilem;* as one calls ships *portatiles domos.*

[m] [Camden, Middl., vol. i. p. 334.]
[n] [Dugdale, Monast., vol. i. p. 292 b.]
[o] [Matth. Par., p. 994.]
[p] [Ep. clxxxv. De correct. Donat., cap. 9. vol. ii. col. 657 G.]
[q] [vol. i. p. 515.]

Now how the christian bishops did hallow and sanctify the heathen churches, particularly may be seen out of Marianus Scotus[r], Rhegino[s], and Sigisbert[t] in the year 607, by Ado and others, when they speak of the dedication of Pantheon by Boniface the fourth; (note, at this day consecration of churches is only reserved unto the bishops; and anciently there was more than one bishop present at the consecration of a church, for Turpinus telleth, to the consecration of a church-yard in Bourdeaux there were seven bishops present.) And that our yew-trees in church-yards was the planting of the heathens, even Verstegan understands. Volateran[u] reports, that about the year 484 pope Felix the third made a canon that temples should only be consecrated by bishops, and that this ceremony of consecrating and hallowing of churches, and dedicating of them, was anciently used by the heathens, both by words and by hand, is plain by Livy, Ovid[x], Tibullus, and Cicero[y] in many places. Livy[z] writeth, Horatius Pulvillus did dedicate the temple of Jupiter capitoline.

2. In this second place, I am to produce some of the ceremonies or policies observed among the heathen *flamines*, or ministers, which are likewise in practice at this day among the christian provinces.

That the heathens had their ministers or priests nothing is more plain; and the priests of our ancestors the british heathens and the Goths were the druids, as at large write Cæsar[a] and Tacitus[b]. And the names of our bishops, *episcopus* and *pontifex*, were used among the heathen. For that he was called *episcopus*, that is, 'overseer' of others, and looked unto the poor, and had care of their diet, is plain by the words of Arcadius[c] the civil lawyer in the Digests, and (as Onuphrius[d] and others note) by Cicero[e] in his epistles, where he writes, Pompey would have him to be bishop of the cities of Asia; and it appeareth by the body of

[r] [col. 373.]
[s] [p. 13.]
[t] [col. 1401.]
[u] [Anthropol., lib. xxii. col. 653.]
[x] [Fast. i. 290. ii. 57. iii. 429. vol. iii. pp. 30, 78, 191, et passim.]
[y] [e.g. De legg. ii. 11. vol. iii. p. 145. Pro dom. 45 sqq. vol. v. p. 384.]
[z] [lib. ii. cap. 8. vid. et lib. vii. cap. 3. vol. i. pp. 91, 403.]
[a] [De bell. gall., lib. vi. cap. 12 sqq. p. 119.]
[b] [Ann., lib. xiv. cap. 30. vol. ii. p. 171. Hist., lib. iv. cap. 54. vol. iii. p. 262.]
[c] [vid. sup., p. 360 not. g.]
[d] [p. 109.]
[e] [vid. sup., p. 360. not. h.]

the common law, the office of the primate came from the heathen. Now for *pontifex*, it is confessed by every one that the christians took that name from the heathen ministers, and so Sozomenus deriveth it; Rhenanus[f] and others note the word 'diocese,' and the jurisdiction in this kind came from the heathen.

Now as among the christian ministers worthily and of necessity there are degrees of the clergy, and one subordinate to another, so likewise was it when our ancestors were pagans, for they had their *pontifex* and *pontifex maximus*, their *flamines* and *archiflamines*, as is plain by Gratian's[g] rhapsody; and as every particular god had his *flamen*, his minister, so, as Gellius[h] notes, *flamen dialis*, Jupiter's priest, was the chiefest among the rest. Beda[i] writes, Coifi was the chiefest heathen priest in the kingdom of king Edwin. Some of our country chroniclers that lived almost four hundred years ago (Ptolemeus Luccensis, who wrote the lives of the popes of Rome, writes in the life of pope Eleutherius how the three *protoflamines* were converted into so many archbishoprics) tell you how many *flamines* and *archiflamines* there were among the Britons, and into what bishoprics and archbishoprics they were afterwards translated; but no wise man will believe their particular, seeing they report actions done a thousand years before their time, having no former author or authority to warrant it. And the heathen priests had some under them which were not priests, and yet to serve in the temples; they were called *camilli*, as appeareth by Plutarch[j] and Dionysius[k]; and these are in the nature of our deacons.

The correspondent power of our clergy to that of the heathen would best appear by opening of the nature of the heathen *pontifices*. To omit Livy, Plutarch, Alciat, Alexander ab Alexandro, Peter Perkins in his comment upon the rules of the common law writeth, the heathens assigned a peculiar jurisdiction to their *pontifices*, namely, to look into the public and private ceremonies of their religion, to defend and interpret

f [Descript. Illyr. provinc., p. 209.]

g [Par. i. Distt. xxi. lxxx. coll. 97—100, 413 sq.]

h [Lib. x. cap. 15. vol. i. p. 348.]

i [vid. sup. p. 375 not. h.]

j [In Num., cap. vii. fin. vol. i. p. 254.]

k [Antiq. rom., lib. ii. cap. 22. vol. i. p. 90. cf. Macrob. Saturn., lib. iii. cap. 8. p. 433. Varro, De ling. lat., lib. vi. p. 71 fin.]

their holy mysteries, to deliver with what altars, to which gods, with what sacrifices, upon what days, at which temples prayers and offerings should be, to see that every one resorted to church, and no new ceremonies to be admitted, that vows be performed, funerals decently bestowed, oaths and faith fulfilled, holy days proclaimed, the gods pleased. And Wolfgangus Lazius[l] particularly noteth out of heathen authors, some the chief of their clergy and *pontifices* were to be skilful, especially in their common or ecclesiastical law; to judge of marriages, of sanctuaries; to consecrate churches, and places of burial; that our clergy hath in like manner most of their particulars, every man must acknowledge.

But to add unto these last recited authors concerning the holy days observed by the christians and heathen, Thucydides[m] notes, it is a matter of necessity to have holy days; that the christians begin their day from midnight, saith Censorinus[n], it is common with the gentiles; and that our clergy foretell and declare the holy days to the people, the like was done by the *pontifices* of Rome, witnesseth Plutarch[o] *in Numâ*. The heathens call the days which are no holy days, *profesti dies*. Yea, that the holy days in the gentiles' calendar lose only their name, having upon the same days christian festivities appointed, (for the apostles made no laws concerning holy days,) is known by Theodoret[p], who writeth that the heathen holy days of Jupiter, Mars, and the rest of the heathen gods, were ordained among the christians' holy days for Peter, Paul, and other saints. Gregorius Nyssenus[q], in the life of Gregory for his great actions surnamed Thaumaturgus, reporteth that it was this Gregory that first made the particular conversion of the heathen into christian holy days. And as among the christians the day of the martyr's or saint's death is the holy day, *dies martyrii, dies natalis,* so was it among the heathens; for by Plutarch *in Camillo*[r], the Romans observe Romulus's death-day for his holy day.

Moreover, as among the christians, before a man can be admitted into the ministry, there is enquiry made by the

l [Lib. iii. cap. 11. p. 351.]
m [Lib. ii. cap. 38. vol. i. p. 265.]
n [cap. xxiii sq. pp. 124, 126.]
o [vol. i. p. 262.]
p [Græc. affect. curat. Disp. viii. prop. fin. vol. iv. p. 923.]
q [vol. iii. col. 574.]
r [vol. i. pp. 137, 567.]

superior clergy of his ability and worthiness, and certain times and solemnities observed at the ordinance of the minister; so likewise was it amongst the infidels our ancestors; for as some of the recited authors mention, the heathen *pontifices* were to be skilful in their profession and clergy discipline; so further it appeareth by Alexander ab Alexandro[s], that if a man were a cripple, or lame in any part of his body, he could not be a *pontifex;* therefore Marcus Sergius being lame, he was not suffered to be a *pontifex;* so Dionysius Halicarnasseus[t] observes, Metellus being a priest, and losing his eyes, he was put out of his priesthood; so Gellius notes[u], their vestals were rejected if they wanted wit or beauty.—The time appointed for their ordination or initiation, as Apuleius[v] writeth, was called *dies natalis sacrorum.*—The ceremonies that were used when the heathen ministers were made, are in part described by Erasmus[x] in his book called Lingua, where he writes their *afflatus* and *exorcismos;* nay as amongst our clergy imposition of hands is almost essential to the office of a minister, so you may see how Livy[y], treating of the ordination of Numa to be *pontifex,* delivered, upon Numa's head hands were laid *ab augure sacerdote.* Julius Pollux[z], in his Onomasticon, discourseth of the manner of the ministers ordaining and ordained.—As at the making or electing of a christian minister no simony is to be used, so is it plain by Dionysius Halicarnasseus no reward was to be given for the making of heathen priests.—And as the minister under the gospel may be deposed or resign, so, that the heathen may be degraded I have already shewed; that he might resign is shewed you by Cicero in his Brutus, where *augures* might resign their *sacerdotium;* and Livy[a] writes, their vestals after they were thirty years old might give over their order.—And as long as our ministers continue of the clergy, we know they have many privileges above the laity; so likewise that the heathen ministers had, is plentifully to be proved out of Aristotle[b], out

[s] [Lib. vi. cap. 14. fin. vol. ii. p. 611.]
[t] [M. Ann. Senec. Controv., lib. iv. contr. 2. p. 55.]
[u] [Lib. i. cap. 12. vol. i. p. 62.]
[v] [Metam., lib. xi. p. 389.]
[x] [vol. iv. col. 747.]
[y] [Lib. i. cap. 18. vol. i. p. 27.]
[z] [Lib. i. cap. 1. vol. i. pp. 4—26.]
[a] [vid. Alex. ab Alex., lib. v. cap. 12. vol. ii. p. 110. et not. Tiraq.]
[b] [Polit., lib. vii. cap. 9. vol. ii. p. 1329.]

of Cæsar[c], out of Plutarch[d] *in Camillo:* not unpoliticly therefore doth cardinal Baronius[e] in one of his tomes, perceiving the argument of the scriptures to prove the pope's supremacy are but straws, at large maintain the superiorities and pre-eminencies of the bishop of Rome to be due unto him, insomuch as he noteth at the conversion of the emperor of Rome from paganism unto christianity, the privileges of the heathen *pontifex maximus* were at last transferred by the emperor unto the pope of Rome.

Again, look into the manner of the government and behaviour of the heathenish priests or sacrificers in their profane churches, and you shall see their good orders are not refused by the christian clergy; for you may learn by Valerius[f] and Philostratus[g], that it is common to the christians with the gentiles to use a white garment upon their bodies in their charges. Because the Egyptians brought no kind of woollen garment into the temple, Gyraldus[h] in his Syntagma notes that they were called *linigeri;* more particularly the priests of the heathen egyptian god Isis wore linen surplices, as witnesseth Nicolaus Leonicenus[i], and Apuleius[k] in his Golden Ass; Alexander ab Alexandro[l] reports, the priests of Arabia were clad in linen garments, having mitres on their heads; and generally that other heathen priests did so, may appear by Virgil, who writeth,

——— fontemque ignemque ferebant
Velati lino ;—

Servius[m] in his comment calleth the surplice a pure religious garment.

To proceed, as our ministers are bare-headed in the saying of service, so generally was it used amongst the heathen priests, as appeareth by Macrobius[n]; and that god Æsculapius was worshipped bare-headed, Plautus[o] may witness,

Quis hic est qui operto capite Æsculapium
Salutat?

[c] [e. g. De bell. gall., lib. vi. cap. 13. p. 121, et passim.]
[d] [e. g. vol. i. pp. 531, 542, 563, et alibi.]
[e] [In A.D. 312. vol. iii. p. 91 sqq.]
[f] [Lib. i. cap. i. exempl. 16. fol. 9.]
[g] [vid. vit. Apollon., lib. viii. p. 387. necnon Apollon., epist. 8.]
[h] [Synt. xvii. vol. i. p. 514.]
[i] [Lib. ii. cap. 21. p. 145.]
[k] [Lib. xi. p. 370.]
[l] [Lib. ii. cap. 8. vol. i. p. 322.]
[m] [Ad Æn. xii. 164.]
[n] [Saturn., lib. i. cap. 8. p. 244.]
[o] [Curc. act. iii. sc. 1. lin. 19. vol. i. p. 214.]

Brissonius[p] notes the manner of the heathen priests being covered to sacrifice, *operto capite,* came first from the Romans; so is the opinion of Servius[q], writing upon the second of the Æneids; and this is formerly noted by Polydore Vergil[r] out of Plutarch; but (saving favour) I take it all Saturn's priests, though Romans, were uncovered at their time of service of sacrifice (for so I learn out of Plutarch[s]) because he was the god of time, and discovereth and layeth open concealed truth. And I remember out of Alexander ab Alexandro[t] that all the priests of Hercules, Honor, Ops, did sacrifice bare-headed; he saith that Æneas[u] was the first that invented any priest should sacrifice covered, or with a veil upon his face, lest their ears and eyes might withdraw them from doing their office; hence Varro's[v] etymology of *flamen* is justified, namely, that in Italy he was so called, *quia capite velato erat.*

Again, as the christian ministers are not to suffer profane or excommunicate persons to come into our churches or sacraments, so likewise would not the heathen clergymen. For as in general appeareth by Theodoret and Sozomenus that the gentiles would not admit christians to their service unless they renounced their religion, and appeased their demons ἀποτροπαίους, 'the drivers away of evil,' which also Julian[x] commanded; Athenæus[y] notes, Demophon would not admit Orestes *ad Choum festum,* because he was an unsanctified person; so in particular at their Eleusine[z] and other sacrifices the heathen priests cried ἑκὰς ἑκὰς ὅστις ἄλιτρος; which words were used by Callimachus[a] in his hymn, and by Lucian[b]; these words exclude especially three sorts of persons, atheists, christians, and epicures. Vives notes out of Servius the words of Virgil's verse, *procul o procul este profani,* were taken from the heathen *pontifices;* which is also further evident out of Alexander ab Alexandro[c], who writeth, when the people came to sacrifice, the *pontifex* or *flamen* asked them, τίς τῇδε; the people answered πολλοὶ καὶ ἀγαθοὶ, 'many

p [Lib. i. p. 36.]
q [vid. ad Æn. iii. 407.]
r [Lib. iv. cap. 13. p. 135.]
s [Quæst. rom., vol. vii. p. 81.]
t [Lib. ii. cap. 22. vol. i. p. 467.]
u [Serv. in Virg. Æn., iii. 407.]
v [De ling. lat., lib. iv. p. 22 fin.]
x [Sozom., lib. v. cap. 5. p. 186.]
y [Lib. x. cap. 49. vol. ii. p. 968.]
z [vid. not. d. inf.]
a [Hymn. in Apoll., lin. 2. p. 9.]
b [vid. De sacrif. ad fin., vol. iii. p. 88.]
c [Lib. iv. cap. 17. vol. i. p. 1080.]

and good men.' Suetonius'[d] saying to this purpose is familiar concerning Nero, the crier using in their temples at sacrificing times to cry that wicked and ungodly persons must not presume to offer sacrifice.

Moreover as we use to preach in our churches, so the very heathen priests, enlightened only by natural reason, made moral exhortations unto the people; for Diodorus Siculus[e] writing that among the Egyptians when the king did offer sacrifice with his ball, the priest out of holy books, after he had prayed for the health and prosperity of the king and state, delivered the counsels and actions of excellent men, by which the king was warned to use his authority and command godly and justly, according to the example of others; he did further entreat, saith Diodorus, of their piety towards their God and religion. And for that purpose I gather out of Valerius Maximus, that the people which were to approach to the heathenish altar were commanded by the priests to lay aside out of their mind all former hatred and malice, or else not to approach.

Likewise the heathen priests had music in their temples in the time of service; wherefore for the general, to omit Livy[f] and Valerius Maximus, in particular Suetonius[g] notes, it is a wonder in Tiberius Cæsar for offering sacrifice unto the gods without music. Now as the christians use in their churches particular psalms, hymns, and prayers for set and festival days; this Gyraldus[h] sheweth in some part, that upon chief and special days the heathen had their particular verses, prayers, and hymns; but more particularly Julius Pollux[i], writing *περὶ ἀρῶν ἐθνικῶν*, namely, the special psalms, if I may so speak, and to what gods they were due. It is worth the remembering how the papists, if a bishop or abbot be canonized and die, they have a glorious and special antiphoneme, which begins *ecce sacerdos magnus*, but if the emperor or king be canonized, his antiphoneme is but the ordinary one for a father; this last I learn out of a treatise called Salem[j] and Byzance.

d [Ner., cap. 34. vol. ii. p. 121.]
e [Lib. i. cap. 70. vol. i. p. 81.]
f [Lib. ix. cap. 30. vol. i. p. 531.]
g [Tib., cap. lxx. vol. i. p. 319.]
h [De poet. hist. Dial. i. vol. ii. p. 35.]
i [Lib. i. cap. 1. fin. vol. i. p. 26.]
j ["Additions of Salem and Byzance," ch. i. fol. 19.]

And as for the bounding of the meres of parishes, our clergy-priests on their rogation-week go on procession; so likewise did the heathen; their perambulations for this purpose were called *ambarvalia*[k].—And it appeareth by Livy[l] that the heathen clergy might not be present at the sentence of death; and Josephus[m] notes that *pontifex maximus* might not behold a dead body; and at this day that this is and hath been the custom of our clergy is full apparent.

To conclude this particular with the nature of the coercive power used by the heathen priests. Julius Cæsar[n] at large delivereth of the heathen clergy of this island and of France, namely the druids: if any private or public person would not stand to their decrees and orders, they used to forbid him their sacrifices, which, saith Cæsar, among them is a most grievous punishment, for the party so interdicted is not only accounted a detested person, and men are to shun his company, but neither shall he be capable of any honour, or shall sue for his own right; hence by good probability came the excommunication used by the british clergy anciently, and continued by our english clergy at this day, seeing the punishment and effect thereof is so lively described, as if Cæsar had been an author of our age. For our excommunication, whether it be *hominis* or *canonis*, (the former may be *clavis ecclesiæ errans*, saith our register, the latter not,) doth not only bar the excommunicated person from entering into the church at service time, and intimate a man not *in osculo communicare cum excommunicato*, as it is in the canon laws, which is the reason Cyprian calls excommunicated persons *abstenti*[o], because men refrain their company; but also it seems unto this day, by the canon laws of this land an excommunicate person cannot bring an action, or implead any other for his right, until he be absolved. I note out of Sophocles'[p] Œdipus, that they which killed king Laius were excommunicated, which took the same effect with the druids' excommunication; and for this also, see Plato, in his ninth[q]

[k] [Alex. ab Alex., lib. iii. cap. 12. vol. i. p. 693. lib. v. cap. 27. vol. ii. p. 377.]

[l] [vid. Serv. in Virg. Æn. vi. 176. Senec. Consol. in Martiam, cap. xv. p. 386.]

[m] [Antiq. Jud., lib. iii. cap. 12. § 2. vol. i. p. 127.]

[n] [De bell. gall., lib. vi. cap. 12. p. 120.]

[o] [e.g. Epp. lix. lxviii. pp. 126, 177.]

[p] [Œd. Tyr., lin. 222 sqq.]

[q] [cap. ix. vol. viii. p. 430 sq.]

and tenth book *De legibus*. Pope Innocent the fourth[r] calleth excommunication the sinew of ecclesiastical discipline; the canonists account excommunication to be the keys of opening and shutting which Christ gave at His departure to His disciples: but the vulgar came not by many hundred years by the travel, and employment, and mission of this good thunderbolt, it is become *brutum* or *salmoneum fulmen*.

3. In the last place I am to speak of the religious ceremonies of the ethnic people in their churches, that they are answerable to ours. It is evident by Tertullian[s], Clement[t], Apuleius[u], and Servius[x] upon Virgil, that the heathens in their churches at the time of their service, praying or sitting, looked into the east, but the Jews[y] in their churches, as appeareth by St. Jerome, praying, looked into the west; and yet we follow the gentiles' custom, and build our churches to that purpose as the heathens did; for Vitruvius[z] the heathen architect commandeth that the face of the temples be built in the west, that they which pray may have their faces looking into the east. St. Basil's[a] opinion then, that it is an apostolical tradition of the christians to pray looking into the east, is not absolutely current; Cælius notes Hermes Trismegistus[b] praying looking upon the south; the Jews looked upon the west[c]; the christians, saith he, looked into the east, which they learned of Pythagoras, as holding (with Ptolemy) the motion of the sun cometh from the east. I read in Athanasius[d] that the apostles appointed the christian churches to be built to the east, that in praying they might behold paradise; but to quit Thomas Aquinas's[e] third reason why the christians in praying look into the east, I fancy the reason of our praying into the east set down in the particular describer of the city of Jerusalem[f]; "the christians in Europe," saith he, "at their prayers looking into the east, behold the country where Christ was conversant on earth, and

r [vid. Concil. reg., vol. xxviii. pp. 399, 408, 451, 467 sqq.]
s [Apol., cap. xvi. p. 16 B.]
t [Strom., lib. vii. vol. ii. p. 856.]
u [Metam., lib. ii. p. 65.]
x [In Æn. xii. 172.]
y [vid. not. c inf.]
z [Lib. iv. cap. 5. p. 70.]
a [De Spir. Sanct., cap. xxvii. § 66. p. 54 E.]
b [Asclep. ad fin. fol. 6 b.]
c [Bona, Psalmod., cap. vi. § 7. p. 165.]
d [Quæstt. ad Antiochum, xxxvii. vol. ii. p. 276.]
e [Sent., lib. iii. dist. 9. quæst. 1. art. 3. fin.—2da 2dæ quæst. 84. art. 3. fin.]
f [Adrichom., p. 120.]

in so beholding may behold the face of Christ upon the cross looking upon them."

Yea the heathens in their prayers not only looked as the christians, and praying held up their hands toward heaven, as Livy[g] sheweth Camillus praying, and Virgil's[h]

tendens ad sidera palmas,

intimateth, but also in some points prayed as we do; to omit their joint order and decency of prayer out of Plutarch[i], *ne Calydonii suis tragœdia renovetur.* And Jamblichus[k], the scholar of Porphyry, as in general he writeth of the force of prayer, so in particular he concludes, all their sacrifices and religion are better joined and perfected by vows and prayers. Yea the wisest of the heathens, as Marsilius Ficinus notes upon Plato's[l] Alcibiades, prayed devoutly and in spirit, *flagrantiâ animi*, offering up their vows without any characters, which were invented to stir up their affection by Orpheus[m] and Zoroaster.—And Alexander ab Alexandro[n] writes, the heathen man which prayed first did confess himself a sinner; that (I observe out of the apothegm of the heathen Lacedæmonian) to God, and not to the priests, which the heathen *pontifex* there confessed.—And that in their prayers Alexander ab Alexandro[o] notes, they thanked the gods for benefits received, and desired aversions of evils: yea, the heathens used to pray in their churches for the afflicted in body and mind, as the christians do; for it appeareth by Lucian[p], if any were hurt, he would sacrifice to the gods to be relieved; and by Plutarch, not only sacrifices were used among the heathen for the health of Pompey, but also cities celebrated holy days in their temples for receiving great benefits of their gods, as the health of Pompey.—And the prayer of Arrianus[q] (the scholar of Epictetus, as Lucian[r] notes) when he would call upon the gods, was in these words, κύριε ἐλέησον, 'Lord, have mercy.'—And as I read Arrianus's book called

[g] [Lib. v. cap. 21. vol. i. p. 314.]

[h] [Æn. i. 97.]

[i] [In vit. Num., cap. 14. vol. i. p. 276.]

[k] [De myst., sect. v. cap. 26. p. 141.]

[l] [In ed. Froben. fol. Basil. 1561. p. 351. "Externas omnes ceremonias auferebant, solam ac puram fragrantiam animi relinquentes."]

[m] [vid. ubi sup.]

[n] [Lib. iv. cap. 17. vol. i. p. 1079.]

[o] [Ubi sup., pp. 1098, 1114.]

[p] [De sacrif., vol. iii. p. 74 sqq.]

[q] [Comment. in Epict., lib. ii. cap. 7. p. 142.]

[r] [Alex., cap. 2. vol. v. p. 62.]

Periplus[s], a phrase of his is, "but now, God willing;" and that *si Deus voluerit* ought to be the prayer of the christians appeareth by James iii.—And if the heathen prayers were not conformable for the present state, the heathen magistrates caused them to be amended; and this I learn out of Valerius[t], that Scipio Africanus, the public prayer being that the gods would make better and more ample the state of Rome, he said, they are already great enough, and devised the form of prayer to be, that the gods would continue and preserve the state of Rome.—Again, as the christian magistrates afore they used to consult of the greatest affairs used to resort to divine service, so that this was an express law to be observed by the roman senators, is noted by Suetonius *in Augusto*[u]; nay, that before every small exercise or recreation, their unchristian men would call unto their gods, I learn out of Hesychius[x], who saith that when they went to play at dice they would call upon their god Mercury in these words, *ἀγαθὸς δαίμων*, 'good god;' (but generally the heathen prayers in their churches were very long, for our Saviour teacheth us, when we pray, "Do not make long prayers, as the heathens do;" for this last see Pererius in his note upon Genesis.)—And if we have not seasonable weather we use particular devotion; to this purpose you may gather out of Dionysius Halicarnasseus[y] that the gentiles proclaimed and kept solemn feasts for the pacifying of their paynim gods.

In this place it were not improper to shew how among the infidels, as well as the christians, the civil magistrate, especially the king, the politic father of the people, made laws to be observed by the heathenish clergy; therefore a common lawyer in his treatise of Salem and Byzance[z] may well note that our king Lucius, buried at Winton, had as much prerogative over his *flamines*, or ministers, being christians, as heathen: and this also appeareth by Aristotle in his Politics[a], by Virgil[b], by Strabo[c]: but this I reserve for another place.

And (to omit Wolfgangus Lazius's[d] discovery of Lent to have

s [Pont. Eux. sig. *iiii.]

t [Lib. iv. cap. 368. fol. 132.]

u [cap. 35. vol. i. p. 156.]

x [In voc. Ἑρμῆς. col. 1438.]

y [e. g. Antiq. rom., lib. vii. cap. 71. vol. i. p. 457.]

z ["Additions of S. and B." ch. ii. p. 34 sqq.]

a [Lib. vii. capp. 8, 9. vol. ii. p. 1328, 9.]

b [e. g. Æn. vi. 645, vii. 86, 750 sqq., viii. 179, xii. 169, et al.]

c [vid. lib. xv. p. 1041. et al.]

d [Lib. xi. cap. 5. p. 881.]

been practised as a policy among the heathen) I shall conclude this particular with the duty of heathen people observed towards their priests in relieving of them, and paying them tithes, as parishioners do to their pastors; but much of this which I or any other can write in this kind, is already quoted in some of the canonists' writings, so covetous men are in advancing their own particular. As the ancient elect people of God afore the law given in mount Sinai paid tithes to their priests, as Gen. xiv., Abraham paid tithes to the greater priest Melchizedec; (but where it is said in Lev. xxvii. 32, the tenth sheep shall go under the rod, a rabbin writes that in those days the tenth sheep was marked with ochre, as they use tithing at this day by putting sheep out of the fold, this I take to be rabbinical, and full of conceit,) so the very heathen priests have by the consent of their people or parishioners always a relief, yea and that with a tenth part of their revenues. Therefore for the first-fruits Pliny[e] writeth, "the Romans were not wont to taste of their fruits or vines afore the heathen priests had sacrificed with them;" and Porphyry confesseth that from all antiquity the first-fruits of the earth were dedicated unto their gods. In particular, Euripides[f] the tragedian saith, that Diana had the first-fruits of every thing that the earth could yield; and Suidas[g], *in verbo ἑρμαῖον*, writeth, The travellers in the highway did use to offer unto the idol of Mercury, that guideth them in their ways, the first-fruits of the earth; and Herodotus[h] discourseth of the image of Delphos, which was made for receiving of *primitias terræ* of the Grecians, who overcame Xerxes; Natalis Comes[i] sheweth out of Aristophanes and Euripides the several first-fruits which were due to their several gods. But in express terms the tenth of their substance was offered unto the heathen gods, and consequently unto the heathen priests; for so it appeareth by Livy[k], Camillus gave the tenth of their corn unto Apollo and the Ephesian Diana: but above all other gods, they were given to Hercules; for not only by Plutarch[l], many men offered the tenth of their substance to Hercules,

[e] [Nat. hist., lib. xviii. cap. 2. vol. iii. p. 342.]
[f] [In fragm. Meleagr., vol. iii. p. 572.]
[g] [col. 1441.]
[h] [Uran., cap. 121 sq.]
[i] [Lib. De anno.]
[k] [Lib. v. cap. 23. vol. i. p. 316.]
[l] [Quæst. rom., vol. vii. p. 84.]

but by Cicero, in his *Natura deorum,* tithes were due unto Hercules; nay, so commonly was the tenth part offered unto Hercules, that Hercules's part and the tenth part were all one in signification: for Plautus[m] writes,

mihi detraxi partem herculaneam;

good reason then I note Tertullian[n] had to speak of tithes that were properly due unto Hercules. Lastly, Dionysius Halicarnasseus[o] noteth that Jupiter and Apollo sent barrenness upon the face of the earth, because men intermitted and neglected the paying of their tithes. Hence then it is more than colourable that the heathen Britons, our ancestors before the time of Julius Cæsar, paid tithes to their priests and druids; whether the tenth part or the eighth, *quota pars,* I have not to define, as holding with a canon lawyer[p] in his treatise, Tithes and maintenance is due by the law of God and man, but not *quota pars,* namely the tenth part, unless in places accustomed to pay it.

Thus having chalked out the paths the christians tread in, having been formerly beaten by the gentiles, but first made (as I told you) by the Jews, in whose steps the gentiles tread, although awry; by this my instant and last place they may perceive that even since the time of the gospel, and that christianity was admitted into the world, the heathens in some things also began to imitate the christians: but it was *diabolicâ instigatione,* as the ordinary phrase in indictments is. A touch of this given by Erasmus; Tertullian[q] in his time complaineth of the devils in heathens imitating christian baptism; *tinget et ipse,* saith Tertullian, *fideles suos;* and after his time you may perceive Sozomenus[r]; but especially by Gregory Nazianzen[s], in his oration against Julian, the damnable politic; Julian the emperor thought it the best way to extirpate christianity, that the heathen in all points of service and adoration should correspond with the christian service; but it could not be effected, say they, because the christians by faith inwardly

m [Truc., act. ii. sc. 7. lin. 11.]

n [Apol., capp. xiv. xxxix. pp. 14, 32.]

o [Antiq. rom., lib. i. cap. 23. vol. i. p. 18 sq.]

p [See the author's tract on tithes, Opusc. p. 155.]

q [De præscr. hær., cap. xl. p. 216 B. vid. et De bapt., cap. v. p. 226 A.]

r [H. E., lib. v. cap. 16. p. 203.]

s [Orat. iv. cap. 111 sq. vol. i. p. 138, 9.]

and in spirit worshipped God. Arnobius[t] notes, because the christians' God was not visible, the heathens call the christians atheists.

Out of this precedent discourse the travelling bee, that is, the honest subject of this realm, with me will reason thus: if our forefathers, which were enlightened only by natural reason, would have so good orders in their temples at their worshipping of false and superstitious gods, what great care should christians have for enjoining and observing of comely and godly ordinances in the worshipping of the true and ever-living God!

[t] [vid. lib. vi. passim, et al.]

INDEX OF TEXTS.

LEVITICUS.

NUMBERS.

DEUTERONOMY.

JOSHUA.

JUDGES.

RUTH.

1 SAMUEL.

PROVERBS.

ECCLESIASTES.

SONG OF SOLOMON.

ISAIAH.

GENERAL INDEX.

D.

E.

F.

G.

H.

I.

O.

P.

Q.

R.

S.

T.

V.

W.

X.

Y.

Z.

LIST OF EDITIONS REFERRED TO.

Abbas Urspergensis, vid. Conradus.
Ado, in vol. xvi. Bibl. max. vett. pat. De la Bigne, fol. Lugd. 1677.
Adrichomius, Urbis Hierosol. descriptio, 8vo. Col. Agr. 1588.
Æschines, in vol. iii. Oratt. Att. ed. Bekker. 8vo. Oxon. 1823.
Æschylus, ed. Wellauer. 8vo. Lips. 1822—4.
Alcuinus, ed. Quercet. fol. Par. 1617.
Alexander ab Alexandro, 8vo. Lugd. Bat. 1673.
Amalarius, ed. Hittorp. fol. Par. 1624.
Ambrosius, ed. Ben. fol. Par. 1686—90.
Andradius (Dieguo Payva), Defens. Trident. fid. cathol. 8vo. Ingolst. 1580.
Andreas Maurus, 12mo. Traj. ad Rhen. 1646.
Apuleius, Opp. 4to. Par. 1688.
Aquinas, Opp. fol. Antuerp. 1512.
Aristoteles, ed. Bekker. 4to. Berol. 1831.
Arnobius, ed. Orell. 8vo. Lips. 1816.
Arrianus, Periplus, fol. Genev. 1577.
Athanasius, Opp. ed. Ben. fol. Par. 1698.
Athenæus, ed. Dindorf. 8vo. Lips. 1827.
Augustinus, Opp. ed. Ben. fol. Par. 1679—1700.
Augustinus Curio, Hist. Saracen. fol. Francof. 1596.
Aulus Gellius, ed. Bipont. 8vo. 1781.
Baronius, Annal. fol. Antuerp. 1597—1630.
Basilius, ed. Garnier. fol. Par. 1721—30.
Beda, Hist. eccles. ed. Hussey, 8vo. Oxon. 1846.
Bellarminus, Opp. fol. Ingolst. 1601—17.
Bernardus, Opp. fol. Antuerp. 1620.
Beza, Nov. Test. cum versione et annott. fol. Basil. 1560.
Blesensis (Petrus), Opp. fol. Par. 1667.
Bona, De div. psalm. 4to. Par. 1663.
—— De reb. liturg. 4to. Par. 1672.
Brissonius, De formulis, &c. 4to. Francof. 1592.
Cæsar, De bell. gall. 8vo. Lond. 1763.
Callimachus, ed. Lösner, 8vo. Lips. 1774.
Calvinus, Inst. fol. Amstel. 1667.
Camden, Britannia, ed. Gibson, fol. Lond. 1772.
Canisius, Opus Catechist. fol. Colon. 1586.
Censorinus, De die natali, ed. Havercamp. 8vo. Lugd. Bat. 1743.
Chemnitius, Exam. Concil. Trident. fol. Genev. 1634.
Chrysostomus, ed. Ben. fol. Par. 1718—38.
Cicero, ed. Olivet. 4to. Par. 1740—2.
Clemens Alexandrinus, ed. Potter, fol. Oxon. 1715.
Codex Theodosianus, vid. Theodosianus.
Concilia, ed. Mansi, fol. Ven. 1759—98.
Conradus à Liechtenaw, Abbas Urspergensis, Chron. fol. Basil. 1569.
Corpus juris canonici, ed. Böhmer. 4to. Hal. Magd. 1747.
———— civilis, ed. Gothofred. fol. Francof. 1688.
Covarruvias (Didacus), Opp. fol. Lugd. 1606.
Cyprianus, ed. Fell, fol. Oxon. 1682.
Cyrillus Alexandrinus, Opp. ed. Aubert. fol. Lutet. 1638.
Cyrillus Hierosolymitanus, Opp. ed. Touttée, fol. Par. 1720.
Damascenus (Joannes), Opp. ed. Lequien, fol. Par. 1712.
Damasus, Opp. ed. Saraz. 4to. Rom. 1638.
Demosthenes, in Oratt. græc. ed. Reisk. 8vo. Lips. 1770.
Didacus Covarruvias, vid. Covarruvias.
Dio Cassius, ed. Leunclav. fol. Hanov. 1605.
Diodorus Siculus, Opp. ed. Wetst. fol. Amst. 1746.
Diogenes Laertius, Opp. ed. Hübner. 8vo. Lips. 1828.

Dionysius Halicarnasseus, Opp. fol. Oxon. 1704.
Dorotheus, Synopsis, in vol. iii. p. 143. Magn. bibl. vett. pat. fol. Col. Agr. 1618—22.
Dubravius, Hist. Boiem. fol. Basil. 1575.
Dugdale, Monasticon, fol. Lond. 1817.
Ephraim Syrus, Opp. ed. Voss. fol. Antuerp. 1619.
Epictetus, Opp. ed. Wolf. 8vo. Colon. 1595.
Epiphanius, Opp. ed. Petav. fol. Par. 1622.
Erasmus, Opp. fol. Lugd. Bat. 1703—6.
Euripides, ed. Musgr. 4to. Oxon. 1778.
Eusebius, Chronicon, ed. Scal. fol. Amst. 1658.
——— Hist. eccl. in vol. i. Eccl. hist. script. ed. Reading, fol. Cantab. 1720.
——— Præp. evangel. ed. Viger. fol. Par. 1628.
Eustathius in Homer. fol. Basil. 1560.
Euthymius, Comment. in quatuor Evang. ed. Matth. 8vo. Lips. 1792.
Galenus, Opp. ed. Kühn, 8vo. Lips. 1821.
Gratianus, Decretum, fol. Par. 1612.
Gregorius Magnus, Opp. ed. Ben. fol. Par. 1705.
——— Nazianzenus, Opp. ed. Ben. fol. Par. 1778, 1840.
——— Nyssenus, Opp. fol. Par. 1638.
Gruterus, Inscript. Rom. fol. in bibliop. Commelin. 1616.
Gyraldus (Lilius), Opp. fol. Basil. 1580.
Hermes Trismegistus, Opuscula, fol. Lond. 1611.
Herodotus, Hist. ed. Gaisford. 8vo. Oxon. 1830.
Hesychius, Lexicon, ed. Albert. fol. Lugd. Bat. 1746—66.
Hieronymus, Opp. ed. Ben. fol. Par. 1693—1706.
Hilarius Pictavensis, Opp. ed. Ben. fol. 1693.
Hooker, Works, ed. Keble, 8vo. Oxon. 1836.
Hosius (Stanislaus), Opp. fol. Colon. 1584.
Hospinianus, De monachis, fol. Genev. 1669.
Jamblichus, De mysteriis, ed. Gale, fol. Oxon. 1678.
Ignatius, Opp. in Patt. apostol. ed. Coteler. fol. Amst. 1724.
Josephus, Opp. ed. Hudson, fol. Oxon. 1720.
Irenæus, Opp. ed. Massuet. fol. Par. 1710.
Isidorus Hispalensis, Opp. 4to. Rom. 1797—1803.
Julius Pollux, Onomasticon, fol. Amst. 1706.
Justinus Martyr, Opp. ed. Maran. fol. Par. 1742.
Juvenalis, ed. Ruperti, 8vo. Lips. 1801.
Lactantius, Opp. ed. Dufresnoy, 4to. Par. 1748.
Lazius (Wolfgangus), Reip. rom. comment. fol. Francof. 1598.
Leo Magnus (cum aliis), Opp. ed. Raynaud, fol. Par. 1639.
Leonicenus (Nicolaus), De variâ historiâ, 4to. Basil. 1531.
Livius (Titus), Hist. Rom. ed. Crevier, 8vo. Oxon. 1821.
Lucianus, Opp. ed. Lehmann, 8vo. Lips. 1822—31.
Macrobius, Saturnalia, 8vo. Lips. 1774.
Marianus Scotus, vid. Scotus.
Matthæus Parisiensis, vid. Parisiensis.
Mutius, German. Chron. fol. Basil. 1539.
Natalis Comes, De anno, 8vo. Ven. 1550.
Nicephorus, ed. Front. Ducæo, fol. Lut. Par. 1630.
Œcumenius, Opp. fol. Veron. 1532.
Onuphrius Panvinius, Interpr. vocc. eccles. ad calc. Hist. Platinæ, fol. Lov. 1572.
Origenes, Opp. ed. Delarue, fol. Par. 1733—59.
Osorius, Opp. fol. Rom. 1592.
Ovidius, Opp. ed. Burmann. 4to. Amst. 1727.
Pansa (Mutius), Osculum &c. 8vo. Marpurg. 1605.
Parisiensis (Matthæus), Hist. miscell. ed. Wats, fol. Lond. 1684.
Paulus Diaconus, in Hist. aug. script. fol. Hanov. 1611.
Pererius, in Genesim, fol. Col. Agr. 1601.
Petrus Blesensis, vid. Blesensis.
Philostratus, vit. Apollon. Tyan. ed. Morell. fol. Par. 1608.
Phocylides, Poett. gr. vet. ed. Lectio. fol. Aurel. Allobr. 1606.
Plato, Opp. ed. Bekker. 8vo. Lond. 1826.
Plautus, ed. Ernest. 8vo. Lips. 1709.
Plinius, Hist. natur. ed. Brotier. 8vo. Par. 1779.
Plotinus, Opp. fol. Basil. 1580.
Plutarchus, Opp. ed. Reisk. 8vo. Lips. 1776.
Polydorus Vergilius, vid. Vergilius.
Pythagoras, Poett. gr. vet. ed. Lectio. Aurel. Allobr. 1606. p. 726.

Rabanus Maurus, Opp. fol. Col. Agr. 1626.

Regino, Chronica, in vol. i. Scriptt. german. Pistorii, fol. Francof. 1583, 4.

Rhenanus, in Tertull. ed. Pamel. fol. Franck. 1597.

——— Descript. Illyrici provinc. ad calc. Notitiæ dignitatum Imp. rom. ex recens. Labb. 12mo. Par. 1602.

Rhodiginus (Ludovicus Cœlius), Lectt. antiq. fol. Col. Allobr. 1620.

Salem and Byzance, Berthel. 8vo. Lond. 1533.

Scotus (Marianus), Chronica, fol. Basil. 1559.

Seneca, L. Ann. Opp. fol. Par. 1587.

——— M. Ann. Controv. cum præced.

Sibyllina Oracula, in Bibl. vett. pat. De la Bigne, Par. 1624. init.

Sigebert, Chronicon, in vol. vii. Bibl. vett. pat. De la Bigne, ed. Par. 1589.

Simplicius, Comment. in Epictet. q. v.

Smith, Sir Thomas, Commonw. of Engl. 12mo. Lond. 1633.

Socrates, Hist. eccl. vol. ii. Hist. eccl. scriptt. ed. Reading, fol. Cantab. 1720.

Sophocles, Opp. ed. Dindorf. 8vo. Oxon. 1832.

Sozomenus, Hist. eccl. ubi Socrates, q. v.

Stapleton, Demonstr. method. fol. Par. 1579.

Strabo, Geogr. fol. Amst. 1707.

Suetonius, Duod. Cæsares, ed. Wolf. 8vo. Lips. 1802.

Suidas, Lexicon, ed. Gaisford. fol. Oxon. 1834.

Tertullian, Opp. ed. Rigalt. fol. Par. 1675.

Theocritus, ubi Phocylides, q. v.

Theodoretus, Hist. eccl. in vol. iii. Hist. eccl. scriptt. ed. Reading, fol. Cantab. 1720.

——— cætera, in Opp. ed. Schultze, 8vo. Hal. 1769—74.

Theodosianus codex, ed. Ritter. fol. Lips. 1736—41.

Thucydides, Hist. ed. Göller, 8vo. Lips. 1826.

Valerius Maximus, Opp. fol. Lutet. 1535.

Varro, Opp. 8vo. Dordr. 1619.

Vergilius (Polydorus), Opp. Froben. fol. Basil. 1525.

Vitruvius, De Archit. ed. De Laet. fol. Elzev. 1649.

Volateranus, Opp. fol. Lugd. 1599.

Urspergensis, vid. Conradus.

Wolfgangus Lazius, vid. Lazius.

Xiphilinus, Dion. Nic. Epitome, 4to. Par. ex offic. Steph. 1551.

ERRATA.

p. 241. line 13. for v. read *5*.
282. line 19. for 53. read 23.
358. line 14. for 24. read 23.

www.ingramcontent.com/pod-product-compliance
Lightning Source LLC
LaVergne TN
LVHW020518100826
845148LV00010B/1276

* 9 7 8 1 6 0 6 0 8 1 2 3 5 *